PMP exam task map

	TASK	CHAPTER
1.0	**INITIATING THE PROJECT (13 PERCENT)**	
1.1	Perform project assessment based upon available information and meetings with the sponsor, customer, and other subject matter experts, in order to evaluate the feasibility of new products or services within the given assumptions and/or constraints.	2
1.2	Define the high-level scope of the project based on the business and compliance requirements, in order to meet the customer's project expectations.	2
1.3	Perform key stakeholder analysis using brainstorming, interviewing, and other data-gathering techniques, in order to ensure expectation alignment and gain support for the project.	11
1.4	Identify and document high-level risks, assumptions, and constraints based on current environment, historical data, and/or expert judgment, in order to identify project limitations and propose an implementation approach.	2
1.5	Develop the project charter by further gathering and analyzing stakeholder requirements, in order to document project scope, milestones, and deliverables.	2
1.6	Obtain approval for the project charter from the sponsor and customer (if required), in order to formalize the authority assigned to the project manager and gain commitment and acceptance for the project.	2
2.0	**PLANNING THE PROJECT (24 PERCENT)**	
2.1	Assess detailed project requirements, constraints, and assumptions with stakeholders based on the project charter, lessons learned from previous projects, and the use of requirement-gathering techniques (e.g., planning sessions, brainstorming, focus groups), in order to establish the project deliverables.	2, 3
2.2	Create the work breakdown structure with the team by deconstructing the scope, in order to manage the scope of the project.	3
2.3	Develop a budget plan based on the project scope using estimating techniques, in order to manage project cost.	5
2.4	Develop a project schedule based on the project timeline, scope, and resource plan, in order to manage timely completion of the project.	4
2.5	Develop a human resource management plan by defining the roles and responsibilities of the project team members in order to create an effective project organization structure and provide guidance regarding how resources will be utilized and managed.	7
2.6	Develop a communication plan based on the project organization structure and external stakeholder requirements, in order to manage the flow of project information.	8, 11
2.7	Develop a procurement plan based on the project scope and schedule, in order to ensure that the required project resources will be available.	10
2.8	Develop a quality management plan based on the project scope and requirements, in order to prevent the occurrence of defects and reduce the cost of quality.	6
2.9	Develop a change management plan by defining how changes will be handled, in order to track and manage changes.	2
2.10	Plan risk management by developing a risk management plan, and identifying, analyzing, and prioritizing project risks in the risk register and defining risk response strategies, in order to manage uncertainty throughout the project life cycle.	9
2.11	Present the project plan to the key stakeholders (if required), in order to obtain approval to execute the project.	2, 11
2.12	Conduct a kick-off meeting with all key stakeholders, in order to announce the start of the project, communicate the project milestones, and share other relevant information.	8, 11

Exam domains, tasks, and knowledge and skill statements The exam domains, tasks, and knowledge and skill statements listed here are current as of this book's publication date. Exam domains, tasks, and knowledge and skill statements are subject to change at any time without prior notice and at the sole discretion of the Project Management Institute (PMI®). Please visit the PMI webpage for the most current information about PMI's Project Management Professional (PMP®) credential: *http://www.pmi.org/en/Certification/Project-Management-Professional-PMP.aspx*.

3.0	**EXECUTING THE PROJECT (30 PERCENT)**	
3.1	Obtain and manage project resources including outsourced deliverables by following the procurement plan, in order to ensure successful project execution.	10
3.2	Execute the tasks as defined in the project plan, in order to achieve the project deliverables within budget and schedule.	2, 8, 11
3.3	Implement the quality management plan using the appropriate tools and techniques, in order to ensure that work is being performed according to required quality standards.	6
3.4	Implement approved changes according to the change management plan, in order to meet project requirements.	2
3.5	Implement approved actions and follow the risk management plan and risk register, in order to minimize the impact of negative risk events on the project.	9
3.6	Maximize team performance through leading, mentoring, training, and motivating team members.	7
4.0	**MONITORING AND CONTROLLING THE PROJECT (25 PERCENT)**	
4.1	Measure project performance using appropriate tools and techniques, in order to identify and quantify any variances, perform approved corrective actions, and communicate with relevant stakeholders.	2, 3, 4, 5, 10, 11
4.2	Manage changes to the project scope, schedule, and costs by updating the project plan and communicating approved changes to the team, in order to ensure that revised project goals are met.	2, 3, 4, 5
4.3	Ensure that project deliverables conform to the quality standards established in the quality management plan by using appropriate tools and techniques (e.g. testing, inspection, control charts), in order to satisfy customer requirements.	6
4.4	Update the risk register and risk response plan by identifying any new risks, assessing old risks, and determining and implementing appropriate response strategies, in order to manage the impact of risks on the project.	9
4.5	Assess corrective actions on the issue register and determine next steps for unresolved issues by using appropriate tools and techniques in order to minimize the impact on project schedule, cost, and resources.	2, 9
4.6	Communicate project status to stakeholders for their feedback, in order to ensure the project aligns with business needs.	8, 11
5.0	**CLOSING THE PROJECT (8 PERCENT)**	
5.1	Obtain final acceptance of the project deliverables by working with the sponsor and/or customer, in order to confirm that project scope and deliverables were met.	2
5.2	Transfer the ownership of deliverables to the assigned stakeholders in accordance with the project plan, in order to facilitate project closure.	2
5.3	Obtain financial, legal, and administrative closure using generally accepted practices, in order to communicate formal project closure and ensure no further liability.	2, 10
5.4	Distribute the final project report including all project closure-related information, project variances, and any issues, in order to provide the final project status to all stakeholders.	2
5.5	Collate lessons learned through comprehensive project review, in order to create and/or update the organization's knowledge base.	2
5.6	Archive project documents and material in order to retain organizational knowledge, comply with statutory requirements, and ensure availability of data for potential use in future projects and internal/external audits.	2
5.7	Measure customer satisfaction at the end of the project by capturing customer feedback, in order to assist in project evaluation and enhance customer relationships.	2

PMP® Training Kit

Sean Whitaker

Published with the authorization of Microsoft Corporation by:
O'Reilly Media, Inc.
1005 Gravenstein Highway North
Sebastopol, California 95472

Copyright © 2013 by Sean Whitaker
All rights reserved. No part of the contents of this book may be reproduced or transmitted in any form or by any means without the written permission of the publisher.

ISBN: 978-0-7356-5780-9

1 2 3 4 5 6 7 8 9 QG 8 7 6 5 4 3

Printed and bound in the United States of America.

Microsoft Press books are available through booksellers and distributors worldwide. If you need support related to this book, email Microsoft Press Book Support at mspinput@microsoft.com. Please tell us what you think of this book at *http://www.microsoft.com/learning/booksurvey*.

Microsoft and the trademarks listed at *http://www.microsoft.com/about/legal/en/us/IntellectualProperty/Trademarks/EN-US.aspx* are trademarks of the Microsoft group of companies. All other marks are property of their respective owners.

The example companies, organizations, products, domain names, email addresses, logos, people, places, and events depicted herein are fictitious. No association with any real company, organization, product, domain name, email address, logo, person, place, or event is intended or should be inferred.

This book expresses the author's views and opinions. The information contained in this book is provided without any express, statutory, or implied warranties. Neither the authors, O'Reilly Media, Inc., Microsoft Corporation, nor its resellers, or distributors will be held liable for any damages caused or alleged to be caused either directly or indirectly by this book.

Acquisitions and Developmental Editor: Kenyon Brown

Production Editor: Melanie Yarbrough

Editorial Production: Online Training Solutions, Inc. (OTSI)

Technical Reviewer: Dan Tuuri

Indexer: BIM Publishing Services

Cover Design: Twist Creative • Seattle

Cover Composition: Karen Montgomery

Illustrator: Online Training Solutions, Inc. (OTSI)

Contents at a glance

	Introduction	xix
	Preparing for the exam	xxiii
CHAPTER 1	Understanding foundational concepts of project management	1
CHAPTER 2	Integration management	31
CHAPTER 3	Scope management	85
CHAPTER 4	Time management	125
CHAPTER 5	Cost management	187
CHAPTER 6	Quality management	229
CHAPTER 7	Human resource management	265
CHAPTER 8	Communications management	311
CHAPTER 9	Risk management	335
CHAPTER 10	Procurement management	387
CHAPTER 11	Stakeholder management	423
CHAPTER 12	Ethics and professional conduct	453
	Glossary	473
	Index	489

Contents

	Introduction	xix
	Preparing for the exam	xxiii
Chapter 1	**Understanding foundational concepts of project management**	**1**

The purpose of the PMBOK® Guide. 2

What is a project, a program, and a portfolio? 4

What is project management? 8

Project management, operations management, and organizational strategy. 10

Organizational influences on project management. 13

The project life cycle. 15

Exercises 20

Chapter review. 22

Answers. 25

    Exercises   25

    Chapter review   28

Chapter 2	**Integration management**	**31**

What is project integration management?. 33

Develop Project Charter 35

    Inputs   39

    Tools and techniques   42

    Outputs   43

What do you think of this book? We want to hear from you!

Microsoft is interested in hearing your feedback so we can continually improve our books and learning resources for you. To participate in a brief online survey, please visit:

www.microsoft.com/learning/booksurvey/

Develop Project Management Plan. 45
    Tools and techniques   48
    Outputs   50

Direct and Manage Project Work 52
    Inputs   53
    Tools and techniques   54
    Outputs   56

Monitor and Control Project Work 58
    Inputs   59
    Tools and techniques   61
    Outputs   63

Perform Integrated Change Control 65
    Inputs   67
    Tools and techniques   68
    Outputs   69

Close Project or Phase 70
    Inputs   72
    Tools and techniques   73
    Outputs   74

Exercises 75

Chapter summary 76

Chapter review. 77

Answers. 80
    Exercises   80
    Chapter review   81

What do you think of this book? We want to hear from you!

Microsoft is interested in hearing your feedback so we can continually improve our books and learning resources for you. To participate in a brief online survey, please visit:

www.microsoft.com/learning/booksurvey/

Chapter 3 Scope management — 85

- What is project scope management? — 86
- Plan Scope Management — 88
  - Inputs — 89
  - Tools and techniques — 90
  - Outputs — 90
- Collect requirements — 93
  - Inputs — 94
  - Tools and techniques — 95
  - Outputs — 97
- Define scope — 99
  - Inputs — 100
  - Tools and techniques — 101
  - Outputs — 102
- Create WBS — 103
  - Inputs — 104
  - Tools and techniques — 105
  - Outputs — 106
- Validate scope — 108
  - Inputs — 109
  - Tools and techniques — 110
  - Outputs — 111
- Control scope — 112
  - Inputs — 113
  - Tools and techniques — 114
  - Outputs — 114
- Exercises — 116
- Chapter summary — 116
- Chapter review — 117
- Answers — 120
  - Exercises — 120
  - Chapter review — 121

Chapter 4 Time management 125

- What is project time management? 126
- Plan Schedule Management. 127
  - Inputs 127
  - Tools and techniques 128
  - Outputs 129
- Define Activities. 131
  - Inputs 132
  - Tools and techniques 132
  - Outputs 133
- Sequence Activities. 135
  - Inputs 136
  - Tools and techniques 137
  - Outputs 140
- Estimate Activity Resources. 142
  - Inputs 143
  - Tools and techniques 144
  - Outputs 145
- Estimate Activity Durations. 147
  - Inputs 148
  - Tools and techniques 149
  - Outputs 155
- Develop Schedule. 157
  - Inputs 158
  - Tools and techniques 160
  - Outputs 166
- Control Schedule. 169
  - Inputs 169
  - Tools and techniques 170
  - Outputs 173
- Exercises 175

Chapter summary	177
Chapter review	178
Answers	181
Exercises	181
Chapter review	183

Chapter 5   Cost management   187

What is project cost management?	188
Plan Cost Management	189
Inputs	189
Tools and techniques	191
Outputs	192
Estimate Costs	193
Inputs	195
Tools and techniques	196
Outputs	200
Determine Budget	201
Inputs	202
Tools and techniques	203
Outputs	205
Control Costs	207
Inputs	208
Tools and techniques	209
Outputs	215
Exercises	217
Chapter summary	218
Chapter review	219
Answers	222
Exercises	222
Chapter review	225

Chapter 6 Quality management — 229

- What is project quality management? 230
- Plan Quality Management. 232
    - Inputs — 233
    - Tools and techniques — 234
    - Outputs — 240
- Perform Quality Assurance 243
    - Inputs — 244
    - Tools and techniques — 245
    - Outputs — 249
- Control Quality 250
    - Inputs — 251
    - Tools and techniques — 252
    - Outputs — 253
- Exercise 256
- Chapter summary 257
- Chapter review 257
- Answers 260
    - Exercises — 260
    - Chapter review — 261

Chapter 7 Human resource management — 265

- What is project human resource management? 266
- Plan Human Resource Management 267
    - Inputs — 267
    - Tools and techniques — 268
    - Outputs — 278
- Acquire Project Team 279
    - Inputs — 279
    - Tools and techniques — 280
    - Outputs — 282

Develop Project Team	284
Inputs	284
Tools and techniques	285
Outputs	294
Manage Project Team	296
Inputs	296
Tools and techniques	297
Outputs	299
Exercises	301
Chapter summary	302
Chapter review	303
Answers	306
Exercises	306
Chapter review	307

Chapter 8   Communications management   311

What is project communications management?	312
Plan Communications Management	313
Inputs	313
Tools and techniques	314
Outputs	318
Manage Communications	320
Inputs	320
Tools and techniques	321
Outputs	322
Control Communications	324
Inputs	324
Tools and techniques	325
Outputs	326
Exercises	328
Chapter summary	328
Chapter review	329

Answers		331
Exercises		331
Chapter review		332

Chapter 9 Risk management 335

What is project risk management?		336
Plan Risk Management		338
Inputs		338
Tools and techniques		339
Outputs		341
Identify Risks		343
Inputs		344
Tools and techniques		347
Outputs		350
Perform Qualitative Risk Analysis		351
Inputs		352
Tools and techniques		353
Outputs		355
Perform Quantitative Risk Analysis		357
Inputs		358
Tools and techniques		359
Outputs		363
Plan Risk Responses		364
Inputs		364
Tools and techniques		365
Outputs		367
Control Risks		368
Inputs		369
Tools and techniques		370
Outputs		372
Exercises		374

Chapter summary 376

Chapter review 376

Answers 380
    Exercises   380
    Chapter review   383

Chapter 10 Procurement management   387

What is project procurement management? 388

Plan Procurement Management 389
    Inputs   389
    Tools and techniques   392
    Outputs   394

Conduct Procurements 397
    Inputs   397
    Tools and techniques   399
    Outputs   401

Control Procurements 405
    Inputs   406
    Tools and techniques   407
    Outputs   409

Close Procurements 411
    Inputs   411
    Tools and techniques   412
    Outputs   413

Exercises 414

Chapter summary 415

Chapter review 415

Answers 418
    Exercises   418
    Chapter review   418

Chapter 11 Stakeholder management　　　　　　　　　　　　423

What is project stakeholder management?..........................424

Identify Stakeholders..425
    Inputs　　　　　　　　　　　　　　　　　　　　　　　　　　　426
    Tools and techniques　　　　　　　　　　　　　　　　　　　426
    Outputs　　　　　　　　　　　　　　　　　　　　　　　　　428

Plan Stakeholder Management 431
    Inputs　　　　　　　　　　　　　　　　　　　　　　　　　　　432
    Tools and techniques　　　　　　　　　　　　　　　　　　　433
    Outputs　　　　　　　　　　　　　　　　　　　　　　　　　434

Manage Stakeholder Engagement 436
    Inputs　　　　　　　　　　　　　　　　　　　　　　　　　　　437
    Tools and techniques　　　　　　　　　　　　　　　　　　　437
    Outputs　　　　　　　　　　　　　　　　　　　　　　　　　439

Control Stakeholder Engagement 441
    Inputs　　　　　　　　　　　　　　　　　　　　　　　　　　　441
    Tools and techniques　　　　　　　　　　　　　　　　　　　442
    Outputs　　　　　　　　　　　　　　　　　　　　　　　　　443

Exercises..445

Chapter summary..446

Chapter review...446

Answers...449
    Exercises　　　　　　　　　　　　　　　　　　　　　　　　　449
    Chapter review　　　　　　　　　　　　　　　　　　　　　　449

Chapter 12 Ethics and professional conduct　　　　　　　　　　453

Responsibility, respect, fairness, and honesty 454

Responsibility..454

Respect...457

Fairness...458

Honesty...460

Exercise...461

Chapter summary 462
Chapter review. 462
Answers. 467
  Exercise   467
  Chapter review   468

Glossary   473

Index   489

Introduction

This training kit is designed for project management practitioners who plan to earn the Project Management Professional (PMP®) credential offered by the Project Management Institute (PMI). It is assumed that before you begin using this kit, you have ensured that you have the necessary eligibility requirements to take the exam.

The material covered in this training kit relates to the PMP® exam based on the PMBOK® Guide, 5th Edition. The topics in this training kit cover what you need to know for the exam.

By using this training kit, you will learn how to do the following:

- Understand foundational project management concepts and terminology.
- Understand and implement tasks associated with initiating a project.
- Understand and implement tasks associated with planning a project.
- Understand and implement tasks associated with executing a project.
- Understand and implement tasks associated with monitoring and controlling a project.
- Understand and implement tasks associated with closing a project.
- Demonstrate an understanding of the PMBOK® Guide knowledge areas.

Refer to the task mapping page in the front of this book to see where in the book each exam task is covered.

Using the companion CD

A companion CD is included with this training kit. The companion CD contains the following:

- **Practice tests** You can reinforce your understanding of the topics covered in this training kit by using electronic practice tests that you customize to meet your needs. You can practice for the PMP® certification exam by using tests created from a pool of more than 400 realistic exam questions, which give you many practice exams to ensure that you are prepared.
- **An eBook** Instructions to download the electronic version (eBook) of this book is included for when you do not want to carry the printed book with you.

> **NOTE COMPANION CONTENT FOR DIGITAL BOOK READERS**
>
> If you bought a digital-only edition of this book, you can enjoy select content from the print edition's companion CD. Visit *http://aka.ms/PMPTK/files* to get your downloadable content.

How to install the practice tests

To install the practice test software from the companion CD to your hard disk, perform the following steps:

1. Insert the companion CD into your CD drive and accept the license agreement. A CD menu appears.

   > **NOTE** **IF THE CD MENU DOES NOT APPEAR**
   > If the CD menu or the license agreement does not appear, AutoRun might be disabled on your computer. Refer to the Readme.txt file on the CD for alternate installation instructions.

2. Click Practice Tests and follow the instructions on the screen.

How to use the practice tests

To start the practice test software, follow these steps:

1. Click Start | All Programs, and then select Microsoft Press Training Kit Exam Prep.

   A window appears that shows all the Microsoft Press training kit exam prep suites installed on your computer.

2. Double-click the practice test you want to use.

When you start a practice test, you choose whether to take the test in Certification Mode, Study Mode, or Custom Mode:

- **Certification Mode** Closely resembles the experience of taking a certification exam. The test has a set number of questions. It is timed, and you cannot pause and restart the timer.
- **Study Mode** Creates an untimed test during which you can review the correct answers and the explanations after you answer each question.
- **Custom Mode** Gives you full control over the test options so that you can customize them as you like.

In all modes, the user interface when you are taking the test is basically the same but with different options enabled or disabled depending on the mode.

When you review your answer to an individual practice test question, a "References" section is provided that lists where in the training kit you can find the information that relates to that question and provides links to other sources of information. After you click Test Results to score your entire practice test, you can click the Learning Plan tab for a list of references for every objective.

How to uninstall the practice tests

To uninstall the practice test software for a training kit, use the Program And Features option in Windows Control Panel.

Acknowledgments

The author's name appears on the cover of a book, but I recognize that I am only one member of a much larger team. This book is the sum total of the efforts of a very skilled and dedicated team. First of all, thanks to Kenyon Brown at O'Reilly Media for allowing me to write this book. During the writing process, I also worked closely with Kathy Krause and Marlene Lambert at OTSI, and O'Reilly Media Production Editor Melanie Yarbrough. All of them contributed in significant ways to making this a great book. Dan Tuuri was the technical reviewer, and he applied a polish to my sometimes raw initial content. Each of these contributed significantly to this book, and I look forward to working with them all in the future.

Support & feedback

The following sections provide information on errata, book support, feedback, and contact information.

Errata

We've made every effort to ensure the accuracy of this book and its companion content. Any errors that have been reported since this book was published are listed on our Microsoft Press site at oreilly.com:

http://aka.ms/PMPTK/errata

If you find an error that is not already listed, you can report it to us through the same page.

If you need additional support, email Microsoft Press Book Support at:

mspinput@microsoft.com

Please note that product support for Microsoft software is not offered through the addresses above.

We want to hear from you

At Microsoft Press, your satisfaction is our top priority, and your feedback our most valuable asset. Please tell us what you think of this book at:

http://www.microsoft.com/learning/booksurvey

The survey is short, and we read every one of your comments and ideas. Thanks in advance for your input!

Stay in touch

Let us keep the conversation going! We are on Twitter: *http://twitter.com/MicrosoftPress*.

Preparing for the exam

The Project Management Professional (PMP®) credential is a great way to build your resume and let the world know about your level of project management expertise. Passing the PMP® exam and gaining the credential validates your on-the-job experience and knowledge of best practices in the profession of project management. Although there is no substitute for on-the-job experience, preparation through study and hands-on practice can help you prepare for the exam. We recommend that you augment your exam preparation plan by using a combination of available study materials and courses. For example, you might use the *PMP® Training Kit* and another study guide such as *PMP® Rapid Review* by Sean Whitaker (Microsoft Press, 2013) for your "at home" preparation, and take a PMP® examination preparation course for the classroom experience. Choose the combination that you think works best for you.

CHAPTER 1

Understanding foundational concepts of project management

This chapter describes foundational concepts of the PMBOK® Guide. It will introduce you to the purpose and content of the PMBOK® Guide, and provide some definitions of projects, project management, program management, portfolio management, organizational project management, operations management, organizational strategy, business value, and the project life cycle. All of these foundational concepts are important to ensure that you understand the terminology used by the PMBOK® Guide, which also appears in the PMP® exam. It is important that you take time to fully understand these foundational concepts, because they underpin many of the processes, tools, and techniques that come later in the book.

EXAM TIP

Remember that the PMP® exam is testing a lot of elements, including your understanding of the PMBOK® Guide terminology and concepts. You may come across questions that have an answer that is what you would actually call something in real life but it is not how the PMBOK® Guide would refer to it. In this instance, always answer according to the PMBOK® Guide. Also, pay close attention to not only the terms but also the various inputs and outputs.

In this chapter, you will learn how to do the following:

- Introduce and outline the key foundational terms, purpose, and contents of the PMBOK® Guide.
- Understand the differences and interrelationships between project, program, and portfolio management.
- Understand the relationship between organizational project management, operations management, and organizational strategy.

- Understand the role that business value and strategic planning have in project management.
- Define organizational process assets and their benefit to project management.
- Define enterprise environmental factors and the ways in which they can assist and constrain a project.
- Define and understand the characteristics of the project life cycle, including project phases.

The purpose of the PMBOK® Guide

> **MORE INFO** THE PMBOK® GUIDE
>
> You can read more about the purpose of the PMBOK® Guide, 5th edition, in the guide itself, in Chapter 1, section 1.1.

The full title of the *PMBOK® Guide* is *A Guide to the Project Management Body of Knowledge*. If you break that down into its component parts, you can get an understanding of what sort of document it is.

First of all, it is a guide. This means that it is not a prescriptive instruction manual that must be followed to the letter, and individuals and organizations can, and do, choose to only implement appropriate portions of the PMBOK® Guide. It presents the information as a guide for you to use when and if it is useful. Obviously, it is a guide to the profession of project management. Because the profession of project management is both relatively young and also very wide in its application, any book purporting to be about it is necessarily going to be both iterative and also broad in the information contained within it. This is the fifth edition of the PMBOK® Guide and represents a major change from previous versions, with an extra knowledge area and more in-depth coverage of foundation topics. The development and updating of the PMBOK® Guide is an ongoing process, with an updated edition being released every three to four years. Make sure you have access to the latest copy of the PMBOK® Guide. It is also aligned with ISO 21500:2012.

> **EXAM TIP**
>
> ISO 21500:2012 is an international standard for project management developed by the International Organization for Standardization (the initials *ISO* come from the French way of saying this). It provides guidance and a high-level description of concepts and processes that are considered to form good or best practice in the profession of project management.

Finally, as a body of knowledge, it contains what is considered to be a fairly complete set of knowledge about the profession of project management. Many professions, including civil engineering, software engineering, contracting, and even massage therapy have bodies of knowledge associated with them.

Overall, the PMBOK® Guide presents what is generally recognized to be good practice in the profession of project management. This means that the processes, tools, and techniques that it presents are useful to most projects most of the time. It is up to the organization or the project management team to determine which, if any, of the processes, tools, or techniques are useful for any project they are working on. This process of selecting only those processes, tools, and techniques that actually provide benefit when managing your projects is called *tailoring*.

Real world

The PMBOK® Guide is not a project management methodology. It is a framework document containing the collection of what is considered good project management practice for projects of any size, complexity, and industry. In order to build a project management methodology, you are directed to take from the PMBOK® Guide only those processes, tools, and techniques that are appropriate and add value to your project via the process of tailoring.

In addition to representing a robust body of knowledge, the PMBOK® Guide also presents standardized terminology. This means that there is generally a single word or phrase to define and describe each element of project management. It allows project managers and project team members within the same organization, and between organizations, to communicate effectively.

Real world

The benefit of a standardized terminology cannot be underestimated. I have been in many situations with people from differing organizations who make simple mistakes because they use different words for the same thing. I remember once I asked a contract manager on my team for the project schedule, and he sent me the schedule of materials. After three requests and increasing confusion on both sides, we finally figured out that I was requesting what he referred to as the project timeframe. On another occasion, I was assisting a firm that was growing rapidly and recruiting project managers every week. The biggest challenge they faced was the different terminology all these experienced project managers used. We worked on developing a common organization-wide project management vocabulary to improve communication between all the project managers and project team members.

Of course, your main interest in the PMBOK® Guide is that it is a very useful text upon which to base your study for the Project Management Professional (PMP®) certification. Passing the PMP® examination requires knowledge of the entire contents of the PMBOK® Guide, as well as knowing the "Project Management Institute Code of Ethics and Professional Conduct."

EXAM TIP

Even if you have a photographic memory and could remember every page of the PMBOK® Guide, you would not necessarily score 100 percent on the PMP® examination because the PMP® examination is based upon the results of a role delineation study about what professional attributes a project manager should have. The PMBOK® Guide presents a very useful text upon which to base your study. This is because the contents of the PMBOK® Guide are built upon the knowledge of many disciplines, and often a single phrase or sentence in the PMBOK® Guide can refer to an entire other subject area. That is why simply studying the PMBOK® Guide is not the best approach to preparing to sit the PMP® examination. This book will not only introduce you to the entire contents of the PMBOK® Guide but also present a lot of other information so you are prepared to pass the examination.

 Quick check

1. How should you use the PMBOK® Guide in your projects?
2. Apart from offering a collection of good practices in project management, what other main benefit does the PMBOK® Guide provide?

Quick check answers

1. By selecting from it only those processes, tools, and techniques that are appropriate for your projects based on size, complexity, and industry.
2. It provides a standardized terminology, or lexicon, for the profession of project management.

What is a project, a program, and a portfolio?

MORE INFO **PROJECT, PROGRAM, PORTFOLIO**

You can read more about the definition of a project, a program, and a portfolio in the PMBOK® Guide, 5th edition, in Chapter 1, section 1.2.

It may seem straightforward to define exactly what a *project* is, but it is important that you know how the PMBOK® Guide defines one. There are several key elements that separate project work from ongoing or operational work.

The first and most important element of a project is that it has a defined start and end, making it a temporary endeavor. On the other hand, operational, or ongoing, work is ongoing and repetitive.

A project also delivers something unique, something that hasn't been done before. Ongoing work is repetitive and delivers the same thing every day or every year.

Finally, a project delivers a product, service, or result. This allows projects to be used to deliver a range of deliverables in many industries, whether they are based on goods or services.

EXAM TIP

There are only two types of work in the world, according to the PMBOK® Guide. All work is either operational work or project work. If it is operational work, then it is repetitive and ongoing. If it is project work, then it has a defined start, middle, and end and delivers a product, service, or result.

> **Real world**
>
> You may find a degree of overlap between project work and operational work. There are certainly some projects that bear a striking resemblance to each other and perhaps could be construed as ongoing work. It is the unique aspect of each—and that it is done slightly differently, in a different location, to produce a slightly different product, service, or result—that makes it a project.

A *portfolio* of projects includes all the projects, whether interdependent or not, that an organization is undertaking. They are only connected by their common goal of delivering the organization's strategic goals.

A *program* of projects describes projects that have some sort of interdependency between them. They may all be part of a larger deliverable; for example, you could have several projects, each of which makes a different part of a new aircraft, but the final deliverable depends on managing the projects together as a program. The projects may also share a common goal, and the program manager needs to monitor and resolve any actual or potential conflicts in the pursuit of those goals.

A project can be part of a program and part of a portfolio. Figure 1-1 shows that all programs are part of a portfolio, but that projects can either be directly part of a portfolio or part of a program.

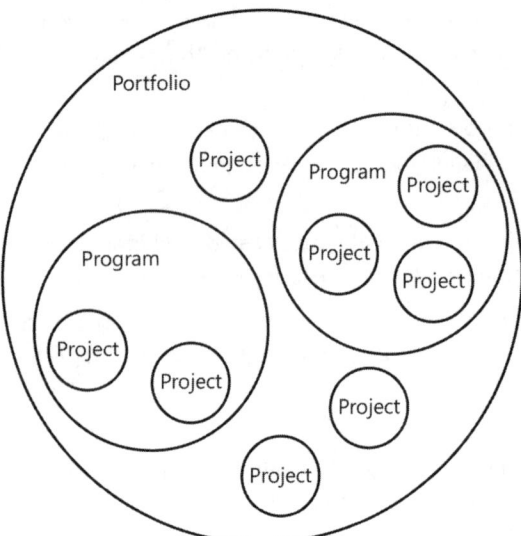

FIGURE 1-1 A portfolio encompasses all projects and programs within an organization.

Project, program, and portfolio management are separate yet interrelated elements of the profession of project management. The combination of the project management, program management, and portfolio management disciplines is viewed as integral and necessary to deliver the organizational strategy and, therefore, any action undertaken in any of the three elements should always align with the organization's strategy.

Portfolio management ensures that all projects selected to be completed by the organization align with the organizational strategy. Portfolio management has an organizational scope that reflects the organizational strategy. Often projects or programs are grouped together into a single portfolio that reflects a specific strategy.

EXAM TIP

The PMBOK® Guide places a great deal of emphasis on the alignment of organizational strategy and the profession of project management as a strategic enabler for delivering the strategy. Always assume that the default position in a question is that an organization has a strategy and is using project management to achieve that strategy.

Program management focuses on managing interdependencies within projects with a common goal or capability. Program managers are skilled at forecasting, anticipating, and dealing with real or perceived conflict between projects in the same program. All programs have projects, but not all projects are part of programs.

EXAM TIP

An interesting distinction made by the PMBOK® Guide is that if the relationship between separate projects is based upon having a shared client or seller, or shared technology or resources, then the projects should be managed as a portfolio rather than a program.

The *project management office* (PMO) is the part of the organization responsible for project management excellence. It provides support for the project manager, which can mean many things, depending on the level of organizational project management maturity. A project management office can simply be a place where a project management methodology is developed and stored, or at the other end of the spectrum, it can be where all the project managers are located, a place that provides common reporting and manages shared resources and it is responsible for portfolio, program, and project management across the entire organization.

The PMBOK® Guide defines three main types of project management office, differentiated by the level of control and influence they have, as shown in Figure 1-2. The supportive project management office provides templates and basic processes and captures lesson learned. The controlling project management office may take responsibility for development and implementation of a project management methodology and provide project governance as well. The directive project management office takes direct control of management of projects within the organization.

Supportive   Controlling   Directive

◄─────────────────────────►

Low   *Level of control and influence*   High

FIGURE 1-2 The types of project management office (PMO) can be shown on a spectrum from supportive to directive.

The type of project management office an organization should have also depends upon the level of organizational project management maturity the organization has attained. *Organizational project management maturity* is a way of assessing where an organization is currently with its level of sophistication and maturity around project management processes, tools, templates, and methodology, and then assessing where they should be. Organizations handling large and complex projects should be at a higher level of project management maturity than organizations managing small and simple projects. Organizations with a high level of project management maturity should have a more directive project management office.

EXAM TIP

If you find a reference to OPM3 in the exam, it is referring to the Organizational Project Management Maturity Model, which is a tool from the Project Management Institute (PMI) for assessing an organization's level of portfolio, program, and project management maturity.

> ✓ **Quick check**
>
> 1. What are the three key elements that distinguish project work from ongoing work?
> 2. What are the key differences between a program and a portfolio of projects?
> 3. How would you describe the main differences between project, program, and portfolio management?
> 4. What function would a project management office play in an organization with a high level of project management maturity?
>
> **Quick check answers**
>
> 1. First, a project has a temporal element defining a start and an end, making it temporary rather than ongoing. Second, it delivers something unique and never done before. Finally, it involves delivery of a product, service, or result.
> 2. In a program of projects the projects share an interdependency, whereas in a portfolio of projects the projects are only united by the fact that they are all being completed by the same organization.
> 3. Portfolio management is the top-level selection process of projects to ensure that they deliver the organization's strategy. A program of projects contains projects that share a common goal or capability, and individual projects are focused on delivering a product, service, or result that will contribute to achievement of the organizational strategy. Remember that all programs have projects, but not all projects are part of programs.
> 4. An organization with a high level of project management maturity will use a directive project management office to take control of the way in which all projects are selected, managed, reported on, and communicated about within the organization.

What is project management?

> **MORE INFO** **PROJECT MANAGEMENT**
>
> You can read more about the definition of project management in the PMBOK® Guide, 5th edition, in Chapter 1, section 1.3.

Project management takes the tools, techniques, and skills contained in the PMBOK® Guide and applies them to the project to deliver the product, service, or result. It is a proactive, rather than a reactive, discipline.

> **EXAM TIP**
>
> Being proactive is a key point about professional project management. If there is any question in the exam that gives you the option to be proactive, it is probably the correct answer.

The PMBOK® Guide, 5th edition, contains a description of 47 project management process in 10 knowledge areas. These 47 processes are placed within five process groups of initiating, planning, executing, monitoring and controlling, and closing to describe the stage in the project in which they are best used. Managing a project means taking the appropriate process and the tools and techniques associated with it and applying them appropriately to the work that needs to be done. Project management, then, is simply the application of any of the PMBOK® Guide knowledge areas with the goal of delivering a product, service, or result.

One of the tasks of project management is the balancing of competing constraints on a project. These constraints can be scope, quality, schedule, budget or cost, resources, and risk. If any one of these constraints changes, it will likely place additional pressure on one or more of the other constraints. For example, if you have to deliver a project in a shorter time period, you may need additional budget to complete the work, and your known risks may increase while quality decreases.

> **EXAM TIP**
>
> You should know that one important aspect of project management is about recognizing and navigating your way through competing constraints on a project. This is evident in planning a project and also when considering a request for a change to a project, where a request for more time may impact schedule, risk, or quality.

An important aspect of project management is that, generally speaking, you cannot know everything there is to know about a project at the outset and, thus, project management is highly iterative. This means that you may be able to accurately define the work to be done for the next few weeks, but you can't plan as well beyond that because there is more uncertainty. So you plan in an iterative manner, meaning that you plan many times, each time with more information. *Progressive elaboration* is an iterative process that acknowledges that you will know more the more you do. For example, at the beginning of a software project you may know the general expected outcome and the first steps on the path to delivering it, but as you move along in the project you become more aware of the magnitude of the work and can plan the project schedule, budget, and risks better.

Rolling wave planning is another type of iterative planning where you plan in detail the next appropriate time period and, as you keep progressing throughout a project, you keep planning that same length of time in detail.

EXAM TIP

If you find the term "progressive elaboration" or "rolling wave planning" in the examination, it is referring to the concept of knowing more about the project the more work you do.

Real world

It is important to let your project stakeholders know that projects are generally iterative and subject to progressive elaboration, to counter the expectation that you can plan everything at the beginning of a project.

 Quick check

1. How would project management differ from managing an ongoing business activity?
2. How does iterative planning differ from progressive elaboration of a project?

Quick check answers

1. Project management uses the process, tools, and techniques of the PMBOK® Guide, is subject to multiple interdependent constraints, and is subject to iterations and progressive elaboration. It is also a temporary endeavor with a defined end. Ongoing operational business activity may or may not be subject to interdependent constraints, and it does not have a defined end.
2. You can deliberately choose to plan iteratively even with a known scope of work. You can decide to focus your detailed planning actives on the immediate future and revisit the planning stages as the project progresses. Progressive elaboration, or rolling wave planning, implies that not everything is known about a project and more will become known as the project moves along.

Project management, operations management, and organizational strategy

MORE INFO PROJECT MANAGEMENT, OPERATIONS MANAGEMENT, AND ORGANIZATIONAL STRATEGY

You can read more about project management, operations management, and organizational strategy in the PMBOK® Guide, 5th edition, in Chapter 1, section 1.5.

As you already know, project management is all about delivering a product, service, or result. After this product, service, or result has been delivered as part of the entire project work or simply as part of a project phase, it normally gets handed over to operational management. Operational management differs from project management in that it is a permanent part of any organization and is focused on the ongoing activities of the business, whereas project management is focused on the temporary activities of project delivery. Operational management also provides the overall strategy for the organization, which is used to help select the right projects.

Obviously, each area intersects at the point where the deliverable is handed over. At this point, the normal operations of the organization may need to change or adapt to accommodate the deliverable. This is one role of operational managers.

EXAM TIP

For the exam, you need to know the difference between operational work and project work, and that operational management often takes responsibility for the deliverable for the project when it has been completed.

Real world

An important tip for any project manager is to include the end users responsible for use and maintenance of any deliverable in the list of stakeholders to be consulted. They will often have real-world experience in the use and ongoing maintenance of the deliverable that perhaps the people who design the deliverable don't.

The *business value* is the sum of all tangible and intangible values in the organization. It can include all capital assets of an organization as well as intangible elements such as brand recognition. Organizations strive to increase their business value, and they can use project management to help them do this. The successful creation of business value is enhanced by having a clear strategy and using the strategy to select projects that deliver appropriate business value. In this way, project management can contribute to the business value of an organization.

More specifically, portfolio management selects the projects that align with organizational strategy, program management manages interconnected projects, and project management delivers unique products, service, and results, all of which contribute to greater business value. The creation of business value is the final link in the process whereby project management can be viewed as a key strategic enabler for a business.

Real world

It is important that project managers have a sound understanding of operational management objectives so they understand why their projects are important and how they fit into the overall organization strategy and add business value. In my own career I have found that a business education has helped my project management and, conversely, my project management experience has helped my operational management efforts.

✓ Quick check

1. Describe the two main points at which the worlds of operational management and project management intersect.
2. What are the key elements that make up business value?
3. How can project management contribute to the creation of business value?
4. How does portfolio management assist in the creation of business value?

Quick check answers

1. The first point of intersection is that operational management provides the overall organizational strategy that is used to select the right projects. The second main point where the two worlds meet is when operational management takes ownership of any project deliverable.
2. Business value is made up of both the tangible and intangible elements of a business.
3. Project management delivers products, services, or results that add either tangible or intangible business value.
4. Portfolio management focuses on ensuring that any projects selected are aligned with the organizational strategy and that the strategy delivers increased business value.

Organizational influences on project management

> **MORE INFO** **ORGANIZATIONAL INFLUENCES**
>
> You can read more about the organizational influences on project management in the PMBOK® Guide, 5th edition, in Chapter 2, section 2.1.

Projects are not completed in a vacuum, devoid of influence by an organization's culture, style, or structure. It is important for a project manager to recognize that each of these elements can positively or negatively influence the outcome of a project. Different organizations have different cultures. These cultures can be observed by noting such things as the values, beliefs, and expectations held by senior management; any relevant policies and procedures that the organization has; its motivation and reward systems; its tolerance toward risk; its attitudes toward hierarchy and power and authority relationships; and such things as the expected work and work hours. The organizational culture is usually established by the founders of the organization, developed by the current employees, and perpetuated through its ongoing recruitment policies.

> **Real world**
>
> Often in the real world you will find organizations that do the same work technically but have completely different organizational cultures. I know of several people who have left one organization to go to a competitor, only to return within a few months because they didn't like the particular organizational culture.

In addition to the internal organizational culture founded by recruitment policies and current employees, an organization's culture can also be influenced by the broader cultural environment in which it operates. This includes factors such as employment market conditions, level of competition, and external political influences. It is up to the project manager to make sure he or she assesses and understands how these cultural factors may impact the project. This creates challenges for the project manager, who must be aware of issues around multiculturalism, particularly with the increase of globalization and the use of project team members from different countries.

> **EXAM TIP**
>
> Both the organization's culture and its structure are enterprise environmental factors because they sit outside of the direct realm of the project and can assist or constrain the project.

So far this chapter has looked at the impact of organizational culture upon projects. Other important aspects of organizational influence upon projects are organizational process assets and enterprise environmental factors.

Organizational process assets, as the name suggests, are any existing plans, procedures, policies, templates, and knowledge bases that the organization owns that can be used to assist the project. Organizational process assets appear as inputs into most of the 47 planning processes in the PMBOK® Guide. Specific examples of organizational process assets include the project management methodology, any blank templates, any change control processes and procedures, any financial control reporting requirements, any defined communication methods, any standardized approach to risk management the organization has, and any project closure guidelines, requirements, or checklists.

Enterprise environmental factors are always external to the project but not necessarily external to the organization; they are just not under the control of the project team. Enterprise environmental factors feature as inputs into most of the 47 planning processes in the PMBOK® Guide. Specific examples of enterprise environmental factors include the organizational culture and structure, any relevant government or industry standards that can affect the project, any personnel administration requirements, any external marketplace conditions, the stakeholder risk tolerances, the external political climate, and any project management information systems, including any software owned by the organization. Many people assume that project management software is an organizational process asset; however, it is generally considered to be an enterprise environmental factor because it is usually licensed rather than owned.

> **Real world**
>
> The most common form of organizational process asset that most project managers encounter is the project management methodology that an organization has. A project management methodology itself can mean many things. It can be as simple as a range of blank templates available to the project manager, or at the other end of the spectrum it can be a fully defined set of processes, procedures, templates, and databases that must be used for all projects.

EXAM TIP

A general rule of thumb for remembering the difference between organizational process assets and enterprise environmental factors is that, generally speaking, organizational process assets can be used to assist a project, whereas enterprise environmental factors will often constrain a project. Additionally, as the name suggests, with organizational process assets the organization must own the assets.

Quick check

1. What are some of the main defining characteristics of an organization's culture?
2. Why should a project manager be aware of the organizational culture?
3. How is an organization's culture established and perpetuated?

Quick check answers

1. The main defining characteristics of an organizational culture can be observed in the organization's visions and values, beliefs, policies, procedures, reward systems, tolerance for risk, work ethic, and view of authority relationships.
2. A project manager needs to be aware of the overall organizational culture and specific elements within it because these will affect the projects he or she is working on, and it is best to leverage those parts of the organizational culture that contribute to project success and mitigate those parts of the organizational culture that may increase the chances of project failure.
3. The culture of an organization generally reflects the values of its founding members. It is then perpetuated and reproduced by both senior managers and leaders, and the organization's recruitment policies.

The project life cycle

> **MORE INFO** **PROJECT LIFE CYCLE**
>
> You can read more about the project life cycle in the PMBOK® Guide, 5th edition, in Chapter 2, section 2.4.

 The *project life cycle* is central to the PMBOK® Guide. It forms the basis for the five PMBOK® Guide process groups. The project life cycle provides a framework and also describes the generally sequential activities undertaken in any project, beginning with the process of starting or initiating the project, organizing and preparing to do the work of the project, then carrying out the defined project work, and finally recognizing the closeout of a project.

 The concept of the project life cycle moving from a project's beginnings to its closure can be applied to an entire project or to the different *phases* within the project. Project phases are best used when there is a clear and defining milestone between activities. For example, a project may have a design phase that requires signoff on the design (which would be the milestone) before the project is allowed to proceed to the implementation phase. Project phases can be performed in a linear, sequential fashion, with successive phases having to wait until a predecessor phase is complete before proceeding. Alternatively, phases can also overlap, with the successive phase able to start prior to the completion of the predecessor phase.

EXAM TIP

Be prepared to find terms such as "milestone," "stage gate," "phase gate," "kill point," or "stop/go point" in questions relating to phases of a project.

A project management *methodology* takes an approach based on the project life cycle and perhaps its phases, and describes the processes that will be followed and the tools and templates to be used. Most project management methodologies are built upon the concept of the project life cycle and have different procedures that reflect different parts of the project life cycle.

Real world

There are many different types of project management methodologies in existence. They range from the highly iterative agile methodologies used in information technology projects to the more predictive methodologies also known as waterfall methodologies, where there is a clear linear progression from start-up through to closure of a project. In developing an appropriate project management methodology for an organization, consideration must be given to the type of projects, the size of projects, the organizational culture, the timeframe for project delivery, and the maturity of the organization. The development of a project management methodology is not a one-size-fits-all proposition. In fact, a good methodology will always be flexible enough to accommodate different projects.

The concept of the project life cycle incorporating the initiation, planning, execution, and closing phases of the project is based upon the Shewhart and Deming *Plan-Do-Check-Act (PDCA) cycle*. This cycle stars with making a plan, then doing what you planned, then checking that what you are doing is what you planned, then acting if you find any variance between what you are doing and what you planned to do, and then going back and planning again. Figure 1-3 shows the Shewhart and Deming Plan-Do-Check-Act (PDCA) cycle.

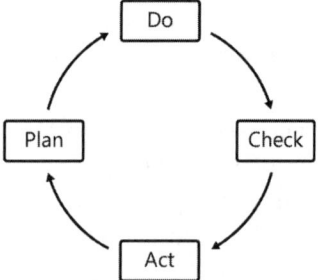

FIGURE 1-3 The Shewhart and Deming Plan-Do-Check-Act cycle shows the iterative nature of project management.

This cycle forms the basis of the initiating, planning (Plan), executing (Do), monitoring and controlling (Check and Act), and closing process groups of the PMBOK® Guide. Figure 1-4 shows the PMBOK® Guide process groups.

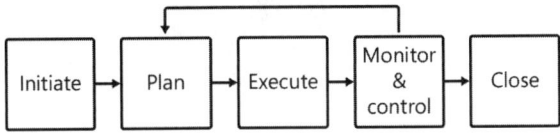

FIGURE 1-4 The PMBOK® Guide process groups can be shown as an iterative cycle of activity.

EXAM TIP

Take care to read any questions about life cycles to determine whether they are referring to the project life cycle or the product life cycle. The project life cycle refers to the project from initiation to closing. The product life cycle refers to the design, manufacturing, use, and obsolescence of the product. The product life cycle can be many years longer than the project life cycle.

The five PMBOK® Guide process groups describe work to be done in each of the 10 specific knowledge areas. Table 1-1 shows how the five process groups and the 10 knowledge areas from the PMBOK® Guide overlap.

TABLE 1-1 The PMBOK® Guide process groups and knowledge areas

	Initiating processes	Planning processes	Executing processes	Monitoring and Controlling processes	Closing processes
Project Integration management	■ Develop Project Charter	■ Develop Project Management Plan	■ Direct and Manage Project Work	■ Monitor and Control Project Work ■ Perform Integrated Change Control	■ Close Project or Phase
Project Scope management		■ Plan Scope Management ■ Collect Requirements ■ Define Scope ■ Create WBS		■ Validate Scope ■ Control Scope	

The project life cycle **CHAPTER 1** **17**

	Initiating processes	Planning processes	Executing processes	Monitoring and Controlling processes	Closing processes
Project Time management		■ Plan Schedule Management ■ Define Activities ■ Sequence Activities ■ Estimate Activity Resources ■ Estimate Activity Durations ■ Develop Schedule		■ Control Schedule	
Project Cost management		■ Plan Cost Management ■ Estimate Costs ■ Determine Budget		■ Control Costs	
Project Quality management		■ Plan Quality Management	■ Perform Quality Assurance	■ Control Quality	
Project Human Resource management		■ Plan Human Resource Management	■ Acquire Project Team ■ Develop Project Team ■ Manage Project Team		
Project Communications management		■ Plan Communications Management	■ Manage Communications	■ Control Communications	
Project Risk management		■ Plan Risk Management ■ Identify Risks ■ Perform Qualitative Risk Analysis ■ Perform Quantitative Risk Analysis ■ Plan Risk Responses		■ Control Risks	

	Initiating processes	Planning processes	Executing processes	Monitoring and Controlling processes	Closing processes
Project Procurement management		■ Plan Procurement Management	■ Conduct Procurement	■ Control Procurements	■ Close Procurements
Project Stakeholder management	■ Identify Stakeholders	■ Plan Stakeholder Management	■ Manage Stakeholder Engagement	■ Control Stakeholder Engagement	

EXAM TIP

Try memorizing this table to help you remember the sequence of processes in the exam. An easy way to remember the knowledge areas is to use a mnemonic. My favorite, after you remove the word *Project* from each one, is: *In Summer The Cruel Queen Hates Cold Runny Porridge Snacks*. Notice that the first letter of each word in the sentence links to the first letter in each of the knowledge areas. Try making up your own mnemonic. If you are a numbers sort of person, try remembering the following number sequence 2 - 24 - 8 - 11 - 2. Those numbers are the number of processes in the Initiating, Planning, Executing, Monitoring and Controlling, and Closing process groups, respectively. Another set of numbers is 6 - 6 - 7 - 4 - 3 - 4 - 3- 6 - 4 - 4, which are the numbers of processes in each knowledge area from Integration Management through Stakeholder Management.

 Quick check

1. What sort of projects benefit from a phased approach?
2. What are the four parts of the Shewhart and Deming cycle?
3. What are the five PMBOK® Guide process groups?

Quick check answers

1. Projects that have well-defined milestones are suitable for a phased approach.
2. The four parts are Plan, Do, Check, and Act.
3. The five PMBOK® Guide process groups are Initiating, Planning, Executing, Monitoring and Controlling, and Closing a project.

Exercises

The answers for these exercises are located in the "Answers" section at the end of this chapter.

1. Consider the following scenarios. For each scenario, decide whether it is a project, a program, a portfolio, or ongoing work.

    A. The implementation of a new piece of software to run an organization's payroll

    B. The construction of a new house

    C. The development of a new housing subdivision

    D. Filming the first movie of a movie trilogy

    E. Increasing sales from the previous year

    F. The design phase of a new piece of software

    G. The range of projects an organization is undertaking to increase market share

    H. The installation of new servers as part of a major upgrade to an organization's software and hardware systems

    I. A new marketing campaign designed to bring in more business

    J. The development of a new product that will increase operational profit

    K. Several different pieces of software being developed that use the same developers

    L. All the new house projects being undertaken by a construction company

2. Practice filling out the following blank table with process groups, knowledge areas, and processes.

The PMBOK® Guide process groups

The PMBOK Guide knowledge area

Chapter summary

- This chapter introduced you to many foundational concepts of the PMBOK® Guide. It began by looking at the purpose and contents of the PMBOK® Guide and then went on to define a project and the unique characteristics that differentiate projects from ongoing or repetitive work. It is important that you understand how project work is different from ongoing or operational work.

- The chapter then looked at the differences between and the relationships among project management, program management, and portfolio management. The link to portfolio management also includes consideration of the link between projects and strategic planning and how project management can be a strategic enabler for an organization. Ultimately, the strategic decisions made and the way in which project management can support them will deliver increased business value.

- The role of the project management office (PMO) in any organization is an important one and reflects the level of organizational project management maturity that the organization has attained. The primary function of a PMO and whether it is supportive, controlling, or directive is a direct reflection of the level of maturity of the organization.

- The role of organizational process assets and enterprise environmental factors in the success or failure of project management is important. Additionally, organizational process assets and enterprise environmental factors feature in many of the 47 processes of the PMBOK® Guide as inputs.

- The concept of the project life cycle, which begins with the start of a project and moves through the organization, preparation, and execution of the planned project work, and finally the closing of the project, is a central concept to many of the processes and knowledge areas in the PMBOK® Guide. The concept of the project life cycle can also be applied to separate project phases.

Chapter review

Test your knowledge of the information in Chapter 1 by answering these questions. The answers to these questions, and the explanations of why each answer choice is correct or incorrect, are located in the "Answers" section at the end of this chapter.

1. What is the primary role of the portfolio manager?
    - **A.** To deliver the unique product, service, or result of the project
    - **B.** To provide project governance and sponsorship
    - **C.** To assess all potential projects against known organizational strategic goals
    - **D.** To directly manage people assigned to several different projects

2. What is the primary purpose of the PMBOK® Guide?
   A. To provide a flexible methodology for all projects, no matter how large or small
   B. To identify a project management framework based on what is generally recognized as good practice
   C. To define a prescriptive approach to managing projects
   D. To present all the known project management information in a concise manner

3. What is the best description of rolling wave planning?
   A. Project management planning activities that become more detailed as you move through the project
   B. Only planning the first phase of a project
   C. Planning the entire project before starting execution
   D. Only planning the next phase in a project

4. What is the relationship between successful projects and an organization's strategic goals?
   A. There is no relationship between the two, because they are separate and distinct parts of an organization.
   B. The successful delivery of projects can be a strategic enabler and deliver strategic goals.
   C. The project selection methodology will determine what an organization's strategic goals are.
   D. Projects deliver programs, which in turn deliver portfolios, which in turn deliver strategy.

5. What is the best role for a project management office in an organization with a low level of project management maturity?
   A. Directive
   B. Controlling
   C. Supportive
   D. Enabling

6. What is the name for a group of related projects managed in a coordinated way to obtain a synergy not found by managing them individually?
   A. Multi projects
   B. Portfolio
   C. Program
   D. Strategy

7. The PMBOK® Guide process groups are based upon which life cycle model?

   A. The Check-Plan-Do-Act cycle

   B. The Plan-Do-Check-Act cycle

   C. The Plan-Check-Act-Do cycle

   D. The Do-Check-Act-Plan cycle

8. How many processes are there in the Risk Management knowledge area?

   A. Three

   B. Four

   C. Five

   D. Six

9. How many processes are there in the Monitoring and Controlling process group?

   A. 9

   B. 10

   C. 11

   D. 12

10. Which knowledge area does not have a Monitoring and Controlling process?

    A. Cost Management

    B. Initiating

    C. Human Resource Management

    D. Closing

Answers

This section contains the answers to the questions for the "Exercises" and "Chapter review" sections in this chapter.

Exercises

1. Consider the following scenarios. For each scenario, decide whether it is a project, a program, a portfolio, or ongoing work.

    A. The implementation of a new piece of software to run an organization's payroll

    This is an example of a project.

    B. The construction of a new house

    This is an example of a project.

    C. The development of a new housing subdivision

    This would generally been viewed as either a very large project or a program. This demonstrates that there is a grey area between projects, programs, and portfolios.

    D. Filming the first movie of a movie trilogy

    The first movie will be viewed as a project; the entire trilogy would be viewed as a program.

    E. Increasing sales from the previous year

    This is an example of ongoing work.

    F. The design phase of a new piece of software

    Because this is a phase, it would best be viewed as part of a program.

    G. The range of projects an organization is undertaking to increase market share

    This is an example of a program with a common goal of increasing market share.

    H. The installation of new servers as part of a major upgrade to an organization's software and hardware systems

    This is an example of a project that is part of a broader program.

    I. A new marketing campaign designed to bring in more business

    Marketing is generally considered to be an ongoing activity rather than a project.

J. The development of a new product that will increase operational profit

This is an example of a project that will be handed over to the operations side of the organization.

K. Several different pieces of software being developed that use the same developers

Merely using the same developers doesn't mean that these projects are part of a program. Instead, they should be considered as individual projects that are part of a portfolio.

L. All the new house projects being undertaken by a construction company

This is an example of a portfolio of projects.

2. Practice filling out the following blank table with process groups, knowledge areas, and processes.

The PMBOK® Guide process groups

		Initiating processes	Planning processes	Executing processes	Monitoring and Controlling processes	Closing processes
The PMBOK Guide knowledge area	**Project Integration management**	■ Develop Project Charter	■ Develop Project Management Plan	■ Direct and Manage Project Work	■ Monitor and Control Project Work ■ Perform Integrated Change Control	■ Close Project or Phase
	Project Scope management		■ Plan Scope Management ■ Collect Requirements ■ Define Scope ■ Create WBS		■ Validate Scope ■ Control Scope	
	Project Time management		■ Plan Schedule Management ■ Define Activities ■ Sequence Activities ■ Estimate Activity Resources ■ Estimate Activity Durations ■ Develop Schedule		■ Control Schedule	

The PMBOK® Guide process groups

	Initiating processes	Planning processes	Executing processes	Monitoring and Controlling processes	Closing processes
Project Cost management		■ Plan Cost Management ■ Estimate Costs ■ Determine Budget		■ Control Costs	
Project Quality management		■ Plan Quality Management	■ Perform Quality Assurance	■ Control Quality	
Project Human Resource management		■ Plan Human Resource Management	■ Acquire Project Team ■ Develop Project Team ■ Manage Project Team		
Project Communications management		■ Plan Communications Management	■ Manage Communications	■ Control Communications	
Project Risk management		■ Plan Risk Management ■ Identify Risks ■ Perform Qualitative Risk Analysis ■ Perform Quantitative Risk Analysis ■ Plan Risk Responses		■ Control Risks	
Project Procurement management		■ Plan Procurement Management	■ Conduct Procurement	■ Control Procurements	■ Close Procurements
Project Stakeholder management	■ Identify Stakeholders	■ Plan Stakeholder Management	■ Manage Stakeholder Engagement	■ Control Stakeholder Engagement	

(The PMBOK Guide knowledge area)

Chapter review

1. **Correct answer: C**

   A. **Incorrect:** The project manager takes responsibility for delivering the product, service, or result of a project.

   B. **Incorrect:** It may be that on occasion a portfolio manager may provide some governance and sponsorship advice, but it is not the portfolio manager's primary role.

   C. **Correct:** The portfolio manager operates at a strategic level within the organization.

   D. **Incorrect:** It would be the program manager or even a functional manager who would take responsibility for managing people on several projects, depending on the type of organizational structure in place.

2. **Correct Answer: B**

   A. **Incorrect:** The PMBOK® Guide does not provide a methodology. You are able to build a methodology from the contents of the PMBOK® Guide via the process of tailoring.

   B. **Correct:** The PMBOK® Guide collects and presents what is generally considered to be good practice across a wide range of industries and presents this information as a framework rather than a methodology.

   C. **Incorrect:** The PMBOK® Guide emphasizes in several places that, through the process of tailoring, you should only take from the PMBOK® Guide what is appropriate to your project.

   D. **Incorrect:** The PMBOK® Guide does not claim to present all known project management information, only that which is generally considered good practice across a wide range of industries.

3. **Correct Answer: A**

   A. **Correct:** Rolling wave planning acknowledges that you will iteratively plan the project as you move along the project life cycle.

   B. **Incorrect:** Only planning the first phase of a project is typical for phased projects, because there may be an important milestone between phases that prevents further planning.

   C. **Incorrect:** Planning the entire project before starting is a very rare occurrence and probably only suitable for small, easily defined projects.

   D. **Incorrect:** Iteratively planning a phase of a project is not an example of rolling wave planning.

4. **Correct Answer: B**

    A. **Incorrect:** There is a strong relationship between successful projects and an organization achieving its strategic goals.

    B. **Correct:** By selecting projects that deliver strategic goals and then successfully delivering these projects, an organization can achieve its strategic goals.

    C. **Incorrect:** It is the organization's strategy that dictates which projects get selected.

    D. **Incorrect:** There is not always a direct linear connection between projects, programs, portfolios, and strategy.

5. **Correct answer: C**

    A. **Incorrect:** Directive project management offices are generally best in an organization with a high level of project management maturity.

    B. **Incorrect:** Controlling project management offices are generally a sign of an organization improving its organizational project management maturity.

    C. **Correct:** Supportive project management offices are generally a sign of a low level of project management maturity, because they do not support a lot of complexity.

    D. **Incorrect:** This is a made-up term and is not from the PMBOK® Guide.

6. **Correct Answer: C**

    A. **Incorrect:** Multi projects is a made-up term that does not describe a coordinated approach to interrelated projects.

    B. **Incorrect:** Portfolios are groups of projects related only by the fact that they are being performed by a single organization.

    C. **Correct:** A program is a group of projects related in some way and that are managed to achieve benefits not gained by managing them independently.

    D. **Incorrect:** Strategy is the organization's future direction and how it is going to achieve this.

7. **Correct Answer: B**

    A. **Incorrect:** The correct order requires planning to come first and checking to come after doing.

    B. **Correct:** The Plan-Do-Check-Act cycle by Shewhart and Deming describes an iterative approach to management.

    C. **Incorrect:** The correct order requires checking to come after doing and before acting.

    D. **Incorrect:** The correct order requires planning to come first.

8. **Correct Answer: D**

    A. **Incorrect:** There are six processes, not three, in the Risk Management knowledge area.

    B. **Incorrect:** There are six processes, not four, in the Risk Management knowledge area.

    C. **Incorrect:** There are six processes, not five, in the Risk Management knowledge area.

    D. **Correct:** The six processes in the Risk Management knowledge area are Plan Risk Management, Identify Risks, Perform Qualitative Risk Analysis, Perform Quantitative Risk Analysis, Plan Risk Responses, and Control Risks.

9. **Correct Answer: C**

    A. **Incorrect:** There are 11 processes, not 9, in the Monitoring and Controlling process group.

    B. **Incorrect:** There are 11 processes, not 10, in the Monitoring and Controlling process group.

    C. **Correct:** The 11 processes in the Monitoring and Controlling process group are Monitor and Control Project Work, Perform Integrated Change Control, Validate Scope, Control Scope, Control Schedule, Control Costs, Control Quality, Control Communications, Control Risks, Control Procurements, and Control Stakeholder Engagement.

    D. **Incorrect:** There are 11 processes, not 12, in the Monitoring and Controlling process group.

10. **Correct Answer: C**

    A. **Incorrect:** The Cost Management knowledge area has the Control Costs process, which is part of the Monitoring and Controlling process group.

    B. **Incorrect:** The Initiating process group is not a knowledge area.

    C. **Correct:** The Human Resource Management knowledge area does not have a Monitoring and Controlling process, because it is usually the functional manager who monitors and controls project staff.

    D. **Incorrect:** The Closing process group is not a knowledge area.

CHAPTER 2

Integration management

This chapter focuses on project integration management. Project integration management recognizes that no part of the profession of project management acts in isolation, and in fact there is a high degree of interdependency between different parts of the profession of project management. Thus, a lot of the information discussed in this chapter reaches across many other knowledge areas within the profession. In addition to recognizing the interdependency of all other knowledge areas, project integration management also specifically addresses those activities, such as change control processes, which are carried out over more than one knowledge area.

> ### The PMBOK® Guide processes
>
> **Project Integration Management knowledge area**
>
> The six processes in the Project Integration Management knowledge area are:
>
> - Develop Project Charter (Initiating process)
> - Develop Project Management Plan (Planning process)
> - Direct and Manage Project Work (Executing process)
> - Monitor and Control Project Work (Monitoring and Controlling process)
> - Perform Integrated Change Control (Monitoring and Controlling process)
> - Close Project or Phase (Closing process)

Domain tasks in this chapter:

- Develop Project Charter process:
    - 1.1 Perform project assessment based upon available information and meetings with the sponsor, customer, and other subject matter experts, in order to evaluate the feasibility of new products or services within the given assumptions and/or constraints.
    - 1.2 Define the high-level scope of the project based on the business and compliance requirements, in order to meet the customer's project expectations.

- 1.4 Identify and document high-level risks, assumptions, and constraints based on current environment, historical data, and/or expert judgment, in order to identify project limitations and propose an implementation approach.
- 1.5 Develop the project charter by further gathering and analyzing stakeholder requirements, in order to document project scope, milestones, and deliverables.
- 1.6 Obtain approval for the project charter from the sponsor and customer (if required), in order to formalize the authority assigned to the project manager and gain commitment and acceptance for the project.
- Develop Project Management Plan process:
  - 2.1 Assess detailed project requirements, constraints, and assumptions with stakeholders based on the project charter, lessons learned from previous projects, and the use of requirement-gathering techniques (e.g., planning sessions, brainstorming, focus groups), in order to establish the project deliverables.
  - 2.9 Develop a change management plan by defining how changes will be handled, in order to track and manage changes.
  - 2.11 Present the project plan to the key stakeholders (if required), in order to obtain approval to execute the project.
- Direct and Manage Project Work process:
  - 3.2 Execute the tasks as defined in the project plan, in order to achieve the project deliverables within budget and schedule.
  - 3.4 Implement approved changes according to the change management plan, in order to meet project requirements.
- Monitor and Control Project Work process:
  - 4.1 Measure project performance using appropriate tools and techniques, in order to identify and quantify any variances, perform approved corrective actions, and communicate with relevant stakeholders.
  - 4.5 Assess corrective actions on the issue register and determine next steps for unresolved issues by using appropriate tools and techniques in order to minimize the impact on project schedule, cost, and resources.
- Perform Integrated Change Control process:
  - 4.2 Manage changes to the project scope, schedule, and costs by updating the project plan and communicating approved changes to the team, in order to ensure that revised project goals are met.
- Close Project or Phase process:
  - 5.1 Obtain final acceptance of the project deliverables by working with the sponsor and/or customer, in order to confirm that project scope and deliverables were met.
  - 5.2 Transfer the ownership of deliverables to the assigned stakeholders in accordance with the project plan, in order to facilitate project closure.

- 5.3 Obtain financial, legal, and administrative closure using generally accepted practices, in order to communicate formal project closure and ensure no further liability.
- 5.4 Distribute the final project report including all project closure-related information, project variances, and any issues, in order to provide the final project status to all stakeholders.
- 5.5 Collate lessons learned through comprehensive project review, in order to create and/or update the organization's knowledge base.
- 5.6 Archive project documents and material in order to retain organizational knowledge, comply with statutory requirements, and ensure availability of data for potential use in future projects and internal/external audits.
- 5.7 Measure customer satisfaction at the end of the project by capturing customer feedback, in order to assist in project evaluation and enhance customer relationships.

What is project integration management?

The other nine knowledge areas in the PMBOK® Guide focus on a specific knowledge area and have key inputs from, and provide outputs for, other knowledge areas. Project integration management is the only knowledge area that actually works across all the other knowledge areas. It has been described as the forest whereas the other knowledge areas are the trees. It is very much a coordination process that recognizes that none of the PMBOK® Guide knowledge areas are isolated and discrete. Project integration management recognizes that the knowledge areas are all interdependent and rely on each other to a greater or lesser extent. They are also able to affect each other and as such, when defining, planning, executing, and controlling the project, a project manager must recognize this and take an integrated point of view. This is true of activity between knowledge areas and also between processes within the same knowledge area. They can also be highly iterative and are not necessarily a direct linear progression from one process to another.

For example, when preparing a cost estimate, you need to have a defined project scope and also be aware of resources available, risks, and any other factors from the other knowledge areas that may affect the cost estimate. If you consider each knowledge area as a separate and discrete activity, then developing cost estimates in isolation would result in highly inaccurate estimates. Project integration management reminds us that all knowledge areas and processes are connected.

The Project Integration Management knowledge area produces the project charter (Develop Project Charter), which is a foundational document for the project and most of the other processes. It also delivers the project management plan in its many iterations (Develop Project Management Plan), takes a coordinated and high-level view of all the work being done on the project to achieve the plans (Direct and Manage Project Work), checks the project progress (Monitor and Control Project Work), and assesses, influences, and controls changes as they occur (Perform Integrated Change Control). In addition to providing the foundational documents that initiate the project this knowledge area also manages the closure of the project, or a phase in a project (Close Project or Phase).

Additionally, the Project Integration Management knowledge area reinforces the fact that there are many successful ways to manage a project. Projects vary considerably in terms of depth, complexity, size, industry, and deliverables. Therefore, the level of interaction between selected processes will also be different. This process is called tailoring, and it involves selecting appropriate processes and ensuring throughout the life of the project that the selected processes and their application are still appropriate. Having a broad oversight of the project via the Project Integration Management knowledge area helps in selecting the right processes and applying them appropriately.

> **Real world**
>
> I am a big advocate of tailoring the tools, techniques, and processes to appropriately fit your organization and your project. There are all sorts of potential problems that arise from simply applying too many, or too few, project management practices to a project. Take the time at the beginning of the project to choose those processes, tools, and techniques that will actually add value to your project and throughout the life of the project be prepared to reexamine your decisions to ensure that they are still correct. For example, on one small IT project I worked on, our project management methodology was tailored to be flexible and very simple because the project was simple and over a short time frame. A larger IT project I worked on had a very rigid methodology with many processes, reflecting the complexity of the project.

EXAM TIP

A high proportion of questions in the PMP exam will expect you to know how one process or knowledge area interacts with, or is dependent on, other processes or knowledge areas. Do not be surprised if you have to read a question several times to determine exactly how many, and which, processes it is referring to. You should also get used to looking not just at the entire process, but also at the way in which inputs become outputs with the application of selected tools and techniques.

Develop Project Charter

> **MORE INFO** **DEVELOP PROJECT CHARTER**
>
> You can read more about the Develop Project Charter process in the PMBOK® Guide, 5th edition, in Chapter 4, section 4.1. Table 2-1 identifies the process inputs, tools and techniques, and outputs.
>
> **TABLE 2-1** Develop Project Charter process
>
> | Inputs | Tools and techniques | Outputs |
> |---|---|---|
> | ■ Project statement of work
■ Business case
■ Agreements
■ Enterprise environmental factors
■ Organizational process assets | ■ Expert judgment
■ Facilitation techniques | ■ Project charter |

The Develop Project Charter process is an initiating process with a single output— not surprisingly, given the name of the process, it is the project charter. The Develop Project Charter process is one of only two initiating processes in the PMBOK® Guide.

The Develop Project Charter process covers the following domain tasks:

- 1.1 Perform project assessment based upon available information and meetings with the sponsor, customer, and other subject matter experts, in order to evaluate the feasibility of new products or services within the given assumptions and/or constraints.
- 1.2 Define the high-level scope of the project based on the business and compliance requirements, in order to meet the customer's project expectations.
- 1.4 Identify and document high-level risks, assumptions, and constraints based on current environment, historical data, and/or expert judgment, in order to identify project limitations and propose an implementation approach.
- 1.5 Develop the project charter by further gathering and analyzing stakeholder requirements, in order to document project scope, milestones, and deliverables.
- 1.6 Obtain approval for the project charter from the sponsor and customer (if required), in order to formalize the authority assigned to the project manager and gain commitment and acceptance for the project.

It is the first process to be completed, and the one that kicks off a project. Unlike most of the other processes in the PMBOK® Guide, the Develop Project Charter process features inputs that are not outputs from other processes. In this case, the inputs come from either the project sponsor (for example, any contracts or agreements, a business case, or the known project statement of work) or from the organization or the environment in which the project must work and is constrained by (such as enterprise environmental factors and organizational process assets). The project sponsor is critical to this process because the sponsor takes responsibility not only for providing some necessary inputs into this process but also for initiating and signing off on the development of the project charter.

EXAM TIP

The Develop Project Charter process is one of two initiating processes in the PMBOK® Guide. The other is the Identify Stakeholders process from Project Stakeholder Identification Management. Because the project charter is an input into the Identify Stakeholders process, it must be done first.

Broadly speaking, many of the inputs used in this process are part of a project selection process that assesses any potential project against the organizational strategic goals and also against financial and non-financial criteria to help the organization make decisions about which project it will undertake and which it won't. Understanding this process will assist your understanding of the Develop Project Charter process. Only projects that are of a compliance nature, or emergency works, should be able to bypass this project selection process, which is illustrated in Figure 2-1. Examples of compliance projects are those that are necessitated when legal reporting requirements are changed and your organization must comply with them, even though there is no business value in doing so. An example of emergency work could be the work you must do after a natural disaster strikes to get your organization up and running again. There is not time to go through a formal process to justify these types of projects.

FIGURE 2-1 This diagram shows how potential projects become approved projects.

The diagram in FIgure 2-1 shows that after an organization has identified all the potential projects it could undertake, it must put each project through a series of filters and criteria to enable it to choose the ones it will undertake. From this approved portfolio of projects it can then prioritize them and begin to develop a project charter. The first step in this selection process is for an organization to choose only those projects that first align with, and deliver, its strategic goals. This is because they will help an organization stay in business and meet its goals, and also because those strategic goals represent the core competencies an organization has.

> **Real world**
>
> The profession of project management is viewed as a critical strategic enabler for organizations. This is because most organizations seek to deliver their strategic goals, and therefore the success or failure of the projects undertaken is a critical indicator of whether or not organizations will achieve their strategic goals.

After a project has been confirmed as meeting the strategic goals of an organization, it may go through either financial or non-financial criteria processes, or both, to further refine and approve or deny projects that will be undertaken as part of the approved portfolio of projects. This is usually done during the preparation of a business case.

The following list describes the most common financial criteria that can be used to determine which projects are suitable:

- **Benefit-Cost Ratio (BCR)** A ratio that looks at the financially quantifiable benefits expected from the project and weighs them against the cost of achieving those benefits. If the benefits outweigh the costs, then the project can be given the go-ahead.
- **Economic Value Add (EVA)** The profit earned by the organization after the cost of capital has been subtracted. Many organizations will set a target for this and approve only projects that meet or exceed this target.
- **Internal Rate of Return (IRR)** The rate of return after the external factors affecting cash flow (for example, interest or cost of capital, and inflation) have been deducted. The higher the IRR, the better the project.
- **Present Value** The value of future cash flows in today's dollars. The formula for calculating it is:

$$PV = \frac{FV}{(1 + r)^n}$$

where *FV* equals the future value of cash flows, *r* equals the interest rate, and *n* equals the number of time periods.

- **Net Present Value (NPV)** The value in today's dollars of future benefits minus the costs to achieve the benefits. The organization's own discount rate is applied to future cash flows to calculate today's value. A positive NPV is good, whereas a negative NPV is bad. NPV is calculated by subtracting the present value of costs from the present value of income and is the sum of all the present value calculations for income generated for a particular time period, subtracted from the initial spend on the project. To calculate NPV, simply add up all the Present Value calculations for the expected income and then subtract this present value from the initial spend. The formula is:

$$\text{NPV} = \text{Initial Outlay} + \frac{\text{Year 1 income}}{(1+r)} + \frac{\text{Year 2 income}}{(1+r)^2} + \frac{\text{Year 3 income}}{(1+r)^3} + \frac{\text{Year 4 income}}{(1+r)^4} + \text{etc.}$$

For example, if your project had an initial spend of $100,000 in the first year, and was supposed to generate income of $30,000 in the second year, $35,000 in the third year, $37,000 in the fourth year, and $39,000 in the fifth year with a discount or interest rate of 10 percent, the Net Present Value of your project would be $10,634.52.

- **Opportunity Cost** The cost of not doing other projects and the profit, or financial surplus, they would bring the organization.

- **Payback Period** The time taken to pay back the investment in the project. An organization may set a required payback period, such as five years, within which time the project must pay back the original investment. Payback period is calculated by dividing the initial investment by the projected annual income.

- **Return on Investment (ROI)** The cost of a project subtracted from dollar gains on a project, divided by the cost of the project, expressed as a percentage. An organization will set criteria specifying that an ROI must first be positive, and the higher the ROI the better. Often organizations will also specify that the ROI must be greater than bank interest rates to reflect the risk in a project. Otherwise, from a commercial point of view, the organization is better off putting its money in a bank.

- **Return on Invested Capital (ROIC)** Used to describe in percentage terms how well an organization is using its money, or capital, on its projects. Positive is good, and the higher the better when it comes to selecting projects.

- **Future Value (FV)** Used to calculate the future value of an asset with a known interest rate to measure accumulation of value over time.

EXAM TIP

If you find "linear programming" or "non-linear programming" referred to in an exam question, the question is referring to a constrained optimization method for project selection. This is a complex mathematical process of maximizing the cost function of any calculation. The other category you will find is the benefit measurement model, in which an organization seeks to compare benefits and features of a particular proposal and make the selection on that basis.

Inputs

The Develop Project Charter process uses some, or all, of the following inputs as part of the development of the project charter for the project.

Project statement of work

The project *statement of work* (SOW) is a high-level narrative description of the work to be done on a project. It reflects what is known about the project work at the early stage of initiating a project. The project statement of work will describe the known scope of work, a description of the business needs, and a description of the product or service to be delivered. The statement of work may also refer to the ways in which the project aligns with, and delivers, the organization's strategic goals. It may also contain information about known milestones and project constraints, as well as any preliminary budget and time estimates. In the absence of this information during this initiating process, the statement of work may describe the work to be done to develop these estimates.

If you are using a statement of work, then it leaves room for further definition of the project scope but gives enough information to authorize the project and do a preliminary assessment of time, cost, and other relevant factors. If a project is based on a signed contract or agreement, then the statement of work will be replaced by the project scope contained in the contract, which tends to be much more detailed in its description of the work to be done.

EXAM TIP

The statement of work is a primary input into the Develop Project Charter process but not a mandatory one. If a business case has been developed, or a fully defined contract or agreement is available, then there will be no need for a statement of work.

Business case

A business case can be used as an input into the project charter, or even as a project charter itself. Typically the *business case* examines the financial and non-financial criteria that are used to assess whether or not the organization will commit to the project. These criteria are best used against a predefined expectation of what constitutes an acceptable project. For example, an organization might require a project to deliver a certain level of Return of Investment or a certain percentage of increase in market share before approving it. Projects that don't deliver these defined metrics are not considered for approval. These predefined metrics can also be further used to prioritize which projects are done first, with the project scoring better being done first. These financial criteria were discussed in greater detail earlier in the chapter.

EXAM TIP

Assume that all projects must go through a rigorous and defined business case process prior to approval.

The business case will also look at any predefined non-financial criteria that the organization wishes to consider. Examples of non-financial criteria an organization may consider are projects that increase market share, those that make it difficult for competitors to enter the market, projects that reduce dependencies on suppliers, and projects focused on delivering social, environmental, health, or educational benefits.

If the project is being executed in several phases with milestones between each phase, the business case can be revisited at these points to ensure it is both still valid and delivering the expected outcomes.

A business case will usually have most of the following elements in it:

- A description of the forecast, or actual, market demand of the product or service
- A description the organizational need for the project
- If it is for an external client, a description of the customer request
- A description of any technical advances that are presenting the opportunity to undertake the project
- Any legal or compliance requirements that are being addressed and met as a result of the project
- Any ecological or natural environmental impacts
- A description of the social need being fulfilled by the project

Clearly, the business case can be a very comprehensive document. If the project is a large and complex project, then the business case should reflect this. However, if the project is relatively simple and straightforward, the business case can be less complex to reflect this.

Agreements

The project charter can be based on any type of agreement between a performing organization and a requesting organization, or customer. An *agreement* can take the form of a signed contract, which in turn may be the result of a procurement process run by an external organization as part of its own project processes. The agreement may also be in the form of a memorandum of understanding (MOU), letter of agreement, or heads of agreement. An exchange of email messages with an offer and acceptance will also form a valid agreement. A valid agreement can also be formed via a verbal exchange, in which case you will want to document the exchange as part of the project charter process.

If an agreement with an external party is used as an input into the Develop Project Charter process, the external party should be able to review and agree to the eventual project charter as it relates to them. This does not mean that they need to view the entire project charter, because there may be commercially sensitive information contained within it, but they should have the opportunity to comment on and agree to the content that relates to any agreement between the parties.

> **NOTE VERBAL AGREEMENTS**
> Projects that are undertaken with a simple verbal agreement must document the agreement at some point to ensure that all parties understand and agree to what was talked about and to ensure everyone's expectations are recorded and communicated. This is best done during the Develop Project Charter process before any planning work is done.

Enterprise environmental factors

Enterprise environmental factors are some of the most common inputs used throughout the PMBOK® Guide. They can refer to many separate and distinct factors that can affect, and be used as inputs to, projects. In the Develop Project Charter process, the specific enterprise environmental factors that can influence the project charter development are any relevant government or industry standards that the project must comply with, any organizational infrastructure issues or constraints, and any known or forecast market conditions affecting the project selection process.

> **EXAM TIP**
> Enterprise environmental factors are some of the most widely used inputs throughout the PMBOK® Guide. The term covers a lot of different factors that can influence a project. The environment referred to is not the ecological environment. It is the financial and human resource market environment, the legislative and legal environment, and the innovation and competitive environment, and it also includes external cultural factors. Take time to understand the variety of factors that are enterprise environmental factors and be able to differentiate them from organizational process assets. Very broadly, enterprise environmental factors can be considered as constraining the project, whereas organizational process assets can be considered as assisting the project.

Organizational process assets

An organizational process asset is any concept, process, or structure documented by the organization for use in project management. For the Develop Project Charter process, the relevant organizational process assets include any organizational processes relating the project selection, business cases, and the development of the project charter, including any templates that the organization may have. It will also include any existing project management methodology that the organization has. Organizational process assets that are useful in the initiation phase and the development of the project charter also include historical information and lessons learned from previous projects.

EXAM TIP

The PMBOK® Guide places a major emphasis on the importance of gathering and referring to historical information and lessons learned. You should always assume that this is done and available to you as a project manager. You should always assume that you will also contribute to the development of an organization's historical information and lessons learned database as part of the project management activities completed on your project. This is an extremely important part of a closeout process and should be part of your closure checklist. You should look to complete closeout interviews and meetings with all stakeholders, complete post-implementation reviews, and also complete benefits realization analysis to measure whether the intended benefits were achieved. All of this information becomes valuable lessons learned and historical information for future projects.

Tools and techniques

The following tools and techniques are available to be used to develop the inputs into this process in order to produce the project charter.

Expert judgment

Expert judgment is the most often used tool in the PMBOK® Guide. Using expert judgment to help you use and optimize the inputs in the process allows you to consult with, and seek guidance from, any person or group who you think can contribute to the process. This expertise may come from within your organization, from individuals, or from the Project Management Office (PMO). You may also choose to seek expert judgment from external consultants, competitors, and trade associations with expertise in the particular area you need guidance on. For example, you may seek guidance from experts in financial analysis as part of the business case.

The client or customer is also a valuable source of expert judgment because they have clear expectations and experience with the product or service being delivered. Professional organizations, such as the Project Management Institute, may be consulted, as well as industry groups and subject matter experts.

Facilitation techniques

The purpose of *facilitation techniques* is to solicit information from team members and other key stakeholders who have a contribution to make in terms of using the process inputs and providing advice or further information to enable you to develop the project charter. There are many facilitation techniques that can be used; the most relevant for the Develop Project Charter process are:

- **Brainstorming** This involves holding structured workshops or sessions where participants are encouraged to think broadly about every possible action or consequence, no matter how strange it may seem. A process of elimination is then used to get to those ideas that are most useful.

- **Conflict resolution** This uses a variety of techniques to ensure that any conflict of opinions between experts does not derail the process. Conflict resolution includes problem-solving techniques that use a wide variety of methods to directly address and permanently resolve any problems that arise.
- **Effective meeting management** Getting your experts together and getting the best from them requires effective meeting management techniques that include structured and purposeful meetings with defined outcomes.

Outputs

After applying the appropriate tools and techniques to the selected inputs, the Develop Project Charter process has the following output.

Project charter

The Develop Project Charter process has only a single output—the project charter. The *project charter* is the foundational document for a project; it is like the birth certificate for a project. It proves the project exists and has financial and political support from the organization, and if applicable, an external client. It should be issued once the project has been through an appropriate project selection process.

The project charter authorizes the initial spend; defines the scope of work known at that time; lists any known constraints, risks, and milestones; and also identifies and authorizes the project manager and project sponsor. Ideally the project manager is identified and authorized in the project charter and assists with its development, but if not, the project manager should definitely be identified before any of the project planning processes begin.

Because the project charter is the foundational document for the project, changing it requires significant consideration and should not be done unless there are serious reasons. For this reason, it can be left broad enough to allow the normal process of change control to take place through the project without having to constantly change the project charter. Any potential changes to the project charter must be referred to the project sponsor.

Not all project charters are created equal, and the size and complexity of the project will determine the size and complexity of the project charter. Additionally, if not much is known about the project, the charter may be big enough to authorize an investigation phase that is part of an iterative planning process. If the scope of the project is well known, the project charter may be a one-off—that is, a complete and complex business case.

> *NOTE* **PROJECT CHARTER**
>
> The foundational document for a project is the project charter. Though in a perfect world it would probably be called a "project charter" by everyone involved in project management, you may call it by other names, such as "project mandate," "business case," or "work order." Remember, though, during the exam you must use the PMBOK® Guide terminology.

EXAM TIP

Always assume that a project has a project charter of some sort and that you will refer to it when seeking answers to why the project exists and what its original goals were.

The project charter is then a key input into the following processes, all of which are planning processes:

- Plan Scope Management
- Collect Requirements
- Define Scope
- Plan Schedule Management
- Plan Cost Management
- Plan Risk Management
- Identify Stakeholders

 Quick check

1. Why is the Develop Project Charter process the first one to be completed in any project life cycle?
2. What is the benefit of choosing projects by a defined project selection process?
3. What is the role of the project sponsor in the Develop Project Charter process?

Quick check answers

1. Because it produces the project charter, which serves as a foundational document for the project as a whole, as well as for many other processes.
2. It enables an organization to select only those projects that assist it in meeting strategic goals, utilize its core competencies, and achieve defined financial and non-financial criteria.
3. The project sponsor provides key inputs, authorizes the project charter, and is responsible for assessing any proposed changes to the project charter.

Develop Project Management Plan

> **MORE INFO** **DEVELOP PROJECT MANAGEMENT PLAN**
>
> You can read more about the Develop Project Management Plan process in the PMBOK® Guide, 5th edition, in Chapter 4, section 4.2. Table 2-2 identifies the process inputs, tools and techniques, and outputs.
>
> **TABLE 2-2** Develop Project Management Plan process
>
> | Inputs | Tools and techniques | Outputs |
> | --- | --- | --- |
> | <ul><li>Project charter</li><li>Outputs from other processes</li><li>Enterprise environmental factors</li><li>Organizational process assets</li></ul> | <ul><li>Expert judgment</li><li>Facilitation techniques</li></ul> | <ul><li>Project management plan</li></ul> |

The Develop Project Management Plan process is a planning process that initiates and encompasses the planning activities of all the other knowledge areas. It is the only planning process for the Project Integration Management knowledge area, and one of 24 planning processes in total.

The Develop Project Management Plan process covers the following domain tasks:

- 2.1 Assess detailed project requirements, constraints, and assumptions with stakeholders based on the project charter, lessons learned from previous projects, and the use of requirement-gathering techniques (e.g., planning sessions, brainstorming, focus groups), in order to establish the project deliverables.
- 2.9 Develop a change management plan by defining how changes will be handled, in order to track and manage changes.
- 2.11 Present the project plan to the key stakeholders (if required), in order to obtain approval to execute the project.

The *project management plan* itself is a document made up of all the other plans, and it provides a centralized means of planning your project. It does not necessarily have to be contained in a single document; different formats, such as word processing, spreadsheets, project management software, and other formats can be used to develop and record the different plans. The Develop Project Management Plan process is a highly iterative process that may start with some blank templates that will eventually become the project management plan for a project.

The primary purpose of this process is to record and document how your project is going to be executed, monitored and controlled, and closed. As such, it should contain plans for each of these elements in the relevant knowledge areas. When your project is under way, you can use the project management plan that has been developed to ensure that progress is as per the plan and act accordingly if there is a variance.

> **Real world**
>
> I have worked for organizations that have a single template for their project management plan; it has sections that need to be filled out and guidance on how to fill these sections out. However, I have also worked for organizations for whom the project management plan was a series of disparate documents held in both hard versions as well as electronic document versions, but when viewed together formed a consolidated plan for managing the project. It is important that a project management plan reflect the complexity, size, and industry of the project. Too small a project management plan for a large, complex project will increase the chances of project failure. On the other hand, too large a project management plan for a simple project will also increase the chances of project failure.

Inputs

The development of the project management plan uses some, or all, of the following four inputs.

Project charter

The project charter is an output from the Develop Project Charter process. It can take many forms, depending on the size and complexity of a project. It acts as the starting point that authorizes and guides the development of the project management plan because it contains the known description of the work to be done and any assumptions, constraints, and milestones.

Outputs from other processes

The Develop Project Management Plan process is an iterative process and uses many of the outputs from other knowledge areas as inputs.

> **EXAM TIP**
>
> Take note of outputs from other planning, executing, monitoring and controlling, and closing processes for project management plan updates that indicate that they will be used as inputs into the Develop Project Management Plan process.

These outputs include, but are not limited to, the successive iterations of the following:
- The requirements management plan
- The requirements documentation
- The schedule management plan
- The schedule baseline
- The cost management plan
- The cost baseline
- The quality management plan
- The process improvement plan
- The human resource management plan
- The staffing management plan
- The communications management plan
- The change management plan
- The risk management plan
- The procurement management plan
- The stakeholder management plan

Enterprise environmental factors

Enterprise environmental factors are both external and internal factors outside the realm of the project (i.e., that a project manager does not have control over) that can influence the processes in a project. Specific enterprise environmental factors that can be used as inputs to aid the development of the project management plan can include the following:

- Any relevant government standards, such as mandatory compliance standards.
- Any relevant industry standards that the project must comply with.
- Any software being used as part of the project management information systems to develop any aspect of the project management plan. Software is considered an external factor because it is generally licensed from a third party.
- The organizational culture and structure of all organizations involved in the project. Organizational culture in terms of acceptable behaviors, attitudes towards risk, the amount of power and authority the project manager has, and a flat versus tall organizational structure are some of the external factors that can all affect how a project management plan is developed.
- Any internal organization policies for the recruitment and release of staff.

Organizational process assets

Organizational process assets are a very common input into many processes. It is also worth remembering that several processes have organizational process assets updates as outputs. The specific organizational process assets that can be used as inputs into the Develop Project Management Plan process include the following:

- Any standard templates or checklists the organization has. For example, they may have a blank template for some or all of the content of a project management plan or a checklist for project closure.
- Any processes, or project management methodology, the organization has that define when, how, and by whom the project management plan is put together.
- Any predefined change control procedures and levels of delegated authority the project manager and team have.
- The organization's standard configuration management system that defines how different version of documents will be recorded, controlled, and updated. This is particularly important to ensure that you are always working on the correct version of any document in what can be a highly iterative process.
- Any historical information from past projects that can be used to assist in the compilation of the current project management plan.

EXAM TIP

The Project Management Institute (PMI) places a great deal of importance on the value of historical information, particularly lessons learned. Even if you work for an organization that does not currently collect historical information about projects, you must remember that it is considered one of the most valuable organizational process assets in project management.

Tools and techniques

The following two tools and techniques are used upon the inputs to deliver the project management plan.

Expert judgment

Expert judgment is a great tool to use, and it is used several times as a tool to help take inputs and use them correctly and wisely in order to generate the outputs from a particular process. The experts providing the judgment can come from any source that is relevant to the needs at hand, and can include you as project manager as well. In this instance, when you are developing the project management plan, expert judgment can first be used to tailor the processes that are applicable and useful to the development of your particular project management plan. You can also use expert judgment during successive iterations of the development of the project management plan to determine if the inputs are still valid and applicable.

Expert judgment can also be used to help evaluate any other aspect of the inputs into this process, particularly the outputs from other processes. Because of the large number of outputs from other processes that can be used as inputs into the Develop Project Management Plan process, you may end up using several experts with skills and experience in different areas.

> **Real world**
> During my career as a project manager, I have made repeated and frequent use of experts with knowledge greater than my own. Not only does it assist with a better output, but it is also a great way to learn. Don't hesitate to gather around you experts who can help you with any aspect of project management. Additionally, don't discount your own experience when it comes to providing an expert opinion.

Facilitation techniques

Facilitation techniques are those techniques you use to gather information from individuals or groups of people in a constructive way that produces positive outcomes for your project. As the name suggests, they are means of facilitating information gathering from people. It is up to you as project manager to initiate, define, and lead many of these facilitation techniques. Depending on whether or not they are useful to you at this point, you may wish to consider using some or all of the following facilitation techniques to help you make sense of, develop, redefine, and use the inputs into this process:

- **Brainstorming** This involves gathering people together in a room and asking them to think about all possible ideas. The ideas can be as wide and as varied as possible with no limitation placed upon the brainstorming process. After all possible options, no matter how seemingly irrelevant, have been gathered, you can then go through a process of refining them.

- **Conflict resolution techniques** These are important because dysfunctional conflict needs to be addressed and dealt with promptly and not swept under the carpet. The other element of conflict is when conflict is used to generate healthy debate, which often results in a more thought-out and considered end result. Problem solving, collaborating, compromise, smoothing, forcing, and withdrawing are all examples of conflict resolution techniques.

- **Productive and effective meetings** Meetings are also an excellent example of facilitation techniques. The use of and adherence to a clear agenda, rules for participants, and clear minutes and action points will greatly assist gathering of information relevant to the development of the project management plan.

Outputs

The Develop Project Management Plan process produces the following output.

Project management plan

There is only a single output from the Develop Project Management Plan process, and that is the project management plan in all its many iterations. The project management plan can be many different things to many different people, depending on the project management maturity of the organization, the size and complexity of its projects, and the industry it is working in. The plan can be a single document or a collection of many documents in different formats. A mature organization will have established organizational process assets that help the project manager complete the project management plan.

> **EXAM TIP**
>
> The project management plan is not a Gantt chart. It is not uncommon for some people to think that the Gantt chart is the project management plan, but it is simply a scheduling and communication tool.

The content and depth of the project management plan will reflect what is known about the project at that time, because you can plan only what is known. Thus, the development of the project management plan is a great example of progressive elaboration and rolling-wave planning on a lot of projects. The project management plan can contain all or some of the following plans and baselines:

- The change control process
- The requirements management plan
- The requirements documentation
- The schedule management plan
- The schedule baseline and milestone list
- The cost management plan
- The cost baseline
- The quality management plan
- The process improvement plan
- The human resource management plan
- The resource calendar
- The communications management plan
- The risk management plan
- The risk register
- The procurement management plan
- The stakeholder management plan

> **Real world**
>
> When putting together a project management plan, I always make sure it is appropriate to the size and complexity of the project I am working on. I also recognize that it is a highly iterative process and you can plan only for those parts of the project you can define. This means that parts of the project off in the distance of time may not be able to be planned as well as parts of the project to be completed in the short term. It is important to communicate this well to stakeholders, who may think it is possible to plan a long-term project in its entirety.

Despite being a singular output, the project management plan is used, either in its entirety or in its component parts and subset plans, as an input into many other processes throughout the PMBOK® Guide. The project management plan is a key input into the following processes:

- Direct and Manage Project Work
- Monitor and Control Project Work
- Perform Integrated Change Control
- Close Project or Phase
- Plan Scope Management
- Control Scope
- Plan Schedule Management
- Control Schedule
- Plan Cost Management
- Control Costs
- Plan Quality Management
- Plan Human Resource Management
- Plan Communications Management
- Control Communications
- Plan Risk Management
- Control Risks
- Plan Procurement Management
- Control Procurements
- Close Procurements
- Plan Stakeholder Management
- Control Stakeholder Engagement

> ✓ **Quick check**
>
> 1. Why is the project charter used as an input into the Develop Project Management Plan process?
> 2. Why do project management plan updates feature so much as outputs from other PMBOK® Guide processes?
> 3. Why does the development of the project management plan appear as part of the Project Integration Management knowledge area?
>
> **Quick check answers**
>
> 1. During the first iteration of the development of the project management plan, the project charter is the document that authorizes time, money, and energy being directed towards the development of the project management plan, and it contains the initial information upon which to base the planning processes.
> 2. The development of the project management plan is a highly iterative process and, therefore, it receives constant updates from other processes as it is fully developed.
> 3. The development of a project management plan requires the development of plans and baselines in all the other knowledge areas in the PMBOK® Guide.

Direct and Manage Project Work

> **MORE INFO** **DIRECT AND MANAGE PROJECT WORK**
>
> You can read more about the Direct and Manage Project Work process in the PMBOK® Guide, 5th edition, in Chapter 4, section 4.3. Table 2-3 identifies the process inputs, tools and techniques, and outputs.

TABLE 2-3 Direct and Manage Project Work process

Inputs	Tools and techniques	Outputs
<ul><li>Project management plan</li><li>Approved change requests</li><li>Enterprise environmental factors</li><li>Organizational process assets</li></ul>	<ul><li>Expert judgment</li><li>Project management information system</li><li>Meetings</li></ul>	<ul><li>Deliverables</li><li>Work performance data</li><li>Change requests</li><li>Project management plan updates</li><li>Project documents updates</li></ul>

The Direct and Manage Project Work process is an executing process. It is one of six processes in the Project Integration Management knowledge area, and one of a total of eight executing processes in the PMBOK® Guide.

The Direct and Manage Project Work process covers the following domain tasks:

- 3.2 Execute the tasks as defined in the project plan, in order to achieve the project deliverables within budget and schedule.
- 3.4 Implement approved changes according to the change management plan, in order to meet project requirements.

The main focus of the Direct and Manage Project Work process is doing instead of planning, which means the execution and completion of the work on the project and the product, or deliverable, you have planned to do. This is why you do all that planning, so when it comes time to start doing work you know what to do.

There are three main components of the Direct and Manage Project Work process, each focused on a slightly different area of project execution. The first and probably largest area is the implementation of the project plans you have made that specify both project and product requirements. The second area of focus for this process is the iterative process whereby you must repair any defects discovered in deliverables in the Monitoring and Controlling processes. The third area is the focus upon implementation of any approved changes. As you can tell, they are all doing something.

EXAM TIP

This process focuses on all the work that has to be done on the project and product, and the integration and interdependencies between all the executing processes. The other executing processes deal specifically with the execution of the quality, human resources, communications, procurement, and stakeholder management plans.

The role of the project manager is extremely important in this process and all the executing processes because, along with the rest of the project team members, the manager is responsible for the execution of the plans. The primary focus of this process is the production of deliverables. The Direct and Manage Project Work process is also where any approved changes are implemented.

Inputs

The inputs used in this process reflect its focus upon doing the work that was planned and also implementing any approved change requests.

Project management plan

The project management plan is the primary input here for obvious reasons. Obviously, you can't execute any project or product work without a proper plan to work to. You can, however, start work without the project management plan being entirely complete due to the iterative nature of the executing process and of the profession of project management generally. You can start work on just those areas you have planned while other areas are still being planned.

> **Real world**
>
> I remember being new to the profession of project management and thinking it was better just to get on with the job and that planning was a negative equation on a cost benefit analysis. It was with the wisdom gained with experience (and mistakes) that I learned that proper planning precedes execution, resulting in a much greater chance of project success.

Approved change requests

The Direct and Manage Project Work process is not just about executing the project and product work detailed in the plans you have prepared. It is also about carrying out the work required as a result of approved changes. Thus, *approved change requests* are an important input because they describe the work to be done. Approved change requests can include a requirement for corrective action, a preventive action, or defect repair. Approved change requests are an output from the Perform Integrated Change Control process.

Enterprise environmental factors

The specific enterprise environmental factors that can influence, or constrain, this particular process are any organizational culture or structure that affects the timing, commitment, and support for the execution process. Other factors that also influence or constrain the speed, timing, and execution of the plans prepared include decisions around project personnel and risk tolerances for stakeholders within and outside the performing organization. Access to adequate and appropriate project management information systems will also affect this process.

Organizational process assets

By now you will have figured out how often organizational process assets appear as a process input. For this process, the specific organizational process assets that can help are things such as standardized guides and work instructions that the organization has to assist the project manager and the project team in doing the planned work. Other organizational process assets that can assist in the execution of the planned work include historical information from similar projects, and any standardized and established communication requirements.

Tools and techniques

The three tools and techniques of this process are all used upon the separate inputs to deliver the planned work or the approved changes.

Expert judgment

Expert judgment as a tool for the Direct and Manage Project Work process is essential for taking the plans and other inputs and carrying out the implementation and execution of those plans. It is the job of the project manager and project team members to provide the expert judgment necessary to carry out the planning work and approved change requests to ensure that this process delivers its expected outputs.

In addition to the expertise of the project manager and project team members, you can also seek guidance from external experts and other stakeholders with skills and experience you require.

Project management information system

The *project management information system* is an automatic or manual system, such as common project management software or databases, used for storing and disseminating project information. Here it is used to track the work being done and communicate it effectively to the correct stakeholders.

> **EXAM TIP**
>
> Project management information systems can include software used for creating and monitoring schedule information such as Microsoft Project. They can also include databases used for cost estimating and control, and range from standalone installations of Microsoft Excel to larger enterprise resource planning systems.

Meetings

Meetings have many purposes throughout the PMBOK® Guide, in this process and also in communications processes. In this instance, meetings are used as a tool by the project manager to discuss and make decisions on matters affecting the execution of the project.

> **Real world**
>
> I have found that a properly organized meeting can be one of the most productive ways of sharing information, getting decisions made, and also building team spirit. To run one well, you need to spend time preplanning the meeting, set a clear agenda, have a real reason for the meeting, and set the expectation of the outcome from the meeting. You also need to invite only those people who need to be present and establish some ground rules. The absence of these basic points will result in a meeting that could potentially be a waste of time for all involved.

Outputs

The major output from the Direct and Manage Project Work process is the project deliverables.

Deliverables

The *deliverables* are often the major focus of any project. It is what the project was set up to do in the first place, and it is the primary output from this process. It can be a single deliverable or one of many deliverables. The product deliverable is the output from this executing process, whereas the other executing processes have outputs focused upon project, not product, work.

The deliverables go on to become an input into the Control Quality process prior to becoming validated deliverables if they are approved. Examples of deliverables include software modules for an IT project. If you are completing a construction project, the deliverable could be the entire building or significant parts of it. Clearly it is important that you are able to measure when a deliverable is complete, so you know when to complete this process.

Work performance data

Another output from this process is the *work performance data,* which is the documented record of observation and measurements of the deliverables taken during this executing process. The work performance data can include any data that records the percent complete, any technical measurements taken, the number of change requests made and approved, the number of defects found and corrected, and start and finish times, both expected and actual. You can probably tell that some of this data is generated by other executing processes, but due to the integrated nature of the Direct and Manage Project Work process, it gets included here as an output because it may affect and be used as an input by the following monitoring and controlling processes:

- Validate Scope
- Control Scope
- Control Schedule
- Control Costs
- Control Communications
- Control Stakeholder Engagement
- Control Procurements
- Control Risks
- Control Quality

Change requests

As a result of doing the planned work, you may discover that there are some changes to part of the project management plan or product requirements. The *change requests* generated as a result of this process go on to become inputs into the Perform Integrated Change Control process.

EXAM TIP

All change requests must go through a documented and agreed-upon change control process and be either approved or declined. Change requests fall into one of the following four categories: corrective action, preventive action, defect repair, or updates.

Project management plan updates

As part of doing the planned work, you may choose to update some or all of the component plans that make up the project management plan. *Project management plan updates* are different from change requests, which signify that there is something new that needs to be considered in an integrated manner. These are simply updates to documents and plans for clarification or revised approaches to executing the planned work.

Project documents updates

As well as updates to specific plans that form the project management plan, you are also able to carry out *project documents updates* to provide clarification or to note any new information such as new issues, assumptions made, and decisions taken.

> ✓ **Quick check**
>
> 1. Why is it important to complete project planning prior to beginning the Direct and Manage Project Work process?
> 2. Why does the Direct and Manage Project Work process appear in the Project Integration Management knowledge area?
> 3. What sort of work do the project deliverables include?
>
> **Quick check answers**
>
> 1. The Direct and Manage Project Work process is a doing process, and before you can do any work you must have planned what it is you are going to do.
> 2. Several other knowledge areas have executing processes that focus on their particular specialty. However, very rarely would there exist an executing process that does not, actually or potentially, have an impact upon other knowledge areas and therefore, the Direct and Manage Project Work process focuses on the integrated nature of project management and the interrelationship between processes.
> 3. The project deliverables include all the project and product work required to be completed by the project management plan.

Monitor and Control Project Work

> **MORE INFO** **MONITOR AND CONTROL PROJECT WORK**
>
> You can read more about the Monitor and Control Project Work process in the PMBOK® Guide, 5th edition, in Chapter 4, section 4.4. Table 2-4 identifies the process inputs, tools and techniques, and outputs.
>
> **TABLE 2-4** Monitor and Control Project Work process
>
> | Inputs | Tools and techniques | Outputs |
> | --- | --- | --- |
> | <ul><li>Project management plan</li><li>Schedule forecasts</li><li>Cost forecasts</li><li>Validated changes</li><li>Work performance information</li><li>Enterprise environmental factors</li><li>Organizational process assets</li></ul> | <ul><li>Expert judgment</li><li>Analytical techniques</li><li>Project management information system</li><li>Meetings</li></ul> | <ul><li>Change requests</li><li>Work performance reports</li><li>Project management plan updates</li><li>Project documents updates</li></ul> |

The key area of focus in the Monitor and Control Project Work process is checking that what you are doing matches what you planned to do. Obviously, to do this you must have done some planning and use these plans and baselines to check that the work you are doing matches what you planned to do. Remember that the work you are doing is not just the product work but also all the project work defined in your project management plan.

The Monitor and Control Project Work process is one of two monitoring and controlling processes in the Project Integration knowledge area and one of a total of 11 monitoring and controlling processes overall. Monitoring and controlling work is done throughout the life of the project from initiation to closure.

The Monitor and Control Project Work process covers the following domain tasks:

- 4.1 Measure project performance using appropriate tools and techniques, in order to identify and quantify any variances, perform approved corrective actions, and communicate with relevant stakeholders.

- 4.5 Assess corrective actions on the issue register and determine next steps for unresolved issues by using appropriate tools and techniques in order to minimize the impact on project schedule, cost, and resources.

EXAM TIP

Hopefully by now you have started the process of immediately trying to determine what sort of inputs would be useful for completing a process and what sort of outputs that process will produce. Before reading any further, think about what sort of inputs would be useful for checking that what you are actually doing is what you planned to do.

Inputs

There are seven inputs into the Monitor and Control Project Work process, all specifically designed to assist you in producing the outputs of change requests, work performance reports, project management plan updates, and project documents updates.

Project management plan

Once again the project management plan forms a key input into a process, this time because if you are going to check that what you are doing is what you planned to do, you should have available to you as an input the project management plan and all its subsidiary plans, because this is what you will be checking your work against. The project management plan is an output from the Develop Project Management Plan process.

Schedule forecasts

Schedule forecasts are an output from the Control Schedule process in the Project Time Management knowledge area. They are obviously useful for determining if what you are actually achieving in terms of your project schedule is accurate and matches what you had planned or forecast.

Cost forecasts

Cost forecasts are an output from the Control Costs process in the Project Cost Management knowledge area. As with the schedule forecasts, they are essential for monitoring and controlling progress on project costs.

Validated changes

Validated changes are an output of the Control Quality process in the Project Quality Management knowledge area. They involve checking that any approved change requests and the associated remedial action have been undertaken as per the approval given. In this process, they are used as part of the baseline of work being done, and you will now monitor and control these approved additional pieces of work.

EXAM TIP

To fully understand what *validated changes* means, you must understand the difference between the words *validate* and *verify*. The PMBOK® Guide has an extensive glossary at the back of the book that describes in detail the different words used throughout. *Validation* means that the product, service, or system meets the needs and requirements of the customer and other important stakeholders. *Verification* means that the product, service, or system complies with documented regulations, specifications, or imposed technical conditions. Think of validation as an external process and verification as an internal process done before validation.

Work performance information

Work performance information is a very common output of a lot of the other monitoring and controlling processes. It is an output from:

- Validate Scope
- Control Scope
- Control Schedule
- Control Costs
- Control Quality

- Control Communications
- Control Risks
- Control Procurements
- Control Stakeholder Engagement

It includes all the data collected during these processes, and as an input into this process, it is valuable for assessing what is actually happening against what you had planned to happen.

EXAM TIP

You may recognize that work performance data becomes work performance information, which in turn becomes work performance reports. Each step is a further refinement of the information.

Enterprise environmental factors

The specific types of enterprise environmental factors that can be used in this process include any relevant government or industry standards, stakeholder risk tolerances, and your project management information system being used to provide information into this process and record and disseminate any results from the process.

Organizational process assets

The specific types of organizational process assets that can be used as inputs into this process include any existing processes and templates the organization has, lesson-learned databases, risk management procedures, documented change control processes and procedures, and issue and defect management procedures.

Tools and techniques

The following tools and techniques are available, if appropriate, to use on the selected inputs.

Expert judgment

Once again expert judgment appears as a key tool to assist in gathering, interpreting, and making sense of the inputs into the process to produce useful and meaningful outputs. In this process, the project manager and members of the project team would be the most relevant and easily accessible experts to consult.

Analytical techniques

Analytical techniques allow you to make sense of the inputs into the processes and the data they contain to forecast potential future scenarios.

The PMBOK® Guide specifically mentions the following analytical techniques:

- **Regression analysis** The analysis of a dependent variable against one or more independent variables to determine the nature of the relationship, if any, between the variables and to extrapolate from this a likely future scenario. In this process it would be used to forecast a likely future state of perhaps time or costs based on past performance and the mathematical trend observed. It is often displayed in graph format, as shown in Figure 2-2.

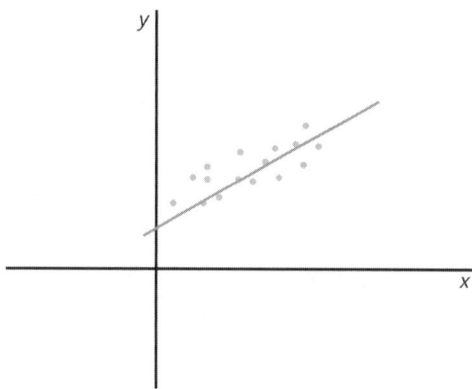

FIGURE 2-2 A graph showing an example of linear regression.

- **Grouping methods** Techniques for taking what you have observed and classifying the data into relevant groups for further study and comparison. A specific type of *grouping method* uses *exploratory study* to compare sets of data and to look for patterns and correlations between the data for causal effects.

- **Multiple equation models** Tools that use simultaneous equations to describe a relationship between variables and forecast likely future outcomes.

- *Failure mode and effect analysis (FMEA)* A widely used technique to examine the consequence of failure in any part of the system and the use of those observations to ensure that failure does not actually occur or that, if it does, the impact is anticipated and mitigated. In this process, you could use this tool to determine the likely effect of failure in the product and prepare to ensure it doesn't happen.

- **Reserve analysis** A tool for determining how much reserve you will need in any of the cost or time management processes or project management plan components.

- **Trend analysis** A technique for observing data, trying to spot a trend in the data and use this observed trend to forecast a future state. You could use this in this process to spot a constant and regular trend in the product deliverable indicating that if the trend continues you will end up with a product that the client doesn't want.

EXAM TIP

All of these analytical tools and techniques feature some form of mathematical modeling and the use of the results to forecast a future state. In the exam, just remember that if you find any tool and technique referred to that is mathematical, and it is in a monitoring and controlling process, then it is probably one of these tools.

Project management information system

The project management information system is used here to record new data, retrieve existing data, and distribute any relevant data to stakeholders.

EXAM TIP

Remember that your project management information system is part of your enterprise environmental factors.

Meetings

Meetings are a useful tool for the project manager, project team members, and relevant stakeholders to exchange and discuss information. They are best held in a face-to-face environment where participants can see each other, but can also be held in virtual formats. Meetings that would be useful during this process are kick-off meetings and review meetings.

The *kick-off meeting* is done on site with all relevant stakeholders as a means of communicating that the project has done enough planning work to begin executing. As such, this meeting is generally done immediately prior to beginning project execution.

Outputs

The following outputs are generated by the Monitor and Control Project Work process.

Change requests

The key outputs from the Monitor and Control Project Work process are change requests, generated as a result of observing and comparing what is actually occurring against what was planned and also generated by changing requirements. There several different categories of change requests that can be made; these include *corrective actions*, *preventive actions*, and *defect repair*.

Change requests become an input into the Perform Integrated Change Control process, where they are assessed and decisions are made as to whether they are approved or declined. They are not acted upon until they have been approved.

Work performance reports

Work performance reports are generated by your project management information system in physical or electronic form and show how the project is progressing against what was planned, and any changes requested and subsequent actions taken. Typically work performance reports include any regular status updates, project memos, explanatory notes, and any other updates to project team members and stakeholders.

> **Real world**
>
> I have always found that not only are reports on work performance information a valuable means of communicating technical information but they are a valuable means of establishing and maintaining effective communications with team members and stakeholders. I have always been selective in what information goes to certain people, and also what the best format is to ensure the information I am distributing is understood by the recipients.

Project management plan updates

As a result of monitoring and controlling the actual results against the planned results, you are going to detect variations, and as a result there will be some changes to your project, probably in several different areas. These need to be captured in updates to the relevant parts of your project management plan.

Project documents updates

Just as there will be updates to parts of your project management plan, there will also need to be updates to project documents that deal with forecast, performance, or issues.

> **Quick check**
>
> 1. How are the Monitor and Control Project Work process and the Perform Integrated Change Control process linked?
> 2. Why is the project management plan an important input into the Monitor and Control Project Work process?
> 3. When would you start the Monitor and Control Project Work process?
>
> **Quick check answers**
>
> 1. The two processes are linked by change requests, which are a primary output from the Monitor and Control Project Work process and are an input in the Perform Integrated Change Control process, where decisions are made about the change request.
> 2. The project management plan provides a description of how the work is expected to be done and can be used to compare with what is actually occurring.
> 3. Monitoring and controlling activities are done throughout the life of the project and begin as soon as the project begins initiation and end when the project is closed.

Perform Integrated Change Control

> *MORE INFO* **PERFORM INTEGRATED CHANGE CONTROL**
>
> You can read more about the Perform Integrated Change Control process in the PMBOK® Guide, 5th edition, in Chapter 4, section 4.5. Table 2-5 identifies the process inputs, tools and techniques, and outputs.

TABLE 2-5 Perform Integrated Change Control process

Inputs	Tools and techniques	Outputs
■ Project management plan ■ Work performance reports ■ Change requests ■ Enterprise environmental factors ■ Organizational process assets	■ Expert judgment ■ Meetings ■ Change control tools	■ Approved change requests ■ Change log ■ Project management plan updates ■ Project documents updates

The Perform Integrated Change Control process is one of two monitoring and controlling processes in the Project Integration Management knowledge area, and one of a total of 11 monitoring and control processes. The other 10 monitoring and controlling processes are focused on discovering any variations between what is planned and what is actually occurring, and generating change requests where appropriate. The Perform Integrated Change Control process deals with these change requests.

The Perform Integrated Change Control process covers the following domain task:

- 4.2 Manage changes to the project scope, schedule, and costs by updating the project plan and communicating approved changes to the team, in order to ensure that revised project goals are met.

This is the process where all changes to any part of the project are considered and decisions are made about whether they are approved or rejected. As such, it receives inputs from all the other monitoring and control processes in the form of change requests that have been generated by these other processes. It is completed throughout the life of the project, as are all monitoring and control processes.

Change requests can come from many sources, including any stakeholder on the project. All changes, no matter how small, should be documented. Many change requests are initiated with a simple verbal request, but even these should be documented and recorded in some way. Documentation of change requests can range from simple email verification of verbal requests to completion of a formal change request document, right up to a complete business case for major changes to a project. Failure to document changes will result in scope creep. "Scope creep" occurs when undocumented change control is allowed to happen, involving small changes that are regarded as insignificant. Individually they may not pose a problem, but collectively they increase the chances of project failure.

"Gold plating" is the process of making small undocumented changes to a project that result in a better outcome for the client. Although it sounds good in theory, the key here is that it is still undocumented changes to a project. This is not to say that you should not pursue better outcomes for the project and the client, but that all changes should be documented and assessed according to an agreed change control process.

EXAM TIP

At all times you should be delivering what is documented and only what is documented. This doesn't mean that you can't change what is being delivered, but that all changes should be documented.

All changes should be recorded in a change log that assigns them a tracking number and records progress and outcomes on the decision-making process.

EXAM TIP

The identification and numbering of the changes in a change log is one example of a configuration management system at work. It is a system whereby you identify all the plans and the version of those plans to ensure you are always working on the latest plans or parts of a project. Configuration verification and audit is the process of checking that the configuration management system is being used correctly and that all changes to it are recorded appropriately. You will find the configuration management system used in several areas throughout the PMBOK® Guide.

Inputs

The following inputs can be used in this process.

Project management plan

The project management plan is a key input into this process because it outlines what is planned to happen on the project. Many change requests are initiated as a result of observing a difference between what was planned and what is actually occurring. The project management plan is an output from the Develop Project Management Plan process.

Work performance reports

If you are going to assess the impact and nature of any changes, it is important that you have the work performance reports to assist you. This will give information about specific areas of the project and also allow the project manager and project team members to consider any impacts of a change in one area upon other areas of the project.

The work performance reports are an output of the Monitor and Control Project Work process.

EXAM TIP

The difference between work performance reports, work performance information, and work performance data is that the work performance data is the raw information work performance information is the raw information after it has been analyzed, and contextualized, and after it incorporates the integrated nature of project management; and the work performance reports are the information presented in a particular way to a particular group of stakeholders.

Change requests

The change requests are an essential input into this process because it is focused upon receiving the change request, considering it in light of the entire project, and making a decision about whether to approve or reject the change request.

As you have already learned, change requests are outputs of the other ten monitoring and controlling processes.

Enterprise environmental factors

The specific enterprise environmental factor that can affect the Perform Integrated Change Control process is primarily the project management information system, because it records all the changes, the work performance information and reports, and the decisions made about the change requests.

Organizational process assets

The organizational process assets that can be used to assist the Perform Integrated Change Control process are any change control processes, templates, and procedures that the organization has that guide assessment, delegated authority, and decision-making.

> **Real world**
>
> I am a strong advocate of documenting very clearly the levels of delegated authority that project managers have when it comes to making assessment and decisions about change requests. It is simply not practical for all changes to go to a change control board that perhaps meets monthly. It is far more sensible to allocate a certain amount of delegated authority to the project manager so the project can keep moving along. This view is reflected in the PMBOK® Guide.

Tools and techniques

The following tools and techniques can be used upon the selected and available inputs to generate the outputs.

Expert judgment

The specific type of expert judgment you will use as a tool in this process is those people with skills and experience to be able to assist in considering the change request and the information that will help decide whether or not to accept or reject the change requests. These experts can be individuals who will be consulted about particular issues, or they can be groups of stakeholders who form the change control board that meets to consider change requests.

Meetings

Meetings, in this case *change control meetings*, are attended by the *change control board* that is responsible for assessing change requests and making the decisions to approve or reject the change requests. Not all changes need to go to the change control board via change control meetings though, only those specified in the documented change control process, which ideally should be part of your project management methodology, itself part of your organizational process assets.

Change control tools

Change control tools used in the Perform Integrated Change Control process can be any automated or manual system for organizing, recording, documenting, assessing, storing, and distributing decisions about change requests and the subsequent decisions made. You can tell that your project management information system will be one example of the sort of change control tool that can be used.

Outputs

The Perform Integrated Change Control process produces some or all of the following outputs.

Approved change requests

Approved change requests are the primary output from the Perform Integrated Change Control process. They are the result of the selected inputs and the tools and techniques applied. All approved change requests will be recorded in the change request log.

The approved change requests go on to be incorporated into existing baselines and become an input in the following processes:

- Direct and Manage Project Work
- Control Quality
- Control Procurements
- Manage Stakeholder Engagement

Change log

The *change log* is the document kept to record the change requests received and their status. It is used as an input in the Manage Stakeholder Engagement process.

Project management plan updates

Approved change requests are added to existing baselines to become new baselines. Additionally, many approved change requests will also affect other subsidiary project management plans. Project management plan updates are used as an input into the Develop Project Management Plan process.

EXAM TIP

According to the PMBOK® Guide, a baseline is the original baseline plus any approved changes. This may differ from your current understanding of the baseline being only what you originally started with.

Project documents updates

Just as approved change requests can change parts of the project management plan, they can also affect other project documents and require them to be updated, particularly those associated with the change control process.

> **Quick check**
>
> 1. Why is the Perform Integrated Change Control process performed after other monitoring and controlling processes?
> 2. During what parts of the project life cycle are the activities associated with Perform Integrated Change Control process performed?
> 3. What is the role of the change control board?
>
> **Quick check answers**
>
> 1. The Perform Integrated Change Control process requires change requests as a key input. These change requests are generated as outputs from other monitoring and controlling processes.
> 2. The activities of the Perform Integrated Change Control process are carried out throughout the entire project life cycle from initiation to closing.
> 3. The change control board is the group of experts who meet to consider change requests. They are defined by the documented change control processes in place within the organization.

Close Project or Phase

> **MORE INFO** **CLOSE PROJECT OR PHASE**
>
> You can read more about the Close Project or Phase process in the PMBOK® Guide, 5th edition, in Chapter 4, section 4.6. Table 2-6 identifies the process inputs, tools and techniques, and outputs.

TABLE 2-6 Close Project or Phase process

Inputs	Tools and techniques	Outputs
<ul><li>Project management plan</li><li>Accepted deliverables</li><li>Organizational process assets</li></ul>	<ul><li>Expert judgment</li><li>Analytical techniques</li><li>Meetings</li></ul>	<ul><li>Final Product, Service, or Result transition</li><li>Organizational process assets updates</li></ul>

The Close Project or Phase process is one of two closing processes in the PMBOK® Guide; the other is Close Procurements in the Project Procurement Management knowledge area.

The Close Project or Phase process covers the following domain tasks:

- 5.1 Obtain final acceptance of the project deliverables by working with the sponsor and/or customer, in order to confirm that project scope and deliverables were met.
- 5.2 Transfer the ownership of deliverables to the assigned stakeholders in accordance with the project plan, in order to facilitate project closure.
- 5.3 Obtain financial, legal, and administrative closure using generally accepted practices, in order to communicate formal project closure and ensure no further liability.
- 5.4 Distribute the final project report including all project closure-related information, project variances, and any issues, in order to provide the final project status to all stakeholders.
- 5.5 Collate lessons learned through comprehensive project review, in order to create and/or update the organization's knowledge base.
- 5.6 Archive project documents and material in order to retain organizational knowledge, comply with statutory requirements, and ensure availability of data for potential use in future projects and internal/external audits.
- 5.7 Measure customer satisfaction at the end of the project by capturing customer feedback, in order to assist in project evaluation and enhance customer relationships.

This process is the only closing process in the Project Integration Management knowledge area and is focused upon the activities involved in completing the work required in a project or a phase of a project. Because it is an integrated process, it involves closure over all the processes being used in the project and not just the deliverable. As the name of the process suggests, it is used when closing a project prior to deliverable handover, or when completing a phase of a project prior to awaiting approval to proceed to the next phase.

The role of the project manager during this process is important because the project manager must take responsibility for closing the project and overseeing the required tasks. He has responsibility for reviewing all the documents created and ensuring that what is being delivered matches what is documented. Having a closeout checklist as part of your organizational process assets is an effective way to document what exactly closure means, the tasks that must be done, the signatures that must be obtained, and the final steps to confirm the project is complete. The role of the project sponsor is also important because that individual officially signs off on project or phase closure.

EXAM TIP

The PMBOK® Guide places a high degree of importance on the value of creating lessons learned during the project and finalizing these during the closeout process through informal means, surveys, interviews, workshops, and post-implementation reviews. You should always assume that you will create lessons learned as part of your project, and always assume that lessons learned are available to you from previous projects when you begin a new one.

One of the key ways to distinguish this process from the Close Procurements process is that the Close Project or Phase process is focused not only on contractual closure but all the aspects of administrative closure as well. Being an integrated process, it considers how contractual closure processes as part of the Close Procurements process may impact other areas of the project, and it also goes through the defined and approved closure process the organization has as part of its organizational process assets.

EXAM TIP

All projects must be closed even if they are ended in less-than-perfect situations. If a project ends suddenly, then you must have a process in place to follow in this instance. If a question in the PMP® exam poses this scenario, you should also assume that whatever the situation, you will enter some form of project closure process.

Real world

Project closure is one of those processes that we know we should do, but usually by the time we move into the part of the project where the bulk of our effort is on project closure, we are being called away to start a new project. I have learned that there are tangible benefits in staying focused on project closure in the face of these calls to join new projects. It is important to make sure you get formal signoff that the project is complete, collect and store lessons learned, and, if possible, hold a post-implementation review sometime later to determine if the deliverable is actually doing what it was supposed to do.

Inputs

The Close Project or Phase process uses the following inputs.

Project management plan

The project management plan defines the work to be done, and so, as part of seeking to close a project or phase of a project, you will need the project management plan and must be able to prove that all the work planned has been completed. The PMBOK® Guide describes the project management plan as the contract between the project manager and the project sponsor, because it is the document that defines what constitutes project completion. The project management plan is an output from the Develop Project Management Plan process.

Accepted deliverables

Accepted deliverables are an output from the Validate Scope process in the Project Scope Management knowledge area. Because they are validated by your documented processes, they are now ready to be handed over as part of the project closure process.

Organizational process assets

The specific organizational process assets that can be used to assist the Close Project or Phase process are any documented closeout checklists, templates, processes, or requirements. Additionally, you can use any relevant historical information or lessons learned to assist you with this process.

EXAM TIP

You should always do your closure planning during the Develop Project Management Plan process and the other planning processes. Along with all your other plans, you should also have a plan for how to close the project.

Tools and techniques

The following tools and techniques can be used upon the inputs into the Close Project or Phase process.

Expert judgment

The type of expert judgment you will want to use during this process will be the project manager, the project team members, the project sponsors, the client, your legal team, and any other stakeholders who can provide advice and opinion on project closure.

Analytical techniques

Analytical techniques were used as a tool or technique in the Monitor and Control Project Work process to analyze data and forecast future trends. As a tool in this process, they are used to substantiate any information that can be used to confirm project or product deliverables. Of the possible analytical techniques that could be used, regression analysis and trend analysis would be the most applicable and useful.

Meetings

Meetings between experts and other stakeholders involved in discussing and deciding on aspects of project or phase closure are an important tool in the process. Specific types of meetings that can be held include lessons-learned meetings, closeout meetings, and post-implementation review meetings.

Outputs

The Close Project or Phase process produces the following outputs.

Final product, service, or result transition

This is the whole point of the project, the reason it was initiated in the first place. This is the deliverable the entire project was planned to provide the customer with. In the case of phase closure, it is the milestone that is expected before approval is given to proceed to the next phase. The *final product, service, or result* is handed over to the customer as the final part of contractual closure.

Organizational process assets updates

The end of a project and the time spent examining what was done well and what was not done so well is a great time to look at updating any relevant organizational process assets as part of your commitment to continuous improvement. The project files, including all the documentation resulting from the completion of the project activities, should be used to update any relevant organizational process assets. The gathering of historical information and lessons learned, and use of this information to update and improve organizational process assets is also an important step. *Organizational process assets updates* are the final act of administrative closure.

> **EXAM TIP**
>
> Know the difference between contractual and administrative closure, and understand that contractual closure is always completed before administrative closure is completed.

> **Quick check**
>
> 1. Why is the completion of the lessons-learned documentation during the Close Project or Phase process so important?
> 2. What is the difference between closing a project and closing a phase of a project?
> 3. What is the role of the project sponsor during the Close Project or Phase process?
>
> **Quick check answers**
>
> 1. The lessons-learned documents ensure that any part of the project that was done well, and any part of the project that was not done well, is documented for future project managers to use so they can take advantage of the strengths and avoid repeating the weaknesses in your project.
> 2. Closing a project means the completion of all work on a project. Closing a phase of a project is the end of one phase and not necessarily the end of the project. The successful end of a phase means waiting for approval to move to the next phase, usually with the output from the phase that is being closed.
> 3. The project sponsor's role in the Close Project or Phase process is to accept the deliverable on behalf of the delivering organization and provide formal signoff for project closure.

Exercises

The answers for these exercises are located in the "Answers" section at the end of this chapter.

1. Calculate the following financial selection criteria for projects:

    A. Calculate Present Value where your Future Value is $300,000, the interest rate is 10 percent, and the time period is three years.

    B. Calculate Net Present Value where the Present Value of Income is $250,000 and the Present Value of Costs is $180,000.

    C. Calculate the Payback Period for a project with an initial cost of $450,000 and annual income of $110,000.

2. All of the following are either inputs, outputs, or both into processes in the Project Integration Management knowledge area. Therefore, it is possible to place them in the order in which they are generally completed so that one is completed prior to it being used as an input in a subsequent process. Place the following in order from first to last in relation to where they appear in the overall flow of inputs and outputs between the processes in the Project Integration Management knowledge area:

   A. Change requests

   B. Agreements

   C. Schedule forecasts

   D. Project management plan

   E. Final product, service, or result

   F. Accepted deliverables

   G. Business case

   H. Deliverables

   I. Project charter

   J. Validated changes

   K. Project statement of work

   L. Cost forecast

   M. Approved change requests

Chapter summary

- The Project Integration Management knowledge area recognizes, and is focused upon, the way in which project work is not completed in separate discrete chunks but that there is both the need to take a high-level view across all project activities, and that activities in one knowledge area may influence activities in another knowledge area.
- The project charter is the foundational document for the project, and all projects must have a project charter.
- The project management plan contains all the elements of integrated project planning and also all the other outputs from the other planning processes.
- The project management plan is an output from the Develop Project Management Plan process and an essential input into the Direct and Manage Project Work, Monitor and Control Project Work, Perform Integrated Change Control, and Close Project or Phase processes.
- The Direct and Manage Project Work process is focused upon completing the work described in the project management plan. The project deliverables are the primary output from this process.

- The Monitor and Control Project Work process is focused upon checking that what is being completed as part of the Direct and Manage Project Work process is what was planned. Any changes are issued as outputs from the process as change requests for the Perform Integrated Change Control process to deal with. Change requests can be outputs from any of the other monitoring and controlling processes in the PMBOK® Guide, with the exception of the Perform Integrated Change Control process for which they are an input.
- The Perform Integrated Change Control process is focused upon receiving and considering all change requests and processing them as per the approved and documented change control process. Change requests can be approved or rejected.
- The Close Project or Phase process is focused upon completing all the activities associated with administrative and contractual closure. It provides the deliverable and closure for a project, or the milestone for a project being delivered in phases.

Chapter review

Test your knowledge of the information in Chapter 2 by answering these questions. The answers to these questions, and the explanations of why each answer choice is correct or incorrect, are located in the "Answers" section at the end of this chapter.

1. Which of the following answers best describes a key benefit of the Develop Project Charter process?
   A. Assess and manage all change requests
   B. Define the project start, and create a formal record of the project
   C. Iteratively prepare plans for execution throughout a project
   D. Ensure all projects are closed

2. The high-level narrative description of the work to be done on the project is known as which of the following?
   A. Strategic plan
   B. Product scope description
   C. Statement of work
   D. Business case

3. Which of the following answers best describes the main purpose of the project management plan?
   A. To initiate and approve the project
   B. To define both project and product scope
   C. To describe how the project will be executed, monitored, and controlled
   D. To assess which projects should be done

4. Which project change requests must go through the approved change control process?

   A. Only those that have an impact on project scope

   B. Any change request that affects scope, time, cost, or quality

   C. Only those change requests that the project managers decides should go through the process

   D. All change requests must go through the change control process

5. What is the name of the group of people responsible for reviewing, evaluating, and deciding on changes to the project?

   A. Change control board

   B. Project steering group

   C. Project team

   D. Stakeholders

6. Which of the following is not an organizational process asset that would be updated as a result of completing project closure?

   A. Historical information

   B. Project files

   C. Project charter

   D. Project closure checklist

7. Consulting stakeholders and project team members, and using your own knowledge, are all examples of what sort of tool or technique used in the Project Integration Management knowledge area?

   A. Stakeholder engagement

   B. Meetings

   C. Expert judgment

   D. Analytical techniques

8. What is the correct order of project activities?

   A. Develop project management plan, execute project, develop project charter, conduct project selection

   B. Conduct project selection, develop project charter, execute project, develop project management plan

C. Conduct project selection, develop project charter, develop project management plan, execute project

D. Develop project charter, develop project management plan, execute project, conduct project selection

9. Which process in the Project Integration Management knowledge area deals with making decisions on change requests?

    A. Monitor and Control Project Work
    B. Develop Project Charter
    C. Direct and Manage Project Work
    D. Perform Integrated Change Control

10. What are the existing change control processes, policies, and templates referred to as?

    A. Organizational process assets
    B. Enterprise environmental factors
    C. Project documents
    D. Project management plan

11. The final product, service, or result is an output of the Close Project or Phase process. Where does it go after this process?

    A. The Monitor and Control Project Work process
    B. The customer
    C. The Perform Integrated Change Control process
    D. The Direct and Manage Project Work process

12. The document that authorizes the project is called what?

    A. Project management plan
    B. Project document
    C. Organizational process asset
    D. Project charter

Answers

This section contains the answers to the questions for the "Exercises" and "Chapter review" sections in this chapter.

Exercises

1. Calculate the following financial selection criteria for projects:

    A. Calculate Present Value where your Future Value is $300,000, the interest rate is 10 percent, and the time period is three years.

    $$PV = \frac{FV}{(1 + r)^n}$$

    Where FV equals the future value of cash flows, r equals the interest rate, and n equals the number of time periods.

    $$PV = \frac{\$300{,}000}{(1 + 0.1)^3} = \$225{,}394$$

    B. Calculate Net Present Value where the Present Value of Income is $250,000 and the Present Value of Costs is $180,000.

    NPV is calculated by subtracting the present value of costs from the present value of income.

    = $250,000 – $180,000 = $70,000

    C. Calculate the Payback Period for a project with an initial cost of $450,000 and annual income of $110,000.

    Payback period is calculated by dividing the initial investment by the projected annual income.

    = $450,000/ $110,000 = 4.09 years

2. The following order presents the inputs before they are required in a process, and subsequent outputs are presented before they are first used as an input.

    A. Project statement of work (input into Develop Project Charter)

    B. Business case (input into Develop Project Charter)

    C. Agreements (input into Develop Project Charter)

    D. Project charter (output from Develop Project Charter; input into Develop Project Management Plan)

    E. Project management plan (output from Develop Project Management Plan; input into all subsequent processes)

    F. Deliverables (output from Direct and Manage Project Work)

G. Change requests (output from Direct and Manage Project Work and Monitor and Control Project work; input into Perform Integrated Change Control)

H. Validated changes (input into Monitor and Control Project Work)

I. Schedule forecasts (input into Monitor and Control Project Work)

J. Cost forecasts (input into Monitor and Control Project Work)

K. Approved change requests (output from Perform Integrated Change Control)

L. Accepted deliverables (input into Close Project or Phase)

M. Final product, service, or result (output from Close Project or Phase)

Chapter review

1. **Correct answer: B**
    A. **Incorrect:** The Perform Integrated Change Control process assesses and manages change requests.
    B. **Correct:** The Develop Project Charter process does result in outputs that define the start of the project and does create a formal record of the project with the project charter.
    C. **Incorrect:** The Develop Project Management Plan process iteratively prepares the different plans to guide project execution.
    D. **Incorrect:** The Close Project or Phase process ensures all projects are formally closed.

2. **Correct answer: C**
    A. **Incorrect:** The strategic plan is developed by the organization and is used to help it select the correct projects.
    B. **Incorrect:** The product scope description is a well-defined description of the deliverable.
    C. **Correct:** The statement of work is a high-level narrative description of the work to be done on the project and is used as an input into the Develop Project Charter process.
    D. **Incorrect:** The business case prepares a justification for undertaking the project.

3. **Correct answer: C**
    A. **Incorrect:** The project charter initiates and approves the project.
    B. **Incorrect:** The scope statement defines both project and product scope.
    C. **Correct:** The project management plan describes how the rest of the project will be executed, monitored, and controlled.
    D. **Incorrect:** The business case can be used to assess which projects should be done.

4. **Correct answer: D**

    A. **Incorrect:** All change requests, not just those that affect project scope, must go through the defined change control process

    B. **Incorrect:** All change requests, not just those that affect scope, time, quality, and cost, must go through the defined change control process.

    C. **Incorrect:** The project manager does play a proactive part in influencing those factors that may lead to change requests being initiated, but once initiated the requests must all go through the approved change control process.

    D. **Correct:** All change requests must be considered as per the approved change control process.

5. **Correct answer: A**

    A. **Correct:** The change control board is responsible for reviewing, evaluating, and deciding on changes to the project.

    B. **Incorrect:** The project steering group is responsible for providing senior-level advice, oversight, and project governance.

    C. **Incorrect:** The project team is responsible for carrying out the project work under the guidance of the project manager.

    D. **Incorrect:** Stakeholders have many roles within the project, and members of the change control board are certainly stakeholders, but the broadest definition includes everyone who can affect or be affected by the project.

6. **Correct answer: C**

    A. **Incorrect:** Historical information would be updated as part of project closure.

    B. **Incorrect:** Many types of project files would be updated as part of project closure.

    C. **Correct:** The project charter is an initiating document and would not be updated as part of project closure, although some historical information may refer to lessons learned about the project charter.

    D. **Incorrect:** The project closure checklist would be completed and updated as part of project closure.

7. **Correct answer: C**

    A. **Incorrect:** Stakeholder engagement is the activity carried out as the focus of the Project Stakeholder Expectation Management knowledge area.

    B. **Incorrect:** Meetings are used to gather groups of stakeholders together to discuss and make decisions.

- **C. Correct:** The description in the question refers to different categories of experts who may be consulted for their advice and opinion.
- **D. Incorrect:** Analytical techniques are mathematical techniques used to interpret raw data.

8. **Correct answer: C**
   - **A. Incorrect:** Project selection and development of the project charter must be carried out before the development of the project management plan.
   - **B. Incorrect:** The development of the project management plan must occur before execution of the work.
   - **C. Correct:** Project selection feeds into the project charter, which in turn feeds into the development of the project management plan. The project management plan is used as the basis for project execution.
   - **D. Incorrect:** Conducting project selection must be done first in the process.

9. **Correct answer: D**
   - **A. Incorrect:** The Monitor and Control Project Work process focuses on monitoring the actual work being done against the planned work. Change requests are an output from this process.
   - **B. Incorrect:** The Develop Project Charter process is focused upon project selection methods and the development of the project charter.
   - **C. Incorrect:** The Direct and Manager Project Work process is focused upon executing the work contained in the project management plan.
   - **D. Correct:** The Perform Integrated Change Control process uses change requests as an input and with the appropriate tools and techniques makes decisions whether to accept or reject the change requests.

10. **Correct answer: A**
    - **A. Correct:** The existing change control processes, policies, and templates are all examples of process assets owned by the organization.
    - **B. Incorrect:** Enterprise environmental factors are external to the project, although they may still be within the performing organization. They can often be viewed as constraining rather than assisting a project.
    - **C. Incorrect:** Project documents are produced as part of many processes. Some documents will be part of the organizational process assets.
    - **D. Incorrect:** The project management plan is the overall combination of subsidiary plans across all the PMBOK® Guide knowledge areas.

11. **Correct answer: B**

    A. **Incorrect:** The Monitor and Control Project Work process uses forecast information and the project management plan to check actual against planned work.

    B. **Correct:** The customer receives the deliverables from the project.

    C. **Incorrect:** The Perform Integrated Change Control process uses change requests and work performance reports as inputs.

    D. **Incorrect:** The Direct and Manage Project Work process uses the project management plan and approved change requests as inputs.

12. **Correct answer: D**

    A. **Incorrect:** The project management plan combines all subsidiary plans from other planning processes. The project charter feeds the development of the project management plan.

    B. **Incorrect:** "Project document" is a generic term for any document used to plan, record, and store information about the project. The project charter is one example of a project document.

    C. **Incorrect:** The process to produce the project charter and the blank template could produce organizational process assets, but are not examples of organizational process assets themselves.

    D. **Correct:** The project charter is the foundation document for any project; it authorizes resources to be used on the project.

CHAPTER 3

Scope management

This chapter looks at the processes focused upon how to plan, define, manage, and control changes to the project requirements, scope, and work breakdown structure (WBS).

The Project Scope Management knowledge area includes six processes. Four of the six processes are planning processes; the other two are monitoring and controlling processes. Properly defining the project scope statement is critical in order to complete other planning activities such as planning the project cost, project time, quality, communications, human resources, and procurement. Without properly defined requirements, scope, and WBS, you simply cannot complete these other activities well.

> **The PMBOK® Guide processes**
>
> **Project Scope Management knowledge area**
>
> The six processes in the Project Scope Management knowledge area are:
>
> - Plan Scope Management (Planning process)
> - Collect Requirements (Planning process)
> - Define Scope (Planning process)
> - Create WBS (Planning process)
> - Validate Scope (Monitoring and Controlling process)
> - Control Scope (Monitoring and Controlling process)

Domain tasks in this chapter:

- Plan Scope Management process, Collect Requirements process, and Define Scope process:
    - 2.1 Assess detailed project requirements, constraints, and assumptions with stakeholders based on the project charter, lessons learned from previous projects, and the use of requirement-gathering techniques (e.g., planning sessions, brainstorming, focus groups), in order to establish the project deliverables.
- Create WBS process:
    - 2.2 Create the work breakdown structure with the team by deconstructing the scope, in order to manage the scope of the project.

- Validate Scope process:
    - 4.1 Measure project performance using appropriate tools and techniques, in order to identify and quantify any variances, perform approved corrective actions, and communicate with relevant stakeholders.
- Control Scope process:
    - 4.2 Manage changes to the project scope, schedule, and costs by updating the project plan and communicating approved changes to the team, in order to ensure that revised project goals are met.

Defining and documenting the project scope is about documenting all the work to be completed, and the work not to be completed, as part of the project and the product. It is important to note that the product scope is a subset of the project scope. Figure 3-1 shows the product scope as a subset of the project scope.

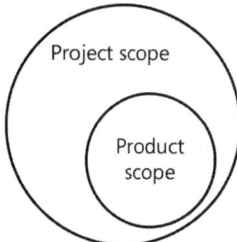

FIGURE 3-1 Product scope is a subset of project scope.

EXAM TIP

Many people are used to focusing on defining the product scope as part of their scope management work. It is important that you realize that there is more to the scope of the project than just the scope of delivering the product and its technical requirements. The project scope includes all the planning work, executing work, monitoring and control work, and closing work that has to be done in addition to the delivery of the product.

What is project scope management?

Project scope management is focused on defining and managing the scope of work to be completed as part of the project. It is a highly iterative process that begins with the initiation of the project and the statement of work contained in the project charter. The project charter is then used as an input into gathering the requirements, which results in requirements documentation; it may also result in a preliminary scope statement. After you have performed these next iterations of defining the scope statement, you will arrive at a project scope statement, which in itself may only define and detail the work to be done in the short term and may leave some of the work to be done in the longer term relatively undefined.

Real world

Most people focus on the three pillars of project management: the scope, the time, and the cost of the project. This is for good reason because it is these three foundational elements that are most often used as the primary metrics of success in a project, and they also feed into the other areas of the profession of project management. Therefore, you should pay extra attention to the time and effort committed to defining the scope of a project because, of the three pillars, it allows you to complete cost and time estimates, and thus, is the most crucial.

There are distinct terms used to describe successive iterations of descriptions of the work to be done on a project. Figure 3-2 shows a hierarchical view of the different terms used to describe successive and progressively more detailed iterations of the scope.

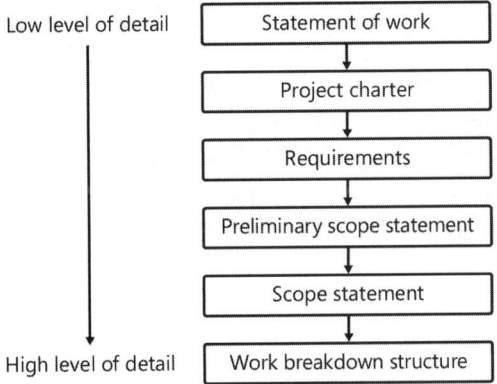

FIGURE 3-2 A hierarchy of project work reflects the level of detail contained in each description.

Real world

When working on a project, I have often found that most people want to spend a lot of time and energy defining the product without giving much thought to planning and defining all the other work that must be done on a project. Not only does the lack of wider project work information create problems with your project as you proceed, it also creates a false impression that all of your work as a project manager is focused upon delivery of the product.

What is project scope management? CHAPTER 3 **87**

EXAM TIP

Make sure when reading a question in the exam that you are careful to look out for the words "project" and "product." This is particularly important in questions relating to the project scope or the product scope. It is also important in the Project Quality Management knowledge area, where there are separate quality processes for the project and the product.

Plan Scope Management

MORE INFO **PLAN SCOPE MANAGEMENT**

You can read more about the Plan Scope Management process in the PMBOK® Guide, 5th edition, in Chapter 5, section 5.1. Table 3-1 identifies the process inputs, tools and techniques, and outputs.

TABLE 3-1 Plan Scope Management process

Inputs	Tools and techniques	Outputs
- Project management plan - Project charter - Enterprise environmental factors - Organizational process assets	- Expert judgment - Meetings	- Scope management plan - Requirements management plan

The Plan Scope Management process is a planning process with two major outputs, the scope management plan and the requirements management plan.

The Plan Scope Management process addresses the following domain task:

- 2.1 Assess detailed project requirements, constraints, and assumptions with stakeholders based on the project charter, lessons learned from previous projects. and the use of requirement-gathering techniques (e.g., planning sessions, brainstorming, focus groups), in order to establish the project deliverables.

The Plan Scope Management process, like most of the other planning processes, sets out and defines your particular approach for further definition of the project and product scope, and the way in which you are going to validate scope and control any changes to the scope. All of these elements are captured in the scope management plan.

EXAM TIP

You may begin to notice that the key output from the initial planning processes in any knowledge area is some form of plan. For example, a key output from the Plan Scope Management process is the scope management plan.

Inputs

The Plan Scope Management process uses some, or all, of the following inputs as part of the development of the scope management plan for the project.

Project management plan

The project management plan, at whatever stage of its development, is used as an input here into planning your approach to managing your scope. Keep in mind that early on in the project, the project management plan, and its subsidiary plans, will be relatively ill defined. As the project progresses and more details are known about the project and the subsidiary elements of the project, the project management plan itself will become more fleshed out. This clearly demonstrates the highly iterative nature of planning how you will manage your project and product scope. The project management plan is the key output from the Develop Project Management Plan process.

> **EXAM TIP**
>
> Keep in mind that the project management plan is the collection of all the other subsidiary plans and baselines.

Project charter

The project charter is used here as an input into the Plan Scope Management processes because it contains the description of the project scope that is known at that point. If the project charter contains a statement of work, this will need to be further developed and defined into a full scope statement. If the project charter is built upon the results of a negotiated contract, it may include a fully defined scope of work. The project charter is the sole output from the Develop Project Charter process.

Enterprise environmental factors

The types of enterprise environmental factors that can play a role in how you manage scope can include things such as the culture of the organization and its attention to detail, risk, and quality, and any external marketplace conditions that the project is being initiated to take advantage of.

> **EXAM TIP**
>
> Enterprise environmental factors are one of the most widely used inputs throughout the PMBOK® Guide. The term covers a lot of different factors that can influence a project. Take time to understand the variety of factors that are enterprise environmental factors and be able to differentiate them from organizational process assets.

Organizational process assets

Once again organizational process assets play an important role as an input into a planning process. The types of organizational process assets that will be most useful in this section are any blank templates, defined policies and procedures, any historical information, lessons learned, and any project management methodology already in place.

Tools and techniques

The following tools and techniques are available to be used to develop the inputs into this process in order to produce the scope management plan.

Expert judgment

Expert judgment is one of the key tools used throughout the entire PMBOK® guide. In relation to the Plan Scope Management process, the experts that you will call upon include your own expert judgment, the expert judgment of team members, and any other experts that you want to consult to help you define your particular approach to scope management.

Meetings

Meetings in which you gather project team members and relevant stakeholders together are an important tool and technique in defining your approach to scope management. Attendees at such meetings should include anyone with responsibility for any part of the scope management process.

EXAM TIP

The way in which you run your meetings will determine how effective they are. Meetings are both an important way to gather technical information and also an important means of distributing information and building a high-performing team. These latter attributes of a meeting will be more fully discussed in the Project Communications Management knowledge area and the Project Human Resource Management knowledge area.

Outputs

After applying the appropriate tools and techniques to the selected inputs, the Plan Scope Management process has the following outputs.

Scope management plan

The *scope management plan* is one of the more important subsidiary plans contained in the project management plan. It outlines your particular process for iteratively defining the detail of the project and product scope, the process of decomposition for the creation of your work breakdown structure (a process that uses the scope statement that has been developed to execute project work), and the process by which any requested changes will be considered and either approved or declined. In addition to these elements, it also sets out the process of validating the project scope and deliverables, and how signoff for closure will be obtained. Again, the detail in the scope management plan will reflect the detail of the project scope. A highly defined scope will result in a well-defined scope management plan, and a loosely defined scope will result in a more flexible scope management plan allowing for further iterations.

The scope management plan is used as an input into the following processes:

- 5.2 Collect Requirements
- 5.3 Define Scope
- 5.4 Create WBS
- 5.5 Validate Scope

Real world

As a general rule of thumb I like to make sure that about one-third of the content of the scope statement refers to what is not included in both the project and product scope of work. If you don't specifically list the exclusions, stakeholders will make assumptions about what is, and what isn't, included in the scope of work, and it is these assumptions that lead to disagreements.

Requirements management plan

The *requirements management plan* is a specific plan that addresses how the product requirements will be documented, defined, tracked, and reported against. It is also in the requirements management plan that detail of the configuration management activities will be defined. The requirements management plan will also contain methods for prioritizing the requirements, and any defined metrics to define the product. The requirements management plan is used as an input into the Collect Requirements process.

Quick check

1. What is the main focus of the Plan Scope Management process?
2. What is the difference between the project scope and the product scope?
3. What are the key differences between the scope management plan and the requirements management plan?

Quick check answers

1. The main focus of the Plan Scope Management process is to develop a scope management plan that will guide your activities in defining the project requirements, scope, and work breakdown structure.
2. The project scope includes a definition of all the work required in the project, whereas the product scope focuses on defining the technical requirements of the expected deliverable.
3. The scope management plan can be viewed as the broader of the two management plans because it focuses on the entire project and product scope and how it will be defined, documented, and controlled. The requirements management plan focuses solely on further iterations and definition of the requirements of the project deliverable.

Collect requirements

> **MORE INFO** **COLLECT REQUIREMENTS**
>
> You can read more about the Collect Requirements process in the PMBOK® Guide, 5th edition, in Chapter 5, section 5.2. Table 3-2 identifies the process inputs, tools and techniques, and outputs.
>
> **TABLE 3-2** Collect Requirements process
>
> | Inputs | Tools and techniques | Outputs |
> |---|---|---|
> | - Scope management plan
- Requirements management plan
- Stakeholder management plan
- Project charter
- Stakeholder register | - Interviews
- Focus groups
- Facilitated workshops
- Group creativity techniques
- Group decision-making techniques
- Questionnaires and surveys
- Observations
- Prototypes
- Benchmarking
- Context diagrams
- Document analysis | - Requirements documentation
- Requirements traceability matrix |

The Collect Requirements process addresses the following domain task:

- 2.1 Assess detailed project requirements, constraints, and assumptions with stakeholders based on the project charter, lessons learned from previous projects, and the use of requirement-gathering techniques (e.g., planning sessions, brainstorming, focus groups), in order to establish the project deliverables.

Requirements can best be defined as a definition of the stakeholders' needs to meet the project's objectives. They can include technical requirements or known constraints. Therefore, the process of collecting requirements will involve stakeholders and documentation of what they believe the project objectives are. It is important to note that the project requirements can be much more than the product requirements.

> **EXAM TIP**
>
> In the exam, you should assume that unless otherwise explicitly stated, you must go through a requirements-gathering process prior to completing the scope statement.

> **Real world**
>
> I have often found that broader project requirements can be captured and documented as key performance indicators for determining the success or otherwise of the project, beyond the strict technical requirements of the product. For example, you could have customer satisfaction, health and safety compliance, environmental management requirements, or any other factors set as key performance indicators of project success, and these factors would be gathered in the requirements documentation.

Inputs

The following inputs are used in the Collect Requirements process.

Scope management plan

Obviously, in order to collect and define the project requirements, it is important that you act according to your scope management plan because the requirements are a subset of the project scope. The scope management plan is a key output from the Plan Scope Management process.

Requirements management plan

The requirements management plan is an important input into this process because it guides you as you seek to further define and document the requirements of the project and product. The requirements management plan is an output from the Plan Scope Management process.

Stakeholder management plan

The *stakeholder management plan* is an important input into this process because you will be approaching stakeholders and asking what the requirements are for the project and the product. Thus, the stakeholder management plan and the information it contains about how you identify and manage stakeholder expectations is a critical part of and input into this process. The stakeholder management plan is a key output from the Plan Stakeholder Management process.

Project charter

The project charter authorizes the project and contains any high level information about the product and project deliverable that can be used to assist the process of collecting more detailed requirements. The project charter is the sole output from the Develop Project Charter process.

Stakeholder register

The *stakeholder register* identifies the known stakeholders, their power and interest in the project, an assessment of their expectations, and an analysis of their communication needs. You're able to use this information to effectively interact with the stakeholders to ensure that you have gathered all the project and product requirements. The stakeholder register is an output from the Identify Stakeholders process.

Tools and techniques

The following tools and techniques can be used to produce the outputs from the Collect Requirements process.

Interviews

When dealing with stakeholders, one of the most effective ways of soliciting information from them is by using *interviews*. Interviews can be formal or informal, and they can be conducted in person or via email or surveys.

Focus groups

Focus groups are a very effective means of bringing together relevant stakeholders and subject matter experts and gathering information from them in a structured way.

Facilitated workshops

Facilitated workshops provide a forum to solicit information from various stakeholders in a controlled manner. They are focused and interactive by their nature and are often facilitated by an independent party. Examples of specific types of facilitated workshops include the joint application design/development sessions (JAD) and the quality function deployment (QFD) facilitated workshops used in new product development.

Group creativity techniques

There are several types of *group creativity techniques* that can be used as tools in this process to further define and document project and product requirements. Brainstorming is particularly popular one, in which you bring together relevant stakeholders with the experience and skills needed and run a free-flowing session where all ideas are considered good ideas and are further refined by the group.

The nominal group technique is a group creativity technique that uses a variety of voting methods by which group members rank the most useful ideas for further brainstorming. Examples include the fist-of-fives, where group members display their support for an idea by raising a number of fingers on their hands; weighted voting systems, where each member is given a certain number of votes to allocate between different ideas; and a simple, straightforward voting system to rank different ideas in terms of validity and prioritization.

Group decision-making techniques

The goal of *group decision-making techniques* is to generate either a consensus among group members or a decision to abide by majority opinion. Obviously, there will be dissenting and differing views on which ideas should have greatest priority. An important part of running any group decision-making process is to establish early on how decisions will be made so that all participants are aware of the process for decision-making. You can agree on any one of the following group decision-making techniques to aid your decision-making process:

- Unanimity or consensus is where everybody agrees on a single course of action.
- The Delphi technique, which gathers information anonymously from experts to avoid peer pressure, can be used if you want to allow experts to provide anonymous feedback.
- You can decide to use a simple majority for any decisions made. If a majority (more than 50 percent of the members of the group) cannot be obtained, you may decide to use plurality, in which the largest bloc in a group decides.
- A final method of obtaining a group decision in the face of dissenting opinions is to agree to allow one individual in the group to make the decision for the group. This is commonly referred to as a dictatorship group decision-making technique.

Questionnaires and surveys

A key element of the Collect Requirements process is the gathering of information that can then be used to further define the requirements for the project and the product. *Questionnaires and surveys* present a very effective means of gathering this information from identified stakeholders. Depending on the development of the questionnaires and surveys, the information gathered may be able to have some statistical analysis applied to it to aid in your requirements-gathering process.

Observations

Observations are a very accurate way of determining how a potential project or product scope will be implemented or used in real life. If the project scope includes certain processes, observing who will use these processes, how they will be used, and any other aspects of it in the real world will help define the process. If part of the project scope includes any product, observing the users of the product in the real world will also help define the product further.

Prototypes

Prototypes are a great way to get fast feedback on any element of the product by producing drafts and seeking feedback from stakeholders as to whether this is what they wanted. The practice of prototyping is quickly gaining support with the rise of technology that allows rapid prototyping. In addition to physical prototypes, storyboarding can be used to show the sequence of processes or product development to solicit feedback from stakeholders, particularly in the production of webpages or user interfaces.

Benchmarking

Benchmarking is a tool used in several processes. It involves comparing what you planned to do against other projects or organizations to determining whether you are better or worse than them. You can gather this important information from competitors, trade and industry associations, and the Project Management Institute.

Context diagrams

A *context diagram* is a simple tool showing visually how a business system and users interact. Figure 3-3 shows an example of a context diagram.

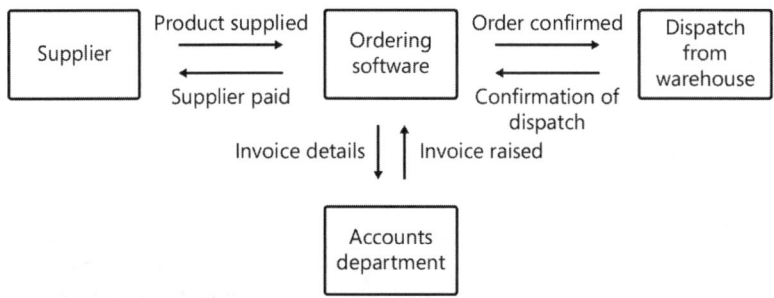

FIGURE 3-3 This context diagram shows the relationship between supplier, ordering software, accounts department, and warehouse.

Document analysis

As part of refining the requirements, you may want to carry out a *document analysis* and examine any relevant documents such as business plans, data models, software documentation, and issues logs to help you summarize the requirements.

Outputs

The following outputs are generated from the Collect Requirements process.

Requirements documentation

The *requirements documentation* itself is highly iterative; you may be able to fully define certain requirements and not yet define other requirements. When requirements are fully defined and documented, they will include a description of how the requirement meets the identified business need, objectives, or stakeholder requirements. They will also include a traceability matrix identifying which stakeholders requested each requirement, defining acceptance criteria, and providing a link back to the business objective that the requirement is intended to meet.

> **EXAM TIP**
>
> You can view the requirements documentation as a subsidiary of the scope statement. Rather than referring to the entire project and product scope, the requirements documentation focuses on individual requirements of parts of the project.

The requirements documentation as an output goes on to be used as an input into the following processes:

- 5.3 Define Scope
- 5.4 Create WBS
- 5.5 Validate Scope
- 5.6 Control Scope
- 8.1 Plan Quality Management
- 12.1 Plan Procurement Management

Requirements traceability matrix

The *requirements traceability matrix* is a valuable tool for ensuring that the documented requirements are mapped directly back to business objectives. A requirements traceability matrix is a table that links the origins of individual product requirements to the expected deliverable that meets those requirements so that you can track requirements throughout the project life cycle. This is particularly important if you want to either change a requirement and assess the impact it will have on deliverables or check that a deliverable still meets the original requirement.

The requirements traceability matrix is used as an input into the following processes:

- 5.5 Validate Scope
- 5.6 Control Scope

Quick check

1. What is the main focus of the Collect Requirements process?
2. How is the requirements documentation different from the project scope statement?
3. Why is consultation with stakeholders critical to successfully documenting project requirements?

Quick check answers

1. The main focus of the Collect Requirements process is to use a variety of means to gather from stakeholders their technical requirements, which will then be used to define the scope of work.
2. The requirements documentation is a subset of the total project scope statement and relates specifically to how requirements of the project and product align with and deliver project objectives. The project scope statement describes and defines the total work to be done in delivering the project and product.
3. Consultation with stakeholders is critical to successfully documenting and defining project requirements; it is the wishes of stakeholders that are driving the project, and by consulting them you can ensure that you meet their expectations by delivering the requirements.

Define scope

> **MORE INFO DEFINE SCOPE**
>
> You can read more about the Define Scope process in the PMBOK® Guide, 5th edition, in Chapter 5, section 5.3. Table 3-3 identifies the process inputs, tools and techniques, and outputs.

TABLE 3-3 Define Scope process

Inputs	Tools and techniques	Outputs
■ Scope management plan ■ Project charter ■ Requirements documentation ■ Organizational process assets	■ Expert judgment ■ Product analysis ■ Alternatives generation ■ Facilitated workshops	■ Project scope statement ■ Project documents updates

The Define Scope process is one of four planning processes in the Project Scope Management knowledge area. The Define Scope process covers the following domain task:

- 2.1 Assess detailed project requirements, constraints, and assumptions with stakeholders based on the project charter, lessons learned from previous projects, and the use of requirement-gathering techniques (e.g., planning sessions, brainstorming, focus groups), in order to establish the project deliverables.

> **Real world**
>
> It is very rare that you will ever begin a project with a complete and detailed description of the scope. Often this will occur only as a result of lengthy contractual negotiations. In almost every other situation, you will begin a project with enough of the scope defined to allow you to begin, and then you will undertake successive iterations of definition and documentation as you go. You may also decide to commit time and energy to defining the scope for the immediate timeframe, and leave definition of the remainder of the scope until you get closer to the time of delivery.

Inputs

The following inputs can be used in the Define Scope process.

Scope management plan

Obviously, in order to define the scope, you are going to have to work according to your scope management plan, which sets out the process you are going to use to iteratively define and document the scope of both your project and the product. The project scope management plan is the key output from the Plan Scope Management process.

Project charter

The project charter can be used as a key input into the Define Scope process because it contains the project approvals and any known description of the project and product scope. The project charter is the sole output from the Develop Project Charter process.

Requirements documentation

The requirements documentation is an output from the Collect Requirements process and contains the defined and documented project and product requirements. These requirements will form an important part of both the project and product scope.

Organizational process assets

Organizational process assets that can be used to define the scope include any project management methodology, policies, and blank templates that the organization has. There is also a high probability that the organization has completed a project with a similar scope in the past, and thus any lessons learned or historical information from previous projects or phases are important organizational process assets that can be used when defining the scope. These resources can also include important internal stakeholders such as the project sponsor.

Tools and techniques

The following tools and techniques can be used on the inputs to generate the process outputs.

Expert judgment

Again we find expert judgment being used as an effective tool to use expert experience and skill to refine process inputs and develop them into the expected outputs. In this instance, as project manager you are one of the more important experts, as are your project team members who are responsible for completing the project work and any other stakeholders with relevant experience and skill in defining the scope.

Product analysis

Product analysis is best used when a project is delivering a product, instead of a service or result, as its major deliverable. Breaking the product down into its component parts and ensuring that each part meets the requirements and technical specifications assists with documenting the product scope. Product analysis can also include value engineering processes in which you try to use innovation to deliver the product as efficiently as possible.

Alternatives generation

The process of *alternatives generation* considers all the potential ways in which the project and product work can be performed in order to determine whether you are using the most efficient way of delivering the project and product scope.

Facilitated workshops

Facilitated workshops involve bringing experts together in a workshop setting and having an independent facilitator guide the group to produce successive iterations of the project and product scope. The role of the independent facilitator is to stay neutral, set and enforce rules about how participants contribute, keep the workshop focused and on track, and make sure expectations are clearly understood.

Outputs

The following outputs are produced by the Define Scope process.

Project scope statement

The major output from the Define Scope process is the *project scope statement*, which describes in increasing detail the deliverables, assumptions, and constraints of the project. The project scope statement defines all the work to be done on the project, and only the work to be done on the project. It includes a detailed description of the exclusions and the work that will not be done as part of the project. The project scope statement also includes a full description of the work to be done to deliver the scope of the product.

> **NOTE SCOPE CREEP AND GOLD PLATING**
>
> One of the primary reasons to conduct scope management planning exercises and produce a clear definition of the scope statement with a documented change control process is to ensure that your project is not subject to scope creep. Scope creep happens because of undocumented scope change. At all times you must be delivering only what is documented for your project and product scope. This does not mean that change will not occur on your project; in fact quite the opposite—you can expect change at all points in your project. What it means is that you consider all changes, no matter how small or large, and if the change is accepted, you document this and incorporate it into your scope statement, thereby stopping scope creep. The other element to watch for with undocumented scope is gold plating. Gold plating occurs when you recognize the opportunity to deliver greater quality for less cost and in less time to the client and decide to proceed with this without documenting it. There is nothing wrong with delivering greater quality and exceeding expectations, but once again, at all times you must be producing only what is documented.

The project scope statement as an output goes on to be used as an input into the following processes:

- 5.4 Create WBS
- 6.3 Sequence Activities
- 6.5 Estimate Activity Durations
- 6.6 Develop Schedule

Project documents updates

The process of defining the scope will probably require *project documents updates* such as updates to the stakeholder register to identify any changes to stakeholder expectations, the requirements documentation to account for any iterative development of the scope that affects requirements, and associated with the requirements documentation, the requirements traceability matrix.

> **Quick check**
>
> 1. How do the Collect Requirements and Define Scope processes interact with each other?
> 2. Why is it important to define the exclusions in the project scope statement?
> 3. How is the information about the project and product scope statement contained in the project charter different from the information contained in the project scope statement?
>
> **Quick check answers**
>
> 1. The Collect Requirements process takes the statement of work and project charter and seeks to gather requirements from stakeholders that are then used as an input into the Define Scope process to help define the scope statement.
> 2. It is important to define the known project and product exclusions as part of the project scope statement in order to avoid ambiguity and assumptions about what is, and what is not, included in the work to be done.
> 3. The project charter contains a description of the project and product work to be done that is known at the time of initiating the project and as such, it may be at a much higher level than the information contained in the project scope statement. Additionally, the project charter contains other information such as the project's purpose, justification, and any required approvals.

Create WBS

> **MORE INFO** **CREATE WBS**
>
> You can read more about the Create WBS process in the PMBOK® Guide, 5th edition, in Chapter 5, section 5.4. Table 3-4 identifies the process inputs, tools and techniques, and outputs.
>
> **TABLE 3-4** Create WBS process
>
> | Inputs | Tools and techniques | Outputs |
> | --- | --- | --- |
> | - Scope management plan
- Project scope statement
- Requirements documentation
- Enterprise environmental factors
- Organizational process assets | - Decomposition
- Expert judgment | - Scope baseline
- Project document updates |

The Create WBS process is the last of the planning processes in the Project Scope Management knowledge area and relies on the Collect Requirements and Define Scope processes to be complete. The Create WBS process covers the following domain task:

- 2.2 Create the work breakdown structure with the team by deconstructing the scope, in order to manage the scope of the project.

> **EXAM TIP**
>
> In the exam, unless it is otherwise stated, you should assume that the processes of collecting requirements and defining the scope have occurred before beginning the process of creating the WBS.

Inputs

The following inputs can be used to generate the outputs of the Create WBS process.

Scope management plan

The scope management plan is a key input because in this plan you have detailed how you will approach the process of decomposing the project scope statement and creating the work breakdown structure (WBS). The scope management plan is a key output from the Plan Scope Management process.

Project scope statement

The WBS is a breakdown of the entire project scope statement into its component parts and therefore, the project scope statement is a key input into the Create WBS process. The project scope statement is the key output from the Defined Scope process.

Requirements documentation

The requirements documentation is a key output from the Collect Requirements process. In addition to the project scope statement, having access to the requirements documentation and the requirements traceability matrix will enable you to ensure that your process of decomposition to create the WBS captures all of the project and product scope and the associated requirements.

Enterprise environmental factors

There are some industry-wide enterprise environmental factors that can be useful as an input into the Create WBS process. For example, the ISO/IEC 15288 standard on systems engineering-system life cycle processes could be used for engineering projects.

Organizational process assets

The most useful organizational process assets to be used as an input into the Create WBS process include any project management methodology, policies, or blank templates for the creation of a WBS, and any historical information or lessons learned from previous projects.

Tools and techniques

There are two techniques used in the Create WBS process.

Decomposition

The process of *decomposition* involves taking a high-level description of the work to be done for the project and product, and successively breaking it down into deliverables, sub-deliverables, and finally down to the level of *work packages*. The work package is the lowest level to which you should break down the work breakdown structure (WBS). A work package is defined as a package of work that can reliably be estimated for time and cost. This means that you can easily allocate the work to one person and that it doesn't make sense to decompose it any further, because at that level you can develop an accurate estimate of the time it will take and the amount of money it will cost to complete the work package. Below the level of work packages are individual activities, which are used in the Project Time Management knowledge area to assist in building a project schedule.

The WBS is a graphical representation of the total project scope and, therefore, work that is not included in the WBS is not part of the project. If the project scope is being developed iteratively, this will be represented in the development of the WBS, and it too will develop iteratively.

> **Real world**
>
> I always use my project team members who are responsible for completing the work to help complete the WBS. Not only does this give me the right technical input from the people responsible for completing the work, but it also creates commitment to the process of completing the work because people feel they have made a significant and personal contribution.

> *NOTE* **DECOMPOSITION**
>
> Decomposition is used in any of the breakdown structures used in project management. It simply describes a process of breaking down a larger concept into its component parts. It is used to create the work breakdowns structure (WBS), the organizational breakdown structure (OBS), the risk breakdown structure (RBS), and another RBS, the resource breakdown structure (RBS).

Expert judgment

Expert judgment is a key tool in the Create WBS process because the creation of the WBS is best done by those experts with knowledge about the work to be done and how it can best be decomposed into its component parts.

Outputs

The following outputs are generated by the Create WBS process.

Scope baseline

The *scope baseline* will be used to measure what is actually being produced against what is expected to be produced in relation to the project and product scope. It is comprised of three key and distinct elements. They are the project scope statement, the WBS, and the WBS dictionary.

EXAM TIP

The scope baseline is what you use to measure progress against in the project. Any baselines in project management can only be changed through the formal change control process. After an approved change is integrated into a baseline, the baseline itself is changed, thus the easiest way to think of a baseline is that a baseline is what you originally started with plus any approved changes.

The *work breakdown structure* (WBS) is often called the backbone of a project. This is because it acts as an input into many other planning processes. Without a complete and accurate WBS your efforts in cost estimating, budget estimating, activity definition, risk identification, and scope validation and all the subsequent processes they provide inputs into would be extremely difficult. Creation of the WBS is done by decomposing the top-level descriptions of project work into their component parts. The highest level is broken down into deliverables, then into sub-deliverables, and then into individual work packages. A work package is an amount of work that can reliably be estimated for time and cost and can generally be performed by one person. Below work packages are activities, which are used in developing a project schedule, as described in the next chapter.

Figure 3-4 shows a WBS for a new house project showing the breakdown of different work streams to work package level. Note that all nodes in the WBS have a unique identifying number that allows you to track work being done and also to allocate costs to specific work packages for better cost reporting. The numbering system should clearly identify each node and relate to the node above so you can easily see related nodes and the way they are decomposed. This numbering system is an example of a configuration management system.

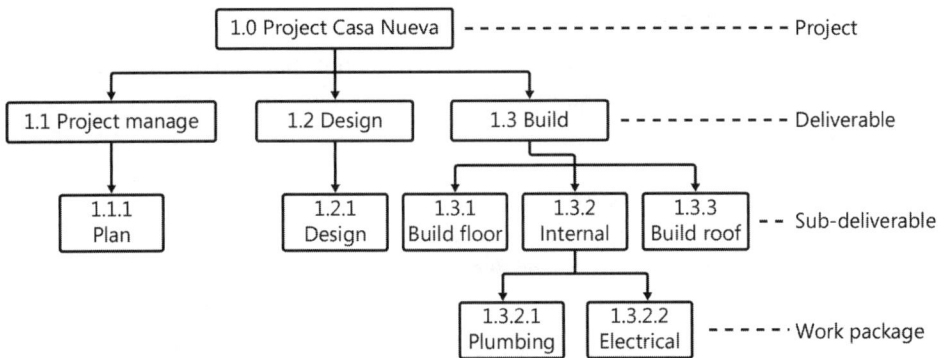

FIGURE 3-4 This work breakdown structure (WBS) shows the total project, deliverables, sub-deliverables, and work packages.

When you are representing a WBS graphically, each node in the WBS can contain only summary information, such as the configuration management details; the name of the deliverable, sub-deliverable, or work package; and summary information about the time, cost, and resources allocated to each node. The *WBS dictionary* is a text-based document that provides additional information about the summary information contained in each WBS node.

The WBS becomes an input into the following processes:

- 5.5 Validate Scope
- 6.2 Define Activities
- 7.2 Estimate Costs
- 7.3 Determine Budget
- 11.2 Identify Risks
- 11.3 Perform Qualitative Risk Analysis

EXAM TIP

There are many exam questions that pose a scenario where something is missing and ask what you should do. In most instances, it is acceptable to continue with the project and develop something in the interim to help tide you over. The only exception to this is if it is the work breakdown structure that is missing. If you are working on a project and you do not have the WBS, you must stop and create the WBS because without it you cannot complete the planning processes of your project.

Create WBS **CHAPTER 3** **107**

Project document updates

As a result of creating the WBS, information may be gathered that requires other project documents to be updated, such as the project scope statement and the requirements documentation.

> **Quick check**
>
> 1. To what level of detail do you decompose the project scope when creating the WBS?
> 2. How would you define the key elements of a work package?
> 3. What elements make up the scope baseline?
>
> **Quick check answers**
>
> 1. The project scope statement is decomposed to major deliverables, sub-deliverables, and down to the work package level.
> 2. A work package can best be defined as an amount of work that can reliably be estimated for time and cost. Going any further in the decomposition process delivers little benefit for the time taken to do the work.
> 3. The three key elements of the scope baseline are the project scope statement, the WBS, and the WBS dictionary.

Validate scope

> **MORE INFO** **VALIDATE SCOPE**
>
> You can read more about the Validate Scope process in the PMBOK® Guide, 5th edition, in Chapter 5, section 5.5. Table 3-5 identifies the process inputs, tools and techniques, and outputs.

TABLE 3-5 Validate Scope process

Inputs	Tools and techniques	Outputs
- Project management plan - Requirements documentation - Requirements traceability matrix - Verified deliverables - Work performance data	- Inspection - Group decision-making techniques	- Accepted deliverables - Change requests - Work performance information - Project documents updates

The Validate Scope process is a monitoring and control process, one of two monitoring and control processes in the Project Scope Management knowledge area.

The Validate Scope process covers the following domain task:

- 4.1 Measure project performance using appropriate tools and techniques, in order to identify and quantify any variances, perform approved corrective actions, and communicate with relevant stakeholders.

> *NOTE* **VALIDATION COMPARED TO VERIFICATION**
>
> The process of validation is an important one to understand, as is the difference between it and the process of verification. Verification is about confirmation that the product, service, or result produced complies with agreed specifications or requirements. It is primarily an internal process that the delivering organization performs prior to submitting the product, service, or result for validation, which involves the customer as well. Validation also involves a check that the product, service, or result meets stakeholder requirements. Verification occurs before validation.

Inputs

The Validate Scope process uses some, or all, of the following inputs.

Project management plan

The project management plan guides how you execute and monitor your project and, as such, it contains plans and baselines useful for validating the project scope. The particular parts of the project management plan that are most useful as inputs into the Validate Scope process are the scope management plan and the scope baseline. The scope management plan is used as an input because it details how you plan to manage your scope in its entirety, including validation. The scope baseline, which includes the scope statement, the WBS, and the WBS dictionary, is absolutely necessary in validating the scope because it represents the baseline against which you are comparing the actual work performed. The project management plan is an output from the Develop Project Management Plan process; the scope management plan is a key output from the Plan Scope Management process; and the scope baseline is the key output from the Create WBS process.

Requirements documentation

The requirements documentation lists the project objectives and the requirements that will deliver those objectives, and as such it is an essential input into validating the scope. Requirements documentation is the key output from the Collect Requirements process.

Requirements traceability matrix

The requirements traceability matrix provides an additional measure of rigor when validating the scope because you are able to link specific requirements back to identified business objectives. The requirements traceability matrix is an output from the Collect Requirements process.

Verified deliverables

The *verified deliverables* are deliverables that have already been completed and checked for correctness against the required specifications through the control quality process and, as such, now need to be validated in order to become accepted deliverables and used in the Close Project or Phase process. Verified deliverables are a key output from the Control Quality process.

> **NOTE DELIVERABLES**
>
> Project deliverables must go through the process of first being verified and then being accepted. Verification is an internal process that ensures correctness against predetermined quality standards, whereas validation is an external acceptance process completed by the project sponsor or customer.

Work performance data

The work performance data indicates whether or not there is compliance with the documented requirements. Work performance data is an output from the Direct and Manage Project Work process.

Tools and techniques

The following two tools and techniques can be used to deliver the process outputs.

Inspection

Inspection as a technique literally means inspecting the deliverables to ascertain whether they meet the documented requirements and acceptance criteria.

Group decision-making techniques

Group decision-making techniques are any techniques used to allow a group of people to reach a decision. It is best if the decision-making technique is outlined to the group prior to the decision-making process being undertaken, to be sure that all group members understand how the decision will be made.

Outputs

The Validate Scope process has the following outputs.

Accepted deliverables

Accepted deliverables meet the acceptance criteria and are signed off and accepted by either the customer or the project sponsor. Accepted deliverables are used as the key input into the Close Project or Phase process.

> **EXAM TIP**
>
> A key role of the project sponsor is to act as the person internal to the performing organization who formally accepts the product. The customer is usually a person external to the organization who accepts the product.

Change requests

If a deliverable is not accepted due to some areas of non-compliance or non-correctness, a change request for defect repair may be generated. Change requests are a key input into the Perform Integrated Change Control process.

Work performance information

Work performance information takes the work performance data and presents it in such a way that project progress can easily be determined and identified. This information is communicated to stakeholders as appropriate. Work performance information is used as an input into the Monitor and Control Project Work process.

> **NOTE WORK PERFORMANCE**
>
> Work performance data is the raw data gathered in any process. Work performance information is the data after it has been interpreted into something meaningful. Work performance data becomes work performance information, which in turn is used in work performance reports.

Project documents updates

The types of project documents that may be updated include requirements documentation, the scope statement, and quality control documents.

> ✓ **Quick check**
>
> 1. What is the main focus of the Validate Scope process?
> 2. What is the difference between validation and verification?
> 3. Who formally accepts the project deliverables?
>
> **Quick check answers**
>
> 1. The main focus of the Validate Scope process is to formally accept the completed project deliverables.
> 2. Verification is an internal process completed by the performing organization measuring the product, service, or result against defined requirements and specifications. It is completed prior to validation. Validation involves taking the verified product, service, or result and in conjunction with key stakeholders confirming that it meets stakeholder requirements.
> 3. The project sponsor formally accepts the project deliverables on behalf of the performing organization. The customer formally accepts the project deliverables on behalf of the external organization requesting the work to be done.

Control scope

> **MORE INFO** **CONTROL SCOPE**
>
> You can read more about the Control Scope process in the PMBOK® Guide, 5th edition, in Chapter 5, section 5.6. Table 3-6 identifies the process inputs, tools and techniques, and outputs.
>
> **TABLE 3-6** Control Scope process
>
> | Inputs | Tools and techniques | Outputs |
> | --- | --- | --- |
> | ▪ Project management plan
▪ Requirements documentation
▪ Requirements traceability matrix
▪ Work performance data
▪ Organizational process assets | ▪ Variance analysis | ▪ Work performance information
▪ Change requests
▪ Project management plan updates
▪ Project documents updates
▪ Organizational process assets updates |

The Control Scope process is a monitoring and control process, one of two monitoring and control processes in the Project Scope Management knowledge area.

The Control Scope process covers the following domain task:

- 4.2 Manage changes to the project scope, schedule, and costs by updating the project plan and communicating approved changes to the team, in order to ensure that revised project goals are met.

Inputs

The following inputs can be used in the Control Scope process.

Project management plan

The project management plan, or more correctly some of the subsidiary plans of the project management plan, are used as inputs to enable you to control the scope. By using a description of what you planned to do and comparing that to what you are actually doing, you can spot any variances. The project management plan is a key output from the Develop Project Management Plan process.

> **EXAM TIP**
>
> Whenever you find the project management plan listed as an input into a process, it indicates that more than one subsidiary plan is used in this process. In this instance, elements of the scope management plan, change management plan, configuration management plan, and requirements management plan are used as inputs to control the scope.

Requirements documentation

The clearly defined requirements documentation for the project and product can be used to detect any deviation in the scope during the Control Scope process. The requirements documentation is a key output from the Collect Requirements process.

Requirements traceability matrix

Using the requirements traceability matrix as an input helps bring an additional level of rigor into the Control Scope process by enabling you to map requirements back to project objectives. The requirements traceability matrix is a key output from the Collect Requirements process.

Work performance data

Work performance data in this instance refers to information about change requests received or the number and type of deliverables completed. Work performance data is the key output from the Direct and Manage Project Work process.

Organizational process assets

Key organizational process assets that can be useful as inputs into the Control Scope process include any change control–related or scope control–related guidelines, policies, or templates, and any documented monitoring and reporting methods.

Tools and techniques

There is a single technique used in the Control Scope process.

Variance analysis

Any *variance analysis* is simply an examination of what is actually occurring against what was planned to occur, and looking for any variances, positive or negative, and acting on them accordingly. If you discover any variance, you can decide to undertake corrective or preventive actions or initiate changes.

> **EXAM TIP**
>
> Variance analysis is a key tool in all the monitoring and controlling processes. Wherever you find variance analysis as a tool in a process, you should also look for some sort of baseline that is being checked for variance.

Outputs

The following outputs are produced by the Control Scope process.

Work performance information

Work performance information as an output from this process will include information relating to the type and category of change requests received and how they may potentially affect other areas of the project. Work performance information goes on to be used as an input in the Monitor and Control Project Work process.

Change requests

Change requests are a result of variances detected. All change requests must be processed according to the predefined change management process. Change requests go on to be used in the Perform Integrated Change Control process.

Project management plan updates

Elements of the project management plan that may be updated as a result of the work done during the Control Scope process include the project scope statement, WBS, and WBS dictionary.

Project documents updates

As a result of performing the Control Scope process you may choose to update the requirements documentation to reflect new or changed information.

Organizational process assets updates

Organizational process assets that may be updated as a result of the Control Scope process include any elements of the project scope management plan, change management plan, or lessons learned that have been gathered.

 Quick check

1. What is the main focus of the Control Scope process?
2. Why is variance analysis important to the Control Scope process?
3. What is the relationship between work performance data and work performance information?

Quick check answers

1. The main focus of the Control Scope process is to check the progress of the project against planned baselines, looking for variances and acting on any that are discovered.
2. Variance analysis is the process of checking what you planned to do against what you are actually doing. If you discover a variance between the two, then you must act.
3. Work performance data is the raw data collected while observing work being performed; it is turned into work performance information by applying metrics, formulas, and other ways of interpreting the data in order for it to make sense and be usable for measuring project progress.

Exercises

The answers for these exercises are located in the "Answers" section at the end of this chapter.

1. Create a WBS.

    You are working on a project, Project BlueTalk, to develop a new piece of software. As part of the development of the scope, you have identified that the four major deliverables are the software design, the testing of the software, the user training of the software, and the implementation of the software. At this early stage in the project, you are only able to further define the software design process and have broken that down into the sub-deliverables for module 1 and module 2. Using your project team members responsible for the software design, you have broken module 1 down into three work packages: database, user interface, and backup.

    Use this information to complete a WBS for the project.

2. Map the following terms to the definition that best fits them:

    a) Project charter
    b) Statement of work
    c) Requirements
    d) Preliminary scope statement
    e) Project scope statement
    f) Product scope

    i. An early iteration of the project scope statement
    ii. A description of all the work to be done on a project
    iii. A description of the product, service, or result to be delivered as part of the project work
    iv. A narrative description of the work to be completed; used as an input into the project charter
    v. The documented list of expectations and specifications from project stakeholders
    vi. The foundational document for a project, which contains a high-level description of the work to be completed

Chapter summary

- The Project Scope Management knowledge area is focused upon the processes of planning, defining, documenting, and managing change to the project requirements, scope, and work breakdown structure.

- Like other knowledge areas, the Project Scope Management knowledge area begins with a process of planning how you will manage the project scope. The key output from this is the scope management plan, which becomes a subsidiary plan of the project management plan.

- The first step in a linear process of defining the full project scope is to collect project requirements from stakeholders and develop both the requirements documentation and requirements traceability matrix.
- The process of defining the project scope is highly iterative and may be subject to rolling wave planning throughout the life of the project. After it is defined, the project scope will be captured in the project scope statement. The scope of the product is a subset of the total project scope.
- The work breakdown structure (WBS) is a graphical representation of the project scope statement, thus any work not included in the WBS is not included as part of the project. The WBS forms one of three key elements of the scope baseline. The scope baseline is made up of the project scope statement, the WBS, and the WBS dictionary.
- The work breakdown structure, after it is completed, serves as a valuable input into several other processes, including Project Cost Management, Project Time Management, and Project Risk Management.
- The process of validating the project scope involves internal and external stakeholders checking that the deliverables conform to stakeholder requirements and expectations. It is performed after scope verification.
- All changes to the project scope or requirements must go through the documented change control process. Any approved changes are incorporated into the scope baseline.

Chapter review

Test your knowledge of the information in Chapter 3 by answering these questions. The answers to these questions, and the explanations of why each answer choice is correct or incorrect, are located in the "Answers" section at the end of this chapter.

1. What is the correct order of activities in the Project Scope Management knowledge area?
    A. Define Scope, Collect Requirements, Plan Scope Management, Create WBS
    B. Plan Scope Management, Define Scope, Collect Requirements, Create WBS
    C. Plan Scope Management, Collect Requirements, Define Scope, Create WBS
    D. Collect Requirements, Define Scope, Create WBS, Plan Scope Management

2. What are the elements of the scope baseline?
    A. The project scope management plan and requirements documentation
    B. The project scope management plan and project scope statement
    C. The scope statement, the WBS, and the WBS dictionary
    D. The project scope statement, the product scope statement, and the WBS

3. What is the correct term for the component of the project management plan that describes how project requirements will be analyzed, documented, and managed?

   A. The requirements management plan
   B. The scope management plan
   C. The project scope statement
   D. The scope baseline

4. Brainstorming is an example of what sort of process tool or technique?

   A. Group decision-making techniques
   B. Observations
   C. Facilitated workshops
   D. Group creativity techniques

5. What is the main purpose of the requirements traceability matrix?

   A. To hold people accountable for work delivery
   B. To let stakeholders know when the project will be delivered
   C. To map individual requirements back to specific business needs and objectives
   D. To describe the work to be completed in the project

6. Which of the following best describes the relationship between the scope of the project and the scope of the product?

   A. The scope of the project includes all the planning work to be done, whereas the scope of the product documents the technical requirements of the deliverable.
   B. The product scope is a subset of the project scope.
   C. The project scope is delivered as part of the delivery of the product scope.
   D. There is no difference between the two terms.

7. What is the lowest level of WBS decomposition?

   A. The deliverable
   B. Project activities
   C. The work package
   D. The scope statement

8. What is the name of the document that provides additional information about each node of the WBS?

    A. The scope management plan
    B. The WBS dictionary
    C. The project scope statement
    D. The requirements documentation

9. What is the key purpose of the Validate Scope process?

    A. It is an internal process to determine whether the product meets strict technical requirements.
    B. It is the process of checking whether the deliverable conforms to requirements.
    C. It is the process of managing changes to the project scope statement.
    D. It is a process that involves internal and external stakeholders checking that the deliverable meets project requirements and stakeholder expectations.

10. Change requests that are generated as part of the Control Scope process are used as inputs into which process?

    A. The Validate Scope process
    B. The Perform Integrated Change Control process
    C. The Control Quality process
    D. The Plan Scope Management process

Answers

This section contains the answers for the "Exercises" and "Chapter review" sections in this chapter.

Exercises

1. Create a WBS.

    Your completed WBS should look like the following diagram shown in Figure 3-5. Did you remember to include the unique number identifiers in each node?

    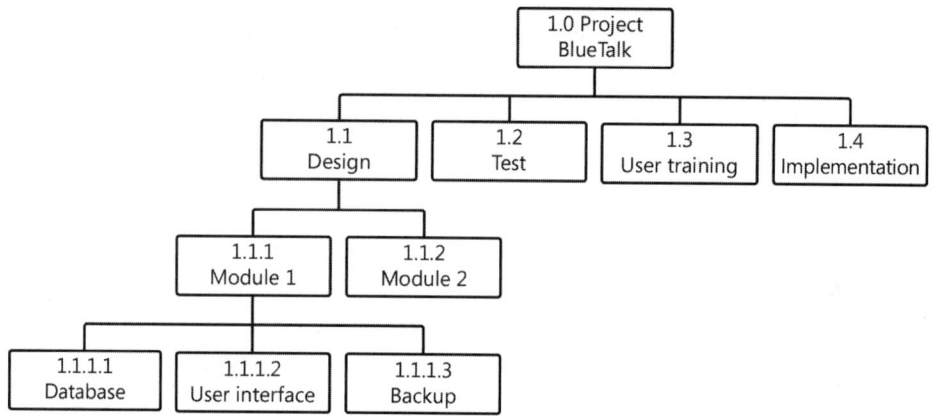

    FIGURE 3-5 A completed work breakdown structure for Project Bluetalk includes clear identifications and numbering.

2. Map the following terms to the definition that best fits them:

    a) Project charter   vi. The foundational document for a project, which contains a high-level description of the work to be completed

    b) Statement of work   iv. A narrative description of the work to be completed; used as an input into the project charter

    c) Requirements   v. The documented list of expectations and specifications from project stakeholders

    d) Preliminary scope statement   i. An early iteration of the project scope statement

    e) Project scope statement   ii. A description of all the work to be done on a project

    f) Product scope   iii. A description of the product, service, or result to be delivered as part of the project work

Chapter review

1. **Correct Answer: C**
   - **A. Incorrect:** Plan Scope Management is the first process to be completed so that you have a guide to completing the others.
   - **B. Incorrect:** Define Scope comes after Collect Requirements.
   - **C. Correct:** The sequence of Plan Scope Management, Collect Requirements, Define Scope, Create WBS describes the iterative development of Project Scope Management processes.
   - **D. Incorrect:** Plan Scope Management is the first process to be completed so that you have a guide to completing the others.

2. **Correct Answer: C**
   - **A. Incorrect:** The project scope management plan and requirements documentation are not part of the scope baseline.
   - **B. Incorrect:** The project scope management plan is not part of the scope baseline.
   - **C. Correct:** The scope statement, the WBS, and the WBS dictionary are the three elements of the scope baseline.
   - **D. Incorrect:** The project scope statement and the product scope statement are a part of, but not all of, the scope baseline.

3. **Correct Answer: A**
   - **A. Correct:** The requirements management plan describes how project requirements will be analyzed, documented, and managed.
   - **B. Incorrect:** The scope management plan describes how the project scope will be defined, documented, and managed.
   - **C. Incorrect:** The project scope statement describes the scope of work to be done as part of the project.
   - **D. Incorrect:** The scope baseline is made up of the scope statement, WBS, and WBS dictionary.

4. **Correct Answer: D**
   - **A. Incorrect:** Group decision-making techniques are techniques to assist groups of people in making decisions in the face of differing, and often dissenting, opinion.
   - **B. Incorrect:** Observations do not require brainstorming.
   - **C. Incorrect:** Facilitated workshops describe focused workshops.
   - **D. Correct:** Brainstorming is an example of a group creativity technique.

5. **Correct Answer: C**

    A. **Incorrect:** The requirements traceability matrix does not hold people accountable for work delivery.

    B. **Incorrect:** Letting stakeholders know when the project will be delivered would be part of your time management plan and communications management plan.

    C. **Correct:** The main purpose of the requirements traceability matrix is to map individual requirements back to specific business needs and objectives.

    D. **Incorrect:** The project scope statement is used to describe the work to be completed in the project.

6. **Correct Answer: B**

    A. **Incorrect:** The project scope includes all the work and only the work to be done, including a description of the product.

    B. **Correct:** The product scope is a subset of the project scope that focuses specifically on the product or deliverable of the project.

    C. **Incorrect:** The project scope is not delivered as part of the delivery of the product scope, it is the other way around.

    D. **Incorrect:** There is a difference between the two terms, because they describe different things.

7. **Correct Answer: C**

    A. **Incorrect:** The deliverable is a high-level description of the work to be done.

    B. **Incorrect:** Project activities are work packages that are further defined and used in developing a project schedule.

    C. **Correct:** The work package is the lowest level of WBS decomposition.

    D. **Incorrect:** The scope statement describes all the work to be done on the project.

8. **Correct Answer: B**

    A. **Incorrect:** The scope management plan describes how the project scope will be defined, documented, and managed.

    B. **Correct:** The WBS dictionary provides additional information to expand on the summary information contained in each node of the WBS.

    C. **Incorrect:** The project scope statement describes all the work to be done on the project.

    D. **Incorrect:** The requirements documentation describes individual requirements for the project.

9. **Correct Answer: D**
    A. **Incorrect:** The Validate Scope process is not simply an internal process.
    B. **Incorrect:** The process of checking whether the deliverable conforms to requirements is a Control Quality process.
    C. **Incorrect:** The change management process describes the process of managing changes to the project scope statement.
    D. **Correct:** The Validate Scope process is a process that involves internal and external stakeholders checking that the deliverable meets project requirements and stakeholder expectations.

10. **Correct Answer: B**
    A. **Incorrect:** Change requests are an output from the Validate Scope process.
    B. **Correct:** Change requests are used as an input into the Perform Integrated Change Control process.
    C. **Incorrect:** Approved change requests, which are change requests that have been through the Perform Integrated Change Control process, are used as an input into the Control Quality process.
    D. **Incorrect:** Change requests are not an input into the Plan Scope Management process.

CHAPTER 4

Time management

This chapter focuses on the topic of project time management. Project Time Management, like the other knowledge areas, begins with a process of planning that produces a schedule management plan. Then there is an iterative, or repeating, process that produces and updates the project schedule. Then, as with all other knowledge areas with the exception of the Human Resource Management knowledge area, there is a controlling process that seeks to measure planned versus actual progress in relation to time and deal with any changes or corrective or preventive actions.

You may need to pay particular attention in this chapter to those activities that lead up to the construction of the network diagram, because there is quite a bit of technical information that you will need to learn.

> **The PMBOK® Guide processes**
>
> **Project Time Management knowledge area**
>
> The seven processes in the Project Time Management knowledge area are:
>
> - Plan Schedule Management (Planning process)
> - Define Activities (Planning process)
> - Sequence Activities (Planning process)
> - Estimate Activity Resources (Planning process)
> - Estimate Activity Durations (Planning process)
> - Develop Schedule (Planning process)
> - Control Schedule (Monitoring and Controlling process)

Domain tasks in this chapter:

- Plan Schedule Management, Define Activities, Sequence Activities, Estimate Activity Resources, Estimate Activity Durations, and Develop Schedule processes:
    - 2.4 Develop a project schedule based on the project timeline, scope, and resource plan, in order to manage timely completion of the project.

- Control Schedule process:
    - 4.1 Measure project performance using appropriate tools and techniques, in order to identify and quantify any variances, perform approved corrective actions, and communicate with relevant stakeholders.
    - 4.2 Manage changes to the project scope, schedule, and costs by updating the project plan and communicating approved changes to the team, in order to ensure that revised project goals are met.

What is project time management?

Project time management is focused upon the processes of developing a schedule management plan, estimating durations for activities and the overall project, preparing your project schedule, ensuring that the project progresses as planned and that milestones are reached on the communicated schedule, and influencing and assessing any changes to the project schedule.

EXAM TIP

There are some industries that use the term "schedule" in reference to a schedule of materials to be used in the execution of the project. For the exam you should note that the word "schedule" is used exclusively to mean project time estimates.

Apart from the Control Schedule process, the processes contained in this knowledge area present what appears to be a wonderfully logical and sequential flow of information, from defining the activities through to development of the project schedule. Figure 4-1 shows the general flow through this linear process.

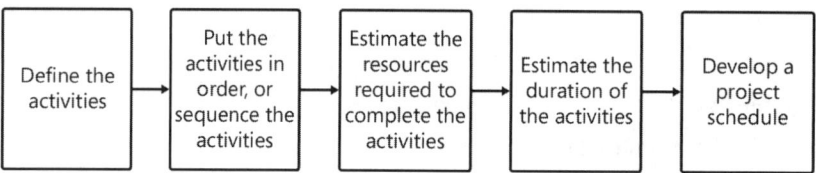

FIGURE 4-1 The sequential flow of the Project Schedule Development process culminates in the development of a project schedule.

Real world

Even though the separate Project Time Management processes are often presented as separate, discrete processes, I have always found that the process of developing a project schedule is in fact done as one process usually at the same time.

EXAM TIP

Remember that the output of the time management processes is the project schedule, which refers to all elements of time management on a project and not just the ubiquitous Gantt chart. Also remember that a project management plan is more than just a Gantt chart.

Plan Schedule Management

MORE INFO PLAN SCHEDULE MANAGEMENT

You can read more about the Plan Schedule Management process in the PMBOK® Guide, 5th edition, in Chapter 6, section 6.1. Table 4-1 identifies the process inputs, tools and techniques, and outputs.

TABLE 4-1 Plan Schedule Management process

Inputs	Tools and techniques	Outputs
- Project management plan - Project charter - Enterprise environmental factors - Organizational process assets	- Expert judgment - Analytical techniques - Meetings	- Schedule management plan

The Plan Schedule Management process is a planning process with a single output—not surprisingly, given the name of the process, it is the schedule management plan. Like all other planning documents, the schedule management plan will guide your efforts in defining and controlling the project schedule. It will form a subsidiary plan to the overall project management plan.

The Plan Schedule Management process covers the following domain task:

- 2.4 Develop a project schedule based on the project timeline, scope, and resource plan, in order to manage timely completion of the project.

Inputs

The Plan Schedule Management process uses some or all of the following inputs as part of the development of the schedule management plan for the project.

Project management plan

Any reference to the project management plan includes a reference to all subsidiary management plans that it contains. Obviously, any aspect of work on the project will incur some time and, therefore, the project management plan, with its information about other areas, provides a useful input into planning your particular approach to schedule management. Any and all information relating to the project scope, project cost, project risk, project communications, project procurement, and stakeholder expectation management will be useful in assisting you develop your schedule management plan.

Project charter

The project charter, which is the foundational document of the project, providing and confirming financial and political support for the project, contains useful information about the known statement of work, any initial known constraints and assumptions, and an assessment of the known risks. This preliminary information contained in the project charter is particularly useful when you first begin defining your project schedule.

Enterprise environmental factors

Enterprise environmental factors are any factors external to the project that can influence the outcome; they can usually be viewed as some sort of constraint on the project. Particular enterprise environmental factors that may assist with development of your schedule management plan include the wider organizational culture and structure, and the inherent skills available throughout the organization. Additional enterprise environmental factors that are useful in developing a project schedule include any external published commercial information that can be used to estimate time on a project, and any company work authorization systems.

Organizational process assets

Organizational process assets that may play an important part as inputs into the development of your schedule management plan include historical information, blank templates, and project management methodology guidelines.

EXAM TIP

Historical information and lessons learned are considered to be two of the most important organizational process assets that any project manager can rely upon in the development of any part of the project management plan. In the exam, you will find an emphasis on historical information and lessons learned as an important input into many processes.

Tools and techniques

The following tools and techniques are available to be used to develop the inputs into this process in order to produce the schedule management plan.

Expert judgment

Again expert judgment is used as a tool. Expert judgment is the advice and opinion of any person or group who holds specific knowledge about a particular area. As project manager, you are considered to be an expert, your project team members are experts, and any other person with specialist knowledge you choose to consult is also an expert.

> **EXAM TIP**
>
> Deciding to use expert judgment is one thing; how you get the information from selected experts is another matter and is the subject of other information-gathering tools and techniques, such as meetings, the Delphi technique, interviews, questionnaires, and surveys.

Analytical techniques

As part of the development of the schedule management plan, you will have to make decisions about which processes, tools, and techniques are best used in your particular project. This process of analyzing the potential options available to you is referred to as using analytical techniques.

Meetings

Meetings are a useful tool to bring together everyone with experience in developing the schedule management plan. When run properly, they are an effective and efficient means of getting work done. The most useful people to invite to these particular meetings are members of the project team and people with experience in developing schedules.

Outputs

After applying the appropriate tools and techniques to the selected inputs, the Plan Schedule Management process has the following output.

Schedule management plan

The Plan Schedule Management process has only a single output—the *schedule management plan*. The schedule management plan is a subsidiary plan of the project management plan. The purpose of the schedule management plan is to guide the project manager and the project team; the plan also guides further activities, such as defining and developing the project schedule, checking for variance between what has been planned and what is actually happening, and managing any changes to the project schedule. As such, it is an important plan to have in place in order to provide oversight, standardization, and best practices to ensure that the project schedule, itself an essential part of any successful project, is well developed, monitored, and controlled.

EXAM TIP

Always assume that any aspect of your project management activities has some form of plan guiding it. The absence of a plan will result in inefficient and ineffective efforts that can increase the chances of project failure.

The schedule management plan is then a key input into the following processes, all of which are planning processes:

- 6.2 Define Activities
- 6.3 Sequence Activities
- 6.4 Estimate Activity Resources
- 6.5 Estimate Activity Durations
- 6.6 Develop Schedule

 Quick check

1. What is the main purpose of the schedule management plan?
2. Why is the project charter an important input into the Plan Schedule Management process?
3. What role does the schedule management plan have in the overall project management plan?

Quick check answers

1. The main purpose of the schedule management plan is to provide a documented guide as to how your project schedule will be defined, documented, and used to check actual versus planned schedule, and to outline how any potential changes will be managed and assessed.
2. At the beginning of the development of your project schedule, the project charter provides a wealth of preliminary information about the statement of work, constraints, assumptions, risks, and other information that will ultimately affect the project schedule.
3. The schedule management plan is a subsidiary plan of the overall project management plan that focuses on the particular area of project time management.

Define Activities

> **MORE INFO** **DEFINE ACTIVITIES**
>
> You can read more about the Define Activities process in the PMBOK® Guide, 5th edition, in Chapter 6, section 6.2. Table 4-2 identifies the process inputs, tools and techniques, and outputs.
>
> **TABLE 4-2** Define Activities process
>
> | Inputs | Tools and techniques | Outputs |
> |---|---|---|
> | - Schedule management plan
- Scope baseline
- Enterprise environmental factors
- Organizational process assets | - Decomposition
- Rolling wave planning
- Expert judgment | - Activity list
- Activity attributes
- Milestone list |

The Define Activities process is a planning process that takes the already-defined work packages from the Create WBS process and breaks them down further into individual activities.

The Define Activities process covers the following domain task:

- 2.4 Develop a project schedule based on the project timeline, scope, and resource plan, in order to manage timely completion of the project.

The difference between an activity and a work package is that an activity is the smallest component of work to be performed during the course of a project. A work package is a convenient level of work to stop at when completing the work breakdown structure (WBS), because at that point the work can reliably be estimated for time and cost. At that point, breaking work packages down into activities for the purposes of the work breakdown structure has a decreasing benefit for the time and effort taken to do this. However, for the purposes of putting together an accurate project schedule, you must break these work packages down even further to the level of activities.

> **Real world**
>
> When completing any decomposition of the project scope statement, it sometimes seems arbitrary to stop the decomposition process at the level of work packages and then come back at some later time to break it down further into activities. Therefore, during the process of decomposition of the scope, whether to show it graphically in a WBS, or to obtain a list of work packages and activities to put into the project schedule, I generally do both processes at the same time.

Inputs

The Define Activities process uses some or all of the following four inputs.

Schedule management plan

The schedule management plan is obviously a key input into the Define Activities process because the schedule management plan contains information about how you will break activities down, and the level of detail expected from the activities listed. The schedule management plan is an output from the Plan Schedule Management process.

Scope baseline

The scope baseline is used to ensure that the project manager captures all of the activities contained in the project scope. When breaking the project scope down into its component parts, you can use the scope baseline and all the information it contains to ensure that you have captured all the activities required to complete the project. The scope baseline is an output of the Create WBS process.

EXAM TIP

Remember that the scope baseline includes the following three elements: the project scope statement, the WBS, and the WBS dictionary.

Enterprise environmental factors

The specific types of enterprise environmental factors that are useful as inputs into the Define Activities process are any aspects of the project management information system, any relevant parts of the organizational culture and structure, and any published information from commercial databases.

Organizational process assets

The specific types of organizational process assets that are useful as inputs into the Define Activities process are any existing project management methodologies, processes, and templates that can assist with the development of the project schedule. Additionally, any configuration management system that defines how different versions of the project schedule will be recorded, controlled, and updated can be used as an input. This is particularly important to ensure that you are always working on the correct version of any document in what can be a highly iterative process. Of course, any historical information from past projects that can be used to assist in the compilation of the current project management plan is also useful.

Tools and techniques

The following three tools and techniques are used upon the inputs to deliver the process outputs.

Decomposition

You have read about the process of decomposition used in the Create WBS process to take the scope of the project and decompose it down to the work package level. As a tool and technique in the Define Activities process, it is used to further decompose the already-defined work packages to activity level.

Rolling wave planning

Rolling wave planning is a key iterative element of the project manager's planning process. It is a form of progressive elaboration in which you can plan in detail work that is in the immediate future, and plan in less detail the work that is further off.

A good example of rolling wave planning is when you have a project that is to go on for two and a half years. You will spend most of your planning activity on the work coming up in the next three months. Work to be done from three months to nine months out will have a lesser level of detail attached to it in the planning, but still enough to give you confidence about project time and cost. Work that is to be done beyond the nine-month period may have a very low level of detail attached to its time and cost elements.

Expert judgment

You may decide to call on the expert judgment of people with skills and experience in this type of project, and in the preparation of project schedules, in order to more accurately define your project activities

Outputs

The Define Activities process produces some or all of the following outputs.

Activity list

The *activity list* is a comprehensive list that includes all currently known activities. In addition to listing the title and brief description of the activity, the activity list can provide additional information such as a unique identification number, which is an example of the configuration management system at work, and any other ancillary information that is relevant.

Is important to note that if you are undertaking any form of progressive elaboration or rolling wave planning, you may only have identified and defined the activities for the next immediate time period, and a definition and documentation of activities beyond this may yet need to be done.

The activity list is used as an input into the following processes:

- 6.3 Sequence Activities
- 6.4 Estimate Activity Resources
- 6.5 Estimate Activity Durations
- 6.6 Develop Schedule

Activity attributes

The *activity attributes* are to the activity list what the WBS dictionary is to the WBS. The activity list contains summary information about each activity, whereas the activity attributes document provides more detailed information about each of the activities. This detailed information can include any requirements, known constraints and assumptions, required milestones, and any other information that helps any person wanting to know more about the activity to understand it fully.

The activity attributes document is used as an input into the following processes:

- 6.3 Sequence Activities
- 6.4 Estimate Activity Resources
- 6.5 Estimate Activity Durations
- 6.6 Develop Schedule

Milestone list

As part of the development of the project schedule, and after the project activities have been defined, the project manager, in consultation with relevant stakeholders, may be able to produce a list of known milestones that should be achieved on the project. The *milestone list* contains these documented milestones.

EXAM TIP

Remember that a milestone has no duration and indicates a particular moment in time, usually when some specific work package or phase of a project has been completed. A milestone is often used as a point in the project where an assessment of work to date is done and decisions made about whether the project will continue.

Real world

Often when I am reporting progress of a project to senior-level stakeholders, the milestone list provides an appropriate means of communicating high-level information quickly. I will often use the milestone list and a description of which milestones have been achieved and which ones have not yet been achieved as a high-level way of communicating project progress quickly to senior stakeholders on the project.

Quick check

1. What is the difference between an activity and a work package?
2. How is rolling wave planning used?
3. What is the primary purpose of the activity attributes document?

Quick check answers

1. A work package is the lowest level of decomposition in the work breakdown structure (WBS). It represents a parcel of work that can reliably be estimated for time and cost. On the other hand, an activity is a decomposed work package, broken down into the actual tasks that need to be done on a project.
2. Rolling wave planning is an important tool to use on long-term projects. With rolling wave planning, planning and detail is done for the immediate time period, and time periods that are further out are planned in less detail.
3. The primary purpose of the activity attributes document is to provide further and more detailed information about each of the activities in the activity list.

Sequence Activities

> **MORE INFO** **SEQUENCE ACTIVITIES**
>
> You can read more about the Sequence Activities process in the PMBOK® Guide, 5th edition, in Chapter 6, section 6.3. Table 4-3 identifies the process inputs, tools and techniques, and outputs.

TABLE 4-3 Sequence Activities process

Inputs	Tools and techniques	Outputs
- Schedule management plan - Activity list - Activity attributes - Milestone list - Project scope statement - Enterprise environmental factors - Organizational process assets	- Precedence diagramming method (PDM) - Dependency determination - Applying leads and lags	- Project schedule network diagrams - Project documents updates

The Sequence Activities process is a planning process that takes the list of activities that have already been defined and starts to put them in the order in which they will be completed.

The Sequence Activities process covers the following domain task:

- 2.4 Develop a project schedule based on the project timeline, scope, and resource plan, in order to manage timely completion of the project.

Inputs

The inputs used in this process allow for sequencing of the already-defined project activities.

Schedule management plan

The schedule management plan is used as a key input into the Sequence Activities process because it outlines and defines how, and when, you will sequence the activities. The schedule management plan is an output from the Plan Schedule Management process

Activity list

The activity list is a very important input into the Sequence Activities process because you need the list of activities to put them in order. The activity list is an output from the Define Activities process.

Activity attributes

The activity attributes document provides additional information about each of the activities that may be useful when it comes to deciding whether they are predecessors or successors for any other activity. The activity attributes document is an output from the Define Activities process.

Milestone list

The milestone list is an important input because it has a description of the known project milestones, and with this you can determine which activities must be completed before the milestone and which must be completed after the milestone. The milestone list is an output from the Define Activities process.

Project scope statement

The project scope statement is used as an input into the Sequence Activities process because it allows you to understand the complete scope of work to be delivered in the project and, thus, you can get a clear idea of which activities must be performed before other activities.

Enterprise environmental factors

The specific types of enterprise environmental factors that will be useful to you during the Sequence Activities process will be scheduling tools, government or industry standards, and any other external factors affecting the order in which work is to be completed on your project.

Organizational process assets

The specific organizational process assets that can assist you in sequencing the activities include any existing processes, templates, historical information, or lessons learned documentation that the organization owns.

Tools and techniques

The three tools and techniques of this process are all used upon the separate inputs to deliver the process outputs.

Precedence diagramming method (PDM)

The *precedence diagramming method* (PDM) is a graphical representation of activities in a project, represented on nodes, with the relationships between them indicated by arrows. This is more commonly called the *activity-on-node (AON)* diagram. It establishes a *predecessor* and *successor* relationship between activities. An activity can be a predecessor of other activities, meaning that it must be done before them. The same activity can also be a successor activity to one or more activities, meaning it must be done after them.

As mentioned already, a predecessor activity is one that comes before another activity, and a successor activity is one that comes after another activity. A predecessor activity may have many successor activities, in which case it is known as a burst activity. A successor activity may have one or more predecessor activities. If the successor activity has more than one predecessor activity, it is known as a merge activity. Figure 4-2 shows an example of Activity A as the predecessor activity, with Activities B and C as the successor activities. Activity A is also a burst activity.

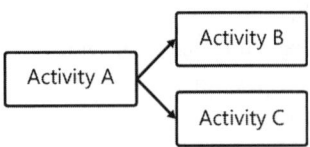

FIGURE 4-2 A predecessor with multiple successors can be shown in a burst activity diagram.

There are four types of relationships that exist between predecessor and successor activities:

- **Finish-to-start (FS)** A finish-to-start relationship is one in which the successor activity cannot start until the predecessor activity has finished. For example, you cannot erect the walls of a house until the foundation has been completed. Figure 4-3 depicts how this would be represented diagrammatically.

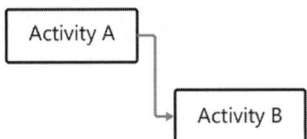

FIGURE 4-3 A finish-to-start relationship is shown with an arrow from the finish of the predecessor activity to the start of the successor activity.

- **Finish-to-finish (FF)** A finish-to-finish relationship is one in which the successor activity cannot finish until the predecessor activity has finished. For example, you cannot finish writing the user manual for a piece of software until the testing is finished. Figure 4-4 depicts how this would be represented diagrammatically.

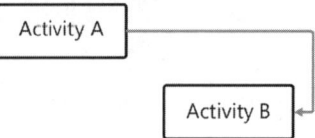

FIGURE 4-4 A finish-to-finish relationship is shown with an arrow from the finish of the predecessor activity to the finish of the successor activity.

- **Start-to-start (SS)** A start-to-start relationship is one in which the successor activity cannot start until the predecessor activity starts. For example, you cannot begin testing a new piece of software until you have started writing the code. Figure 4-5 depicts how this can be represented diagrammatically.

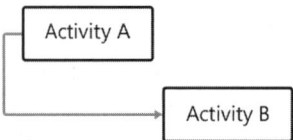

FIGURE 4-5 A start-to-start relationship is shown with an arrow from the start of the predecessor activity to the start of the successor activity.

- **Start-to-finish (SF)** A start-to-finish relationship indicates that the successor cannot finish until the predecessor starts. For example, you may have an activity to send the invoice for a product, but the invoice cannot be sent (finished) until delivery of the product has started. This type of relationship is almost never used because it seems to indicate that the successor should be the predecessor and vice-versa. Figure 4-6 depicts how this would be represented diagrammatically.

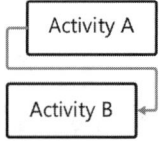

FIGURE 4-6 A start-to-finish relationship is shown with an arrow from the start of the predecessor activity to the finish of the successor activity.

> **Real world**
>
> In project management scheduling software such as Microsoft Project, the default relationship for activities is finish-to-start. Check it out: if you enter *FS* after a predecessor, the *FS* disappears. However, if you enter *FF*, *SS*, or *SF*, they remain.

Dependency determination

In addition to the types of relationships that exist between predecessor and successor activities, there are also four types of dependencies that determine the nature of the relationship between the two activities.

- In mandatory dependencies, the successor activity must always occur after the predecessor activity. For example, you must develop the code for a piece of software before you begin testing it.
- In discretionary dependencies, the successor activity should occur after the predecessor activity, although the two activities can be performed in another sequence if necessary.

> **EXAM TIP**
>
> Be aware that discretionary dependencies have some flexibility built into them in terms of how they are scheduled. Generally they should be performed in sequence, with successor activities after their predecessor activities, but they can be performed in parallel if necessary. Generally there is an increased risk associated with performing discretionary dependencies in parallel rather than in sequence, and this additional risk would need to be considered when putting together the project schedule.

- In external dependencies, the activity is dependent upon an activity being completed outside of the project. For example, you cannot start construction on the house until you have received building consent.
- In internal dependencies, the activity relies upon another activity that is external to the project but internal to the broader organization. For example, the recruitment of people on your project may be done by the human resources department, and you have to wait until they complete the work.

Applying leads and lags

As you start to put together your project network diagram by beginning with the sequencing of the activities, you can also choose to apply *leads* and *lags*. A lead is the amount of time that a successor activity can start before its predecessor activity finishes. For example, generally speaking, you do not start building the walls of a house until construction of the foundation has been completed. However, you can get a lead on the construction of the walls by having them built off site.

The opposite of a lead is a lag. A lag is the amount of time that a successor activity must wait after its predecessor activity has finished before it can start. For example, in the case of pouring concrete for a house foundation, you must wait several days while the concrete cures before you can start building on it. Because the concrete curing period has neither resources nor costs assigned to it, it cannot be included as an activity in your network diagram. Instead, you indicate that the successor activities must wait via a lag before they can begin.

Real world

If you want to indicate a lead between a successor and its predecessor by using Microsoft Project, this can be done by using the relationship acronym, such as finish-to-start (FS), and a minus sign followed by the number of time periods the activity can start before the completion of its predecessor. For example, *FS -4* means that the successor activity has a finish-to- start relationship with its predecessor activity and can start 4 days before the predecessor activity ends. If you want to indicate a lag, you can do this by the use of a plus sign after the relationship acronym. For example, if you want to indicate a lag of 3 days, you would simply write the task ID number of the predecessor and then, for a finish-to-start relationship, *FS +3*.

Outputs

The major outputs from the Sequence Activities process are the following.

Project schedule network diagrams

The *project schedule network diagram* represents all the activities in the project and the relationships between them all.

The process of completing the sequencing of activities is the first step in the completion of the project schedule network diagram. This first pass, which indicates the relationships between the activities, will be further fleshed out with more information in the coming processes as you use the resource estimates to define the durations of each of the activities. Then you will be able to calculate the total project duration, the amount of slack or float in the project, and the critical path or paths.

Figure 4-7 shows what an activity-on-node (AON) network diagram might look like at the end of the sequencing process. Information about each activity is represented in the nodes on the diagram, and the arrows indicate the relationship between the activities. In this case they are all finish-to-start (FS) relationships. The activity-on-node (AON) diagram is the most popular graphical way of representing a network diagram, but there is another, less intuitive way, called the *activity-on-arrow (AOA)* diagram.

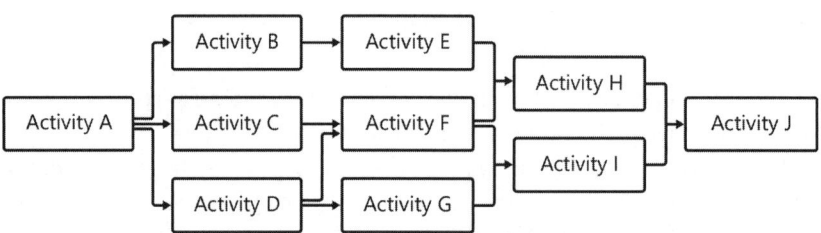

FIGURE 4-7 An activity-on-node network diagram shows activity nodes connected by arrows.

Real world

It is highly unlikely that you will need to know how to construct a network diagram manually in the real world. I have found that the main benefit in knowing how to put together a network diagram, calculate the project duration, calculate any slack in the network diagram, and determine a critical path is for understanding and appreciating how project management software works. Perhaps the only time you will need to know how to do this manually is for a small part of your project schedule at short notice when software isn't available.

EXAM TIP

The other way of graphically representing a network diagram is what is called the Arrow diagramming method or the activity-on-arrow (AOA) diagram. The activity-on-arrow diagram is not used very much at all within the project management world because it seems to run counter to the logical representations of activities and the relationships between them. Because the activities themselves are represented by arrows, it becomes a problem to also use arrows to show relationships between activities, so where there are multiple predecessors to an activity, a dummy activity is used, represented by a dotted line. Figure 4-8 shows an example of an activity-on-arrow diagram with a dummy activity showing a relationship between Activities B and G. In the exam, if you find a reference to a dummy activity, you know it is referring to activity-on-arrow diagrams.

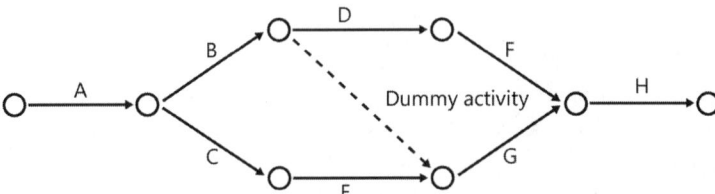

FIGURE 4-8 An activity-on-arrow (AOA) diagram shows the activities on arrows instead of nodes.

Project documents updates

The types of project documents that may be updated as a result of the Sequence Activities process are the activity list, activity attributes, and any other relevant documents.

> ✓ **Quick check**
>
> 1. What is the most commonly used type of relationship between predecessor and successor activities?
> 2. What is the difference between a lead and a lag?
> 3. What is the difference between an activity-on-node diagram and an activity-on-arrow diagram?
>
> **Quick check answers**
>
> 1. The most commonly used type of relationship between predecessor and successor activities is a finish-to-start relationship.
> 2. A lead is the amount of time that a successor activity can start before its predecessor finishes, whereas a lag is the amount of time a successor activity must wait after its predecessor activity finishes.
> 3. An activity-on-node diagram represents the project activities on nodes, with the arrows between the nodes representing the types of relationships. An activity-on-arrow diagram shows the activities of the project occurring on the arrows themselves, with nodes representing where multiple activities join.

Estimate Activity Resources

> **MORE INFO** **ESTIMATE ACTIVITY RESOURCES**
>
> You can read more about the Estimate Activity Resources process in the PMBOK® Guide, 5th edition, in Chapter 6, section 6.4. Table 4-4 identifies the process inputs, tools and techniques, and outputs.
>
> **TABLE 4-4** Estimate Activity Resources process
>
> | Inputs | Tools and techniques | Outputs |
> | --- | --- | --- |
> | ▪ Schedule management plan
▪ Activity list
▪ Activity attributes
▪ Resource calendars
▪ Risk register
▪ Activity cost estimates
▪ Enterprise environmental factors
▪ Organizational process assets | ▪ Expert judgment
▪ Alternative analysis
▪ Published estimating data
▪ Bottom-up estimating
▪ Project management software | ▪ Activity resource requirements
▪ Resource breakdown structure
▪ Project documents updates |

The key area of focus in the Estimate Activity Resources process is to consider the defined activities and carry out the process of estimating what resources will be required to complete the work.

The Estimate Activity Resources process covers the following domain task:

- 2.4. Develop a project schedule based on the project timeline, scope, and resource plan, in order to manage timely completion of the project.

> **NOTE DEFINING RESOURCES**
> A resource can be defined as any person, team, machinery, equipment, material, or funds used to do work on the project.

Inputs

There are eight inputs into the Estimate Activity Resources process, all specifically designed to assist you in producing the outputs.

Schedule management plan

Again the schedule management plan appears as a primary input into a process devoted to producing the project network diagram. This is because the schedule management plan is the document that describes and defines your approach to producing a project schedule. The schedule management plan is an output from the Plan Schedule Management process.

Activity list

The activity list provides information about all the activities that you have defined. You will use this information to estimate individual resources assigned to each activity. The activity list is an output from the Define Activities process.

Activity attributes

The activity attributes document provides additional information about each activity on your activity list. This information can refer to which resources are available. The activity attributes document is an output from the Define Activities process.

Resource calendars

Resource calendars are a key input into this process because they define constraints on when resources are available to work. They define such things as normal working times, holidays, and any other constraints on when resources may be available. Resource calendars are an output from the Acquire Project Team process in the Human Resource Management knowledge area.

Risk register

The *risk register* is used to assist with estimating activity resources because it documents any known risks that might affect resources that you plan to use on the project. The risk register is an output from the Identify Risks process in the Risk Management knowledge area.

Activity cost estimates

You are able to use *activity cost estimates* to determine the cost of the resources you might be considering for each activity. Activity cost estimates are an output from the Estimate Costs process in the Cost Management knowledge area.

Enterprise environmental factors

The specific types of enterprise environmental factors that can be used in this process include any constraints imposed upon resource availability for the project, such as government regulations on mandatory types of resources that must be used, or perhaps regulations of health and safety that affect the number of people who must be present in a workplace.

Organizational process assets

The specific types of organizational process assets that can be used as inputs into this process include any existing processes and templates, any relevant human resource policies, and any relevant policies in relation to procurement of supplies and equipment that the organization has. Additionally, a key organizational process asset is always historical information from previous projects.

Tools and techniques

The following tools and techniques are available, if appropriate, to use on the selected inputs.

Expert judgment

Expert judgment is a key tool because you will use the judgment of experts to help produce the activity resource estimates. The types of experts you should consult are those people with prior, and specialized, knowledge in resource planning on a project similar to your own.

Alternative analysis

The process of *alternative analysis* considers all the different permutations of delivering an activity by using different combinations of resources, quantities of resources, and types of resources, and whether you will rent or buy the resources you require.

Published estimating data

Published estimating data is a convenient means of getting reliable data from commercial sources. This published estimating data can give you information on what resources are available, the cost of these resources, and the work rate of the resources.

EXAM TIP

You will use published estimating data as a tool for cost estimating processes as well.

Bottom-up estimating

Bottom-up estimating is an estimating process that begins at a low level of the WBS, such as at individual work packages or even at activity level, and works upward by aggregating, or adding up, resource estimates in each level of the WBS to arrive at a high-level estimate. Bottom-up estimating is generally considered to be more accurate than top-down estimating, but it involves more time and effort to complete.

Project management software

Most projects plan to use many different types of resources, and therefore it is neither effective nor efficient to do this process manually. This is where using *project management software* provides a definite advantage, because it can process information more quickly.

Outputs

The following outputs are generated by the Estimate Activity Resources process.

Activity resource requirements

The *activity resource requirements* list is the documented list of the resources that you will require to complete every activity on your activity list. The activity resource requirements list goes on to be used as an input into the Plan Human Resource Management process and the Plan Procurement Management process.

Resource breakdown structure

The *resource breakdown structure*, like other breakdown structures, is used to decompose the categories of resource required and the specific resources required for the project. The resource breakdown structure then goes on to be used as an input into the Estimate Activity Durations process and the Develop Schedule process. Figure 4-9 shows an example of a resource breakdown structure.

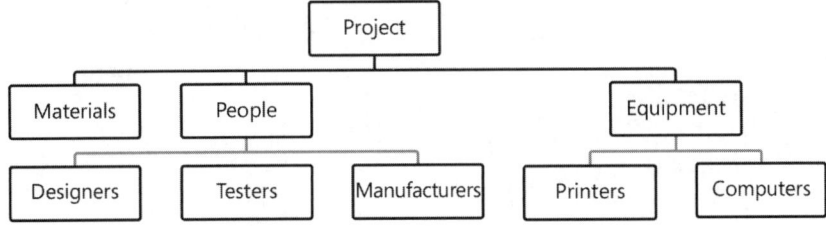

FIGURE 4-9 A resource breakdown structure is one of the outputs of the Estimate Activity Resources process.

Estimate Activity Resources **CHAPTER 4** 145

EXAM TIP

The resource breakdown structure is one of four breakdown structures that you should know for the exam. The other three are the organizational breakdown structure, the risk breakdown structure, and of course, perhaps the most important, the work breakdown structure (WBS).

Project documents updates

Types of project documents that might be updated as a result of the Estimate Activity Resources process are the activity list, activity attributes, resource calendars, and project schedule management plan.

 Quick check

1. What is the definition of a project resource?
2. What is the benefit of using published estimating data?
3. What is the advantage of using bottom-up estimating techniques?
4. Why is it important to use resource calendars as an input into the Estimate Activity Resources process?

Quick check answers

1. A project resource is any person, material, funding, or piece of equipment that is being used to complete activities, and subsequently work, on a project.
2. The benefit of using published estimating data is that it is reliable and is generally prepared by using relevant commercially available data.
3. Bottom-up estimating techniques are generally more accurate than top-down techniques because they aggregate estimates at a low level in the WBS and roll them up.
4. Resource calendars provide information about resource availability and, as such, they are an essential input into the Estimate Activity Resources process because they let you know when resources are available and when resources are not available to work on a project.

Estimate Activity Durations

> **MORE INFO** **ESTIMATE ACTIVITY DURATIONS**
>
> You can read more about the Estimate Activity Durations process in the PMBOK® Guide, 5th edition, in Chapter 6, section 6.5. Table 4-5 identifies the process inputs, tools and techniques, and outputs.
>
> **TABLE 4-5** Estimate Activity Durations process
>
> | Inputs | Tools and techniques | Outputs |
> | --- | --- | --- |
> | - Schedule management plan
- Activity list
- Activity attributes
- Activity resource requirements
- Resource calendars
- Project scope statement
- Risk register
- Resource breakdown structure
- Enterprise environmental factors
- Organizational process assets | - Expert judgment
- Analogous estimating
- Parametric estimating
- Three-point estimating
- Group decision-making techniques
- Reserve analysis | - Activity duration estimates
- Project documents updates |

The Estimate Activity Durations process is focused upon taking the previous data you have produced in defining the activities, sequencing the activities, and estimating the resources required for each activity, and then estimating the duration of each activity so that you can roll these individual estimates up into a total estimate for the project duration.

The Estimate Activity Durations process covers the following domain task:

- 2.4 Develop a project schedule based on the project timeline, scope, and resource plan, in order to manage timely completion of the project.

> **EXAM TIP**
>
> The reason that the Estimate Activity Resources process comes before the Estimate Activity Durations process is that generally you need to know what resources are available for you to be able to estimate how long activity will take because the more resources you have, the faster an activity will be completed.

Inputs

The following inputs can be used in the Estimate Activity Durations process to generate the outputs.

Schedule management plan

The schedule management plan is again a key input into this process because it outlines the way in which you are going to complete your estimate of activity durations. The schedule management plan is an output from the Plan Schedule Management process.

Activity list

The activity list provides information about all the activities on a project and is an essential input because you are now going to be estimating the duration of each of these activities. The activity list is an output from the Define Activities process.

Activity attributes

Though the activity list provides you with a list of all the activities, and some summary information about each of them, the activity attributes document provides detailed information about each of the activities, including the resources allocated to them, any known constraints or assumptions, and any risks about them. Activity attributes are an output from the Define Activities process.

Activity resource requirements

The activity resource requirements match each activity in your activity list with allocated resources that have been estimated to complete the activity. The activity resource requirements are an output from the Estimate Activity Resources process.

Resource calendars

Resource calendars provide you with information about constraints on resource availability. They specify when resources are available and when they are not available. If they are referring to people, they may outline holidays and known non-working times so that you can build these into your duration estimates. Resource calendars are also useful for indicating when resources are allocated to other projects and are thus not available to work on your project. Resource calendars are an output from the Acquire Project Team process.

Project scope statement

The use of the project scope statement as an input into the Estimate Activity Durations process provides a great level of oversight to ensure that you have captured the entire project scope. Furthermore, the project scope statement will contain additional information that you may need to be aware of when estimating activity durations, such as any pre-identified skilled resources and any known contract terms and requirements affecting duration estimates. The project scope statement is an output from the Define Scope process in the Scope Management knowledge area.

Risk register

The project risk register includes an analysis of the risks associated with resource use on the project and, as such, will contain important information about uncertainty in your activity duration estimates. The risk register is an output from the Identify Risks process in the Risk Management knowledge area.

Resource breakdown structure

The resource breakdown structure provides you with a comprehensive decomposition of the types of resources you will require on the project, and with this information you can estimate durations better. The resource breakdown structure is an output from the Estimate Activity Resources process.

Enterprise environmental factors

The specific types of enterprise environmental factors that may be used as inputs into this process are any estimating databases that the organization has accumulated or that are available from external sources, and any known productivity metrics useful in determining the durations of particular activities when completed by specific resources.

Organizational process assets

The organizational process assets that can be used to assist in the Estimate Activity Durations process are any historical information you have from previous projects, any lessons learned from previous projects specifically in relation to estimating, activity durations, and any organizational methodology and processes that can assist you in this process.

Tools and techniques

The following tools and techniques can be used upon the selected inputs to generate the outputs.

Expert judgment

The specific type of expert judgment you will use as a tool in this process will be from anyone with specific knowledge about how long activities should take. This expert judgment can come from team members, others within the organization, or external people with specific experience.

Analogous estimating

Analogous estimating is an estimating technique in which you take a similar activity and extrapolate from that a current estimate based on the relationship between the other activity and this activity. For example, you may know that a similar activity took three days to complete, and the one you are currently estimating is twice as big; therefore, you would estimate a total duration of six days by using an analogous estimating technique.

> **NOTE ACCURACY OF ESTIMATES**
>
> Any estimating technique is simply an attempt to forecast what the future may hold. The better the information that goes into the estimating process is, the better the estimate will be. For example, let's say that you are trying to forecast the weather for tomorrow, for one week from now, for one month from now, and for one year from now. In order to estimate the weather for tomorrow, you have available to you a lot of data, including quantitative data on what today's weather pattern is doing and what historical information, and computer simulations, tell you this weather pattern will do tomorrow. As a result of this detailed information going into the estimating process, you can be reasonably sure that your estimate about tomorrow's weather will be fairly accurate. As you move out in time with your weather forecasts, the data available to you and the ability of computer simulations and historical information will provide less valuable input, and thus your weather forecast for a year away will basically just be a guess based on the seasonal expectations.

Parametric estimating

Parametric estimating uses known quantities and known units of measurement, and multiplies them together to arrive at an estimate. For example, you may know that each person can write 300 lines of code per day and that there are 3,000 lines of code to be written; therefore, your duration estimate using parametric estimating is 10 days.

Three-point estimating

Three-point estimating is part of the *Program Evaluation and Review Technique* (PERT), a technique that uses a weighted average scenario to arrive at an estimate where there are most likely, optimistic, and pessimistic durations for an activity. If you were to take a simple average of three numbers, you would simply add the three numbers together and then divide by 3. The three-point estimating technique gives a higher weighting to the most likely estimate (tM) and assigns it a weight of 4, while assigning a weight of 1 to each of the optimistic (tO) and pessimistic (tP) duration estimates. With six numbers now instead of three, you divide by 6 to get the weighted average. Therefore, the formula for calculating a three-point estimate using this technique is:

$$\frac{tO + (tM \times 4) + tP}{6}$$

EXAM TIP

The same formula is used to estimate project costs. In this section, the letter t is used to denote the variable being used to estimate time. When you are using this formula to estimate costs, the letter c is used instead. You may find it easier just to remember the formula without the t or c. Expert judgment, analogous estimating, parametric estimating, and three-point estimating are also used in the Estimate Costs process.

For example, if you had an optimistic estimate of 4 days, a most likely estimate of 7 days, and a pessimistic estimate of 12 days and put these estimates into the three-point estimating formula, your three-point estimate for this activity is 7.33 days.

$$\frac{4 + (7 \times 4) + 12}{6}$$

$$= \frac{4 + 28 + 12}{6}$$

$$= \frac{44}{6}$$

$$= 7.33$$

In addition to calculating the expected duration, you can also calculate the *standard deviation* and variance. The standard deviation is a calculation of how far away from the average duration, or the expected duration using the three-point estimating formula, your data is spread. A smaller standard deviation means that the data is tightly grouped, while a larger standard deviation means that the data is more widely spread.

The standard deviation calculation used in the three-point estimating technique is essentially a heuristic, or rule-of-thumb, way of calculating standard deviation rather than the full formula used by statisticians. The formula subtracts the optimistic from the pessimistic and divides the result by 6. So, using the previous example, the standard deviation is 8 divided by 6, which equals 1.33 days.

$$\text{Standard deviation} = \frac{P - O}{6}$$

A benefit of calculating the standard deviation is that you can then estimate the confidence interval for a range of estimates. The confidence interval states the amount of the data that you expect to fall between the number of standard deviations above and below the mean. 1 standard deviation either side of the mean represents a confidence interval of 68 percent, 2 standard deviations either side of the mean gives a confidence interval of 95 percent, and 3 standard deviations either side of the mean gives a confidence interval of 99.7 percent.

EXAM TIP

Six standard deviations either side of the mean contains 99.999 percent of the population. More commonly known as *Six Sigma*, it is used as a quality management tool in the Project Quality Management knowledge area.

Figure 4-10 shows a normal distribution and the range of a population you would expect to find with either one, two, or three standard deviations (SD) either side of the mean.

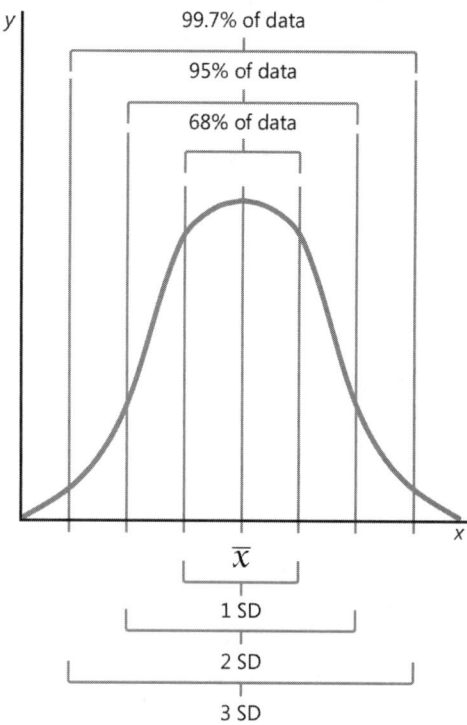

FIGURE 4-10 A curve shows standard deviations.

For example, in the previous scenario, you could say that you have a 95 percent degree of certainty that the estimate for the activity duration is between 7± 2.66 days. This is calculated by realizing that 95 percent certainty will reflect two standard deviations either side of the mean. The standard deviation, as already calculated, equals 1.33 days; therefore, two standard deviations equals 2.66 days.

EXAM TIP

In the exam, you may be asked a question about a range of estimates of which you are either 68 percent, 95 percent, or 99.7 percent certain, which means that the question is asking you to calculate 1, 2, or 3 standard deviations either side of the mean or average.

There is one more formula that you need to be aware of, and that is calculating the *variance*. The variance is calculated by multiplying the standard deviation by itself. Using the previous example, the variance is the standard deviation squared, which equals 1.33 × 1.33, which equals 1.77.

$$\text{Variance} = \left(\frac{P - O}{6}\right)^2$$

> **NOTE ORIGINS OF THREE-POINT ESTIMATING**
>
> The origins of the three-point estimating technique are reportedly from the U.S. Navy Polaris submarine program in the 1950s. The technique was developed to help improve the delivery of large and complex projects. It is a subset of the Program Evaluation and Review Technique (PERT), which was one of the first analytical techniques to sequence activities and show the relationship between them.

> **EXAM TIP**
>
> In the exam, you will probably have to do some calculations using formulas. You should always round your answer to two decimal places. However, you may arrive at an answer that is a fractionally different from one of the ones presented. If this is the case, it is probably a safe bet, if you have used the right equation, that the answer closest to yours is correct.

Group decision-making techniques

There are many ways to gather information from groups of people, each with their own benefits and drawbacks. The most common group decision-making techniques used are *brainstorming*, *nominal group techniques*, and the *Delphi technique*.

Brainstorming is an excellent way of getting a group of people to think about many possible options. If you are facilitating a brainstorming session, you should encourage all ideas. The *nominal group technique* takes all the ideas and uses the group to vote on which ideas are worthy of further investigation.

The *Delphi technique* is a technique for soliciting information from experts on an anonymous basis. The reason for this is that often, bringing experts together into a room to provide expert opinion and advice results in the loudest being heard, or peer pressure influencing the opinions of those present. The Delphi technique aims to get around these potential problems and allow experts to contribute freely by asking each expert anonymously, via a structured questionnaire, for his or her opinion. After the first round of opinions has been gathered, your summarized results are often circulated again to all experts taking part in the process. They can then review results and, if they want, change their original opinion.

Real world

The Delphi technique is a very effective way of getting accurate information from experts, however it is also time consuming and can cost a significant amount of money to do successfully. I have been part of a Delphi technique being used to determine the level of risk on IT projects, I never knew how many other experts were being consulted, but the whole process took about three weeks to complete.

NOTE **ORIGINS OF THE DELPHI TECHNIQUE**
The Delphi technique is named after the oracle of Delphi, who was a priestess at the Temple of Apollo in ancient Greece who would go into a trance and provide advice on what the future may hold.

Reserve analysis

A *reserve analysis* is the process of determining a justifiable reserve, or buffer, to be added to activities based on quantitative analysis carried out as part of developing the risk register. This process will develop a *contingency reserve*, which is used for known unknowns, or identified uncertainty, in your project. It is a justifiable means of adding in extra time or cost. For example, if during your quantitative risk assessment you discovered that there was a 25 percent chance of a time delay of 10 days to a particular activity, you would add in a contingency reserve of 2.5 days to your estimates. If the risk did not manifest, you would not need this contingency reserve anymore.

The other sort of reserve that may be available to a project is a *management reserve*, which is a figure determined at the start of the project that management and the project sponsor control for unknown unknowns, or unforeseen risks. A project can apply to use the management reserve. Use of the management reserve will result in a change to the schedule baseline, because it is not factored into your duration estimates. *Padding* of estimates is unjustifiable additions to cost or time estimates and is considered unethical.

> **Real world**
>
> It can be extremely difficult to convince the project sponsor and members of the project steering group to approve a contingency reserve for either time or cost, because they need to be convinced that your methodology for determining it is sound and based on quantitative data. I have always argued for the provision of a contingency reserve on the basis of "no surprises," and this has generally been successful. When the identified activity has been completed, if there was no need to use the contingency reserve, this is reported and the overall contingency reserve is decreased.

Outputs

The Estimate Activity Durations process produces some or all of the following outputs.

Activity duration estimates

The main output from the Estimate Activity Durations process is the *activity duration estimates*, which define and record the individual assessments for the time required to complete each activity on the activity list. The individual activity durations estimates will include an expected duration for each activity and, if calculated, the range of uncertainty in each activity, which can be aggregated to provide an expected duration with the total range of uncertainty for the entire project. For example, you could report that the total project duration is expected to be 89 days with a 10 percent probability that it will take 95 days based upon the reserve analysis. The activity durations estimates go on to be used as an input into the Develop Schedule process.

Project documents updates

The specific types of project documents that may be updated as a result of completing the Estimate Activity Durations process are the activity list, the activity attributes, and any other documents relating to expected durations of activities that the organization has.

Quick check

1. Using the three-point estimating technique, what is the expected duration of an activity with an optimistic duration of 8 days, a most likely estimate of 10 days, and a pessimistic estimate of 16 days?
2. What is the main benefit of using the Delphi technique as an estimating tool?
3. What is the main difference between analogous and parametric estimating techniques?
4. What percentage of a data population would you expect to find within two standard deviations either side of a mean?
5. What are the two types of justifiable reserve that may be used on a project?

Quick check answers

1. If you apply the three-point estimating formula to this scenario, you will arrive at a three-point estimate of 10.66 days.
2. The main benefit of using the Delphi technique is to allow experts to contribute their opinions anonymously and without peer pressure.
3. Analogous estimating uses similar scenarios to extrapolate a current estimate, whereas parametric estimating uses a known quantity and multiplies it by a known metric.
4. You would expect to find approximately 95 percent of a population within two standard deviations either side of a mean.
5. Both the contingency reserve, for "known unknowns," and the management reserve, for "unknown unknowns," are developed by using quantitative data and historical information and, therefore, provide justifiable reserves.

Develop Schedule

> **MORE INFO** **DEVELOP SCHEDULE**
>
> You can read more about the Develop Schedule process in the PMBOK® Guide, 5th edition, in Chapter 6, section 6.6. Table 4-6 identifies the process inputs, tools and techniques, and outputs.
>
> **TABLE 4-6** Develop Schedule process
>
> | Inputs | Tools and techniques | Outputs |
> | --- | --- | --- |
> | - Schedule management plan
- Activity list
- Activity attributes
- Project schedule network diagrams
- Activity resource requirements
- Resource calendars
- Activity durations estimates
- Project scope statement
- Risk register
- Project staff assignments
- Resource breakdown structure
- Enterprise environmental factors
- Organizational process assets | - Schedule network analysis
- Critical path method
- Critical chain method
- Resource optimization techniques
- Modeling techniques
- Leads and lags
- Schedule compression
- Scheduling tool | - Schedule baseline
- Project schedule
- Schedule data
- Project calendars
- Project management plan updates
- Project documents updates |

The Develop Schedule process takes all the information you have gathered in the previous processes—Define Activities, Sequence Activities, Estimate Activity Resources, and Estimate Activity Durations—and combines them into the project network diagram, which graphically represents the project schedule.

The Develop Schedule process covers the following domain task:

- 2.4 Develop a project schedule based on the project timeline, scope, and resource plan, in order to manage timely completion of the project.

> ## Real world
>
> On most projects that I've been involved in, the Develop Schedule process has been our primary focus and the preceding processes have all been completed at the same time, rather than as discrete, separate processes.

Inputs

The Develop Schedule process uses the following inputs.

Schedule management plan

The schedule management plan is an essential input into the Develop Schedule process because it outlines the way in which you are going to develop the project schedule. The schedule management plan is an output from the Plan Schedule Management process.

Activity list

The activity list provides you with a list of all the activities that you have defined for the project that need to be completed. Each activity needs to be represented on the completed project schedule, and thus the activity list is a key input into this process. The activity list is an output from the Define Activities process.

Activity attributes

The activities attributes give you more detailed information about the activities on the activity list, which only provides summary information about each activity. The activity attributes are an output from the Define Activities process.

Project schedule network diagrams

The project schedule network diagrams present each of the activities and the relationship each has with predecessors and successors. The full development of the project schedule takes this preliminary information and adds additional detail to it, such as the estimate of activity resources and the individual estimate of activity durations, to produce the final project schedule. The project schedule network diagrams are an output from the Sequence Activities process

Activity resource requirements

The activity resource requirements are used to allocate resources to each of the activities identified in the project. Activity resource requirements are an output from the Estimate Activity Resources process.

Resource calendars

The resource calendars give you information about any known constraints upon the use of resources on your project that may affect scheduling. The resource calendars are an output from the Acquire Project Team process in the Human Resource Management knowledge area.

Activity durations estimates

The activity durations estimates are absolutely essential if you want to complete a project schedule. You will use these individual estimates and aggregate them to determine your total project duration. Activity durations estimates are an output from the Estimate Activity Durations process.

Project scope statement

The project scope statement gives you information about the project and product scope of work to be completed, and it also provides information about known constraints and assumptions and any known contractual obligations that will affect your project schedule. The project scope statement is an output from the Develop Project Scope process in the Scope Management knowledge area.

Risk register

The risk register contains information about known schedule risks and known resource risks of the project. As part of the analysis of these risks, there may be the development of contingencies relating to time that must be taken into account in developing a project schedule. The risk register is an output from the Identify Risks process in the Risk Management knowledge area.

Project staff assignments

The *project staff assignments* specify which organizational employees are to be allocated to each activity and provide an analysis of experience and skills that each particular person brings. The project staff assignments are an output from the Acquire Project Team process in the Human Resource Management knowledge area.

Resource breakdown structure

The resource breakdown structure is used as an input because it provides the details of the categories of individual skills that resources must be able to bring to the project to complete the assigned activities. The resource breakdown structure is an output from the Estimate Activity Resources process.

Enterprise environmental factors

The specific enterprise environmental factors that may be used as inputs, if appropriate, are any external standards, regulations, contractual obligations, or licensed scheduling tools that you will use to develop the project schedule.

Organizational process assets

The specific organizational process assets that may be useful in developing your project schedule include any existing project management methodology, blank templates, tools, and other techniques owned by the organization for the preparation of a project schedule.

Tools and techniques

The following tools and techniques can be used upon the inputs into the Develop Schedule process.

Schedule network analysis

Schedule network analysis is a primary tool used to bring together all the previous information you have gathered when you defined the activities, sequenced the activities, estimated the activity resources, and estimated the activity durations. You use all of this information to put together your full schedule network diagram and, when it is completed, you can use the critical path method, critical chain method, what-if analysis, and resource leveling to determine the total project duration and the amount of *total float or slack* between specific activities and in the overall project.

> **Real world**
>
> There are many ways of drawing the information contained in each node of an activity-on-node network diagram, and there are at least two ways of representing the numbering systems used to calculate durations between activities.

Critical path method

The *critical path* method focuses on identifying all the paths through a project and, with the aid of a network diagram, determining which of these paths presents the shortest duration and also the least amount of scheduling flexibility as indicated by the length of slack or float. The path with the shortest duration and the least slack or float through the project represents the path of most risk to the project, hence the name *critical path*.

There can be many paths through a project, as Figure 4-11 shows.

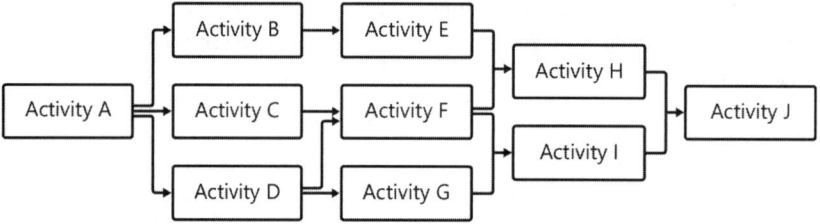

FIGURE 4-11 An activity node diagram can show many network paths.

There are the following paths through this network diagram:

- A-B-E-H-J
- A-C-F-H-J
- A-C-F-I-J
- A-D-F-H-J
- A-D-F-I-J
- A-D-G-I-J

However, you are not able to determine which path or paths are the critical paths until you complete a full schedule network analysis.

> **NOTE SLACK AND FLOAT**
>
> There are not many instances in the PMBOK® guide for which a single word has two meanings. The case of *slack* and *float* is one of the only times when two words are used to mean the same thing. There are two types of slack or float: free slack or free float, and total slack or total float. Free slack, or free float, indicates the amount of time an activity can be delayed before that affects the next activity on the path. Total slack, or total float, indicates the amount of time an activity can be delayed before it affects the total project duration. If an activity has zero total float, it means that if it is delayed, it will automatically increase the duration of the project. The critical path or paths through a project are those upon which there is no slack or float.

In order to complete a full schedule network diagram you must understand how to complete an activity-on-node (AON) diagram. This next section will take you through the process of completing a schedule network diagram, completing a *forward pass* to determine the project duration, and completing a *backward pass* to determine the critical path or paths.

To calculate the critical path on an activity-on-node diagram, this example will use the node to represent the information about the activity. The information contained in the node will be the task ID, the duration of the activity, the *early start (ES)*, the *early finish (EF)*, the *late start (LS)*, the *late finish (LF)*, and the amount of total float in the activity. Figure 4-12 represents a typical node; however, be aware that in the real world and in the exam many different forms of node may be used with information displayed in different locations, yet they all display the same information, just in different ways.

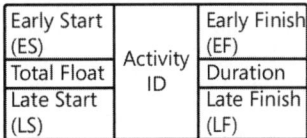

FIGURE 4-12 An activity node can contain information about the activity.

Now if you take the information contained in Table 4-7 and map that out over an entire network diagram, you will be up to calculate the project duration and the critical path or paths.

TABLE 4-7 Activity information

Activity ID	Duration (days)	Predecessor
A	3	-
B	5	A
C	4	A
D	2	B, C
E	6	C
F	5	D, E
G	4	E
H	7	F, G

The first step in the process is to construct a network diagram showing the relationships between the activities. In this instance, assume that all activities have a finish-to-start relationship and there are no leads and lags. Figure 4-13 shows the network diagram.

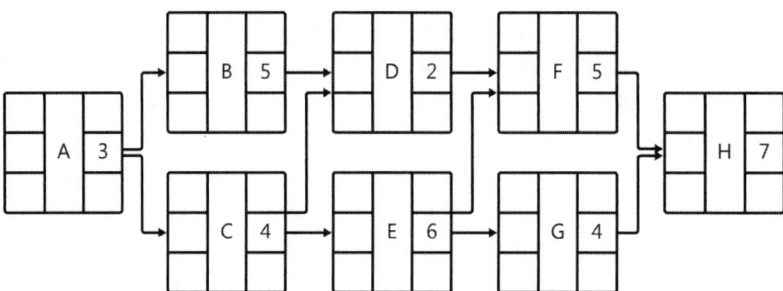

FIGURE 4-13 This network diagram example shows the relationships between activities.

By examining this network diagram, you can now write out the paths through the diagram as follows:

- A-B-D-F-H
- A-C-D-F-H
- A-C-E-F-H
- A-C-E-G-H

The next step in the process is to complete a forward pass. The forward pass is completed by working from left to right and calculating the early start and the early finish for each task.

The earliest a task can start is immediately after the latest early finish of all its predecessor activities. For example, if Activity A has an early finish of day 3 (which means it finishes at the end of day 3), then Activity B has an early start of day 4 (which means it starts at the beginning of day 4). If an activity has more than one predecessor, the earliest it can start is immediately after the latest early finish of all its predecessors. Figure 4-14 shows the network diagram with the forward pass completed. You can now determine that the project duration is 25 days.

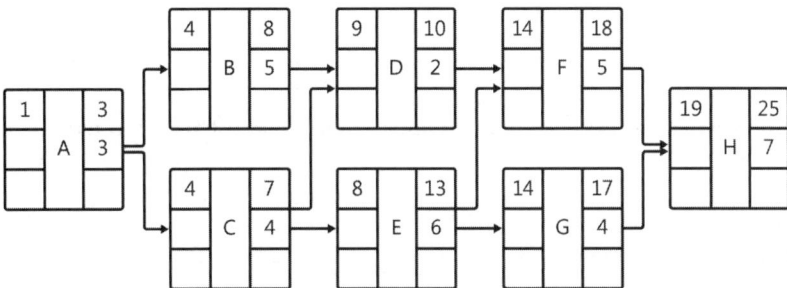

FIGURE 4-14 The forward pass is completed.

The next step in the process is to complete a backward pass. This time, you work from right to left, and you calculate the late finish and the late start for each activity. This time, when calculating the late finish for an activity, you must look to its successor activities; the late finish for an activity is immediately prior to the earliest of all successor late start dates. For example, if Activity D is the successor to Activity B, and activity D has a late start of day 12, then Activity B has a late finish of day 11. As you complete the backward pass, you can also calculate the total slack for each task by subtracting the late start from the late finish. Figure 4-15 shows a completed backward pass.

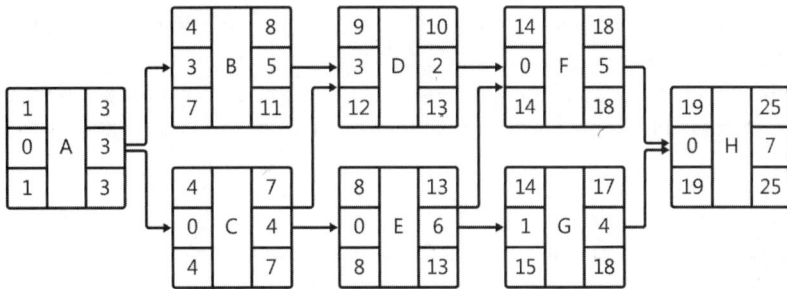

FIGURE 4-15 The backward pass is completed.

To calculate which of the paths through the network diagram is the critical path, you simply look at all the activities that have zero total float because these represent activities that if delayed will affect the total project duration. If you do this, you can determine that the critical path in this network diagram is A-C-E-F-H.

Critical chain method

The *critical chain method* is a means of purposely adding in buffer time to identified activities, usually on the critical path, to account for limited resources and project uncertainties. The amount of buffer is usually worked out by using historical information or quantitative risk analysis. The purpose of adding buffer is to ensure that activities on the critical path that are identified as important feeder activities—that is, those that produce work for successor activities—always have float to ensure that they don't slip and cause the project duration to extend.

EXAM TIP

If you find a question in the exam asking about the application of buffer time, it is referring to the critical chain method.

Resource optimization techniques

Often the first pass through any estimate of activity resources—either equipment, supplies or people—is what could be referred to as the optimal use of resources. However, this may not be the most efficient use of resources, and there may be times when resources are either overallocated or underallocated. If resources are overallocated, you may not be able to use them, and if they are underallocated, you may be paying for resources to sit around unused. Through the processes of *resource leveling* and *resource smoothing* you can attempt to make more efficient use of your resources, but this may have an impact on project cost and project duration.

Resource leveling involves moving the allocation of resources between time periods to level out either periods when a resource will be overused or periods when a resource will be underused. For example, you may have forecast one person to be working 60 hours in a week, while someone else will work 15 hours. Obviously, after you start moving a resource around to get more efficient use, you may end up changing the duration of activities or even the sequence of activities. Resource smoothing is a less intensive form of resource leveling because it adjusts resources only within the total float for each activity so as not to extend the total project duration.

Real world

Typically, resource leveling is best left to sophisticated project management software such as Microsoft Project. If you try and do it manually, you may end up spending too much of your time completing it and not obtaining the optimal results.

Modeling techniques

Modeling techniques typically use computers to present a model of a potential outcome. They are particularly useful when you are developing your project schedule because you can examine all potential options and easily find problems or opportunities within the project schedule.

A particular type of modeling technique is the *what-if scenario analysis*. What-if scenario analysis is a form of statistical and mathematical analysis that looks at the potential probabilities and likely outcomes of different scenarios occurring. For example, you may be able to use this technique to analyze what would happen to your project schedule if certain events occurred, and from this analysis, choose the scenario that best suits your project duration goals. Of all the what-if scenario analysis techniques, the most common is *Monte Carlo analysis*. Monte Carlo analysis applies statistical analysis to examining a possible distribution of outcomes and extrapolates from this the likelihood of specific outcomes. Due to its complex use of mathematical modeling, this type of analysis is most often performed by a computer.

EXAM TIP

Often in the exam, if you find a question that relates to mathematical analysis of different scenarios, or the probability of different outcomes, the answer will most likely be what-if scenario analysis or Monte Carlo analysis.

NOTE **ORIGIN OF MONTE CARLO ANALYSIS**

Monte Carlo analysis was used to assist with modeling potential effects of the atomic bomb during the Manhattan Project, and was reportedly so named because the uncle of one of the lead scientists using the method liked to gamble at the casino in Monte Carlo.

Leads and lags

In completing your entire project schedule with the use of a schedule network diagram, you may choose to use leads and lags, as appropriate, to represent either the amount of time an activity can start before its predecessor finishes or the amount of time an activity must wait after its predecessor ends before starting, respectively.

Schedule compression

Often the first pass through the development of your project schedule results in an optimal timeframe. However, there may be existing schedule constraints, legislation requiring a set date for compliance, market conditions, or stakeholder expectations that mean that your original estimate of total project duration is too long. In this case, you will need to consider undertaking a variety of *schedule compression* techniques to shorten the duration of the project. The two most common and most often used techniques are crashing and fast tracking. *Crashing* involves adding extra resources to an activity in order to complete it in a shorter time period, which often involves extra cost. *Fast tracking* allows activities that would normally be done in sequence to be done in parallel for all, or at least a portion, of their duration. Obviously, the type of dependency between the two activities would need to be a discretionary dependency, and you may need to take into account extra risk analysis in relation to starting an activity early.

Scheduling tool

A *scheduling tool* can be a piece of project management software dedicated entirely to project scheduling, or it can be a module of a larger piece of project management software, such as Microsoft Project.

Outputs

The Develop Schedule process produces the following outputs.

Schedule baseline

The schedule baseline is the final approved version of the project schedule used to track actual progress against planned progress.

EXAM TIP

There are four baselines in project management that are used to monitor progress after project execution has begun. They are the scope baseline, the time or schedule baseline, the project budget, and the quality baseline. All project baselines form part of the overall project management plan because they provide information about what is intended.

> **Real world**
>
> The most often used form of schedule baseline is the Gantt chart. However, be aware that the Gantt chart is also an exceptional communications tool. On many projects I have worked on, I have used the Gantt chart for both reasons with great success. This is because it presents different levels of information graphically, which means it is easily understood by both technically minded and non-technically minded stakeholders.

Project schedule

The *project schedule* can be represented in a number of ways. It is most commonly presented graphically by using either a Gantt chart, which is often called a horizontal bar chart, or a horizontal histogram. The project schedule can also be represented by a milestone chart or, less commonly, by the project schedule network diagram. Figure 4-16 shows an example of a Gantt chart.

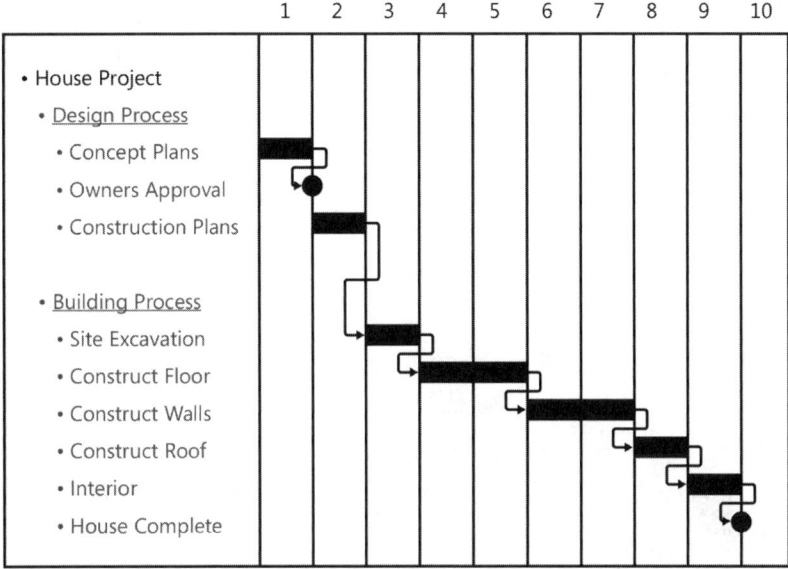

FIGURE 4-16 A Gantt chart is a graphical representation of a schedule.

> **NOTE** **ORIGIN OF THE GANTT CHART**
>
> Many people think that Gantt is an acronym for something. I did have a student once who was absolutely convinced that it stood for *graphical analysis and numerical tracking tool*. I think that student was just making that up because it is actually the surname of Henry Gantt, a mechanical engineer credited with using the chart to plot durations on a project.

Schedule data

The *schedule data* refers to all the data that makes up the project schedule, and it refers to data relating to activity duration estimates, resources, reserves, constraints, and any resource leveling undertaken.

Project calendars

The *project calendar* refers to the working time available for the project resources over the life of the project. If the project calendar is for people, then it may refer to the working week; if the project calendar is for machinery, it may refer to a 24-hour, seven-day-a-week schedule.

Develop Schedule   **CHAPTER 4**   **167**

Project management plan updates

The parts of the project management plan that may be updated as a result of developing a project schedule are the schedule management plan and the schedule baseline.

Project documents updates

The types of project documents that may be updated as a result of completing the Develop Schedule process iteratively are any of the documents that feed into any part of the previous processes, such as activity resource requirements, activity attributes, project calendars, or the risk register.

 Quick check

1. Why is identifying the critical path so important?
2. After completing a forward pass you will have calculated what?
3. After completing a backward pass you will have calculated what?
4. What method uses time buffers to ensure that feeder activities don't extend the project duration?
5. What is the key purpose of leveling resources?
6. What is the main difference between crashing and fast tracking?

Quick check answers

1. Activities on the critical path have no total float and therefore, if they are delayed, they will extend the overall project duration. Therefore, they represent a high degree of risk on the project.
2. After completing a forward pass, you will have calculated the project duration.
3. After completing a backward pass, you will have identified the total float for each activity and be able to determine the critical path.
4. The critical chain method uses time buffers inserted into the project schedule to ensure that high-risk activities do not cause the overall project duration to extend.
5. The key purpose of resource leveling is to maximize the efficient use of resources.
6. The main difference between crashing and fast tracking is that, generally, crashing costs more because it involves allocating more resources to a particular activity to shorten the duration.

Control Schedule

> **MORE INFO** **CONTROL SCHEDULE**
>
> You can read more about the Control Schedule process in the PMBOK® Guide, 5th edition, in Chapter 6, section 6.7. Table 4-8 identifies the process inputs, tools and techniques, and outputs.
>
> **TABLE 4-8** Control Schedule process
>
> | Inputs | Tools and techniques | Outputs |
> |---|---|---|
> | <ul><li>Project management plan</li><li>Project schedule</li><li>Work performance data</li><li>Project calendars</li><li>Schedule data</li><li>Organizational process assets</li></ul> | <ul><li>Performance reviews</li><li>Project management software</li><li>Resource optimization techniques</li><li>Modeling techniques</li><li>Leads and lags</li><li>Schedule compression</li><li>Scheduling tool</li></ul> | <ul><li>Work performance information</li><li>Schedule forecasts</li><li>Change requests</li><li>Project management plan updates</li><li>Project documents updates</li><li>Organizational process assets updates</li></ul> |

The Control Schedule process is focused mainly on monitoring any variations between what was planned in terms of individual activity durations and the overall project duration, and what is actually occurring. It is also focused upon documenting any requested changes to the project schedule as per the agreed change control procedure.

The Control Schedule process covers the following domain tasks:

- 4.1 Measure project performance using appropriate tools and techniques, in order to identify and quantify any variances, perform approved corrective actions, and communicate with relevant stakeholders.
- 4.2 Manage changes to the project scope, schedule, and costs by updating the project plan and communicating approved changes to the team, in order to ensure that revised project goals are met.

Inputs

The Control Schedule process uses the following inputs.

Project management plan

Obviously, in order to control any process, you are going to need a plan, or plans, that guide you in determining your particular approach to monitoring and controlling. In this instance, the project management plan contains the plans and documents that are required to control the schedule. First and foremost among these will be the schedule management plan and the schedule baseline. In addition, your change management plan and other subsidiary plans will be useful in guiding you in this process. The project management plan is an output from the Develop Project Management Plan process.

Project schedule

The project schedule is an absolutely essential input into the Control Schedule process because you are going to use this to check for any variance. The project schedule outlines what you had planned to achieve in terms of time progress on the project. Through your efforts of checking this against what is actually happening, you will be a spot any variances and, as a result, raise any requested changes or corrective or preventive actions. The project schedule is an output from the Develop Schedule process.

Work performance data

Work performance data is the information you gather about progress on the activities that have started, what the actual duration is, and the status of any activities considered finished. You use this work performance data as a key input into the Control Schedule process. Work performance data is an output from the Direct and Manage Project Work process.

Project calendars

Project calendars, which outline the times that the project will carry out the planned activity, are useful particularly when there is more than one project calendar assigned to different resources being used on the project. Project calendars are an output from the Develop Schedule process.

Schedule data

Schedule data is the raw data that was used to develop the project schedule model and includes the known milestones, activities, activity attributes and, if known, any identified constraints and assumptions. You will use the schedule data to measure variance of planned versus actual. The schedule data is an output from the Develop Schedule process.

Organizational process assets

The types of organizational process assets that will be useful as inputs into the Control Schedule process are any existing policies or procedures that the organization has that assist with measuring and reporting on project schedule progress, any manual or automated schedule control tools, and any established reporting templates that can be used.

Tools and techniques

The following tools and techniques can be used upon the inputs into the Control Schedule process.

Performance reviews

Performance reviews are the key tool used to control the schedule because the focus is on analyzing what you had planned to do in terms of project schedule performance and what you are actually doing. There are several techniques that may be used as part of applying performance reviews. One of these techniques, *trend analysis*, gathers data about your project performance to date and then, by using graphs that extrapolate from this information, what likely future performance will be. Another important tool or technique used for performance reviews is the critical chain method, which you also saw used as a tool in the Develop Schedule process. In the Control Schedule process it is used to continually asses the allocated time buffers against what is actually occurring, and make adjustments as necessary.

Project management software

Given the in-depth nature of variance analysis and its focus on actual versus planned durations and completion of activities, completing the work manually would be tedious and inefficient. This is where the use of project management software is very helpful.

> **Real world**
>
> One of the key tasks I've always given to project administrators working on my projects is to take responsibility for using the project management software to keep track of both time and cost performance on the project. On one particularly complex project I was working on, I had our wonderful project administrator out on site nearly every day, checking what was actually being accomplished and recording this in the project management software against what we had planned to do. We were then able to use the project management software's forecasting abilities to get early indicators of where we might end up if we continued at the same pace. This is one of the key benefits of using forecasting. A simple forecast of where you might end up is not a predetermination of the actual outcome; instead, it should be viewed as a warning of what may happen if you continue doing what you have been doing. If the results show that you will end up either over budget or over time, you have plenty of warning to implement strategies to make sure this doesn't happen.

Resource optimization techniques

After the project is underway and resources are being used to complete activities, you may want to utilize resource optimization techniques and use either resource leveling or resource smoothing to obtain a more efficient allocation of the resources.

Modeling techniques

Modeling techniques are used to forecast different schedule scenarios based on the different possibilities that could happen with the schedule. The most common one is what-if scenario analysis.

The what-if scenario analysis and Monte Carlo analysis are useful mathematical tools for forecasting future outcomes based on performance to date. A what-if scenario analysis uses known probabilities of work done to date and uses estimated probabilities of potential work paths to be done to calculate the likelihood of all possible scenarios. After this has been completed, you are able to discover what the most likely scenarios are and judge their impact, as well as discovering the least likely scenarios and their impact. Monte Carlo analysis extrapolates from existing work performance data what likely future outcomes will be.

Leads and lags

In the Develop Schedule process you also saw this tool used. The purpose of this is to be able to adjust leads and lags between activities to more efficiently achieve the expected activity duration and total project duration.

Schedule compression

In the process of examining planned versus actual time performance on the project, you may detect that some activities are taking longer than planned, and therefore threaten the total project duration. At this point, you may want to consider the application of schedule compression techniques in order to shorten the duration of particular activities, a sequence of activities, or the total project overall. The two most commonly used schedule compression techniques are crashing, which involves the use of more resources and usually costs more, and fast tracking, which involves the scheduling of activities in parallel that were previously scheduled in sequence.

EXAM TIP

In the exam, if any schedule compression technique being used involves more cost, you can be certain that this is referring to crashing. Conversely, if the question poses a scenario where you are asked to compress a project schedule but do not have access to any more budget, you will not be able to select crashing as an option.

Scheduling tool

A scheduling tool is a specific piece of software dedicated to project scheduling only. It is often part of a more robust piece of project management software such as Microsoft Project.

EXAM TIP

Did you notice that these last five tools listed in the Control Schedule process are the same as the last five tools listed in the Develop Schedule process, with the exception that the Develop Schedule process uses *applying* leads and lags as a tool, whereas the Control Schedule process uses *adjusting* leads and lags as a tool?

Outputs

The Control Schedule process produces the following outputs.

Work performance information

As a result of investigating how your project is doing in terms of individual activities durations, and the overall project duration, you will develop work performance information. If you recall, work performance data was used as an input into this process, and with the application of the selected tools and techniques, that data has been refined into work performance information. The work performance information can be presented as schedule variance (SV) and schedule performance index (SPI) values for individual activities and work packages. The work performance information itself goes on to be used as an input into the Monitor and Control Project Work process.

EXAM TIP

Work performance data is used to create work performance information, which in turn is used to produce work performance reports.

NOTE EARNED VALUE MANAGEMENT

In Chapter 5, "Cost management," you will look in depth at the earned value management system and the associated formula for measuring current progress and forecasting likely future progress on a project. Two of the indicators you will look at are the schedule variance (SV) and schedule performance index (SPI) formulas. Both of these formulas and earned value management analysis focus on assessing current performance in relation to time and are useful for detecting variance from what was planned.

Schedule forecasts

Schedule forecasts are what you obtain by examining current performance and using this to extrapolate likely future performance. Chapter 5 looks in depth at the earned value management system. Of the earned value management system, it is the formula for calculating *estimate at completion* (EAC) and *estimate to complete* (ETC) that would be useful in forecasting the schedule. Schedule forecasts go on to be used as inputs into the Monitor and Control Project Work process.

> **NOTE ESTIMATE AT COMPLETION**
> As you will read in the next chapter, in its focus on the earned value management system, the estimate at completion (EAC) activity is one formula that can be calculated in a large number of ways. There are different formulas that take into account different parameters, and if you want to use estimate at completion (EAC) and take into account the time performance to date, you would select one of the formulas that uses the schedule performance index (SPI).

> **Real world**
> Usually immediately after you inform key stakeholders about how well the project is going to date, the next question they ask is how well it will go in the future. To answer this question, you are going to need to forecast future performance of the project. In relation to the time or cost performance, the best way to forecast future performance is simply to analyze past performance. I have always used earned value management on projects I work on in order to give people an indication—because that is all it is—of the likely future outcomes based on past performance.

Change requests

If, during the process of examining actual versus planned performance in relation to project time, you discover any variances, one of your options is to submit a change request as per your documented and approved change control process. Change requests go on to be used as inputs into the Perform Integrated Change Control process in the Integration Management knowledge area.

Project management plan updates

If, as a result of monitoring and controlling the project schedule, you do discover any variances, you may choose to update specific elements of the project management plan. Of these, the most common updates will be to the schedule management plan and the schedule baseline. Given the integrated nature of project management, though, any changes to the project schedule may also result in changes to the project cost baseline, project risks, project quality, and elements of the project scope. Project management plan updates are used in turn as inputs into the Develop Project Plan process.

Project documents updates

In addition to elements of the project management plan and its subsidiary plans, there are specific project documents that may be updated as a result of information gathered during the Control Schedule process. You may want to update the project schedule data, and as a result, the project schedule.

Organizational process assets updates

Specific organizational process assets that may be updated as a result of the Control Schedule process are historical information, lessons learned, records of corrective actions, and updates to any organizational templates and policies in order to ensure they are still relevant.

> **Quick check**
>
> 1. What is the key focus of the variance analysis tools and techniques used in the Control Schedule process?
> 2. What is the relationship between work performance data and work performance information?
> 3. What is the key earned value management formula used for schedule forecasts?
>
> **Quick check answers**
>
> 1. The focus of variance analysis tools and techniques used in the Control Schedule process is to look at what you had planned to achieve against what you are actually achieving and determine if there is a variance between the two.
> 2. Work performance data is the raw data gathered that gets filtered to become useful work performance information.
> 3. The key earned value management formula used for schedule forecasts is the estimate at completion (EAC) formula when it incorporates the schedule performance index (SPI) into its calculation.

Exercises

The answers for these exercises are located in the "Answers" section at the end of this chapter.

1. Based upon the information in the following table, complete a network diagram showing the project duration and calculate the critical path or paths.

Activity ID	Duration (days)	Predecessor
A	4	-
B	3	A
C	6	A, B
D	5	B
E	3	C, D

Activity ID	Duration (days)	Predecessor
F	7	D
G	2	D, E
H	9	F, G

2. Using three-point estimating, what is the expected mean, standard deviation, and variance of the following scenarios?

Optimistic	Most likely	Pessimistic
6	8	12
3	10	15
12	14	18
27	35	48

3. You have been asked by your project sponsor to provide a date range for which you are 99.7 percent certain the project will be delivered, with an optimistic duration of 35 days, a most likely duration of 45 days, and a pessimistic duration of 60 days. What is your answer to your project sponsor?

4. Match up the estimating technique on the left with the appropriate description on the right.

Estimating technique	Definition
1. Analogous estimating	a. An estimating technique that multiplies a known quantity by a known metric
2. Parametric estimating	b. An estimating technique that takes the weighted average of the optimistic, most likely, and pessimistic estimates
3. Bottom-up estimating	c. An estimating technique that gathers information from experts anonymously
4. Delphi technique	d. An estimating technique using information from a similar activity
5. Three-point estimating	e. An estimating technique that takes low-level detailed estimates and aggregates them

Chapter summary

- The Time Management knowledge area is focused upon the development and checking of the project schedule.
- As with all the other knowledge areas, the Time Management knowledge area begins with an initial planning process, which in this instance produces the schedule management plan. The schedule management plan sets out how you will go about completing the planning, execution, and control of the project schedule.
- There is then a five-step iterative process that culminates in the development of a project schedule.
- The first of these five steps is to define the activities, which are a further level of decomposition of already-identified work packages from the Scope Management knowledge area.
- After the activities have been identified and documented in the Define Activities process, they can then be put in sequence with the relationships between the activities clearly identified and defined. This Sequence Activities process constitutes the beginning of the development of the schedule network diagram.
- The Estimate Activity Resources process then seeks to provide an estimate of the type and quantities of material, people, equipment, or supplies that will be required to complete each of the activities.
- After an estimate of the type and quantities of resources for each activity has been prepared, an estimate of the duration of each activity can then be completed. This is the main focus of the Estimate Activity Durations process.
- The Develop Schedule process takes the information from the previous four planning processes and combines them into the project schedule. Because it is a highly iterative process and subject to rolling wave planning, it may focus more on the immediate future, and leave further detail to be defined as the project progresses.
- After the planning activities have been completed and project execution is underway, the control schedule process seeks to monitor the schedule status of the project and what was planned against what is actually occurring by using the schedule baseline. Any variances from what was planned can be dealt with in a change request, corrective action, or preventive action recommendation.

Chapter review

Test your knowledge of the information in Chapter 4 by answering these questions. The answers to these questions, and the explanations of why each answer choice is correct or incorrect, are located in the "Answers" section at the end of this chapter.

1. What is the correct order of processes in the Time Management knowledge area?

    A. Define Activities, Sequence Activities, Estimate Activity Resources, Estimate Activity Durations, Develop Schedule

    B. Define Activities, Sequence Activities, Estimate Activity Durations, Estimate Activity Resources, Develop Schedule

    C. Sequence Activities, Define Activities, Estimate Activity Resources, Estimate Activity Durations, Develop Schedule

    D. Sequence Activities, Define Activities, Estimate Activity Durations, Estimate Activity Resources, Develop Schedule

2. What is the document that provides additional information about activities identified on the activity list?

    A. Project charter

    B. Activities attributes

    C. Resource breakdown structure

    D. Scope statement

3. What is the BEST definition of rolling wave planning?

    A. It is the breakdown of work packages into activities.

    B. It is a form of progressive elaboration that focuses on defining work in the immediate future in more detail than work further off.

    C. It is the process of first defining, then sequencing, then estimating durations in the preparation of the project schedule.

    D. It is the process of comparing actual progress against planned progress.

4. What is the name of the document that will guide the definition, documentation, execution, and control of the project schedule?

    A. Project management plan

    B. Scope statement

    C. Organizational process assets

    D. Schedule management plan

5. Why are activity resources generally estimated before activity durations?
   A. Because that is the way the PMBOK® Guide sets them out.
   B. Because in order to estimate activity durations you must know in what sequence they occur.
   C. Because you need to know how many resources are available to complete an activity as this will affect how fast the activity can be completed.
   D. They don't—it's better to estimate activity durations first, then estimate activity resources.

6. What is the form of estimating that uses known quantities and multiplies them by known metrics?
   A. Analogous estimating
   B. Parametric estimating
   C. Three-point estimating
   D. The Delphi technique

7. You are obtaining information from a group of experts about your project durations, and each expert is being asked individually for their opinion without knowing who else is being interviewed. What sort of estimating technique are you using?
   A. Alternatives analysis
   B. Parametric estimating
   C. Three-point estimating
   D. The Delphi technique

8. Which of the following estimating techniques is part of the PERT technique?
   A. Analogous estimating
   B. Parametric estimating
   C. Three-point estimating
   D. Bottom–up estimating

9. If a successor activity cannot start until its predecessor activity has started, what sort of relationship is this?
   A. Finish-to-start
   B. Start-to-start
   C. Finish-to-finish
   D. Start-to-finish

10. What is the name of the process of considering whether an additional amount of time should be provided based on quantitative risk analysis?

    A. Expert judgment

    B. Parametric estimating

    C. Reserves analysis

    D. Monte Carlo analysis

11. The path, or paths, through a project schedule network that represent the most risk because there is no total float is called what?

    A. Critical chain

    B. Network diagram

    C. Gantt chart

    D. Critical path

12. If you are compressing the project schedule by using a technique that generally does not increase project costs, which of the following techniques are you using?

    A. Fast tracking

    B. Crashing

    C. Resource optimization

    D. Resource leveling

13. The amount of time a successor activity must wait after the completion of its predecessor activity is known as what?

    A. Lead

    B. Resource leveling

    C. Lag

    D. Float

Answers

This section contains the answers for the "Exercises" and "Chapter review" sections in this chapter.

Exercises

1. Based upon the information in the following table, complete a network diagram showing the project duration and calculate the critical path or paths.

Activity ID	Duration (days)	Predecessor
A	4	-
B	3	A
C	6	A, B
D	5	B
E	3	C, D
F	7	D
G	2	D, E
H	9	F, G

The project duration is 28 days.

The critical path is A-B-D-F-H.

The completed network diagram is shown in Figure 4-17.

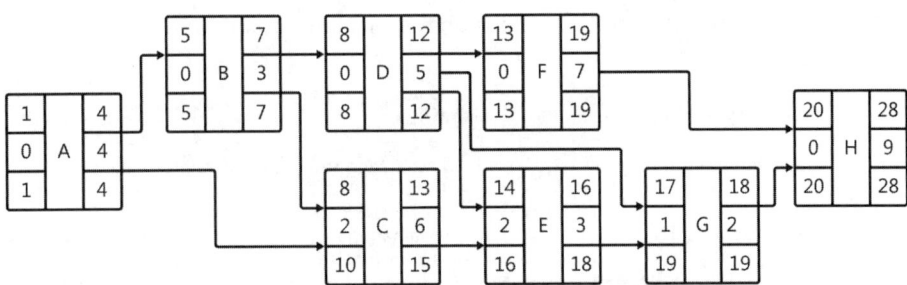

FIGURE 4-17 The activity-on-node diagram is completed.

2. Using three-point estimating, what is the expected mean, standard deviation, and variance of the following scenarios?

Optimistic	Most likely	Pessimistic	Mean	Standard deviation	Variance
6	8	12	8.33 days	1	1
3	10	15	9.67 days	2	4
12	14	18	14.33 days	1	1
27	35	48	35.83 days	3.5	12.25

3. You have been asked by your project sponsor to provide a date range for which you are 99.7 percent certain the project will be delivered, with an optimistic duration of 35 days, a most likely duration of 45 days, and a pessimistic duration of 60 days. What is your answer to your project sponsor?

To calculate the answer, first determine the standard deviation:

$$\frac{P - O}{6}$$

$$= \frac{60 - 35}{6}$$

$$= \frac{25}{6}$$

$$= 4.17$$

The question is asking for 99.7 percent certainty, which is 3 standard deviations either side of the mean, so multiply the standard deviation by 3: 4.17 × 3 = 12.51.

Therefore, the answer is 45±12.51 or 32.49–57.21 days

4. Match up the estimating technique on the left with the appropriate description on the right.

Estimating technique	Definition
1. Analogous estimating	d. An estimating technique using information from a similar activity
2. Parametric estimating	a. An estimating technique that multiplies a known quantity by a known metric
3. Bottom-up estimating	e. An estimating technique that takes low-level detailed estimates and aggregates them
4. Delphi technique	c. An estimating technique that gathers information from experts anonymously
5. Three-point estimating	b. An estimating technique that takes the weighted average of the optimistic, most likely, and pessimistic estimates.

Chapter review

1. **Correct answer: A**
   - **A. Correct:** First define activities, then sequence them, then estimate resources prior to estimating durations, then develop the schedule.
   - **B. Incorrect:** Estimate Activity Durations generally occurs after Estimate Activity Resources.
   - **C. Incorrect:** Sequence Activities occurs after Define Activities.
   - **D. Incorrect:** Sequence Activities occurs after Define Activities.

2. **Correct answer: B**
   - **A. Incorrect:** The project charter contains high-level information.
   - **B. Correct:** The activities attributes document provides additional detail about identified activities.
   - **C. Incorrect:** The resource breakdown structure provides a breakdown of categories and types of resources required on the project.
   - **D. Incorrect:** The scope statement describes all the work to be done on the project.

3. **Correct answer: B**
   - **A. Incorrect:** The breakdown of work packages into activities is the process of decomposition.
   - **B. Correct:** It is a form of progressive elaboration that focuses on defining work in the immediate future in more detail than work further off.
   - **C. Incorrect:** The process of first defining, then sequencing, then estimating durations in the preparation of the project schedule broadly outlines the Time Management processes.
   - **D. Incorrect:** The process of comparing actual progress against planned progress is variance analysis.

4. **Correct answer: D**
   - **A. Incorrect:** The project management plan is the overall plan containing many subsidiary plans and documents.
   - **B. Incorrect:** The scope statement defines the work to be done on the project.
   - **C. Incorrect:** The organizational process assets are process polices, templates, and methodologies the wider organization owns that can assist project management.
   - **D. Correct:** The schedule management plan defines how the project schedule will be developed, executed, and controlled.

5. **Correct answer: C**

   A. **Incorrect:** The PMBOK® Guide is not prescriptive.
   B. **Incorrect:** This answer links two processes that are separated by the Estimate Activity Resources process.
   C. **Correct:** You need to know how many resources are available to complete an activity because this will affect how fast the activity can be completed.
   D. **Incorrect:** Generally it's better to estimate activity resources first, then estimate activity durations.

6. **Correct answer: B**

   A. **Incorrect:** Analogous estimating uses a similar activity to estimate the resources or duration of a current activity.
   B. **Correct:** Parametric estimating uses known quantities and multiplies them by known metrics.
   C. **Incorrect:** Three-point estimating uses a weighted average of an optimistic, most likely, and pessimistic estimate.
   D. **Incorrect:** The Delphi technique solicits information from experts anonymously.

7. **Correct answer: D**

   A. **Incorrect:** Alternatives analysis considers a range of alternative approaches in order to determine the most appropriate one.
   B. **Incorrect:** Parametric estimating uses known quantities and multiplies them by known metrics.
   C. **Incorrect:** Three-point estimating uses a weighted average of an optimistic, most likely, and pessimistic estimate.
   D. **Correct:** The Delphi technique solicits information from experts anonymously.

8. **Correct answer: C**

   A. **Incorrect:** Analogous estimating uses a similar activity to estimate the resources or duration of a current activity.
   B. **Incorrect:** Parametric estimating uses known quantities and multiplies them by known metrics.
   C. **Correct:** Three-point estimating uses a weighted average of an optimistic, most likely, and pessimistic estimate and is part of the Program Evaluation and Review Technique (PERT).
   D. **Incorrect:** Bottom–up estimating aggregates low-level estimates and rolls them up to obtain higher-level estimates.

9. **Correct answer: B**
   A. **Incorrect:** A finish-to-start relationship means the successor cannot start until the predecessor finishes.
   B. **Correct:** A start-to-start relationship means a successor activity cannot start until its predecessor activity has started.
   C. **Incorrect:** A finish-to-finish relationship means the successor cannot finish until the predecessor finishes.
   D. **Incorrect:** A start-to-finish relationship means the successor cannot finish until the predecessor starts.

10. **Correct answer: C**
    A. **Incorrect:** Expert judgment is a technique for getting information from acknowledged experts.
    B. **Incorrect:** Parametric estimating uses known quantities and multiplies them by known metrics.
    C. **Correct:** Reserves analysis considers whether an additional amount of time should be provided based on quantitative risk analysis.
    D. **Incorrect:** Monte Carlo analysis uses sophisticated mathematical modeling to forecast future states from observed data.

11. **Correct answer: D**
    A. **Incorrect:** The critical chain method places time buffers around high-risk activities to mitigate any potential adverse impact on the project duration.
    B. **Incorrect:** The network diagram is a graphical representation of the project activities and the relationship between them.
    C. **Incorrect:** The Gantt chart is a graphical representation of the project schedule.
    D. **Correct:** The critical path is the path, or paths, through a project schedule network that represent the most risk because there is no total float.

12. **Correct answer: A**
    A. **Correct:** Fast tracking schedules activities in parallel that would normally be done in sequence.
    B. **Incorrect:** Crashing adds more resources to an activity to shorten its duration, but it usually costs money.
    C. **Incorrect:** Resource optimization is a technique of making most efficient use of resources on a project.
    D. **Incorrect:** Resource leveling is a type of resource optimization.

13. **Correct answer: C**

   A. **Incorrect:** The lead is the amount of time a successor can start before completion of the predecessor activity.

   B. **Incorrect:** Resource leveling is a type of resource optimization.

   C. **Correct:** The lag is the amount of time a successor activity must wait after the completion of its predecessor activity.

   D. **Incorrect:** The float is the amount of time an activity can be delayed before it has an impact upon successor activities or the total project duration.

CHAPTER 5

Cost management

This chapter focuses on project cost management. Project cost management, like the other knowledge areas, begins with a process of planning that produces a cost management plan. Then there is an iterative process that produces and updates the cost estimates and cost baseline. After these have been developed, a monitoring and controlling process is used to measure actual versus planned cost performance and to manage any change requests.

You may need to pay particular attention in this chapter to those activities of calculating earned value management; there is quite a bit of technical information that you will need to learn.

> ## The PMBOK® Guide processes
>
> ### Project Cost Management knowledge area
>
> The four processes in the Project Cost Management knowledge area are:
>
> - Plan Cost Management (Planning process)
> - Estimate Costs (Planning process)
> - Determine Budget (Planning process)
> - Control Costs (Monitoring and Controlling process)

Domain tasks in this chapter:

- Plan Cost Management, Estimate Costs, and Determine Budget processes:
    - 2.3 Develop a budget plan based on the project scope using estimating techniques, in order to manage project cost.
- Control Costs process:
    - 4.1 Measure project performance using appropriate tools and techniques, in order to identify and quantify any variances, perform approved corrective actions, and communicate with relevant stakeholders.
    - 4.2 Manage changes to the project scope, schedule, and costs by updating the project plan and communicating approved changes to the team, in order to ensure that revised project goals are met.

What is project cost management?

Project cost management is focused upon the processes of developing a cost management plan, the processes of estimating costs for activities and the overall project, preparing your project budget or cost baseline, recording performance, and influencing and assessing any changes to the project budget.

EXAM TIP

Although presented as discrete processes, the two processes of estimating costs and determining budget are usually done concurrently.

The processes contained in this knowledge area present a logical and sequential flow of information from estimating the costs through to controlling changes to your project budget. Figure 5-1 shows the general flow through this linear process without the general initial Plan Cost Management process.

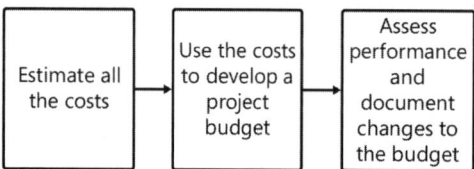

FIGURE 5-1 This flow shows the process of developing project costs, then a project budget, and then monitoring the budget.

Real world

I have always found that the development of the project cost estimates and the approved cost budget is one of the most iterative parts of project management. You start out with high-level estimates based on incomplete information and constantly revise and refine both the information you have and the estimates that are based on the information. When you check how progress is going, you may need to revisit your estimates and revise individual costs estimates. It is because of this iterative nature and the high expectations that stakeholders have upon project costs that I pay extra attention to the cost management processes.

Plan Cost Management

> **MORE INFO** **PLAN COST MANAGEMENT**
>
> You can read more about the Plan Cost Management process in the PMBOK® Guide, 5th edition, in Chapter 7, section 7.1. Table 5-1 identifies the process inputs, tools and techniques, and outputs.

TABLE 5-1 Plan Cost Management process

Inputs	Tools and techniques	Outputs
- Project management plan - Project charter - Enterprise environmental factors - Organizational process assets	- Expert judgment - Analytical techniques - Meetings	- Cost management plan

> **EXAM TIP**
>
> Did you notice that the inputs, tools, and techniques for the Plan Cost Management process are identical to the inputs, tools, and technique for the Plan Schedule Management process? The only difference between the two processes is the single output.

The Plan Cost Management process is a planning process with a single output—the cost management plan. Like all other planning documents, the cost management plan will guide your efforts in defining and controlling the project budget. It will form a subsidiary plan to the overall project management plan.

The Plan Cost Management process covers the following domain tasks:

- 2.3 Develop a budget plan based on the project scope using estimating techniques, in order to manage project cost.

Inputs

The Plan Cost Management process uses some or all of the following inputs as part of the development of the cost management plan for the project.

Project management plan

The distinct elements of the project management plan that will be useful in developing your own cost management plan are the scope and schedule information contained in the scope baseline and schedule baseline, respectively. After it is created, the cost management plan will become part of the project management plan. The project management plan is an output from the Develop Project Management Plan process.

Project charter

The project charter contains the approved initial budget for the project at the time of project initiation. It also contains known constraints, assumptions, and risks that may affect project costs and their management. The project charter is an output from the Develop Project Charter process.

Enterprise environmental factors

Particular enterprise environmental factors that may assist with development of your cost management plan include the particular organizational culture and structure, any external market conditions that may affect project costs, and any published commercially available cost information that you may use to develop and check your cost estimates.

Organizational process assets

Organizational process assets that may play an important part in the development of your cost management plan include any historical information, and any established financial control procedures, policies, and templates for defining and controlling project costs and budget.

EXAM TIP

It is important to note that in your day-to-day work you may use the terms "cost" and "budget" interchangeably. However, for the purposes of this examination you must understand that the two words have separate meanings. "Cost" refers to the actual costs of each activity or work package which, when aggregated, form a total project cost. "Budget," on the other hand, refers to costs over time.

Real world

One way to keep your accounts people very happy is to be proactive with the development of your project budget. If you are able to tell them clearly when you expect to spend money, and when you expect to have money come in, they are able to better plan the organization's cash flow requirements. It is important that you realize that as a project manager your project may impose serious cash flow problems upon the wider organization, and it is the accounts people who have to figure out how to make sure money is available when you need it. I have always found that giving the accounts people information early and often about when I plan to use money is a great way of managing this particular group of stakeholders.

Tools and techniques

The following tools and techniques are available to be used to develop the inputs into this process in order to produce the cost management plan.

Expert judgment

Expert judgment is used as a tool and technique in the Plan Cost Management process as again we rely on the experience, opinion, and expertise of individuals to assist the development of a cost management plan. The experts that you consult may be members of your project team, other employees in your organization, or people from outside your organization with particular experience in putting together an appropriate cost management plan.

Analytical techniques

The use of analytical techniques in the development of your cost management plan is an important tool because you, or your financial department, will have to analyze options and make decisions about how the project will be funded. You may be able to fund the project with cash reserves, bank loans, funding with equity from shareholders, or funding with debt from other sources. Each of these options has its own benefits and drawbacks. In making the decision, you're able to use a number of techniques, such as payback period, return on investment, internal rate of return, discounted cash flow, and net present value. Each of these terms was discussed in more detail in the Develop Project Charter process as part of the project selection process.

> **Real world**
>
> I have often found that many project managers are completely oblivious to how the project is going to be funded. I believe an important skill that any project manager should have is to have an understanding of project financing methods and the implications that the different finance sources have upon project costs. One of the first places you will look for guidance about funding criteria and sources of potential funding is the project charter.

Meetings

Meetings are a great way to bring together members of the project team who have expertise and skill in development of the cost management plan because they are the people completing the work. You may also choose to invite selected stakeholders from outside the project team who have specialist knowledge and skills in this particular area. An example of this would be inviting members of your organization's financial or accounts department to contribute to the development of the cost management plan.

Outputs

After the appropriate tools and techniques have been applied to the selected inputs, the Plan Cost Management process has the following output.

Cost management plan

The Plan Cost Management process has only a single output—the cost management plan. The *cost management plan* is a subsidiary plan of the project management plan and is used as a guide for the other cost management processes. The purpose of the cost management plan is to provide guidance to the project manager and the project team on how the organization expects costs to be estimated, budgets to be determined, cost performance to be assessed, and any potential changes assessed, documented, and reported upon. It will also outline the process of reporting progress in relation to forecast cost versus actual cost on the project and will prescribe acceptable tools, techniques, processes, and any other relevant information relating to how costs will be managed on the project.

The cost management plan is then a key input into the Estimate Costs and Determine Budget processes, both of which are planning processes.

 Quick check

1. What is the main purpose of the cost management plan?
2. What is the main reason for using analytical techniques during the Plan Cost Management process?
3. What sort of organizational process assets would be useful as inputs into the Plan Cost Management process?

Quick check answers

1. The main purpose of the cost management plan is to provide guidance on further planning of project costs, estimating costs, developing a project budget, checking planned cost performance against actual cost performance, and managing any potential changes to the cost baseline.
2. Analytical techniques are used as a tool to help assess the different options, and the pros and cons of each, for funding or financing the project.
3. The types of organizational process assets that would be useful as inputs into the Plan Cost Management process include any existing organizational financial control procedures, blank templates, established processes, gathered historical cost information, and any internal financial databases.

Estimate Costs

> **MORE INFO** **ESTIMATE COSTS**
>
> You can read more about the Estimate Costs process in the PMBOK® Guide, 5th edition, in Chapter 7, section 7.2. Table 5-2 identifies the process inputs, tools and techniques, and outputs.
>
> **TABLE 5-2** Estimate Costs process
>
> | Inputs | Tools and techniques | Outputs |
> | --- | --- | --- |
> | - Cost management plan
- Human resource management plan
- Scope baseline
- Project schedule
- Risk register
- Enterprise environmental factors
- Organizational process assets | - Expert judgment
- Analogous estimating
- Parametric estimating
- Bottom-up estimating
- Three-point estimating
- Reserve analysis
- Cost of quality
- Project management software
- Vendor bid analysis
- Group decision-making techniques | - Activity cost estimates
- Basis of estimates
- Project documents updates |

The Estimate Costs process is a planning process that uses the cost management plan for guidance and takes the defined activities and work packages, and assigns a cost estimate for each one using a variety of tools and techniques. In order to easily track which estimates are for which particular work package, you can use the numbering systems from the work breakdown structure (WBS). This process is a highly iterative process that is repeated throughout the life of the project.

The Estimate Costs process covers the following domain task:

- 2.3 Develop a budget plan based on the project scope using estimating techniques, in order to manage project cost.

In assessing the estimate for each activity, it is important to have a basic understanding of different types of costs that may be estimated.

- **Variable costs** These are costs that change with the amount of production. The more you produce, the more costs you incur. For example, if you increase the amount of homes you are building, you will use more home building materials. If you use more electricity as a result of greater amounts of work, then your costs will increase.
- **Fixed costs** These are costs that are fixed no matter how much you produce. For example, the rental you pay for your warehouse storage space is constant whether or not the warehouse is full or empty. Also, the costs you pay for any consents you require or equipment needed to complete the job are fixed costs.

- **Direct costs** These are costs attributable directly to the actions of the project. For example, the materials you use on your project are direct costs.
- **Indirect costs** These are costs that are not incurred directly by the project but which the project may have to account for. For example, the project may have to make provision for paying a share of corporate overheads such as office rental space and shared services. Your cost management plan may contain guidelines on what portion, if any, of indirect costs you must account for in your cost estimates. These are often referred to as overheads.

> **Real world**
>
> Indirect costs, or overheads, are often overlooked by project managers when preparing their cost estimates. Unless there are clear guidelines from the organization about what portion, if any, of indirect costs the project must account for, a lot of project managers simply do not think about this. Many organizations will account for indirect costs in required margins or profits. Hopefully, your organizational process assets include guidance on how you are expected to manage this issue.

- **Sunk costs** These are costs spent on the project to date that cannot be recovered if the project was to stop. For example, the money you have spent developing code for a new piece of software is sunk cost if you stop halfway through, because it has no recoverable value. Your cost management plan may contain guidelines on how sunk costs are treated in determining whether to continue on a troubled project.

All estimates are simply your best guess at the future, based on the information you have available to you. The better the information you have, the better the estimates will be. Thus, there is nearly always an element of uncertainty inherent in any estimate. It is often important to express this range of uncertainty inherent in any estimate. As a rule, the accuracy of cost estimates will improve as the project progresses, and your organization may have, as part of its organizational process assets, guidelines on the necessary level of accuracy required before proceeding. Table 5-3 shows the typical description of a variety of estimate ranges.

TABLE 5-3 Range of estimates

Estimate type	Estimate range
Order of Magnitude Estimate	-50% to +100%
Rough Order of Magnitude Estimate	-25% to +75%
Conceptual Estimate	-30% to +50%

Estimate type	Estimate range
Preliminary Estimate	-20% to +30%
Definitive Estimate	-15% to +20%
Control Estimate	-10% to +15%

Inputs

The Estimate Costs process uses some, or all, of the following seven inputs.

Cost management plan

The cost management plan is obviously a key input into the Estimate Costs process because it provides the guidance for how you are going to complete this process and, therefore, without it you would not be able to complete the process. The cost management plan is an output from the Develop Cost Management Plan process.

Human resource management plan

The *human resource management plan* is used as an input into the Estimate Costs process because it contains information about the project staff who will be working on the project and the chargeout rates, remuneration packages, and any other financial rewards to be paid to them. In order to develop the project cost, you will need to know this information. The human resource management plan is an output from the Plan Human Resource Management process.

Scope baseline

The scope baseline is composed of the project scope statement, the work breakdown structure (WBS), and the WBS dictionary, and it contains a full and detailed description of all the work to be done on the project. By using this information you can then attribute costs to each of the work packages and also the activities taken from the project schedule, and aggregate these costs into a total project cost estimate. The scope baseline is an output from the Create WBS process.

Project schedule

The project schedule is an important input into the Estimate Costs process because it gives an indication of when the work packages and activities are to be completed. The sequencing, timing, and duration of distinct project work packages and activities will affect the costs. The project schedule is an output from the Develop Project Schedule process, which in itself is the culmination of the other schedule management planning processes.

Risk register

The risk register is used as an input into the Estimate Costs process because it contains information around defined and documented uncertainty relating to specific work packages. This uncertainty is captured in the contingency reserve for each activity work package and needs to be taken into account in developing the project cost estimates. The risk register is an output from the Identify Risks process.

Enterprise environmental factors

The specific types of enterprise environmental factors that are useful as inputs into the Estimate Costs process are external market conditions that will affect the prices of products and services being procured for the project, and any published commercially available estimating data.

> **Real world**
>
> It is worthwhile to carefully subscribe to, and pay for access to, reputable published estimating databases. These databases are usually very accurate sources of information about the costs of particular materials and resources, and they are often separated into regional areas to determine variances at a local level. Many organizations, industry associations, and professional bodies compile these databases and will allow access for a fee.

Organizational process assets

The specific types of organizational process assets that are useful as inputs into the Estimate Costs process are any relevant templates and processes useful in the development of project cost estimates, including any historical information and lessons learned owned by the organization.

Tools and techniques

The following 10 tools and techniques are used upon the inputs to deliver the process outputs.

Expert judgment

The use of experts is an acknowledged tool in the preparation of project cost estimates. It is the experts, or people working on the project, who have an intimate knowledge of the work to be done and the likely cost of that work. In addition to project team members with expert judgment on the work to be done, you may also choose to consult external experts, such as those involved in the quantity surveying profession, who can provide expert advice on the expected costs of materials and resources to be used.

Analogous estimating

Analogous estimating is a quick means of estimating what a likely cost is to be for a particular material or resource by comparing your current requirements with the requirements of a previous project that you have information on, and then looking at the similarities between the two instances to determine what your current estimate will be. For example, if on a previous project you used a particular amount of concrete and it cost you $1,500, and on this project you expect to use twice as much, you would assume that your cost estimate is $3,000, by using analogous estimating. Because you are using an analogy from previous experience, there is a certain degree of expected inaccuracy in this form of estimating.

Parametric estimating

Parametric estimating is generally considered to be more accurate than analogous estimating because it uses known quantities of materials for resources and multiplies them by known financial rates. For example, you may know that you require 50 hours of work to be done by a business analyst, and that a business analyst costs $80 an hour; therefore, multiplying 50 hours by $80 an hour, you will arrive at a cost estimate of $4,000 by using parametric estimating.

Bottom-up estimating

Bottom-up estimating is generally considered to be quite an accurate form of estimating, because what you are doing is taking cost estimates from lower-level information—for example, the bottom level of the WBS—and then adding up, or rolling up, to higher levels and aggregating those costs to report a total cost.

Three-point estimating

You saw the use of three-point estimating in Chapter 4, "Time Management," in the discussion of the Estimate Activity Durations process from the Schedule Management knowledge area. Here it is used again as a method of determining an estimate where there is a most likely (cM), optimistic (cO), and pessimistic (cP) cost estimate for an activity.

> **EXAM TIP**
>
> Although the correct name for the formula is the "three-point estimate," and it is part of the Program Evaluation and Review Technique (PERT), it is often simply called the "PERT formula."

To get a *simple average* you take these three figures and add them together and divide by three. However, if you want to get a *weighted average* that gives greater weight to the most likely (cM) figure, then the formula to use is

$$\frac{cO + (4 \times cM) + cP}{6}$$

For example, if you have an optimistic cost estimate of $10, a most likely cost estimate of $16, and a pessimistic cost estimate of $25, then the weighted average using three-point estimating is $16.50.

You can also calculate the standard deviation which indicates how far from the average the optimistic and pessimistic figures are. A smaller standard deviation means they are closer to the average than a larger standard deviation. The formula for standard deviation is

$$\frac{cP - cO}{6}$$

For example, using the numbers from the previous example, the standard deviation would be $2.50.

After you have determined the standard deviation, you can then express your certainty about a cost estimate range. You express this certainty as a confidence interval where one standard deviation either side of the mean represents a confidence interval of 68 percent, two standard deviations either side of the mean gives a confidence interval of 95 percent, and three standard deviations either side of the mean gives a confidence interval of 99.7 percent.

For example, using the numbers from the previous example, you could say that you have a 95 percent certainty that the cost for the activity will be between $11.50 and $21.50.

> **Real world**
>
> In reality, when you are completing any sort of estimating process in the project, you are going to use a variety of estimating techniques. The type of estimating technique that you choose to use will depend on how much information you have. At the beginning of a project, when information is generally less available, you may choose to use less accurate forms of estimating. As the project progresses and you have more information available, you may choose to use more accurate and time-consuming forms of estimating for that work that you have greater information for, and still use less-accurate forms of estimating. In relation to rolling wave planning, you will most likely use more accurate forms of estimating on the work to be done in the immediate future, and less accurate forms of estimating on work to be done further off in the future.

Reserve analysis

Reserve analysis looks at the contingency reserves, or contingency allowances, provided for in the project cost estimates. The contingency reserve is an amount that reflects and allows for identified uncertainty in estimating particular costs. It is commonly known as "accounting for the known unknowns" in any project and is usually calculated during quantitative risk analysis performed as part of the Risk Management knowledge area. For example, you may determine that a particular activity has a 10 percent chance of experiencing a $1,750 cost overrun, and therefore you would allow a $175 figure ($1750 x 10 percent) in the contingency reserve. By aggregating, or adding up, all of the individual amounts allowed for in the contingency reserve analysis, you will arrive at a total contingency reserve for the entire project.

The management reserve for unknown unknowns is also able to be calculated during risk assessment, or by expressing the range of uncertainty in your estimates as a total amount. The management reserve is controlled by senior managers, and the project manager must apply to use it; it is not part of the approved budget.

> **Real world**
>
> In theory, the contingency reserve should be part of the approved project budget and under the control of the project manager, and the management reserve under the control of senior management or members of the steering group. In reality, you may find that your approved budget may just be for known costs and that sponsors can sometimes be reluctant to approve reserve budgets, because they view it as endorsing inaccuracy and sloppy estimating practices. My argument is that I would prefer to go forward on a "no surprises" basis and release the reserves once the identified uncertainty has been defined or has been passed.

Cost of quality

As part of the preparation of your quality management plan, you will consider the issue of cost of quality, because any decisions made about what this means to you will affect cost on the project immediately, and for the organization after the project is handed over. *Cost of quality* refers to the quality attributes of the project and the product over the life of the product. For example, you may need to take into account the cost of future product returns or warranty claims because of decisions made to manufacture lower quality to lower the project costs.

Project management software

Project management software should be considered essential for any large and complex projects because trying to collect and aggregate many cost estimates manually is simply not possible.

Vendor bid analysis

The *vendor bid analysis* process is a way of double-checking the bids received from vendors to make sure that they are neither overinflated nor underinflated. You can think of vendor bid analysis as your quality check on the prices people are submitting to you.

Group decision-making techniques

Good cost estimates are prepared by people familiar with the activities being estimated, and when you get a group of these people together you are going to need some effective group decision-making techniques to make sense of the expert opinions supplied. These techniques are also used when estimating elements of the project schedule and include brainstorming, nominal group techniques, and the Delphi technique.

Outputs

The Estimate Costs process produces some, or all, of the following outputs.

Activity cost estimates

The activity cost estimates are the individual estimates for each activity identified. They are the entire focus of this process and will be used to put together your cost baseline. The activity cost estimates are used as an input into the Determine Budget process.

Basis of estimates

The *basis of estimates* is a useful document, because it outlines the assumptions made, the type of estimating technique used, any known constraints, and an indication of the range of uncertainty and of the confidence level of the final estimates for each activity, and indeed the entire project. The basis of estimates is used as an input into the Determine Budget process.

> **EXAM TIP**
>
> There are several supporting documents that provide additional information to summary documents. For the requirements documentation you have the requirements traceability matrix. For the WBS, you have the WBS dictionary, providing additional information. For the activity list, you have the activity attributes, providing more detailed information. For the activity cost estimates, you have the basis of estimates. You can recognize that the summary document and the document containing greater detail are both important to provide a full picture.

Project documents updates

The specific project documents that may be updated as a result of estimating costs will include such things as the statement of work, which may be updated as a result of the cost estimates, and elements of the risk register that are refined and updated as a result of specific cost estimates.

> ✓ **Quick check**
>
> 1. What is the difference between a simple average and a weighted average?
> 2. What is the difference between a contingency reserve and a management reserve?
> 3. What information does the basis of estimates contain?
>
> **Quick check answers**
>
> 1. A simple average divides the most likely (cM), the optimistic (cO), and the pessimistic (cP) cost estimates by 3, whereas a weighted average gives a higher weighting of 4 to the most likely cost estimate and then divides by 6.
> 2. A contingency reserve is prepared for the known uncertainty, or known unknowns on a project, and should be under the control of the project manager. A management reserve is prepared for the unknown uncertainty, for unknown unknowns, and is generally under the control of senior management.
> 3. The basis of estimates contains information about the assumptions made in preparing cost estimates, the types of estimating techniques used, and the amount of uncertainty in the final activity cost estimates.

Determine Budget

> **MORE INFO** **DETERMINE BUDGET**
>
> You can read more about the Determine Budget process in the PMBOK® Guide, 5th edition, in Chapter 7, section 7.3. Table 5-4 identifies the process inputs, tools and techniques, and outputs.
>
> **TABLE 5-4** Determine Budget process
>
> | Inputs | Tools and techniques | Outputs |
> | --- | --- | --- |
> | - Cost management plan
- Scope baseline
- Activity cost estimates
- Basis of estimates
- Project schedules
- Resource calendars
- Risk register
- Agreements
- Organizational process assets | - Cost aggregation
- Reserve analysis
- Expert judgment
- Historical relationships
- Funding limit reconciliation | - Cost baseline
- Project funding requirements
- Project documents updates |

The Determine Budget process is a planning process that takes the individual activity cost estimates and aggregates them into a total project cost, then applies the project schedule to determine the timing of when costs will be incurred in order to develop the project budget, or cost baseline.

The Determine Budget process covers the following domain task:

- 2.3 Develop a budget plan based on the project scope using estimating techniques, in order to manage project cost.

Inputs

The inputs used in this process take the individual cost estimates and aggregate them into the project budget.

Cost management plan

The cost management plan is used as a key input into the Determine Budget process because it is the cost management plan that sets out the processes, policies, rules, and regulations that you are going to apply in order to determine a project budget. The cost management plan is an output from the Plan Cost Management process.

Scope baseline

The scope baseline is a very important input into this process because it outlines all the work to be done, and the work not to be done, as part of the project. It is by breaking the scope baseline down into its component parts via the work breakdown structure (WBS), and subsequently down to activity level with the schedule work, that you are then able to estimate individual activity costs. The scope baseline consists of the project scope statement, the work breakdown structure, and the WBS dictionary, and it is an output from the Create WBS process.

Activity cost estimates

The activity cost estimates provide you with individual estimates of cost for identified activities by using a variety of tools and techniques from the Estimate Costs process. In order to put together your project budget you will take these individual activity estimates, aggregate them, and determine the time period in which those costs will be incurred. The activity cost estimates are an output from the Estimate Costs process.

Basis of estimates

The basis of estimates is an important input because it provides further information about each of the estimates you have determined for the individual activities. The basis of estimates is an output from the Estimate Costs process.

Project schedule

The project schedule is used as an input into the Determine Budget process because you need to know when each activity will be performed so that you can determine when the costs of activity will be incurred. This is the essence of developing a project budget, which is taking the project costs and applying them over time. The project schedule is an output from the Develop Schedule process.

Resource calendars

The resource calendars are used as an input into the Determine Budget process because they provide additional and more detailed information about when specific resources are available to work on the project. They are an output from the Acquire Project Team process.

Risk register

The risk register is used as an input into this process because it will identify risks associated with both individual activity cost estimates and elements of the project schedule that need to be taken into account when developing the project budget. It is an output from the Identify Risks process.

Agreements

Any existing agreements are used by the project manager as an input into this process, because they will outline any agreement between parties to the project about costs, payments, and any other matters, such as retention payments, that need to be included in the project budget. For example, you may have an agreement for paying suppliers that requires payment regularly each month, or one that requires progress payments at certain project milestones. These agreements are an output from the Conduct Procurements process.

Organizational process assets

The specific organizational process assets that can assist in the development of the project budget include any organizational policies and procedures relating to the development and presentation of the project budget, and any blank templates for preparing budgets and for reporting the budget.

Tools and techniques

The five tools and techniques of this process are all used upon the separate inputs to deliver the process outputs.

Cost aggregation

Cost aggregation is the process of taking the individual estimates for each of the activities and aggregating upward to work package level, then rolling these estimates up to high level, sub-deliverable level, and deliverable level, in order to arrive at a bottom-up estimate for portions of the project or the entire project. Figure 5-2 shows how individual activities are added up, or aggregated.

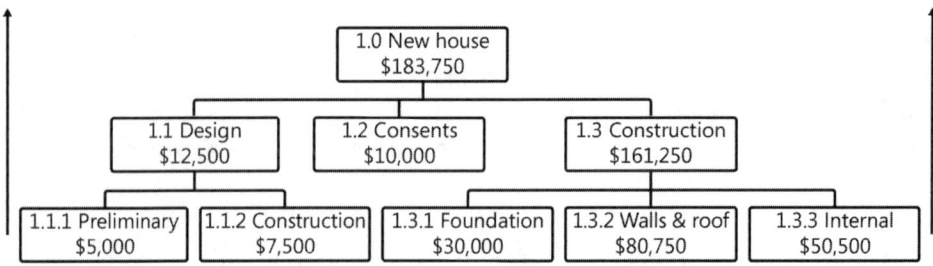

FIGURE 5-2 In bottom-up cost aggregation, individual activities are added up, or aggregated.

Reserve analysis

The reserve analysis is the method of looking at both the contingency reserve and the management reserve required for the project and the timing of access to those reserves. Contingency reserves will be identified for specific activities, and access to the contingency reserve for this will be required when the activity is being performed. Access to the management reserve could be required at any time in the project because it is for the purpose of unknown unknowns, or for elements that could not reasonably have been foreseen.

Expert judgment

Again expert judgment is a key tool and technique in determining the budget. The experts should be from the project team and also from outside the project team; for example, from the organization's finance or accounts department.

Historical relationships

If the organization is mature enough to have been recording information about *historical relationships* and the reliability and range of uncertainty in its cost estimating process, it can then use this information to further refine its current cost estimates, or to acknowledge a quantifiable amount of uncertainty in those estimates.

Funding limit reconciliation

As part of the Determine Budget process, you may find that there are *funding limit reconciliation* issues that need to be considered. For example, you may want to do a great amount of work but simply might not have the funds until a later period in time; therefore, you will have to limit the activity on the project until funds to complete the work become available.

> **Real world**
>
> Is it important that you are able to determine how the project will be funded early on, and whether this funding process imposes any constraints upon your project schedule. I have often found that there are constraints on when funds will be available, which is generally related to the financial years into which the funds are allocated. This is the reason why the finance department of an organization is so interested in how much of your project budget you are spending, how much you are carrying over to the next financial year, or how much you want to bring forward into this financial year. You may not realize that someone has to find the finances to complete not only your project but all other projects that the organization is completing.

Outputs

The major outputs from the Determine Budget process are the following.

Cost baseline

The *cost baseline* is one of four baselines that you will use to measure progress on the project. The other three are the scope baseline, the time baseline, and the quality baseline. The key element of the cost baseline is that it takes the aggregated individual estimates of cost for each activity and applies them to the time periods in which the costs will be accrued. This is the baseline against which you are going to measure project cost performance. Figure 5-3 shows an example of a cost baseline represented graphically. It shows the total amount of spend for each time period, in this case in months. Additionally, it shows the cumulative spend over the life of the project. This is represented by the line, which is often referred to as the "S-curve" (it is in the shape of the letter S) because there is little spend at the beginning of a project, a lot of spend in the middle section of the project, and a decrease in spending toward the end of the project.

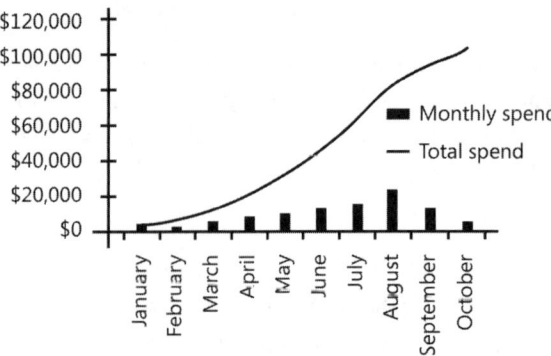

FIGURE 5-3 This cost baseline shows the total amount of spend for each month.

EXAM TIP

Individual contingency reserve figures are added to the individual activity cost estimates. These are then aggregated and rolled up to work package level, with the aggregated contingency reserve applied against individual work packages. The management reserve is added to the total cost baseline. The only way that you're able to use funds from the management reserve is to obtain approval by the documented and approved change control process. Management reserves are not usually part of the project budget.

Project funding requirements

The *project funding requirements* acknowledge when the funding for the project will be available; for example, annually, quarterly, or monthly. This recognizes that funding for a project often occurs in incremental amounts, whereas expenditure on a project may be continuous.

> **Real world**
>
> Matching up when funds will be available against when money will be spent is an important aspect of sound and prudent financial management for the project. You do not want to be in a situation where you have spent more than your ability to pay, because this may mean delays in paying creditors and ultimately delays to the project.

Project documents updates

The types of project documents that may be updated as a result of the Determine Budget process are the individual cost estimates, project schedule, and risk register.

Quick check

1. Why is the project schedule an important input into the Determine Budget process?
2. How would you describe cost aggregation?
3. Why are funding limits reconciliations and the project funding requirements important aspects of any project cost baseline?

Quick check answers

1. The project schedule allows you to view the time period within which the project activities will be performed and their costs incurred.
2. Cost aggregation is the process of adding up individual activity cost estimates up to the work package level, then the sub-deliverable level, and then the deliverable level.
3. Both the technique of funding limits reconciliation and the output of project funding requirements recognize that funds for the project may be incremental while spending may be continuous, and therefore there may be times when there are not enough funds to pay accrued expenses.

Control Costs

> **MORE INFO CONTROL COSTS**
>
> You can read more about the Control Costs process in the PMBOK® Guide, 5th edition, in Chapter 7, section 7.4. Table 5-5 identifies the process inputs, tools and techniques, and outputs.
>
> **TABLE 5-5** Control Costs process
>
> | Inputs | Tools and techniques | Outputs |
> |---|---|---|
> | - Project management plan
- Project funding requirements
- Work performance data
- Organizational process assets | - Earned value management
- Forecasting
- To-complete performance index (TCPI)
- Performance reviews
- Project management software
- Reserve analysis | - Work performance information
- Cost forecasts
- Change requests
- Project management plan updates
- Project documents updates
- Organizational process assets updates |

EXAM TIP

Did you notice that the outputs from the Control Costs process are the same as the outputs from the Control Schedule process, with the exception of the cost forecasts instead of schedule forecasts?

The Control Costs process is focused mainly on measuring actual against planned cost performance, forecasting likely future cost performance, and managing any changes to the cost baseline. The Control Costs process covers the following domain tasks:

- 4.1 Measure project performance using appropriate tools and techniques, in order to identify and quantify any variances, perform approved corrective actions, and communicate with relevant stakeholders.
- 4.2 Manage changes to the project scope, schedule, and costs by updating the project plan and communicating approved changes to the team, in order to ensure that revised project goals are met.

Inputs

The Control Costs process uses the following inputs.

Project management plan

The project management plan, and its subsidiary plans, guide you in the process of controlling any potential changes to your cost baseline or any of the individual estimates that were prepared. As such, it is an important input into the Control Costs process. The project management plan is an output from the Develop Project Management Plan process.

Project funding requirements

The project funding requirements are an important input into the Control Costs process because they enable you to determine when expenditures will be incurred and when funding for the project will be available, and to therefore assess actual versus planned project funding requirements and control any changes to these elements. The project funding requirements are an output from the Determine Budget process.

Work performance data

By now you should have picked up that work performance data is an important input into several controlling processes. Work performance data is the information you gather about what is actually occurring on the project down to the level of which activities have started, the costs associated with completing those activities, and any estimates for completing the remainder of the work to be done. Work performance data is an output from the Direct and Manage Project Work process.

Organizational process assets

The types of organizational process assets that will be useful as inputs into the Control Costs process are any existing organizational policies, procedures, templates, or any other element relating to how costs will be monitored and reported on in your project.

Tools and techniques

The following tools and techniques can be used upon the inputs into the Control Costs process.

Earned value management

The earned value management (EVM) system provides you with an effective and efficient way to establish what has occurred in the past and use this information to forecast likely future scenarios by using a range of mathematical equations. It is better than simply taking one or two elements of past performance and simply expecting that performance to continue. For example, imagine that you are a project sponsor on a project, and your project manager tells you that the project is 50 percent of the way through and has spent only 40 percent of the budget. Is this a good situation or not? It might be, but without knowing how much of the actual work has been completed and how much value has been earned, you don't really know if this is a positive statement or not. This is exactly the scenario that earned value management is able to get around.

Earned value management takes the original project cost baseline, the planned value of the work you had expected to have completed by now, the earned value of the work you have completed now, and the actual cost of delivering that value to determine what the project cost and schedule performance to date is, and then forecast what the likely costs at completion will be. It does this by using the following formulas:

- **Budget at completion (BAC)**   The original forecast budget for the project.

- **Planned value (PV)**   The amount of value that you should have earned by this time in the project. Because the total *planned value (PV)* for a project equals the budget at completion (BAC), you can determine the planned value by simply determining how far through the project you are in relation to time, and mapping this back to the approved cost baseline to establish the planned value. Figure 5-4 demonstrates how to determine the PV from the BAC.

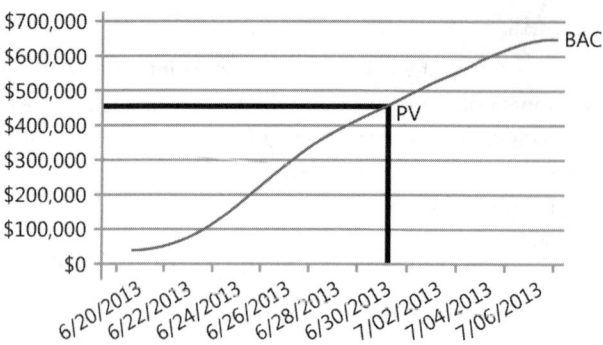

FIGURE 5-4 The project cost baseline shows Planned value (PV) and budget at completion (BAC).

- **Earned value (EV)**   The value of the work that has been completed. This is not the actual cost of the work that has been completed but rather the original ascribed value from your approved cost baseline for the value of the work.

- **Actual cost (AC)**   The actual realized cost you incurred for the work that you have done to date. You will be able to get a record of this from your accounts system.

Figure 5-5 shows the budget at completion (BAC), planned value (PV), earned value (EV), and actual cost (AC) on a single graph. Incidentally, it shows a project in trouble in terms of both time and cost because the actual cost is above the planned value, and the earned value is less than the planned value.

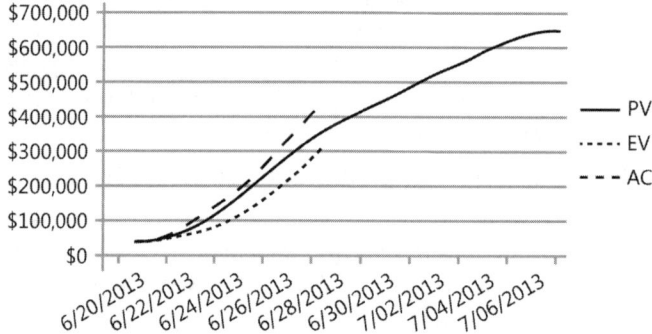

FIGURE 5-5 This graph shows a record of project planned value, earned value, and actual cost.

EXAM TIP

On most questions you will be challenged to extract the BAC, PV, EV, and AC from the scenario given. Take your time to ensure that you are extracting the correct figures.

Real world

I've often found that when calculating the actual cost it is important to remove from this calculation the value of any material held in stock. On some projects, you may decide to procure a lot of required materials early to avoid potential cost increases over time. Therefore, you will have paid for these materials, and this will show up in your accounts. However, incorporating this amount into your actual cost figure for the purposes of earned value management will skew the results negatively. Therefore, I recommend that you do regular stock takes and remove the value of material held in stock from the actual cost figure that you use for the earned value management calculations.

- **Cost variance (CV)**   This is simply the difference between the value of what you expected to have earned (EV) at this point and the actual cost (AC) at this point. A positive *cost variance* is good and shows that the project is under budget, a negative cost variance is bad and shows that the project is over budget. The formula is:

    $CV = EV - AC$

- **Cost performance index (CPI)**   One of the limitations of the cost variance equation is that it gives you a simple gross figure. You are not able to tell whether a $10,000 cost variance is significant on your project. If you are working on a $50,000 project it would be significant; if you are working on a $10 million contract, it may not be so significant. The *cost performance index* calculation tells you the magnitude of the variance. A cost performance index of more than 1 is good because it means that the project is under budget; a cost performance index of less than 1 is bad because it means that the project is over budget. For example, if you have a cost performance index of 1.1, it means that for every dollar you spend on the project you are getting a $1.10 return. The formula is:

    $CPI = EV/AC$

- **Schedule variance (SV)**   This tells you whether you are ahead or behind your planned schedule. It is the difference between the earned value (EV) and the planned value (PV). A positive schedule variance is good and means that you are ahead of schedule; a negative schedule variance is bad and means that you are behind schedule. The formula is:

    $SV = EV - PV$

- **Schedule performance index (SPI)**   This is a ratio of the earned value and planned value that allows you to better determine the magnitude of any variance. A schedule performance index of more than 1 is good because it means that the project is ahead of time; a schedule performance index of less than 1 is bad because it means that the project is behind schedule. For example, if you have a schedule performance index of 0.95, it means that every day you spend working on the project you are getting a 0.95 day return. The formula is:

SPI = EV/PV

EXAM TIP

A quick and easy way to remember the formula for CV, CPI, SP, and SPI is that each of the formula starts with EV. If it is a formula relating to variance, CV or SV, then the next symbol is a minus sign. If it is a formula relating to a performance index, CPI or SPI, then the next symbol is a divide sign. If the formula is in relation to cost, CV or CPI, then the final part of the formula is AC. If the formula is in relation to schedule, SV or SPI, the final part of the formula is PV.

Forecasting

Forecasting is the process of taking time and cost performance to date and using this information to forecast a likely future scenario. The time and cost performance measurements are the cost variance (CV), schedule variance (SV), cost performance index (CPI), and schedule performance index (SPI). You can use these measurements and the following formulas to forecast a likely project cost at completion, the amount of money required to complete the project, and the difference between what you originally thought it would cost and what you now think it will cost.

- **Estimate at completion (EAC)**   There are many ways to calculate a forecast estimate at completion (EAC). Keep in mind that in order to forecast a likely future cost or time frame for the project, you are going to be using historical information. Therefore, the quality of your EAC calculation will depend entirely on the quality of the historical information that you are using. The following four formulas use different inputs to calculate the EAC. Each one will give a difference answer for the same project.

    - **EAC = BAC/CPI**   This is perhaps the simplest of the estimate at completion calculations because it simply takes your original budget at completion (BAC) and divides that by your cost performance index (CPI). Obviously, this is a useful calculation if your cost performance to date is indicative of your likely cost performance going forward, and by the same measure will not be a great calculation to use if your cost performance to date is not indicative of your cost performance in the future.

    - **EAC = AC+ ETC**   Simply adding your estimate to complete (ETC) to your actual cost (AC) spent to date is an effective way to determine your estimate at completion (EAC). However, the method by which you determine your estimate to complete calculation will have a great effect on whether or not this formula is accurate.

    - **EAC = AC + (BAC–EV)**   This formula takes the actual costs (AC) spent to date and adds to them the total budget at completion (BAC) with your current earned value (EV) subtracted.

- **EAC = AC + ((BAC–EV)/(CPI × SPI))**   This formula takes into account both your cost performance and your schedule performance and applies it to the value of the work you have left to complete.

EXAM TIP

Memorize all these formula, and as soon as you are allowed to start the exam, write them all down.

> **NOTE CUMULATIVE VERSUS NON-CUMULATIVE**
>
> When using either the CPI or SPI formula you are able to choose whether you use cumulative or non-cumulative variations of these. The cumulative calculation calculates right from the start of the project to where you are now in the project, and obviously if you use this you are assuming that that particular range is indicative and typical of your cost or schedule performance going forward. If, however, for some reason there have been some atypical variances experienced in either time or cost on your project in the past, you may want to avoid using these when you use either CPI or SPI for forecasts. In this case, you will use non-cumulative CPI or SPI calculations taken from a specific period of time that you feel is a more accurate representation of likely future performance.

> ### Real world
>
> When using an EAC formula, as a general rule of thumb, I tend to use the BAC divided by CPI calculation for the first third of the project because the information coming out at this point tends to be less accurate. After I get past the halfway point on a project, I will use the AC + ((BAC-EV)/(CPI × SPI)) formula because it takes into account all parameters and is generally more accurate.

- **Estimate to complete (ETC)**   The estimate to complete calculation is simply your forecast of the remaining costs to be incurred on the project. The easiest way to calculate this is simply to subtract your actual cost (AC) spent to date from your estimate at completion (EAC). The formula is:

    ETC = EAC − AC

- **Variance at completion (VAC)**   The *variance at completion* calculation is simply the difference between what you originally thought the project was going to cost (BAC) and what you now think it is going to cost (EAC). A negative variance is bad, and a positive variance is good. The formula is:

    VAC = BAC − EAC

EXAM TIP

There are occasions when the three-letter acronyms used here to outline the earned value management system are represented by an older set of four-letter acronyms as follows:

Planned value (PV) = Budgeted cost of work scheduled (BCWS)

Actual cost (AC) = Actual cost of work performed (ACWP)

Earned value (EV) = Budgeted cost of work performed (BCWP)

EXAM TIP

In the exam you will often be presented with a scenario that requires you to work out one set of figures before you can work out another set of figures. For example, you may be required to work out the EAC by using either CPI or SPI but will not be given the CPI figures or SPI figures. You will instead be given figures for EC, AC, and PV, and be expected to work out either the CPI or the SPI first. Also, when looking at a question that requires you to calculate any formula, be on the lookout for any irrelevant information because sometimes not all the information presented in the scenario is relevant.

To-complete performance index (TCPI)

The *to-complete performance index* (TCPI) tells you the rate at which you have to work to achieve either your estimate at completion (EAC) or your budget at completion (BAC), depending on which one you are targeting. A to-complete performance index of less than 1 is good, whereas a to-complete performance index of more than 1 is bad. If you are using the original budget at completion as your target, the formula is:

TCPI = (BAC-EV)/ (BAC-AC)

If you are using the estimate at completion as the target, the formula for TCPI is:

TCPI = (BAC-EV)/ (EAC-AC)

EXAM TIP

When doing any calculations in the exam, round your answer to two decimals places but be prepared for an answer that is slightly different due to slight differences in the approach to rounding of decimal places.

Performance reviews

Performance reviews are conducted via a variety of means, including earned value management variances and trend analysis. You already have learned about the use of earned value management variances for the calculation of both the cost variance (CV) and schedule variance (SV) using earned value management. These are the most frequently used methods of determining variance and performance.

In addition to earned value management variances as a performance review tool, you can also use trend analysis, which looks at past performance and extrapolates from that a likely future performance, usually by using graphs and linear regression.

Project management software

Project management software is very useful in monitoring the performance of cost on a project as it is able to quickly do what would take a lot of time if done manually. Additionally, it can take both the original data and any data from calculations and display it graphically for easy interpretation and communication.

Reserve analysis

Reserve analysis in this monitoring and controlling process is the process of re-examining the original reserves calculated, both the contingency and management reserves, and checking whether the assumptions made when calculating them are still valid, and also releasing any unused portions of contingency reserves from the approved project budget in order to enable other projects to access the pool of funds.

Outputs

The Control Costs process produces the following outputs.

Work performance information

The easiest way to display work performance information based on the work performance data is by using the earned value calculations for cost variance (CV), schedule variance (SV), cost performance index (CPI), schedule performance index (SPI), and the to-complete performance index (TCPI). The work performance information goes on to be used as an input into the Monitor and Control Project Work process.

Costs forecasts

Cost forecasts are obtained from the estimate at completion (EAC) values. Cost forecasts go on to be used as an input into the Monitor and Control Project Work process.

> **Real world**
>
> It is important to emphasize to project stakeholders that any estimate at completion calculation is just that, it is your estimate about what it will cost to complete the project. When calculating the estimate at completion, you are using historical information to try to forecast a likely future outcome. If project stakeholders consider that your estimate at completion figure is an absolute figure that you definitely achieve, this will create unrealistic expectations.

Change requests

One of the key outputs from any controlling process is change requests that arise as a result of either variances detected or additional information provided. Change requests may include preventive or corrective actions. All change requests are processed as per your documented and approved change control process.

Change requests go on to be used as an input into the Perform Integrated Change Control process from the Integration Management knowledge area.

Project management plan updates

Specific parts of the project management plan that may be updated as a result of the Control Costs process include the cost baseline and the cost management plan. Project management plan updates are used in turn as an input into the Develop Project Plan process.

Project documents updates

Specific project documents that may be updated as a result of the Control Costs process include any documentation relating to how you build up your cost estimates, such as the cost baseline and the basis of estimates document.

Organizational process assets updates

Specific organizational process assets that may be updated as a result of the Control Cost process are historical information, records of financial information kept, lessons learned, records of corrective actions, and updates to any organizational financial templates and policies in order to ensure that they are still relevant.

Quick check

1. What is the difference between work performance data and work performance information?
2. If a project has a CPI of 1.1 and an SPI of .90, how is it performing in relation to time and cost?
3. What is the key difference between each of the four formulas for estimate at completion?

Quick check answers

1. Work performance data is the raw information collected by checking on cost and time performance. Work performance information applies filters to this data to make it useful information.
2. This project is under budget because the CPI is greater than 1, but behind schedule because the SPI is less than 1.
3. Each of the four formulas uses different historical information about the project to forecast a likely future outcome.

Exercises

The answers for these exercises are located in the "Answers" section at the end of this chapter.

1. (A) You are the project manager on a project to build 10 identical offices. You expect to spend $50,000 per office to complete the work and take 20 months to finish. You are 12 months into the work and have completed five offices and spent $310,000 in total. Use this information to calculate the following:

    A. Budget at completion (BAC)
    B. Actual cost (AC)
    C. Planned value (PV)
    D. Earned value (EV)
    E. Cost variance (CV)
    F. Cost performance index (CPI)
    G. Schedule variance (SV)
    H. Schedule performance index (SPI)
    I. Estimate at completion (EAC)

J. Estimate to complete (ETC)

   K. Variance at completion (VAC)

   L. To-complete performance index (TCPI)

   (B) Based on the information gained from the calculations you have performed, how is the project performing in terms of both cost and time?

2. (A) You are the project manager on a project to complete 15 miles of road. Your approved budget for the project is $930,000, and you have forecast that the project will take 35 weeks to complete. You are 13 weeks into the project, and have constructed 7 miles of road at a cost of $58,000 per mile. Use this information to calculate the following:

   A. Budget at completion (BAC)

   B. Actual cost (AC)

   C. Planned value (PV)

   D. Earned value (EV)

   E. Cost variance (CV)

   F. Cost performance index (CPI)

   G. Schedule variance (SV)

   H. Schedule performance index (SPI)

   I. Estimate at completion (EAC)

   J. Estimate to complete (ETC)

   K. Variance at completion (VAC)

   L. To-complete performance index (TCPI)

   (B) Based on the information gained from the calculations you have performed, how is the project performing in terms of both cost and time?

Chapter summary

- The Cost Management knowledge area is focused upon the development and checking of the project costs and begins with a planning process that produces the cost management plan, which then guides the individual cost estimating process and development of the cost baseline. It also provides guidance on monitoring actual versus planned cost performance and managing any changes to the cost baseline.

- The Plan Cost Management process focuses on the production of the cost management plan, which is a subsidiary plan of the project management plan.

- The Estimate Costs process is a highly iterative process repeated throughout the project that uses a variety of estimating techniques to developed individual activity cost estimates.
- The Determine Budget process aggregates the individual activity cost estimates and determines exactly when the costs will be incurred to produce a time-phased project budget, or cost baseline.
- The Control Costs process assesses planned cost performance against actual cost performance and forecasts a likely future state by using the earned value management systems. Any changes to the project cost baseline or individual activity cost estimates are managed through the approved change control process.

Chapter review

Test your knowledge of the information in Chapter 5 by answering these questions. The answers to these questions, and the explanations of why each answer choice is correct or incorrect, are located in the "Answers" section at the end of this chapter.

1. What is the correct order of processes in the Cost Management knowledge area?
   A. Plan Cost Management, Estimate Costs, Determine Budget, Control Costs
   B. Plan Cost Management, Determine Budget, Estimate Costs, Control Costs
   C. Plan Cost Management, Control Costs, Estimate Costs, Determine Budget
   D. Plan Cost Management, Estimate Costs, Control Costs, Determine Budget

2. What is the single output from the Plan Cost Management process?
   A. Activity cost estimates
   B. Cost baseline
   C. Cost management plan
   D. Cost forecasts

3. All of the following could be included in the cost management plan EXCEPT?
   A. A description of the accuracy of estimating.
   B. The cost reporting formats to be used.
   C. A description of the units of measure used to estimate costs.
   D. The dates each activity will occur.

4. If you are estimating the cost for an activity by comparing the current activity with similar ones you have completed in the past, what sort of estimating technique are you using?

    A. Analogous estimating
    B. Parametric estimating
    C. Three-point estimating
    D. Bottom–up estimating

5. If you are aggregating the individual activity cost estimates up to the work package level, then the sub-deliverable level, and then the deliverable level to arrive at a total project cost estimate, what sort of estimating technique are you using?

    A. Analogous estimating
    B. Parametric estimating
    C. Three-point estimating
    D. Bottom–up estimating

6. If you are applying to senior management to obtain extra funds for unforeseen costs on your project, what are you using?

    A. Contingency reserve
    B. Funding limit reconciliation
    C. Management reserve
    D. Cost aggregation

7. If you have a project with a schedule performance index (SPI) of 1.05 and a cost performance index (CPI) of 0.92, how is your project performing?

    A. The project is over budget and behind schedule.
    B. The project is over budget and ahead of schedule.
    C. The project is under budget and behind schedule.
    D. The project is under budget and ahead of schedule.

8. If the budget at completion for your project is $70,000, the earned value is $30,000, and the actual cost is $32,000, what is your estimate at completion?

    A. $70,000.00
    B. $65,625.00
    C. $74,468.08
    D. $62,000.00

9. If the budget at completion for your project is $70,000, the earned value is $30,000, and the actual cost is $32,000, what is your variance at completion?

    A. $0.00

    B. $7,375.00

    C. −$4 468.08

    D. $8 000.00

10. If the to-complete performance index calculated for the budget at completion for your project is 1.1, what does this mean?

    A. Your project is doing well and you can slow down and still achieve the budget at completion.

    B. Your project is right on track to achieve the budget at completion.

    C. You need to produce $1.10 worth of effort for every $1.00 spent to achieve the budget at completion.

    D. You need to speed up the schedule but slow down the spending.

11. Which of the following is an example of work performance information?

    A. Reserve analysis

    B. Activity cost estimates

    C. Project funding requirements

    D. Schedule variance

Answers

This section contains the answers to the questions for the "Exercises" and "Chapter review" sections in this chapter.

Exercises

1. (A) You are the project manager on a project to build 10 identical offices. You expect to spend $50,000 per office to complete the work and take 20 months to finish. You are 12 months into the work and have completed five offices and spent $310,000 in total. Use this information to calculate the following:

    A. **Budget at completion (BAC):** 10 offices × $50,000 each = $500,000
    B. **Actual cost (AC):** You have spent $310,000 in total so this is your actual cost.
    C. **Planned value (PV):** You are 12 months into a 20-month work program, so you planned to have created value equivalent to 12/20, or 60%, of your total planned value, or budget at completion. Therefore, your planned value (PV) is $500,000 × 60% = $300,000.
    D. **Earned value (EV):** You have built five offices, each with a value to you of $50,000, so your earned value is 5 × $50,000 = $250,000.
    E. **Cost variance (CV):** CV = EV − AC: $250,000 − $310,000 = −$60,000
    F. **Cost performance index (CPI):** CPI = EV/AC: $250,000/$310,000 = 0.81
    G. **Schedule variance (SV):** SV = EV − PV: $250,000 − $300,000 = −$50,000
    H. **Schedule performance index (SPI):** SPI = EV/PV: $250,000/$300,000 = 0.83
    I. Estimate at completion (EAC)
        1. **EAC= BAC/CPI:** $500,000/0.81 = $617,283.95
        2. **EAC = AC + ETC:** $310,000 + $307,283.95 = $617,283.95
        3. **EAC = AC + (BAC − EV):** $310,000 + ($500,000 − $250,000) = $560,000
        4. **EAC = AC + ((BAC−EV)/(CPI × SPI)):** $310,000 + (($500,000 − $250,000)/(0.81 × 0.83)) = $681,857.80
    J. **Estimate to complete (ETC):** The estimate to complete answer will depend on which estimate at completion figure you choose to use in the formula ETC = EAC − AC. If you use the estimate at completion (EAC) from the BAC/CPI formula, the answer is $307,283.95.

K. Variance at completion (VAC): The variance at completion answer will depend on which estimate at completion you choose to use in the formula VAC = BAC − EAC. If you use the estimate at completion (EAC) from the BAC/CPI formula, the answer is −$117,283.95.

L. To-complete performance index (TCPI): The to-complete performance index answer will depend on whether your target is your budget at completion (BAC) or the estimate at completion (EAC), and if it is the estimate at completion (EAC), it will depend on which formula you use to calculate that. The following example uses BAC/CPI to calculate EAC.

1. TCPI for EAC = (BAC − EV)/(EAC − AC) = 0.81
2. TCPI for BAC = (BAC − EV)/(BAC − AC) = 1.31

(B) Based on the information gained from the calculations you have performed, how is the project performing in terms of both cost and time?

Based on the information calculated, the project is over budget because the cost variance (CV) is negative and the cost performance index (CPI) is less than 1. The project is behind schedule, because the schedule variance (SV) is negative and the schedule performance index (SPI) is less than 1.

2. (A) You are the project manager on a project to complete 15 miles of road. Your approved budget for the project is $930,000, and you have forecast that the project will take 35 weeks to complete. You are 13 weeks into the project, and have constructed seven miles of road at a cost of $58,000 per mile. Use this information to calculate the following:

A. Budget at completion (BAC): $930,000

B. Actual cost (AC): You have built seven miles of road at a cost of $58,000 so your actual cost is 7 × $58,000 = $406,000.

C. Planned value (PV): You are 13 weeks into a 35-week work program, so you planned to have created value of 13/35, or 37%, of your total planned value, or budget at completion. Therefore, your planned value (PV) is $930,000 × 37% = $344,100.

D. Earned value (EV): You are building 15 miles of road for $930,000, so each mile of road has a value of $930,000/15 = $62,000. You have built seven miles of road each with a value to you of $62,000, so your earned value is 7 × $62,000 = $434,000.

E. Cost variance (CV): CV = EV − AC: $434,000 − $406,000 = $28,000

F. **Cost performance index (CPI): CPI = EV/AC:** $434,000/$406,000 = 1.07

G. **Schedule variance (SV): SV = EV – PV:** $434,000 – $344,100 = $89,900

H. **Schedule performance index (SPI): SPI = EV/PV:** $434,000/$344,100 = 1.26

I. Estimate at completion (EAC)

1. **EAC = BAC/CPI:** $930,000/ 1.07 = $869,158.88
2. **EAC = AC + ETC:** $406,000 + $464,158.88 = $870,158.88
3. **EAC = AC + (BAC – EV):** $406,000 + ($930,000 – $434,000) = $902,000
4. **EAC = AC + ((BAC – EV)/(CPI × SPI)):** $406,000 + (($930,000 – $434,000)/(1.07 × 1.26)) = $773,407.41

J. **Estimate to complete (ETC):** The estimate to complete answer will depend on which estimate at completion figure you choose to use in the formula ETC = EAC – AC. If you use the estimate at completion (EAC) from the BAC/CPI formula, the answer is $463,158.88.

K. **Variance at completion (VAC):** The variance at completion answer will depend on which estimate at completion you choose to use in the formula VAC = BAC – EAC. If you use the estimate at completion (EAC) from the BAC/CPI formula, the answer is $60,841.12.

L. **To-complete performance index (TCPI):** The to-complete performance index answer will depend on whether your target is your budget at completion (BAC) or the estimate at completion (EAC), and if it is the estimate at completion (EAC), it will depend on which formula you use to calculate that. The following example uses BAC/CPI to calculate EAC.

1. TCPI for EAC = (BAC – EV)/(EAC – AC) = 1.07
2. TCPI for BAC = (BAC – EV)/(BAC – AC) = 0.95

(B) Based on the information gained from the calculations you have performed, how is the project performing in terms of both cost and time?

Based on the information from the earned value calculations, the project is ahead of schedule because the schedule variance (SV) is positive and the schedule performance index (SPI) is greater than 1. The project is also under budget because the cost variance (CV) is positive and the cost performance index (CPI) is greater than 1.

Chapter review

1. **Correct answer: A**
   A. **Correct:** First plan your approach to cost management, then estimate costs, then determine your budget, then control the costs.
   B. **Incorrect:** Estimate Costs occurs before Determine Budget.
   C. **Incorrect:** Control Costs occurs after Determine Budget.
   D. **Incorrect:** Control Costs occurs after Determine Budget.

2. **Correct answer: C**
   A. **Incorrect:** Activity cost estimates are an output from the Estimate Costs process.
   B. **Incorrect:** The cost baseline is an output from the Determine Budget process.
   C. **Correct:** The cost management plan is the sole output from the Plan Cost Management process.
   D. **Incorrect:** Cost forecasts are an output from the Control Costs process.

3. **Correct answer: D**
   A. **Incorrect:** A description of the accuracy of estimating would be included in the cost management plan.
   B. **Incorrect:** A description of the cost reporting formats to be used would be included in the cost management plan.
   C. **Incorrect:** A description of the units of measure used to estimate costs would be included in the cost management plan.
   D. **Correct:** The dates each activity will occur would be included as part of your project schedule, not the cost management plan.

4. **Correct answer: A**
   A. **Correct:** Analogous estimating uses similar activities from the past and extrapolates from them a likely current cost estimate.
   B. **Incorrect:** Parametric estimating multiplies a known quality by a known dollar amount to arrive at a cost estimate.
   C. **Incorrect:** Three-point estimating takes the weighted average of a most likely, optimistic, and pessimistic cost estimate.
   D. **Incorrect:** Bottom-up estimating aggregates lower-level cost estimates.

5. **Correct answer: D**
   A. **Incorrect:** Analogous estimating uses similar activities from the past and extrapolates from them a likely current cost estimate.
   B. **Incorrect:** Parametric estimating multiplies a known quality by a known dollar amount to arrive at a cost estimate.
   C. **Incorrect:** Three-point estimating takes the weighted average of a most likely, optimistic, and pessimistic cost estimate.
   D. **Correct:** Bottom-up estimating aggregates lower-level cost estimates up to higher levels to arrive at a total project cost estimate.

6. **Correct answer: C**
   A. **Incorrect:** The contingency reserve is for known unknowns on the project.
   B. **Incorrect:** The funding limit reconciliation is an output from the Determine Budget process.
   C. **Correct:** The management reserve is available for truly unforeseen costs that arise on a project and is controlled by senior management.
   D. **Incorrect:** Cost aggregation is the technique of adding up lower-level costs to obtain higher-level cost estimates.

7. **Correct answer: B**
   A. **Incorrect:** The project would need a CPI less than 1 and an SPI less than 1 to be over budget and behind schedule.
   B. **Correct:** A CPI less than 1 and an SPI greater than 1 indicate that the project is over budget and ahead of schedule.
   C. **Incorrect:** The project would need a CPI greater than 1 and an SPI less than 1 to be under budget and behind schedule.
   D. **Incorrect:** The project would need a CPI greater than 1 and an SPI greater than 1 to be under budget and ahead of schedule.

8. **Correct answer: C**
   A. **Incorrect:** $70,000 is the budget at completion.
   B. **Incorrect:** You would arrive at this figure if you reversed the calculation for cost performance index (CPI).
   C. **Correct:** If you calculate the cost performance index (CPI) first by dividing the earned value (EV) by the actual cost (AC), then divide the budget at completion (BAC) by the cost performance index (CPI), this is the answer you get.
   D. **Incorrect:** This is the answer you get if you add the earned value (EV) to the actual cost (AC).

9. **Correct answer: C**
   A. **Incorrect:** There is a variance at completion, according the formula VAC = BAC − EAC.
   B. **Incorrect:** This is the answer you arrive at if you calculate estimate at completion (EAC) incorrectly.
   C. **Correct:** Variance at completion (VAC) equals budget at completion (BAC) minus estimate at completion (EAC), which is -$4 468.08.
   D. **Incorrect:** If you got this answer, you probably guessed or used the wrong equation.

10. **Correct answer: C**
    A. **Incorrect:** A to-complete performance index (TCPI) of 1.1 is a bad thing and means you need to work faster or more efficiently to achieve your goal of either budget at completion (BAC) or estimate at completion (EAC).
    B. **Incorrect:** A to-complete performance index (TCPI) of 1.1 shows that the project is not on track.
    C. **Correct:** A to-complete performance index (TCPI) of 1.1 means that you have to work harder or more efficiently to achieve the goal of the budget at completion (BAC).
    D. **Incorrect:** A to-complete performance index (TCPI) of 1.1 means that you must pay attention to both schedule and spending, but neither one is in a good position because the index is greater than 1.

11. **Correct answer: D**
    A. **Incorrect:** Reserve analysis is the process of determining and monitoring contingency and management reserves.
    B. **Incorrect:** Activity cost estimates are an output of the Estimate Costs process.
    C. **Incorrect:** Project funding requirements are an output of the Determine Budget process.
    D. **Correct:** Schedule variance, cost variance, schedule performance index, and cost performance index are all examples of work performance information.

CHAPTER 6

Quality management

This chapter focuses on the topic of project quality management. Project Quality Management, like the other knowledge areas, begins with a process of planning that produces a quality management plan. It then has an executing process, Perform Quality Assurance, which is focused on defining and checking the quality of the processes in the project. It also has a monitoring and controlling process, Control Quality, which is focused upon defining and inspecting the quality of the project deliverables.

You may need to pay particular attention in this chapter to those activities and the range of different quality tools that are described because many of them may be new to you.

> ### The PMBOK® Guide processes
>
> **Project Quality Management knowledge area**
>
> The three processes in the Project Quality Management knowledge area are:
>
> - Plan Quality Management (Planning process)
> - Perform Quality Assurance (Executing process)
> - Control Quality (Monitoring and Controlling process)

Domain tasks in this chapter:

- Plan Quality Management process:
  - 2.8 Develop a quality management plan based on the project scope and requirements, in order to prevent the occurrence of defects and reduce the cost of quality.
- Perform Quality Assurance process:
  - 3.3 Implement the quality management plan using the appropriate tools and techniques, in order to ensure that work is being performed according to required quality standards.
- Control Quality process:
  - 4.3 Ensure that project deliverables conform to the quality standards established in the quality management plan by using appropriate tools and techniques (e.g., testing, inspection, control charts), in order to satisfy customer requirements.

What is project quality management?

Project quality management is focused upon the processes of developing a quality management plan, defining and checking particular processes that affect the entire project, and inspecting the quality of project deliverables. The general process of quality management in the PMBOK® Guide is aligned to the International Organization for Standardization (ISO) guide to quality management. Therefore, if you have experience with the standards, you will find this section easier to understand.

Let's start with the formal definition of what *quality* is. It is defined as the degree to which a set of inherent characteristics fulfills requirements. You should remember this definition because it may be different from how you define quality. It has two key elements: the first is a defined set of observed characteristics, which are then measured against the second element, a predefined set of requirements. The closer these two elements are, the higher the level of quality. As a result of defining the characteristics of quality and the requirements that will be met, you are seeking to satisfy customer and stakeholder expectations. The responsibility for establishing a professional approach to quality management within an organization, and within a project, lies with management.

In addition to the exact definition of what quality is, there are some basic foundational concepts of quality management that you must be aware of.

A key foundational concept of the approach to quality management is that, generally speaking, it costs less to prevent a mistake than it does to correct a mistake. This concept of prevention over inspection informs much of the approach to quality management. You should always assume that you have the ability to prevent mistakes rather than spend time and money correcting them once they are discovered. In addition to costing time and money to fix mistakes, poor quality will result in the client not accepting the product, and therefore it can also adversely affect your reputation.

You need to be aware that quality management is not something that happens only once; it is ongoing throughout the life of the project, and it is iterative. Not only is quality management highly iterative, like other project management processes, one of its central elements is the concept of *continuous improvement*, or *kaizen*. Continuous improvement is an iterative process of always seeking to improve your approach to, and results obtained from, quality management processes, and has the goal of improving the quality of the project processes as well as the project deliverables.

EXAM TIP

Kaizen is a loose Japanese translation of the term *continuous improvement*. So in the exam, if you find either term, you will know what it means.

Precision and *accuracy* are two separate terms; you will need to be aware of the definition of each. Precision relates to how tightly clustered results are. The closer the results are, the more precise the measurements being taken are. Accuracy, on the other hand, refers to how close the results are to the actual value. An example to illustrate the concepts would be a shooting target and 10 shots taken at the target. Accuracy would refer to how close the shots are to the bullseye, which is the intended target. Precision would refer to how tightly grouped the 10 shots are, no matter how close to the bullseye they are. If they are tightly grouped, then they demonstrate a high level of precision. Obviously, the preferred mix is high degrees of both accuracy and precision.

In your workplace, you may use the two terms *quality* and *grade* interchangeably. However, for the purposes of the exam, it is important that you realize that they are actually quite distinct concepts. Quality is defined as the degree to which a set of inherent characteristics fulfills requirements. Grade, on the other hand, refers to the amount of features that a particular product has. For example, there are several manufacturers that choose different brands to indicate the difference between low-grade and high-grade products. The products themselves are manufactured to the same quality standards, but some have fewer features or are of a lower grade, than others.

Most people know *just in time* as an inventory control system in which suppliers provide materials just before they are required. It is often seen as an efficient way to manage organizational finances because it does not require funds to be tied up in stock or materials being stored. However, just in time (JIT) can also be used as a quality management approach; the absence of materials in stock forces an organization to maintain a high level of quality because it cannot depend on simply going to its warehouse for more stock when poor quality is produced.

Total quality management (TQM) is a particular approach to quality management that means that everybody within an organization takes responsibility for quality within the organization or project. It is led by management, and everyone at all levels of the organization is expected, encouraged, and trained to participate in constantly improving all aspects of quality.

Six Sigma is a particular approach to quality management that offers credentials such as green belt and black belt. Six Sigma practitioners are focused upon reducing quality defects to as close to zero as possible.

> **Real world**
>
> When I was working in the telecommunications industry, we had to build telephone networks reliable enough that when someone dialed the emergency number for police, ambulance, or fire, it would connect 99,999 times out of every 100,000 attempts. This was known as *five nines* reliability; that is, 99.999 percent of the time it had to work. This is an example of a Six Sigma approach.

> **NOTE DEMING, JURAN, AND QUALITY MANAGEMENT**
>
> Much of the modern history of the profession of quality management is rooted in the seminal works of William Edwards Deming. It was Deming who, through his approach to quality management, contributed greatly to the rise of the post–World War II Japanese economy based on competing on quality. Deming is also known for his collaboration with Walter Shewart in producing and refining the Plan-Do-Check-Act cycle, which forms the basis not only of quality management but also of the profession of project management. At the same time that Deming was influencing Japanese industry, Joseph Juran was also working the same area and is most well known for his approach to quality as a management activity, the Pareto analysis, and the cost of quality analysis. If you want to know more about quality management, I highly recommend reading the work of these researchers.

Plan Quality Management

> **MORE INFO PLAN QUALITY MANAGEMENT**
>
> You can read more about the Plan Quality Management process in the PMBOK® Guide, 5th edition, in Chapter 8, section 8.1. Table 6-1 identifies the process inputs, tools and techniques, and outputs.

TABLE 6-1 Plan Quality Management process

Inputs	Tools and techniques	Outputs
▪ Project management plan ▪ Stakeholder register ▪ Risk register ▪ Requirements documentation ▪ Enterprise environmental factors ▪ Organizational process assets	▪ Cost-benefit analysis ▪ Cost of quality ▪ Seven basic quality tools ▪ Benchmarking ▪ Design of experiments ▪ Statistical sampling ▪ Additional quality planning tools ▪ Meetings	▪ Quality management plan ▪ Process improvement plan ▪ Quality metrics ▪ Quality checklists ▪ Project documents updates

The Plan Quality Management process is a planning process with a range of outputs including, most importantly, the *quality management plan*. Similar to the other planning documents, the quality management plan will guide your efforts in defining and controlling the quality of both the project processes and the deliverables. It will form a subsidiary plan to the overall project management plan. Another important output from the Plan Quality Management process is the process improvement plan, which is also a subsidiary of the project management plan and details how you will define and continuously improve all the processes on your project.

The Plan Quality Management process covers the following domain task:

- 2.8 Develop a quality management plan based on the project scope and requirements, in order to prevent the occurrence of defects and reduce the cost of quality.

Inputs

The Plan Quality Management process uses some or all of the following inputs as part of the development of the quality management plan for the project.

Project management plan

The distinct elements of the project management plan that will be useful in developing your own quality management plan are the scope, schedule, and cost baselines, because they contain useful information against which to measure quality. The project management plan is an output from the Develop Project Management Plan process.

Stakeholder register

Given that the purpose of quality management is to deliver processes and products that meet customer and stakeholder expectations, the stakeholder register—which describes stakeholders, their interest in the project, the impact they have on the project, and their expectations in relation to the project generally and quality specifically—can be considered a very important input into the Plan Quality Management process.

The stakeholder register is an output from the Identify Stakeholders process in the Stakeholder Management knowledge area.

Risk register

The risk register documents and assesses specific risks that may have an impact upon any quality management issues and decisions you are making. The risk register is an output from the Identify Risks process in the Risk Management knowledge area.

Requirements documentation

Given that the definition of quality is the degree to which a set of inherent characteristics fulfills requirements, it is important to use the requirements documentation as an input because it describes and documents the requirements. Requirements documentation is an output from the Collect Requirements process in the Scope Management knowledge area.

Enterprise environmental factors

Particular enterprise environmental factors that may assist with the development of your quality management plan include any external local or broader government regulations pertaining to quality specifications, and any other industry rules or guidelines.

Real world

One of the key enterprise environmental factors affecting the quality management plans that I have worked on are external standards that different products and deliverables must meet. These are often set by industry organizations or government departments and may change during the duration of your project. Local governments may set building or manufacturing quality standards or health and safety standards, or industry or professional bodies may set employment standards. There are many examples of external enterprise environmental factors relating to quality. If you are getting accredited as an ISO 9001 compliant organization or obtaining the PMP® credential because it is a government or industry requirement for you to work as a project manager, this is an example of an enterprise environmental factor at work.

Organizational process assets

Organizational process assets that may be important inputs into the development of your quality management plan include relevant organizational policies and guidelines relating to the organization's approach and expectations of quality, and any historical information or lessons learned from previous projects relating to quality.

Tools and techniques

The following tools and techniques are available to be used to develop the inputs into this process in order to produce the quality management plan.

Cost-benefit analysis

Cost-benefit analysis is used as a tool in the Plan Quality Management process because you need to look at the costs of meeting quality requirements, which generally increase as you seek to improve the quality and avoid re-work and decreasing stakeholder satisfaction. The pursuit of quality is always a trade-off between the costs involved and the benefits obtained and, therefore, using cost-benefit analysis is an important tool for producing a quality management plan.

Cost of quality

Cost of quality considers the total cost of quality over the life of the product, which is well beyond the life of the project and examines the cost of low quality, the subsequent warranty claims, any negative effect on brand or reputation, and loss of future work.

EXAM TIP

Cost of quality is mirrored by, and sometimes referred to as, cost of poor quality. Whatever the term used, it is the concept of assessing what the implications are for producing, or not producing, quality products far beyond the life of the project.

Seven basic quality tools

The catchall phrase, *seven basic quality tools*, refers to the graphical representation of tools used to measure, assess, and determine causes of quality issues. They are a convenient and graphical way to represent what can often be quite complex text-based or numerical information to allow quick communication and assessment of quality issues.

EXAM TIP

Each of the seven basic quality tools refers to a particular type of diagram.

The *cause-and-effect diagram*, which is also called the *Ishikawa* or *fishbone diagram*, is used to describe a known defect and assess the variety of possible causes. It enables you to consider multiple causes for a single problem. Figure 6-1 shows a cause-and-effect diagram with one level of analysis done. You start by identifying a particular defect, then look at all the possible causes of that defect and, if you want, you can also go on to seek further root causes of each identified cause. After you have identified the potential causes, you can then use more quantifiable analysis, such as counting the number of times that cause is responsible for the defect, and come up with a prioritized list of causes.

EXAM TIP

This is one of those instances where there are multiple terms that mean the same thing in the exam. This diagram may be referred to as the cause-and-effect, Ishikawa, or fishbone diagram.

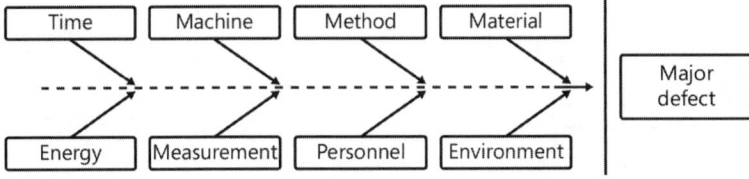

FIGURE 6-1 This type of diagram is known as a cause-and-effect, Ishikawa, or fishbone diagram.

Flowcharts are a convenient way to show the flow of information, or the sequence of steps, in a particular process. Figure 6-2 shows an example of a flowchart.

Plan Quality Management **CHAPTER 6** **235**

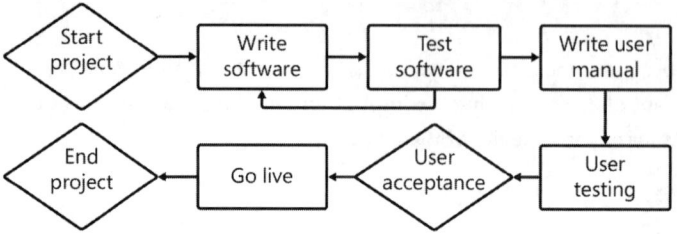

FIGURE 6-2 A flowchart is a clear way to show many types of processes.

Real world

Each shape used in a flow chart has a specific meaning attached to it. For example, the rectangle shape refers to a process, and the diamond shape refers to a decision point. Each and every shape used has a different meaning so that you can quickly look at the flowchart and get information about it very fast.

EXAM TIP

In the exam you may notice the acronym *SIPOC* used. If so, then it is referring to a particular type of flowchart used for documenting the flow of goods and information between suppliers and customers. The acronym *SIPOC* stands for *Suppliers, Inputs, Process, Outputs, and Customers*.

Checksheets are a convenient way to document the activities that must be done and provide a way of checking that they have been done. Checksheets are sometimes called tally sheets. Figure 6-3 shows an example of a checksheet.

Activity	Status	Date
Produce first draft of quality management plan	Closed	4/8/14
Submit first draft for team feedback	Open	4/12/14
Finalize quality management plan	Not yet started	
Distribute quality management plan	Not yet started	

FIGURE 6-3 Checksheets are useful for listing activities and tracking their status.

EXAM TIP

The difference between a checksheet and a checklist is that a checksheet documents what is to be done, whereas a checklist documents what has been done. Additionally, a checksheet is a tool whereas a checklist is an input or output.

A *Pareto diagram* is a way of using a histogram to document the frequency of particular events in descending order and then adding up the cumulative percentage of the quality defects in order to assess which subset of defects causes the greatest amount of problems. The purpose of this Pareto analysis is to focus your attention and energy upon those 20 percent of problems that are causing 80 percent of the issues. Figure 6-4 shows an example of a Pareto diagram.

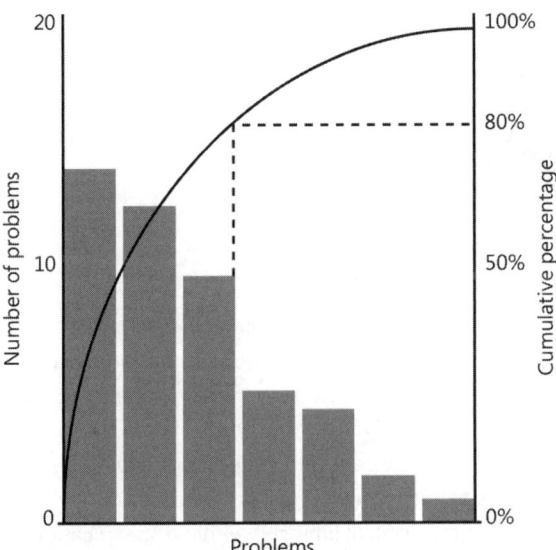

FIGURE 6-4 A Pareto diagram allows you to focus on the 20 percent of the problems that are causing 80 percent of the issues.

NOTE PARETO PRINCIPLE

Joseph Juran first used the term *Pareto principle* to refer to what is now more commonly referred to as the 80:20 rule. It was called the Pareto principle because in the early part of the 20th century an economist by the name of Wilfried (or Vilfredo, if you are Italian) Pareto observed that 80 percent of the land in Italy was owned by 20 percent of the people. This 80:20 rule has come to be used in a wide variety of disciplines to describe any situation where a small amount of a population is responsible for a lot of the observations made.

Histograms, or bar charts, are a simple way of representing frequency, or occurrence, of particular events. Figure 6-5 shows an example of a histogram.

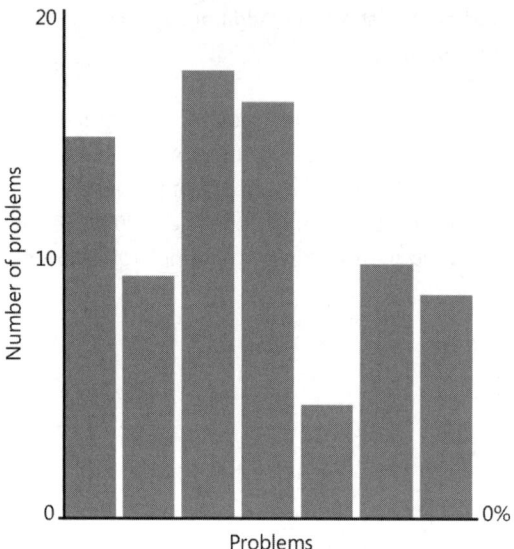

FIGURE 6-5 A histogram is also known as a bar chart.

 Control charts are an effective way of recording data and determining whether or not a manufacturing process is still in control or is about to go out of control. Information is gathered and plotted on the control chart around an expected average, or mean. Using standard deviations, you can then set the upper and lower control limits, three standard deviations either side of the mean. Beyond these *control limits*, the upper and lower *specification limit* is set. Any data point that appears outside of the specification limit will not be accepted by the customer. Any data point that appears outside of the control limit but within a specification limit indicates that the process is out of control and investigation should commence immediately as to the cause of this. Any information or data gathered within the control limits is acceptable.

 The exception to this rule is when seven consecutive data points appear on either side of the mean. This is called the *rule of seven*, and it is statistically improbable that you will get seven consecutive points on either side of the mean. An easy way to understand the rule of seven is to consider a coin being tossed and the chances of it landing with either a head or tail facing up. You would expect a random distribution of heads and tails, but would consider it statistically improbable that you would get seven consecutive heads or tails. If you do note seven consecutive data points above or below the mean, it signals that you should investigate the cause, because the process may be about to go out of control. Figure 6-6 shows an example of a control chart. Note the appearance of seven consecutive data points above the mean, indicating the rule of seven.

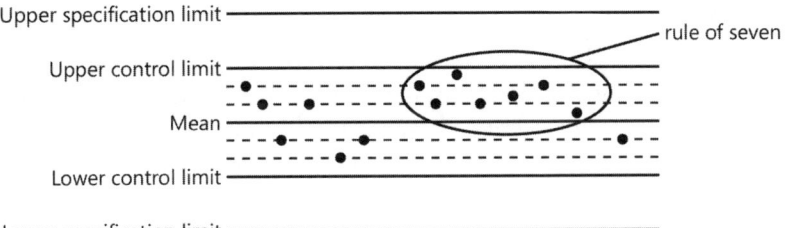

FIGURE 6-6 A control chart can tell you whether or not a process is going out of control.

Scatter diagrams simply record the relationship between two variables in graphical form. Figure 6-7 shows an example of the scatter diagram.

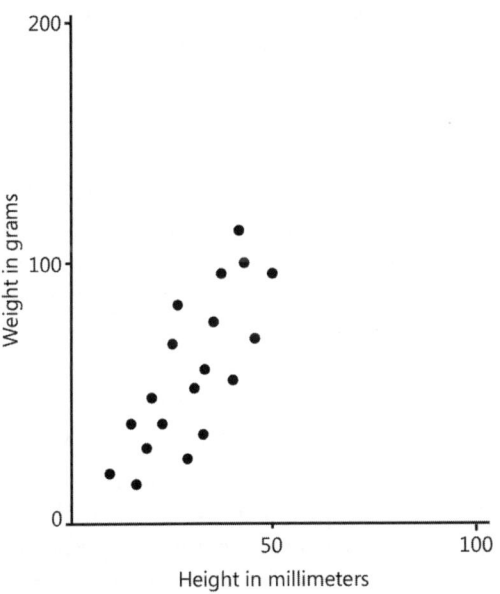

FIGURE 6-7 A scatter diagram shows the relationship between two variables on an x and y axis.

> **NOTE ISHIKAWA AND QUALITY MANAGEMENT**
>
> The development of the seven basic quality tools is attributed to the work of Kaoru Ishikawa, a Japanese professor and one of the great quality management advocates and developers.

Benchmarking

Benchmarking is the process of comparing your quality practices to those of other projects or other organizations and seeing how you compare.

Plan Quality Management   **CHAPTER 6**   **239**

Design of experiments

Design of experiments is a tool to assist with developing useful and reliable experiments to test quality. Key considerations in the design of experiments include the identification and control of variables and the understanding of how the testing process itself may affect observed outcomes. A well-designed experiment will be able to independently control different variables to determine which ones are causing problems.

Statistical sampling

Statistical sampling is used when there are either too many quality checks to do, or quality checks involve destructive testing. For example, you may want to do testing on lines of software code being written, but there are more than 100,000 lines of code. Instead of checking every line of code, you could simply select 100 lines of code and check them for accuracy. One constraint of statistical sampling is the assumption that the result from a small population is representative of the entire population.

Additional quality planning tools

In addition to the tools and techniques listed previously are *additional quality planning tools* that can be used to plan your particular approach to quality management. These include brainstorming and nominal group techniques, both of which you have seen as tools and techniques in other areas. In addition to these two tools, you can use force field analysis, affinity diagrams, process decision program charts, interrelationship diagrams, tree diagrams, prioritization matrices, activity network diagrams, and matrix diagrams. All of these quality management and control tools are covered in more depth in the Perform Quality Assurance process.

Another quality planning tool that can be used is failure mode and effect analysis (FMEA). FMEA is a widely used technique that examines the consequence of failure in any part of the system and uses those observations to ensure that failure does not actually occur or that, if it does, the impact is anticipated and mitigated. In this process you could use this tool to determine the likely effect of failure of the product and prepare to ensure that it doesn't happen.

Meetings

Meetings are a useful way to bring together members of the project team and other stakeholders so that they can contribute to the development of the quality management plan.

Outputs

After applying the appropriate tools and techniques to the selected inputs, the Plan Quality Management process has the following outputs.

Quality management plan

The Plan Quality Management process has the *quality management plan* as its primary output. Similar to other management plans, the quality management plan provides a description of the overall approach to quality management, guidelines for all project processes and how they will be implemented, and a description of expected quality, testing, and inspection of project deliverables. The detail contained in the quality management plan will reflect the size and complexity of the project, and it should be updated and reviewed regularly to ensure that it is still accurate. The quality management plan is then a key input into the Perform Quality Assurance and Control Quality processes.

EXAM TIP

According to the PMBOK® Guide, every project should have a quality management plan. The quality management plan itself can be formal and documented, or it can be an informal set of policies and guidelines. It will reflect the size and complexity of the project but should always be done.

Real world

Many organizations, after they reach a certain size, are able to appoint a particular person to manage quality within the organization and also within projects. I believe that this is an important step for an organization to take because a focus on quality is often a much more important element than a focus on cost. A simple way to remember why quality is so important to your project is that if you don't care about quality your competitor will. I remember on one large project I was managing, I wanted the quality of the project to be the legacy that I left rather than coming in under budget and ahead of time. We still focused on measuring cost and time performance, and we did come in under budget and ahead of time, but the element I was most proud of was the extra quality that we were able to deliver.

Process improvement plan

The *process improvement plan* is a subsidiary of the project management plan that focuses specifically on analyzing quality processes and describing ways in which continuous improvement can be applied to these processes. The process improvement plan is used as an input into the Perform Quality Assurance process.

EXAM TIP

Note that the process improvement plan is not used as an input into the Control Quality process because its primary focus is on project processes, which are the main focus of the Perform Quality Assurance process.

Quality metrics

The development and documentation of specific *quality metrics* are necessary in order to be able to measure progress against what has been planned. The more specific the quality metric, the more detailed the measurement and reporting can be. The most common quality metrics developed include performance measurements relating to schedule, cost, defects, failure, and reliability. The quality metrics are used as an input into the Perform Quality Assurance and the Control Quality processes.

Quality checklists

The *quality checklist* is a specific type of checklist that you can use to determine whether defined steps of the quality process have been performed. A quality checklist should both document the steps to be taken and incorporate acceptance criteria from the project requirements and scope baseline. The quality checklists are used as an input into the Control Quality process.

Project documents updates

The specific project documents that may be updated as a result of completing the Plan Quality Management process are the stakeholder register and the responsibility assignment matrix.

> **Quick check**
>
> 1. What is the key function of a quality management plan?
> 2. What does it mean when a data point is outside the control limit but within the specification limit?
> 3. Under what circumstances would you use statistical sampling?
>
> **Quick check answers**
>
> 1. The key function of a quality management plan is to describe your particular approach to quality in your project, the relevant policies, your approach to quality assurance and process improvement, and quality metrics and how you will control and measure quality of the project deliverables.
> 2. If a data point is outside of the control limit but within the specification limit, this indicates that the process may be out of control and requires immediate investigation.
> 3. You would use statistical sampling to determine the level of quality when there are too many samples to investigate individually or when investigating the quality of the sample involves destructive testing.

Perform Quality Assurance

> **MORE INFO** **PERFORM QUALITY ASSURANCE**
>
> You can read more about the Perform Quality Assurance process in the PMBOK® Guide, 5th edition, in Chapter 8, section 8.2. Table 6-2 identifies the process inputs, tools and techniques, and outputs.
>
> **TABLE 6-2** Perform Quality Assurance process
>
> | Inputs | Tools and techniques | Outputs |
> |---|---|---|
> | - Quality management plan
- Process improvement plan
- Quality metrics
- Quality control measurements
- Project documents | - Quality management and control tools
- Quality audits
- Process analysis | - Change requests
- Project management plan updates
- Project documents updates
- Organizational process assets updates |

The Perform Quality Assurance process is an executing process that uses the quality management plan for guidance and is focused on implementing processes across the entire project and checking that these processes are being adhered to and continuously improved. The processes that you define and audit won't only be processes around quality management. For example, you could decide to have a process about setting up and choosing the right projects, culminating in a signed project charter, all of which would be covered in the Develop Project Charter process. The Perform Quality Assurance process will check that you have followed this process correctly.

The Perform Quality Assurance process covers the following domain task:

- 3.3 Implement the quality management plan using the appropriate tools and techniques, in order to ensure that work is being performed according to required quality standards.

> **EXAM TIP**
>
> A simple way to remember the difference between quality assurance and quality control is that quality assurance uses audits and focuses on processes, whereas quality control focuses on inspections and the project deliverables.

> **Real world**
>
> The ISO 9000 standard is an excellent example of quality assurance at work. This standard requires processes to be in place and regular audits to occur to ensure that the processes are being followed. The standard does not focus on the quality of the product being produced. Thus, there are some unscrupulous companies that have ISO 9000 accreditation but produce low-quality products.

Inputs

The Perform Quality Assurance process uses some or all of the following inputs.

Quality management plan

The quality management plan is obviously a key input into the Perform Quality Assurance process because it guides how the process will be carried out. The quality management plan is an output from the Plan Quality Management process.

Process improvement plan

The process improvement plan is used as an input into this process because it is focused on detailing the processes that will be put in place, and how they will be checked and improved. The process improvement plan is an output from the Plan Quality Management process.

Quality metrics

The quality metrics are specific variables that can be measured as part of checking whether or not you are implementing and adhering to particular quality processes. The quality metrics are an output from the Plan Quality Management process.

Quality control measurements

Quality control measurements are generated by the Control Quality process and are used in the Perform Quality Assurance process to analyze and evaluate the particular quality standards relating to the quality processes that are supposed to have been followed.

Project documents

The specific types of *project documents* that are useful as inputs into the Perform Quality Assurance process are any documents relating to requirements or quality processes, or those that define stakeholder expectations.

> **EXAM TIP**
>
> Did you notice that neither environmental enterprise factors nor organizational process assets are used as inputs into this process?

Tools and techniques

The following tools and techniques are used upon the inputs to deliver the Perform Quality Assurance process outputs.

Quality management and control tools

The Perform Quality Assurance process uses all of the tools and techniques featured throughout the Quality Management knowledge area. It uses the seven basic tools of quality already covered in the Plan Quality Management process, as well as statistical sampling, inspection, benchmarking, design of experiments, cost-benefit analysis, and cost of quality.

 Additionally, there are the following *seven new quality tools* and techniques that can be used. Each of these additional quality management and control tools is used to document and represent particular measurements taken during the Perform Quality Assurance process.

> **NOTE SEVEN NEW QUALITY TOOLS**
>
> The seven new quality tools come from the book *Seven New QC Tools: Practical Applications for Managers* by Yoshinobu Nayatani, Toru Eiga, Ryoji Futami, and Hiroyuki Miyagawa (Productivity Press, 1994). Both these seven and the basic seven tools all represent data in graphical format for easy interpretation and communication.

 Affinity diagrams, or KJ Methods diagrams, can be used during a brainstorming session to create cause-and-effect diagrams because they group data in logical relationships. Figure 6-8 shows an example of an affinity diagram.

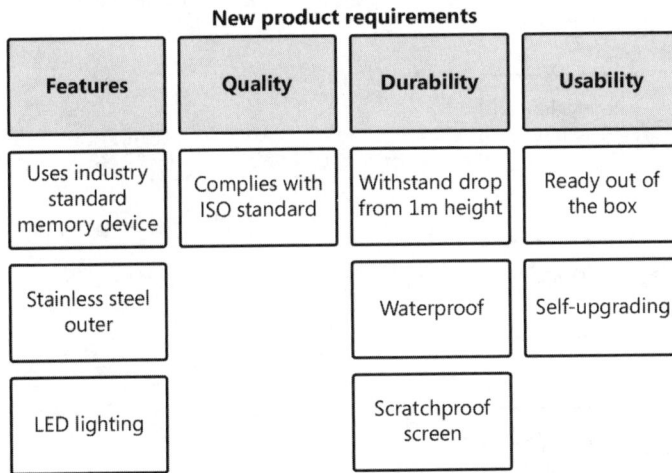

FIGURE 6-8 An affinity diagram groups data in logical relationships.

A *process decision program chart* (PDPC) displays in graphical and hierarchical form the steps in a process in order to understand the issues that may positively or negatively affect the sequence of activities to reach a goal. In this sense, it is a cross between a flowchart and a breakdown structure. Figure 6-9 shows an example of a process decision program chart.

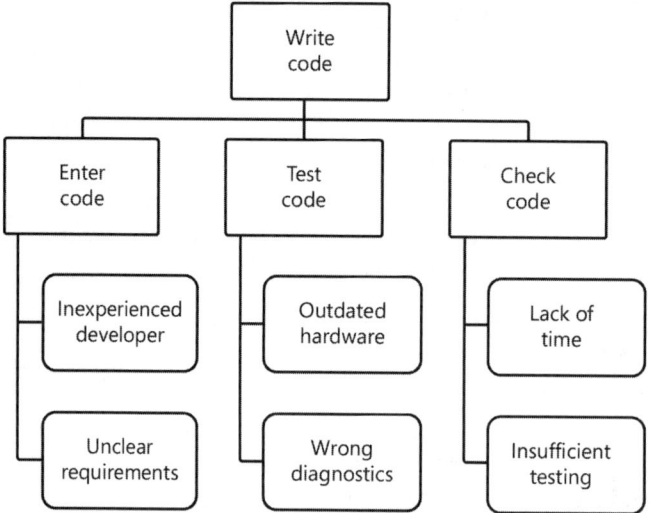

FIGURE 6-9 A process decision program chart can show steps in a process and the issues that might affect those steps.

 Interrelationship digraphs are useful to graphically show multiple cause-and-effect relationships between various factors. Figure 6-10 shows an example of an interrelationship digraph.

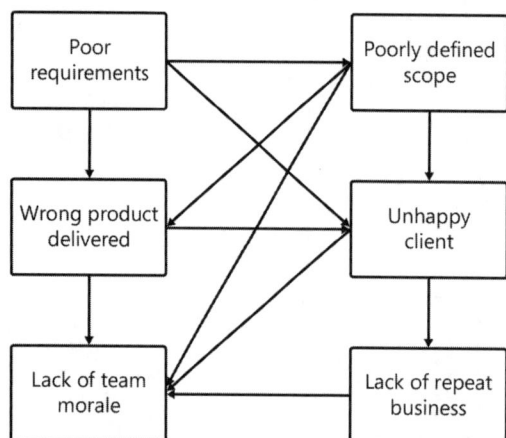

FIGURE 6-10 An interrelationship digraph shows cause and effect relationships among multiple factors.

A *tree diagram* is a very useful graphical representation of hierarchical relationships and parent-to-child relationships. You have seen the tree diagram as a work, risk, and organizational breakdown structure. In managing quality, the tree diagram can be used to describe nested relationships between steps in the quality assurance process. Figure 6-11 shows an example of a tree diagram.

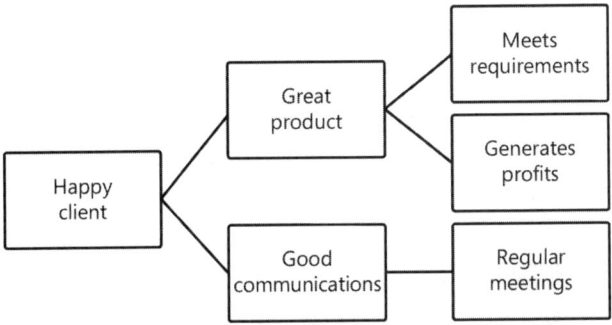

FIGURE 6-11 A tree diagram is useful for showing hierarchical relationships.

 Prioritization matrices use a variety of weighted criteria to determine the priority of quality actions to enable the key issues to be determined. Figure 6-12 shows an example of a prioritization matrix.

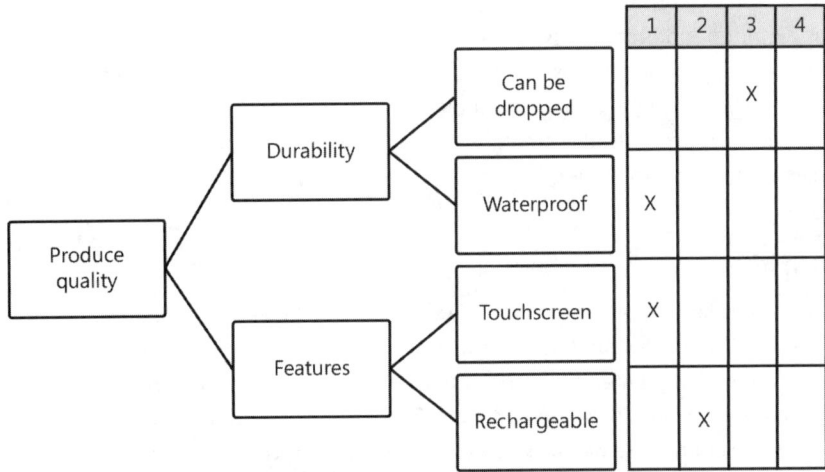

FIGURE 6-12 A prioritization matrix is used to determine the priority of quality actions.

 Activity network diagrams are used to show relationships between activities to be completed. You have already seen these diagrams used in the managing the project schedule and determining the tasks on the critical path with activity-on-node (AON) diagrams. In quality management, they are used to show the sequence of, and interrelationships between, various quality activities. Figure 6-13 shows an example of an activity network diagram.

Perform Quality Assurance **CHAPTER 6** **247**

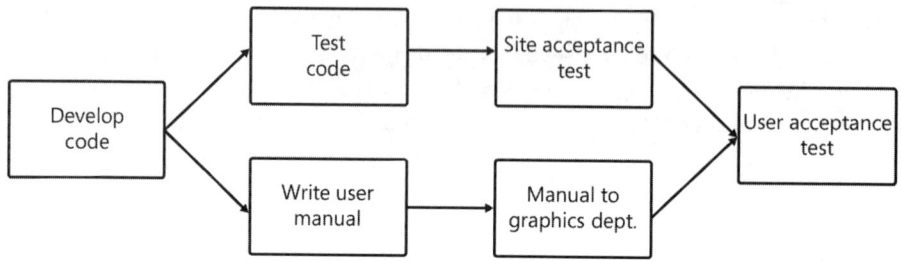

FIGURE 6-13 An activity network diagram shows relationships between activities.

 Matrix diagrams are used to indicate whether a relationship exists between two variables. Figure 6-14 shows an example of a matrix diagram.

	Customer A	Customer B	Customer C	Customer D
Durability	High	High	Moderate	High
Features	Low	High	High	Moderate
Price	Low	Moderate	Low	High
Size	Small	Med	Large	Small

FIGURE 6-14 A matrix diagram shows whether a relationship exists between two variables.

Quality audits

 A *quality audit* is an independent process that seeks to determine whether the defined project processes are being carried out as per the quality management plan. Quality audits are carried out by using the quality management plan as a guideline and should generally be done by people not involved with the project who can independently assess whether the required processes are in place and whether or not they are being followed.

> **Real world**
>
> On one particularly large project that I was managing, we had it as part of the contract that regular audits would occur on all our project processes. We had an independent assessor appointed from one of the large global auditing companies, and every six months, that assessor would show up in person and spend several days requesting proof that we had processes in place and that we followed those processes correctly. The assessor would then produce a report detailing both areas of compliance and noncompliance. As the project manager, it was my responsibility to ensure that any areas of noncompliance were addressed promptly. The costs for completing these quality audits were part of the overall project budget.

EXAM TIP
Wherever you find an audit being used as a tool, it will be checking that processes are in place, that they are being followed as per the requirements, and that any deviation from the processes is documented and dealt with. Audits do not check the quality of any deliverables or products.

Process analysis

Process analysis takes the steps in the process improvement plan and executes them in order to identify and improve existing processes.

Outputs

The Perform Quality Assurance process produces some or all of the following outputs.

Change requests

The change requests are generated as a result of information discovered by audits and process analysis that then requires changes to be considered as per the agreed change management process. The change requests are used as an input into the Perform Integrated Change Control process.

Project management plan updates

The specific parts of the project management plan that may be updated as a result of the Perform Quality Assurance process are the quality management plan, the process improvement plan, the schedule management plan, and the cost management plan.

Project documents updates

The specific project documents that may be updated as a result of the Perform Quality Assurance process include such things as the project-specific policies and guidelines relating to preparation and execution of processes.

Organizational process assets updates

The specific organizational process assets that may be updated as a result of the Perform Quality Assurance process are any templates, policies, or guidelines relating to quality audits, and training and appointment of independent auditors.

> ✓ **Quick check**
>
> 1. What is the difference between quality assurance and quality control?
> 2. What is it that both the seven basic quality tools and the seven new quality tools are attempting to do?
> 3. What is the purpose of a quality audit?
>
> **Quick check answers**
>
> 1. The difference between quality assurance and quality control is that quality assurance is focused upon the processes of the project, whereas quality control is focused upon the project deliverables.
> 2. All of the quality tools described seek to take what can be quite complex text, verbal, or numerical information and collate and present it in an easy-to-understand graphical form.
> 3. The purpose of the quality audit is to independently check that required processes are in place and are being followed.

Control Quality

> **MORE INFO** **CONTROL QUALITY**
>
> You can read more about the Control Quality process in the PMBOK® Guide, 5th edition, in Chapter 8, section 8.3. Table 6-3 identifies the process inputs, tools and techniques, and outputs.

TABLE 6-3 Control Quality process

Inputs	Tools and techniques	Outputs
- Quality management plan - Quality metrics - Quality checklists - Work performance data - Approved change requests - Deliverables - Project documents - Organizational process assets	- Seven basic quality tools - Statistical sampling - Inspection - Approved change requests review	- Quality control measurements - Validated changes - Validated deliverables - Work performance information - Change requests - Project management plan updates - Project documents updates - Organizational process assets updates

The Control Quality process is a monitoring and controlling process that uses the quality management plan and checks that the project deliverables will meet the documented requirements and stakeholder expectations.

The Control Quality process covers the following domain task:

- 4.3 Ensure that project deliverables conform to the quality standards established in the quality management plan by using appropriate tools and techniques (e.g., testing, inspection, control charts), in order to satisfy customer requirements.

Inputs

The following inputs are used in the Control Quality process.

Quality management plan

The quality management plan is a critical input into the Control Quality process because it sets out and describes how this process will occur. The quality management plan is an output from the Plan Quality Management process

Quality metrics

The quality metrics are a required input into the Control Quality process because they describe the attributes that are expected in the project deliverables and how these attributes will be measured. Quality metrics are an output from the Plan Quality Management process

Quality checklists

Quality checklists provide a documented and structured list of steps, attributes, and guidelines that can be used to ensure that all the quality control work is done correctly. Quality checklists are an output from the Plan Quality Management process.

Work performance data

In order to measure whether or not the project is being delivered as per the desired quality requirements, you will need the work performance data. Work performance data is an output from the Direct and Manage Project Work process.

Approved change requests

Approved change requests can have an impact upon the project deliverables and may require modifications, such as defect repairs, and thus are an important input into this process. Approved change requests are an output from the Perform Integrated Change Control process.

Deliverables

Given that the control quality process is focused upon checking the quality of the deliverables, having the deliverables as an input into the process can be viewed as quite critical.

Project documents

The specific types of project documents that may be used as inputs into this process include any contracts that specify deliverable requirements and attributes, and any relevant quality audit reports.

Organizational process assets

The specific organizational process assets that can assist with the Control Quality process are any guidelines, processes, policies, or blank templates that the organization has relating to quality control.

Tools and techniques

The following tools and techniques of this process are able to be used upon the separate inputs to deliver the process outputs.

Seven basic quality tools

The seven basic quality tools have been described in detail earlier in the Plan Quality Management process. They can be used in the Control Quality process to graphically represent and analyze any of the data gathered.

EXAM TIP

By now you have probably realized that the seven basic quality tools can be used as a tool or technique in any of the quality management processes.

Statistical sampling

As part of completing a check on the quality of the deliverables, you may choose to use statistical sampling as a tool or technique, if the number of deliverables is too great to test each one individually, or if the sampling would involve destructive testing.

Inspection

Inspection is one of the key tools of the control quality process. It is a physical examination of the deliverable to measure and determine whether it complies with the required standards. As a result of completing inspection, you will generally produce a variety of measurements indicating compliance or noncompliance with the required deliverable standards.

Approved change requests review

It is one thing to have approved change requests; it is another to ensure that they have been implemented as per the change documentation. The way to do this is via the use of an *approved change requests review*.

> **Real world**
>
> I have often seen assumptions made about approved change requests being carried out. Some people seem to think that simply because the change has been requested, considered, and a decision made to approve it, that the change is automatically carried out. Unfortunately, this isn't always the case. This is one of the reasons you should record all change requests, their status, any decisions made, and any required follow-up actions on your change request log. Furthermore, assigning someone to be responsible for not only carrying out the change but checking that it was carried out correctly is an important factor in making sure all your approved change requests are implemented.

Outputs

The major outputs from the Control Quality process are the following.

Quality control measurements

The quality control measurements are the documents that you produce as a result of carrying out the Quality Control processes and activities. They should be concise and presented in an appropriate format for easy communication, presentation, and tracking. Quality control measurements go on to be used as an input into the Perform Quality Assurance process.

Validated changes

The validated changes output involves checking that the approved change requests, and any required modifications, have been inspected and comply with the change request documentation. Validated changes go on to be used as an input into the Monitor and Control Project Work process.

EXAM TIP

The process of validation occurs after the process of verification. The process of validation is an important one to understand, as well as how it is different from the process of verification. Verification is about confirmation that the product, service, or result produced complies with agreed specifications or requirements. It is primarily an internal process performed by the delivering organization prior to submitting the product, service, or result for validation, which involves the customer as well. Validation also involves a check that the product, service, or result meets stakeholder requirements. Verification occurs before validation.

Validated deliverables

You will recall that deliverables were one of the inputs into the Control Quality process. After they have been subjected to the appropriate tools and techniques to check that they conform to the required standards, and if they are accepted, *validated deliverables* will become an output from the process. Validated deliverables go on to be used as an input into the Validate Scope process.

Work performance information

You will recall that work performance data was used as an input into the Control Quality process. This is the raw data collected about work performance to date. After it is subjected to the appropriate tools and techniques, it becomes work performance information. Work performance information then goes on to be used as an input into the Monitor and Control Project Work process.

Change requests

As a result of carrying out the Control Quality process, there may be a reason to raise a change request to deal with defect repairs, required modifications, or corrective or preventive actions. All change requests should be prepared, submitted, and assessed as per the documented and defined change control process. Change requests go on to be used as an input into the Perform Integrated Change Control process.

Project management plan updates

Specific parts of the project management plan that may be updated as a result of the Control Quality process are the quality management plan and the process improvement plan.

Project documents updates

Specific project documents that may be updated as a result of the Control Quality process are any relevant quality standards or agreements relating to any aspect of the quality management process.

Organizational process assets updates

Specific organizational process assets that may be updated include lessons learned databases and any blank templates for any aspect of the organization's quality management process.

Quick check

1. What is the main focus of the Control Quality process?
2. Which three inputs into the Control Quality process are further refined and are outputs from the same process in a more refined state?
3. How does inspection differ from audits?

Quick check answers

1. The main focus of the Control Quality process is to check that the project deliverables meet the required and documented standards. This is in contrast to the Perform Quality Assurance process, which is focused on the processes of the project.
2. The three inputs are approved change requests, deliverables, and work performance data. Each is used as an input into the Control Quality process and after the application of appropriate tools is further refined so that approved change requests become validated changes, deliverables become validated deliverables, and work performance data becomes work performance information.
3. Inspection is one of the tools of the Control Quality process and involves physical examination of the deliverables produced by the project to determine whether they conform to the required standards. On the other hand, audits are used as a tool in the Perform Quality Assurance process to check whether processes are in place and that they are being followed correctly.

Exercise

The answer for this exercise is located in the "Answers" section at the end of this chapter.

1. Match up the quality tool on the left with the description on the right.

Quality tool	Definition
1. Histogram	a. A diagramming technique showing relationships and sequencing of quality activities so you can determine the critical path of activities
2. Tree diagram	b. A diagram that groups similar concepts under relevant headings that can then be used to generate cause-and-effect diagrams
3. Pareto diagram	c. A process of comparing your quality activities to those of other projects or organizations
4. Flowchart	d. A standardized and documented list of quality activities to be carried out and confirmed as completed
5. Prioritization matrix	e. A graphical representation of data points measured against an expected mean with control limits set three standard deviations either side of the mean
6. Affinity diagram	f. A diagram showing the sequence of steps within a process using standardized shapes to represent different activities
7. Matrix diagram	g. A bar chart showing frequency of discrete data
8. Scatter diagram	h. A graphical representation showing multiple cause-and-effect relationships between various factors
9. Ishikawa diagram	i. A diagrammatic way of representing effects and their possible causes
10. Activity network diagram	j. A diagram that shows how multiple variables interact with each other
11. Control chart	k. A diagram showing the individual and cumulative frequency of events to determine which 20% of events cause 80% of the problems
12. Process decision program chart	l. A diagram showing the weighted scoring of variables to determine the priority of activities
13. Interrelationship digraph	m. A graphical way to show the hierarchy of steps in a process in order to understand the sequence of activities to reach a goal
14. Benchmarking	n. A diagram with data points showing the correlation between two variables, each represented on a vertical or horizontal axis
15. Statistical sampling	o. A process of testing that takes a small population and extrapolates the result to a larger population
16. Checksheet	p. A diagram of hierarchical relationships and parent-to-child relationships

Chapter summary

- The Quality Management knowledge area is focused upon the development of the quality management plan, then using this quality management plan to carry out quality assurance to check the project processes, and quality control to check the project deliverables.
- The quality tools and techniques are common to all three quality processes.
- The Plan Quality Management process produces the quality management plan for the project, which sets out guidelines and processes for checking both the processes and deliverables for the project.
- The Perform Quality Assurance process focuses on checking that processes are in place and are being followed. It uses a variety of tools and techniques, including audits.
- The Control Quality process is focused upon checking project deliverables and approved change requests for conformity to requirements.

Chapter review

Test your knowledge of the information in Chapter 6 by answering these questions. The answers to these questions, and the explanations of why each answer choice is correct or incorrect, are located in the "Answers" section at the end of this chapter.

1. What are the three processes in the Quality Management knowledge area?
   A. Control Quality, Perform Quality Assurance, Plan Quality Management
   B. Plan Quality Management, Control Assurance, Perform Quality Control
   C. Perform Quality Control, Determine Quality, Plan Quality Management
   D. Plan Quality Management, Assure Quality, Control Quality

2. Which of the following is *not* one of the seven basic quality tools?
   A. Benchmarking
   B. Scatter diagram
   C. Control chart
   D. Pareto diagram

3. What does it mean if a single data point appears above the upper specification limit on a control chart?

   A. The process is in control and the customer is happy.

   B. The process may be out of control, and consideration should be given to checking the process in the near future.

   C. A single data point outside the upper specification is okay. You only need to be concerned if there are seven consecutive data points outside either of the specification limits.

   D. The process is out of control and requires immediate action, because the customer will not accept any deliverables outside the specification limit.

4. What is the best definition of quality?

   A. Quality is whatever the customer says is right.

   B. Quality is the degree to which a product can be used for its intended purpose.

   C. Quality is the degree to which a set of inherent characteristics fulfills requirements.

   D. Quality is the number features that the product has.

5. What is the best definition of the principle of kaizen?

   A. Defining quality processes and checking that they are being used

   B. Continuously improving

   C. Checking the quality of the product

   D. Having a quality management plan

6. If you are considering the impact of potential future warranty claims as part of your quality management plan, what are you considering?

   A. Cost of quality

   B. Quality assurance

   C. Benchmarking

   D. Prevention over inspection

7. If you are using a diagram to determine the potential causes of quality issues, what would you be using?

   A. Control chart

   B. Histogram

   C. Checksheet

   D. Fishbone diagram

8. If you are testing and measuring a small sample and extrapolating those results to be indicative of a total population, what tool or technique are you using?

    A. Benchmarking

    B. Statistical sampling

    C. Design of experiments

    D. Brainstorming

9. If you are conducting an audit to check whether processes are being followed correctly, what process are you involved in?

    A. Plan Quality Management

    B. Control Quality

    C. Perform Quality Assurance

    D. Perform Quality Audit

10. What are the variables and allowable variations called that should be measured as part of the Perform Quality Assurance and Control Quality processes?

    A. Quality control measurements

    B. Quality checklists

    C. Quality metrics

    D. Cost of quality

11. Which quality process uses inspection as a tool or technique?

    A. Plan Quality Management

    B. Control Quality

    C. Perform Quality Assurance

    D. Perform Quality Inspection

Answers

This section contains the answers for the "Exercises" and "Chapter Review" sections in this chapter.

Exercises

1. Match up the quality tool on the left with the description on the right.

Quality tool	Definition
1. Histogram	g. A bar chart showing frequency of discrete data
2. Tree diagram	p. A diagram of hierarchical relationships and parent-to-child relationships
3. Pareto diagram	k. A diagram showing the individual and cumulative frequency of events to determine which 20% of events cause 80% of the problems
4. Flowchart	f. A diagram showing the sequence of steps within a process using standardized shapes to represent different activities
5. Prioritization matrix	l. A diagram showing the weighted scoring of variables to determine the priority of activities
6. Affinity diagram	b. A diagram that groups similar concepts under relevant headings that can then be used to generate cause-and-effect diagrams
7. Matrix diagram	j. A diagram that shows how multiple variables interact with each other
8. Scatter diagram	n. A diagram with data points showing the correlation between two variables, each represented on a vertical or horizontal axis
9. Ishikawa diagram	i. A diagrammatic way of representing effects and their possible causes
10. Activity network diagram	a. A diagramming technique showing relationships and sequencing of quality activities so you can determine the critical path of activities
11. Control chart	e. A graphical representation of data points measured against an expected mean with control limits set three standard deviations either side of the mean
12. Process decision program chart	m. A graphical way to show the hierarchy of steps in a process in order to understand the sequence of activities to reach a goal
13. Interrelationship digraph	h. A graphical representation showing multiple cause-and-effect relationships between various factors
14. Benchmarking	c. A process of comparing your quality activities to those of other projects or organizations
15. Statistical sampling	o. A process of testing that takes a small population and extrapolates the result to a larger population
16. Checksheet	d. A standardized and documented list of quality activities to be carried out and confirmed as completed

Chapter review

1. **Correct answer: A**
   - **A. Correct:** The three processes in the Quality Management knowledge area are Plan Quality Management, Perform Quality Assurance, and Control Quality.
   - **B. Incorrect:** There is no process called Control Assurance.
   - **C. Incorrect:** There is no process called Perform Quality Control or Determine Quality.
   - **D. Incorrect:** There is no process called Assure Quality.

2. **Correct answer: A**
   - **A. Correct:** Benchmarking is a tool that is used in quality management, but it is not one of the seven basic quality tools.
   - **B. Incorrect:** The scatter diagram is one of the seven basic quality tools, which include cause-and-effect diagrams, flowcharts, checksheets, Pareto diagrams, histograms, control charts, and scatter diagrams.
   - **C. Incorrect:** The control chart is one of the seven basic quality tools.
   - **D. Incorrect:** The Pareto diagram is one of the seven basic quality tools.

3. **Correct answer: D**
   - **A. Incorrect:** A data point outside the specification limit does not mean that the process is in control; the customer will not pay for anything that is outside the specification limit.
   - **B. Incorrect:** A data point outside the specification limit indicates that the process is definitely out of control.
   - **C. Incorrect:** A single data point outside the specification limit indicates that something is wrong. The rule of seven applies to consecutive data points within the control limits.
   - **D. Correct:** Any data point outside the specification limits indicates that the process is out of control and should be investigated immediately.

4. **Correct answer: C**
   - **A. Incorrect:** Quality doesn't necessarily relate to what the customer says is right, unless what the customer says is right is captured in the requirements.
   - **B. Incorrect:** Quality is more than the degree to which a product can be used for its intended purpose.
   - **C. Correct:** Quality is the degree to which a set of inherent characteristics fulfills requirements—remember this definition for the exam.
   - **D. Incorrect:** The amount of features product has, or does not have, refers to grade, not quality.

5. **Correct answer: B**
   A. **Incorrect:** Defining quality processes and checking that they are being used is the process of quality assurance.
   B. **Correct:** Kaizen is the loose Japanese translation of the term *continuously improving*.
   C. **Incorrect:** Checking the quality of the product is the process of quality control.
   D. **Incorrect:** Have a quality management plan is the process of planning quality management.

6. **Correct answer: A**
   A. **Correct:** Cost of quality, mirrored by the cost of low quality, considers the impacts of quality decisions over the entire life of the product.
   B. **Incorrect:** Quality assurance is the process of defining processes and checking that you are using them as planned.
   C. **Incorrect:** Benchmarking is the process of comparing your efforts against other projects or organizations.
   D. **Incorrect:** Prevention over inspection is a key concept of the overall approach to project quality management.

7. **Correct answer: D**
   A. **Incorrect:** A control chart maps data points against an expected mean, upper and lower control limits set three standard deviations either side of the mean, and upper and lower specification limits.
   B. **Incorrect:** A histogram, or bar chart, is a graphical way of representing frequency or total occurrences of data.
   C. **Incorrect:** A checksheet is a standardized description of processes, steps. and information to be completed or gathered.
   D. **Correct:** A fishbone diagram, also called an Ishikawa diagram or cause-and-effect diagram, shows a graphical representation of potential causes of a particular event.

8. **Correct answer: B**
   A. **Incorrect:** Benchmarking is the process of comparing your efforts against other projects or organizations.
   B. **Correct:** Statistical sampling means taking a small sample of a total population for testing and then assuming those results apply to the entire population. It is used when there are simply too many tests to be done or when the testing involves destructive testing.

- **C. Incorrect:** Design of experiments is the process of designing, and considering the implications and effects upon the results, of experiments to determine quality.
- **D. Incorrect:** Brainstorming is a technique that gathers a group of people together and encourages them to think laterally about a particular issue.

9. **Correct answer: C**
   - **A. Incorrect:** Plan Quality Management is the initial planning process and delivers the quality management plan.
   - **B. Incorrect:** Control Quality uses inspection to determine the quality of the product.
   - **C. Correct:** Perform Quality Assurance is the process of establishing processes and checking that you are following them by conducting audits.
   - **D. Incorrect:** Perform Quality Audit is a made-up process name.

10. **Correct answer: C**
    - **A. Incorrect:** Quality control measurements are the measurements taken that allow you to assess whether quality metrics are being achieved.
    - **B. Incorrect:** A quality checklist is a standardized description of processes, steps, and information to be completed or gathered.
    - **C. Correct:** Quality metrics are defined during the Plan Quality Management process and set out the variables and allowable variations that should be measured as part of the Perform Quality Assurance and Control Quality processes.
    - **D. Incorrect:** Cost of quality considers the impact of quality decisions over the entire life of the product.

11. **Correct answer: B**
    - **A. Incorrect:** Plan Quality Management is the initial planning process and delivers the quality management plan. It does not use inspection as a tool or technique.
    - **B. Correct:** The Control Quality process is focused on checking the quality of the product or deliverable and uses inspection as a tool.
    - **C. Incorrect:** Perform Quality Assurance is the process of establishing processes and checking that you are following them by conducting audits. It does not use inspection as a tool or technique.
    - **D. Incorrect:** Perform Quality Inspection is a made-up process name.

CHAPTER 7

Human resource management

This chapter focuses on Project Human Resource Management. Similar to the other knowledge areas, it begins with a planning process, which in this case produces a human resource management plan. It then has three executing processes that focus on carrying out the contents of the human resource management plan. The three executing processes focus on acquiring your project team members, developing your project team members, and managing your project team members.

You may need to pay particular attention in this chapter to the many different theories relating to management, motivation, and development of people, because many of them may be new to you.

> ### The PMBOK® Guide processes
>
> **Project Human Resource Management knowledge area**
>
> The four processes in the Project Human Resource Management knowledge area are:
>
> - Plan Human Resource Management (Planning process)
> - Acquire Project Team (Executing process)
> - Develop Project Team (Executing process)
> - Manage Project Team (Executing process)

EXAM TIP

Did you notice that this knowledge area is the only one without a monitoring and controlling process? This is because the assumption is that functional managers will carry out monitoring and controlling activities associated with human resources, because they generally have final authority over human resources working on your project. Even in a strong matrix structure, although the project manager has authority, the people allocated to the project will eventually go back to the functional manager.

Domain tasks in this chapter:

- Plan Human Resource Management process:
    - 2.5 Develop a human resource management plan by defining the roles and responsibilities of the project team members in order to create an effective project organization structure and provide guidance regarding how resources will be utilized and managed.
- Acquire Project Team, Develop Project Team, and Manage Project Team processes:
    - 3.6 Maximize team performance through leading, mentoring, training, and motivating team members.

What is project human resource management?

Project human resource management is focused upon the processes of developing a human resource management plan, which allows you to identify how you will recognize which people you want as part of your project team, when you will require them and for how long, and how you will get those people, develop those people, and reward, motivate, and manage those people. It covers all the aspects relating to your project team, including you as a project manager.

> **Real world**
>
> I have always found the term "human resource" to be a little too technical and clinical for my liking. Machines are resources, and there is an element of expected decay, obsolescence, and replacement with the term. People are not resources. So, if you are having the same trouble, I suggest using the much friendlier term "project people management" for this section. Of course, for the exam, you will use "project human resource management."

> **EXAM TIP**
>
> In considering all the issues and topics relevant to human resource management, there are a host of ancillary topics around interpersonal skills, leadership, ethics, and organizational and motivational theories that you must also know for the exam. This chapter will cover a wide range of topics relating to all these different aspects of project human resource management.

Plan Human Resource Management

> **MORE INFO** **PLAN HUMAN RESOURCE MANAGEMENT**
>
> You can read more about the Plan Human Resource Management process in the PMBOK® Guide, 5th edition, in Chapter 9, section 9.1. Table 7-1 identifies the process inputs, tools and techniques, and outputs.
>
> **TABLE 7-1** Plan Human Resource Management process
>
> | Inputs | Tools and techniques | Outputs |
> |---|---|---|
> | ■ Project management plan
■ Activity resource requirements
■ Enterprise environmental factors
■ Organizational process assets | ■ Organizational charts and position descriptions
■ Networking
■ Organizational theory
■ Expert judgment
■ Meetings | ■ Human resource management plan |

The Plan Human Resource Management process is a planning process with a single output, the human resource management plan.

The Plan Human Resource Management process covers the following domain task:

- 2.5 Develop a human resource management plan by defining the roles and responsibilities of the project team members in order to create an effective project organization structure and provide guidance regarding how resources will be utilized and managed.

Inputs

The Plan Human Resource Management process uses some or all of the following inputs as part of the development of the human resource management plan for the project.

Project management plan

The key elements of the project management plan that will be useful as inputs into the Plan Human Resource Management process are a description of the work to be completed to determine what skills will be required, and elements from the project schedule and schedule management plan, which are useful for determining time constraints. The project management plan is an output from the Develop Project Management Plan process.

Activity resource requirements

Activity resource requirements contain information about the specific activities to be completed and the resources, particularly human resources, needed to complete the work. Activity resource requirements are an output from the Estimate Activity Resources process.

Enterprise environmental factors

The specific enterprise environmental factors that will be useful as inputs into this process are the external organization culture, existing employees, existing organizational employment and personnel policies, and external marketplace conditions affecting availability and cost of hiring people.

Organizational process assets

The specific organizational process assets that may be important inputs into the development of your human resource management plan include any specific organizational policies, process, or guidelines for the recruitment, reward, and retention of people, and any historical information on what has and has not worked on previous projects.

Tools and techniques

The following tools and techniques are available to be used to develop the inputs into this process in order to produce the human resource management plan.

Organizational charts and position descriptions

A foundational concept of the Plan Human Resource Management process is the need to define a role for everyone on the project and define the responsibilities for each role. In order to do this, you can use *organizational charts and position descriptions* to clearly show what roles there are, how they are linked by reporting lines, and what their expected experience, technical skills, duties, and responsibilities are.

Before we go any further, let's focus on describing all the roles that can exist in a typical project. In addition to the individual and defined project team member roles, the primary roles in the world of project management are the project manager, sponsor, functional manager, program manager, and portfolio manager.

The *project manager* is one of the key roles in the successful delivery of any product, service, or result because this role takes full responsibility for the project. The project manager works closely with the program manager because the project manager's project may be part of a program; she also works closely with the portfolio manager because the project will be part of a portfolio. The role of project manager is obviously central to the profession of project management. The project manager is the person assigned to lead the project team and take responsibility for the delivery of the project's objectives. This is different from the work of a *functional manager*, who takes responsibility for a functional unit within an organizational structure. In some instances, a project manager may report to a functional manager, but at other times the role may report to a program or portfolio manager.

EXAM TIP

Not all organizations have program managers or portfolio managers, nor should they. Those roles are generally reserved for large, mature organizations. For the exam, unless you are specifically told otherwise in the question, you should, however, assume that the scenario has all three roles in an organization.

A competent project manager must have a wide range of skills and experience to be successful. These include specific skills for the industry in which the manager is working, and general management skills; the manager must also demonstrate a high degree of expertise in and knowledge about project management, the ability to self-motivate and achieve results through high performance, and great personal effectiveness while leading the project. It is key to the success of the project manager that this person not only possess the right technical skills but also the right interpersonal skills, which will be covered in a later section.

EXAM TIP

In the exam, you must always assume that the role of the project manager is proactive and in control of the project. The project manager takes responsibility entirely for the project, which may differ from your experience.

> **Real world**
>
> In my opinion, the easiest way to describe the role of the project manager is to simply replace the title "project manager" with "general manager of a project." We all know what a general manager does, and a project manager really is the general manager of a project and must take the same senior role.

In addition to the role of project manager, there are also the roles of *project coordinator* and *project expeditor*. A project coordinator has less power and authority than a project manager, and a project expeditor has little or no power and authority.

EXAM TIP

For the exam, look for any project role description that differs on the basis of the amount of power and authority. High levels of both refer to a project manager; mid-levels refer to a project coordinator; and low levels refer to a project expeditor.

The project team is made up of the staff that have been assigned, or recruited, to the project to provide technical skills. It includes at its core the project manager, the direct members of the project team, and also the members of the wider project team. The difference between direct members of the project team and members of the wider project team relate to whether they are assigned full-time or part-time to the project. If you are working within a matrix organizational structure, team members will come from different functional areas. If it is a strong matrix organization, the team members will report solely to the project manager; if it is a weak matrix organization, the team members will still report to the functional managers.

The exact composition of any project team is dependent upon the organizational culture, organizational structure, the scope of work, the geographic location of the work to be done, and the availability of team members. There are four categories of project team. The first is the dedicated project team, where the majority of the team members are working full-time on the project. A second type of project team is the part-time project team, where generally the functional managers have more power and authority and assignment to the project is generally part-time for both the project manager and the project team members. A third type of project team is created from the partnership between two or more organizations who agree to assign staff to the project team. This offers great flexibility and the ability to secure resources and technical experience that any one organization may not have. The fourth and final form of project team is the virtual team, which is increasingly used with the broadening geographical spread of team members throughout the world. Bringing together and getting a virtual team to perform well is a challenge for any project manager and will require special attention to overcome some of the potential obstacles.

> **Real world**
>
> It is increasingly common in the real world that team members are drawn from differing geographical locations. These locations can be different parts of the same city, the same country, or even from different countries. In addition to the problems faced in developing a high-performing team presented by a lack of colocation and face-to-face communication, there are also a number of other problems that can potentially adversely affect the outcome of the project. A project manager working in or with a virtual team needs to be mindful and aware of the potential problems that can arise, and address them early and consistently throughout the life of the project.

A *program manager* leads a program of projects. A program of projects is a group of projects that are linked in some way. They may share resources or they may be contributing to a greater deliverable. The role of the program manager is to manage competing interests between the projects. A *portfolio manager* has responsibility for all the projects an organization is undertaking and is usually in charge of project selection processes to ensure that all projects align with organizational strategy and meet documented financial and nonfinancial criteria. A portfolio of projects includes all projects that an organization is undertaking.

A project *sponsor* is the person responsible for providing the initial statement of work, approving the financial spend on the project, signing the project charter and approving any changes to it, and being the project champion. The person in this role is internal to the organization and will sit on the *project steering committee* or group. The role of the project steering committee or group is to provide high-level support, oversight, and if required, governance.

EXAM TIP

Don't get the roles of the project sponsor and client mixed up. The project sponsor is always internal, whereas the client may be internal or external but is the recipient of the deliverable.

Real world

Many people assume that the client is responsible for financing a project. This isn't true. The client pays the bills after the costs have been incurred. Someone within the organization, usually the project sponsor, must approve the organization's incurring the costs, such as wages or salaries and materials purchased to complete the work, and financing these costs until such time as the client pays the bills.

Figure 7-1 shows the hierarchy of roles from project steering committee down to members of the wider project team.

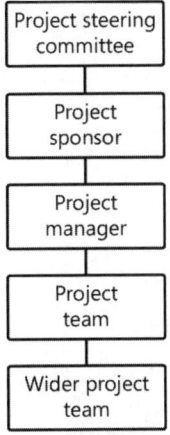

FIGURE 7-1 The descending hierarchy of groups and individuals in a project often starts with the project steering committee at the top.

The functional manager is a role that a project manager needs to be mindful of because the majority of organizations are organized around functional areas, even if they are acting as matrix organizations. The functional manager is usually a general manager or team leader of a particular group of technical experts, and this manager will assign his or her staff members to the project for the duration of the project. The project manager must negotiate with the functional manager for the people and, depending on who has the most power in the relationship, this will affect availability of people for the project. This issue is discussed in more depth in an upcoming section.

Now that the typical roles in an organization have been covered, you can use the organizational charts and position descriptions to help produce the human resource management plan. There are several graphical and text-based formats for doing this. The most popular of these are organizational charts, matrix charts such as the RACI chart, or text-based descriptions, such as those often used for job descriptions.

The *organizational chart* is another example of a breakdown structure such as the work breakdown structure (WBS). It takes high-level concept, in this case the organization, and breaks it down into its component roles. It starts at the top with the chief executive officer (CEO) or general manager, and breaks it down into lower-level roles such as line manager, team leader, team member, and specific technical roles. In addition to using the chart to break down organization-wide roles, you can also use it to break down project roles, in which case you would have the project manager at the top, and lower-level project roles beneath this. Figure 7-2 shows an example of an organization chart.

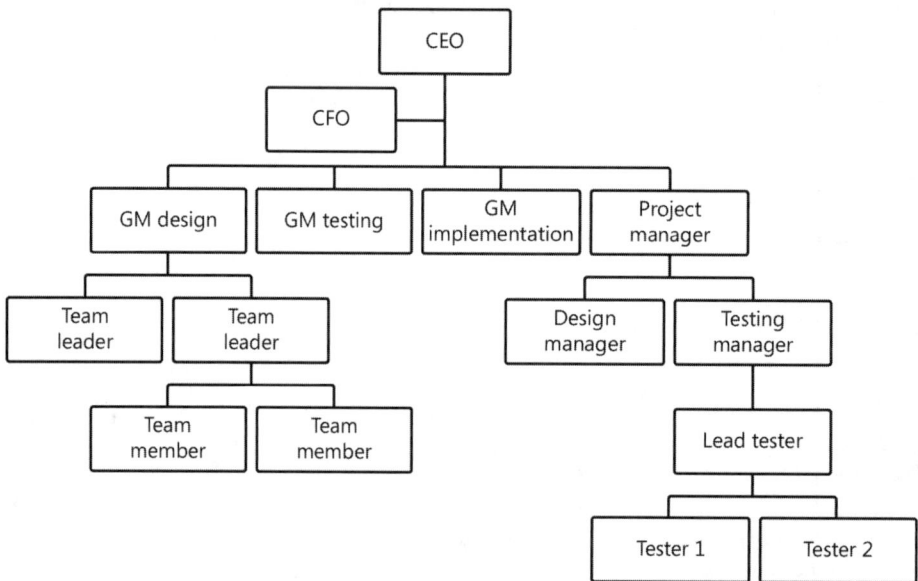

FIGURE 7-2 An organizational chart shows the breakdown of roles in an organization.

Another popular way of displaying not only roles but also the responsibility different roles have is a matrix-based chart called a *RACI chart*. A RACI chart is a type of *responsibility assignment matrix* (RAM). A RACI chart describes who is responsible, who is accountable, who will be consulted, and who will be informed on different activities. The difference between the "responsible" and "accountable" designations is that being responsible for an activity means producing or actually completing the work, whereas being accountable for an activity means having to answer for the work being done or not being done on time. A single person can be both responsible and accountable for an activity, and if your project is large enough to have many team members, you can split the responsibility and accountability as a means of ensuring better management of activities. Figure 7-3 shows an example of a RACI chart.

	Team member			
Activity	David	Thomas	Jayne	Mark
Collect requirements	R/A	C	C	I
Design prototype	C	A	R	
Test		I	R	A

FIGURE 7-3 A RACI chart shows team member responsibility and accountability.

> **Real world**
>
> I have used several forms of the RACI chart on different projects. Some smaller projects simply have an RA chart. I also did some work for a large company that had their own variant, a RASCI chart, with the "S" standing for "Support," to indicate which team members were providing technical support.

Networking

Networking is the action of interacting with, and building relationships with, other people for political and influencing purposes. Networking can be undertaken in both informal and formal ways. Networking is important because getting the people you want, when you want them, will usually involve negotiation with other managers.

> **Real world**
>
> I have always found that networks are a great way to increase your influence and reputation. At the heart of any network connection is a strong personal relationship and reputation. Take time to build genuine relationships, and your networking efforts will pay off more.

Organizational theory

As part of your efforts to produce an appropriate human resource management plan for your project, you will need to have a good grasp of *organizational theory* and how it affects human resource management and project success. The way in which an organization is structured can influence its culture, strategy, personnel recruitment, and the projects it chooses to do. Different organizational structures have different strengths and weaknesses when it comes to successful project management. The main types of organizational structures are the functional organization, the matrix organization, and the projectized organization. The organizational structure is usually demonstrated in the organizational breakdown structure or organization chart.

In a *functional organizational* structure, there is a chief executive officer (CEO), or similar, at the top. Underneath the CEO are general managers, or functional managers, of each functional area. Below the general managers are team leaders. There may also be shared services, such as human resources and finance, directly reporting to the CEO as well. In this sort of organizational structure, staff report directly to the functional manager, who is responsible for assigning them to work or deciding on their remuneration packages and ensuring that they are part of the team; thus, the functional manager has all the power and authority. If an organization wants to undertake a project, generally the project is staffed by members from one functional area, and there can be little cooperation and coordination between the different functional areas. A project manager working in this sort of organizational structure will have great difficulty in obtaining the people and finances needed to complete the project without first getting approval from the functional manager. Figure 7-4 shows an example of a functional organizational structure.

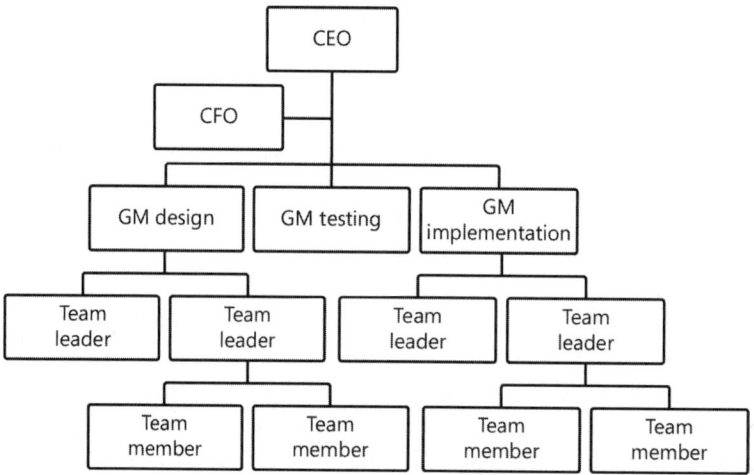

FIGURE 7-4 An organizational chart can be used to show a functional organizational structure.

A *matrix organization* is one in which a functional structure exists, but the organization has decided to do projects by using people and resources from different functional areas. The project manager is assigned a team and access to resources from these different functional areas, and both the project manager and functional manager have power and authority in deciding the allocation and use of people.

   In a *weak matrix* organization, most of the power and authority resides with the functional manager, and due to the low levels of power and authority that the project manager has in a weak matrix organizational structure, the role may more appropriately be described as a project expeditor or project coordinator. In a *strong matrix* organization, most of the power and authority is with the project manager. Between strong and weak forms of the matrix organization is the *balanced matrix*, where power and authority is shared between functional managers and project managers. Figure 7-5 shows an example of a matrix organization with the dotted lines around roles indicating which people are assigned to the project.

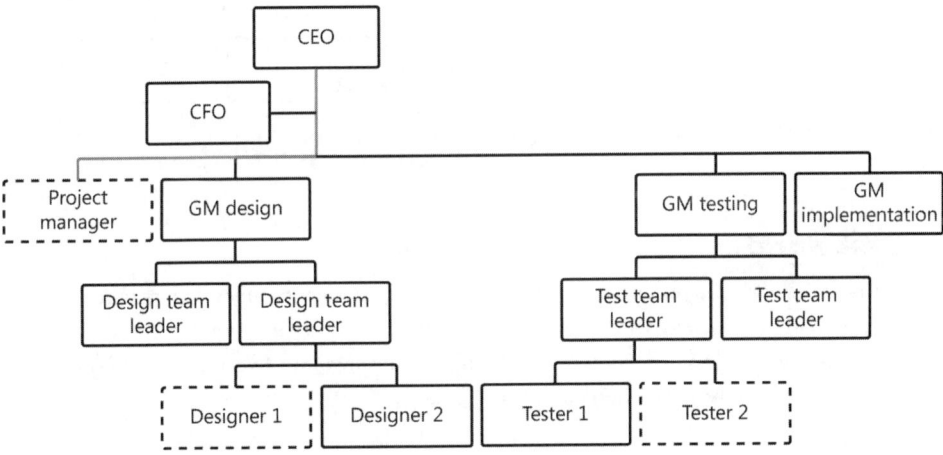

FIGURE 7-5 An organizational chart can show a matrix organizational structure.

   Projectized organizations are organized according to the projects they undertake. In this instance, the project manager acts almost as a functional manager, but instead of having a team of specialists and a functional area reporting to him or her, the project manager has the project team, which may consist of several different technical specialties. In this instance, the project manager acts as general manager of the project and has full power and authority. Figure 7-6 shows an example of a projectized organization.

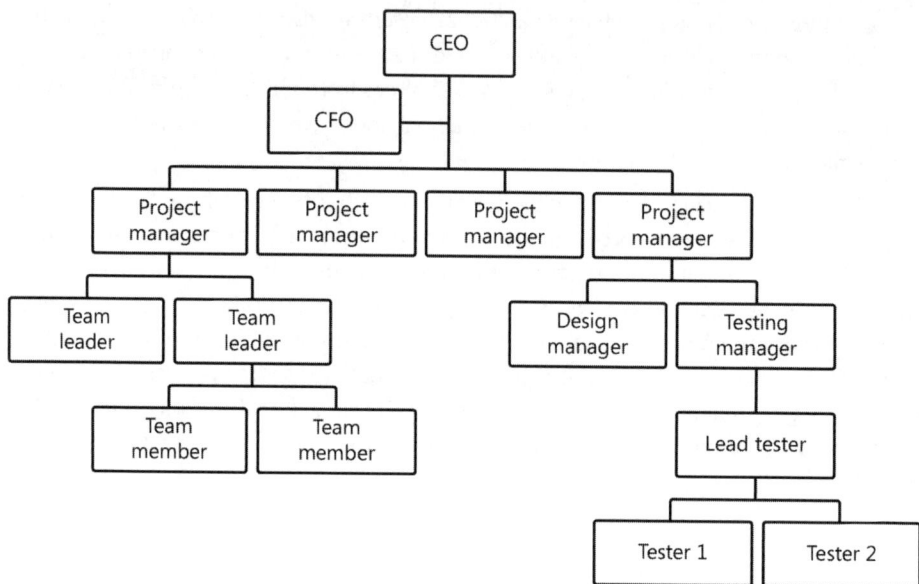

FIGURE 7-6 An organizational chart can show a projectized organizational structure.

> **Real world**
>
> In the real world, you are often going to have to negotiate with functional managers for access to resources and money. Your ability to be a skilled communicator, influencer, and negotiator will come to the fore in this instance to enable you to get the resources you require when you need them.

Table 7-2 shows the allocation of power and authority between functional managers and project managers in the different types of organizational structures.

TABLE 7-2 Organizational structures, authority, and power

Functional	Weak matrix	Balanced matrix	Strong matrix	Projectized
■ Project manager may be part-time and has very little power and authority ■ Functional manager has most authority over people and budget	■ Project manager may be part-time and has low levels of power and authority ■ Functional manager has most authority over people and budget	■ Project manager may be part-time or full-time and has equal levels of power and authority with functional manager ■ Functional manager has equal levels of authority with project manager over people and budget	■ Project manager will be full-time and has more power and authority than functional manager ■ Functional manager has less authority over people and budget than project manager	■ Project manager will be full-time and have high to almost total power and authority ■ Functional manager has very little, if any, authority over people and budget

EXAM TIP

It is important for the exam that you understand the differences in power and authority in each of the different organizational structures. In the absence of any further information provided in the question, any questions in relation to this topic will assume first that you are working in a matrix form of organizational structure, and second that it is a strong matrix.

Expert judgment

Expert judgment from functional managers, current and potential team members, the project sponsor, and other stakeholders will be useful as you put together your human resource management plan.

Meetings

Meetings are a useful way to bring together members of the project team and other stakeholders so they can contribute to the development of the human resource management plan.

Outputs

After applying the appropriate tools and techniques to the selected inputs, the Plan Human Resource Management process has the following outputs.

Human resource management plan

The Plan Human Resource Management process has the human resource management plan as its sole output. Similar to other management plans, this plan provides a description of the overall approach to human resource management, and details specific guidelines on acquiring, developing, training, motivating, rewarding, and managing your project team members. In addition to the text describing all of these aspects, the human resource management plan will also include diagrams such as organizational charts and RACI charts.

An important sub-plan of the human resource management plan is the *staffing management plan*, which describes when and how project team members are to be recruited. The staffing management plan will identify whether project team members are to be recruited from internal or external sources, and the process by which they will be described, contacted, assessed, and appointed.

The human resource management plan is a subsidiary of the project management plan and is used as an input into the three human resource management executing processes. It is also used as an input into the Estimate Costs process because it provides information about personnel costs, and it is also used as an input into the Identify Risks process.

 Quick check

1. What is the purpose of the human resource management plan?
2. What is the primary role of the project sponsor?
3. If you always have to ask the functional manager for permission to use staff to work on your project, what sort of matrix organization are you working in?

Quick check answers

1. The main purpose of the human resource management plan is to guide your actions in identifying, obtaining, rewarding, training, motivating, and managing your project team members.
2. The primary role of the project sponsor is to provide financial support, provide project charter approval, appoint the project manager, and provide political support for the project.
3. In this instance you would be working in a weak matrix because the functional manager has the power and authority.

Acquire Project Team

> **MORE INFO** **ACQUIRE PROJECT TEAM**
>
> You can read more about the Acquire Project Team process in the PMBOK® Guide, 5th edition, in Chapter 9, section 9.2. Table 7-3 identifies the process inputs, tools and techniques, and outputs.
>
> **TABLE 7-3** Acquire Project Team process
>
> | Inputs | Tools and techniques | Outputs |
> |---|---|---|
> | ■ Human resource management plan
■ Enterprise environmental factors
■ Organizational process assets | ■ Preassignment
■ Negotiation
■ Acquisition
■ Virtual teams
■ Multicriteria decision analysis | ■ Project staff assignments
■ Resource calendars
■ Project management plan updates |

The Acquire Project Team process is an executing process that uses the human resource management plan for guidance to check and confirm the availability of project team members and have them assigned to, or recruited to, the project for the period of time their services are required. If you can't get the human resources you require, with the skills you need them to have, at the time you need them, this will greatly affect the chances of project success. Additionally, in acquiring project team members you will need to be aware of any local or national employment legislation, collective bargaining agreements, typical employment contracts, and any other relevant guidelines.

The Acquire Project Team process covers the following domain task:

- 3.6 Maximize team performance through leading, mentoring, training, and motivating team members.

Inputs

The Acquire Project Team process uses some or all of the following inputs.

Human resource management plan

The human resource management plan is obviously a key input into the Acquire Project Team process because it provides a description of how you will carry out acquiring the people that you need for your project team. More specifically, the human resource management plan includes a description of the roles and responsibilities required during the life of the project to complete the project activities, and the project organizational chart showing the number and reporting lines of people on the project team.

One of the most important parts of the human resource management plan to be used as an input into the Acquire Project Team process is the staffing management plan because it specifically addresses how project team members are to be acquired. The human resource management plan is an output from the Plan Human Resource Management process. The staffing management plan is a subsidiary plan of the human resource management plan.

Enterprise environmental factors

The specific types of enterprise environmental factors that will be useful in acquiring your project team are any local government or industry regulations affecting the employment of project personnel. Other enterprise environmental factors may also include general organizational structure issues.

Organizational process assets

The specific types of organizational process assets that will assist you in acquiring your project team members include any relevant organizational policies, processes, and guidelines relating to the acquisition and employment of people. Additionally, historical information and lessons learned from previous projects are also useful organizational process assets.

Tools and techniques

The following tools and techniques are used upon the inputs to deliver the Acquire Project Team process outputs.

Preassignment

Preassignment is the advanced allocation of project team members to your project. This can happen as a result of both internal and external processes in which specific people are assigned to the project as a result of the skills and experience they may have, or because of particular contractual arrangements.

> **Real world**
>
> I've often found that as a general rule, up to half of my project team members are allocated on a preassigned basis due to the particular skills and knowledge they have. This can be quite a good thing because you know that you have people with the right skills allocated to your project from the beginning. There can be a high degree of uncertainty in the process of trying to acquire people for your project via either negotiation with functional managers or by some external recruitment process.

Negotiation

Negotiation for your project team members will occur in several ways. First, you will need to negotiate with functional managers to get the staff you want, when you want them. Your ability to negotiate in the circumstances reflects the power and authority that you have. If you are working in a weak matrix environment, you will have little power and authority, and the allocation of project team members to your project will be at the discretion of the functional manager. However, if you are working in a strong matrix organization, you will have the power and authority to get the project team members you need, when you need them.

The process of negotiation also occurs with external providers of project team members, or during the process of recruiting a project team member and the negotiation of a particular employment contract.

Given the importance of negotiation in acquiring project team members in a timely and cost-effective manner, it is important that you have good negotiation skills.

Acquisition

The term *acquisition* in this instance means an external process of advertising for, interviewing, and negotiating employment contracts with project team members. Often this process is best left to professionals with experience in advertising and recruitment.

Virtual teams

The use of *virtual teams* is becoming increasingly common throughout the world as technology allows people to work together in ways they previously couldn't. These virtual teams can be separated by different floors in building, can be in different cities, or can even be in different countries. The advantages of the virtual team are that it allows you to use the skills and experience of people who may not be able to co-locate in the same area, and also to cater to individual preferences in terms of work hours or work locations. The use of virtual teams is also a legitimate option when a project may incur large travel expenses in order to host face-to-face meetings. A drawback to virtual teams is that it is difficult to maintain effective communication by using any sort of technology, such as e-mail, telephone, or video conference.

Multicriteria decision analysis

The process of acquiring project team members can also use *multicriteria decision analysis* so that you can take into account a variety of criteria in order to make the best decision about who should be selected to work on the project. In this instance, you would choose the criteria that were relevant; these criteria could be such things as cost, experience, and availability. You would give each of these a weight, and then score individual candidates, multiply their scores by the weightings, and arrive at a total score. By ranking each candidate by their total scores, you will be able to determine your preferred candidates.

Outputs

The Acquire Project Team process produces some or all of the following outputs.

Project staff assignments

A key output from the Acquire Project Team process is, of course, the *project staff assignments*. Project staff assignments provide documentation of project team members' names, their roles and responsibilities, contact details, and other relevant information that allows all interested stakeholders to view who is part of the project team, their roles, and how to contact them. The project staff assignments go on to be used as an input into the Manage Project Team and Develop Project Team processes.

Resource calendars

The resource calendars are a useful output from the Acquire Project Team process because they document when people are available to work on the project. At a high level, they will include such things as weekends or public holidays; at a lower and more specific level they will include when personnel actually work according to their individual work agreements, and any known holidays they are taking. The resource calendars go on to be used as an input into the Develop Project Team process, as well as the Estimate Activity Resources, Estimate Activity Durations, Develop Schedule, and Determine Budget processes.

Project management plan updates

The specific parts of the project management plan that may be updated as a result of the Acquire Project Team process are the human resource management plan, and any document affected by the human resource management plan.

Quick check

1. Why is the human resource management plan an important input into the Acquire Project Team process?
2. What is meant by the term "preassignment"?
3. Why are negotiation skills useful during the Acquire Project Team process?
4. What is the advantage gained in using multicriteria decision analysis?

Quick check answers

1. The human resource management plan and the staffing management plan provide specific guidance on how the process of acquiring your project team members will be carried out.
2. Preassignment involves having team members allocated to your project before the project begins as a result of specific skills and experience or as a result of contractual negotiations.
3. Negotiation skills are important because, when you are recruiting project team members, you may have to negotiate with their functional managers or, if you are recruiting team members from the open employment marketplace, you will have to negotiate employment contracts with them directly.
4. Using multicriteria decision analysis allows you to rank prospective team members based upon important attributes to decide who should be recruited.

Develop Project Team

> **MORE INFO** **DEVELOP PROJECT TEAM**
>
> You can read more about the Develop Project Team process in the PMBOK® Guide, 5th edition, in Chapter 9, section 9.3. Table 7-4 identifies the process inputs, tools and techniques, and outputs.
>
> **TABLE 7-4** Develop Project Team process
>
> | Inputs | Tools and techniques | Outputs |
> |---|---|---|
> | - Human resource management plan
- Project staff assignments
- Resource calendars | - Interpersonal skills
- Training
- Team-building activities
- Ground rules
- Co-location
- Recognition and rewards
- Personnel assessment tools | - Team performance assessments
- Enterprise environmental factors updates |

The Develop Project Team process is an executing process that uses the human resource management plan to improve individual and team performance so that the team members will be able to contribute to a greater chance of project success. The goal is to develop a high-performing team, and a key concept is that the project manager has responsibility for this, must lead by example, and must actively seek to continuously develop the team. Thus, it is important that any project manager actively develop and practice his leadership skills and knowledge of how to build a high-performing team.

The Develop Project Team process covers the following domain task:

- 3.6 Maximize team performance through leading, mentoring, training, and motivating team members.

Inputs

The following inputs are used in the Develop Project Team process.

Human resource management plan

The human resource management plan is a critical input into the Develop Project Team process because it sets out and describes how the process of developing a high-performing team will occur. The human resource management plan is an output from the Plan Human Resource Management process.

Project staff assignments

The project staff assignments describe who the individual project team members are and their current roles, experience, and ability. This information is useful for identifying team members and deciding who needs training. Project staff assignments are an output from the Acquire Project Team process.

Resource calendars

Resource calendars, which identify when the project team members are available to work, are an important input into the Develop Project Team process because they let you know when people are available to participate in team-building activities. Resource calendars are an output from the Acquire Project Team process.

Tools and techniques

The following tools and techniques of this process are able to be used upon the separate inputs to deliver the process outputs.

Interpersonal skills

Interpersonal skills are key skills for any project manager to have so that the manager can effectively contribute to the development of the team. Team development is not a mechanical exercise; it is one built upon relationships between people. Thus, interpersonal skills, or soft skills, are useful in building these relationships and contributing toward a high-performing project team.

There are a wide range of interpersonal skills that a project manager must develop and learn to use at the appropriate time. These include the following eight skills:

1. Leadership is the purposeful influencing of followers. A leader must have a clear vision of where she wants to take the followers. In relation to a project, a vision can be a successful project in terms of time, cost, and quality. Because leadership is essentially a relationship between the leader and follower, it must be built like any other human relationship, upon respect and trust, which are key elements of effective leadership. Project managers are responsible for developing their own leadership abilities, and must realize that different situations call for different leadership styles or the demonstration of a different set of leadership competencies. Because leadership is situational, the type of leadership required over time can change. Figure 7-7 shows how different leadership styles can change from a more autocratic style at the beginning of a project to a more participatory, or supporting, style of leadership toward the end of the project. This model indicates that a leader trusts the team members and gives away some of her power. Both trust and the ability to give away power are important attributes of a good leader.

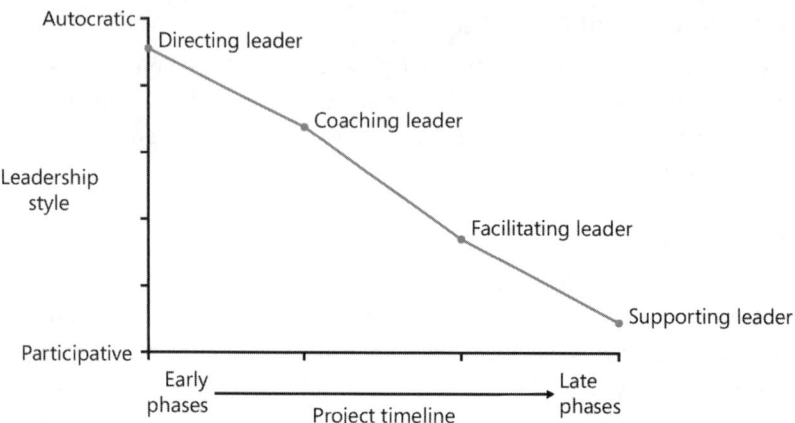

FIGURE 7-7 Different types of project leadership are required at different points of a project.

Fielder's Contingency theory states that a leader's effectiveness is contingent on two sets of factors: whether the leader is task-oriented or relationship-oriented and whether the environment is stressful or calm. A task-oriented leader is more effective in stressful situations, and a relationship-oriented leader is more effective in calm situations.

Being in a position of leadership gives power to the project manager, and a good project manager will recognize the responsibility that comes with power. If used well, power can be a great way to lead project team members, inspire people, and motivate people. If used incorrectly by a project manager, power can create hostility, demotivate an entire team, and cause staff to leave. There are five forms of power that a project manager can use to assist both in his or her leadership of, and negotiation for, the project team. The five leadership styles are:

- Formal or legitimate power, which is based on the position that you hold as a manager. It should be viewed as an interim form of power because people may respect you initially because of the fact that you are the manager, but your subsequent actions could cause this form of power to become invalid; therefore, it is not the best form of power to use.
- The power to reward people, which is a good form of power to use because you are using it to incentivize good performance and discourage poor performance. It should not be used to blackmail or manipulate people.
- The power to impose penalties or punishment upon people, which is never the best form of power to use, because it will always generate negative feedback in both explicit and subtle ways.
- Expert power, which is an excellent form of power to use because it is one that is ascribed to you by others because of your respected position as a technical expert. You are viewed as the expert in a particular area and, as such, people look up to you.
- Referent power, which is a result of your own personality and whether or not you are liked and respected by other people.

2. The ability to build teams is a key interpersonal skill for any project manager and leader. This topic is covered in more detail in a later section in this chapter. Team-building activities go together with good leadership to build a high-performing team.

3. The ability to motivate people, and understand what motivates different people, is a key interpersonal skill for a project manager to have. Different people are motivated by different things, and it is important that a project manager have an understanding of different motivation theories. The following are the most popular motivation theories that a project manager should be aware of:

Maslow's hierarchy of needs describes a situation whereby people perform at their best when they have the opportunity to be what Maslow refers to as "self-actualized." This is the top of the needs pyramid he describes. However, people want to fulfill the bottom needs first and cannot fulfill higher needs until lower ones are fulfilled, and the current need will always take precedence. So if people are concerned about their physiological well-being—for instance, if they can't afford groceries—then they will not be able to gain acceptance and esteem. Figure 7-8 shows the levels in Maslow's hierarchy of needs.

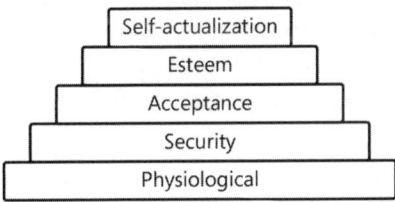

FIGURE 7-8 Maslow's hierarchy of needs extends from physiological at the base to self-actualization at the top.

Vroom's Expectancy Theory states that the expectation of receiving a reward for a certain accomplishment will motivate people to work harder, but it only works if the accomplishment is perceived to be achievable. People will make a conscious decision to work harder if they believe there are achievable outcomes. For a project manager, this means that some people will respond to rewards offered in return for higher productivity, but that those rewards need to be available, specific, measurable, and relevant to the individual. If not, they can prove to be a disincentive.

Herzberg's Motivation-Hygiene Theory states that hygiene factors (such as company policies, good supervision, and safe and pleasant working conditions) will not motivate, but their absence will make staff unsatisfied. Motivation factors (such as achievement, work, responsibility, and advancement) will motivate, but only if hygiene factors are in place. For the project manager leading a project team, this means that if the working conditions are unpleasant or unsafe, then offering up greater responsibility to people in return for more work will not succeed. They will first want the basic workplace environment conditions improved.

McClelland's Human Motivation, Achievement, or Three Needs Theory states that people will work not for more money but instead for achievement, power, and affiliation, and a manager should use these three needs to motivate employees.

Real world

It is often thought that money is the prime motivator for people. This is only true up to the point where you pay people enough to take the issue of money off the table. The specific amount differs between regions and countries, but at a certain point, people have enough money to take care of their essential and basic needs and have some discretionary income to be able to afford nonessential things. Above a certain amount of money, people will be motivated by more intrinsic things such as prestige, responsibility, recognition, and authority. I have always found that when working with experienced, educated professionals as I often do in a project, these latter factors are much more productive ways to motivate people.

McGregor's Theory X and Theory Y describe a manager's attitude towards staff or team members. A theory X manager believes that team members are inherently unmotivated to work, require constant supervision, and can't be trusted. A theory Y manager believes that people want to work, can be trusted, and are naturally ambitious and self-motivated.

Following on from McGregor's Theory X and Theory Y comes *Ouchi's theory Z*, which tries to increase worker loyalty and raise worker productivity by offering a job for life and providing support for the employee both in and out of the workplace.

Real world

I'm sure we have all dealt with managers who exhibit some theory X attributes. It is important to realize that it has been proven that management in a theory X style is extremely counterproductive and will lead to lower productivity, decrease staff morale, and increased staff turnover. As you develop your own managerial style, I encourage you to model yourself after those managers you have admired most; they probably displayed theory Y attributes.

> **NOTE MOTIVATION THEORIES**
>
> As part of your own professional development, you may want to read both the seminal works by the authors mentioned in this section and the works of authors influenced by these people.

EXAM TIP

Make sure you know the basics of each of these theories for the exam. Don't get confused by an answer with just any old surname in it. If you know the basics, you will be able to differentiate between a right answer, a wrong answer, and a made-up answer.

4. Excellent communication skills are an essential interpersonal skill for a project manager to have, because communication forms the basis of any relationship. We will cover communication skills in more detail in Chapter 8, "Communications management."

5. The ability to proactively influence people is an important interpersonal skill that a project manager must have. It is achieved through being genuine, leading by example, establishing networks, and adjusting communication styles to suit the audience.

EXAM TIP

A project manager must always be proactively influencing all aspects of the project, potential change requests, and stakeholder expectations.

Real world

There is a fine line between influencing and manipulation. Manipulation usually has a secret agenda and seeks to force people to do something they wouldn't normally do. Influencing is a political act that is built on relationships, mutual understanding, and an attempt to elicit cooperation from others.

6. Decision-making skills are essential for any project manager. In making a decision, there are four basic decision styles normally used by project managers depending on the time constraints present, trust between team members, quality of information, and ability to get acceptance. They are command, consultation, consensus, and if all else fails, coin flip. In addition to these reactive means of making a decision, there is a more formal six-phase decision-making model developed by Morris and Sashkin. In this model, the six phases in making a decision are:

   - Problem solving
   - Problem solution generation
   - Ideas to action
   - Solution action planning
   - Solution evaluation planning
   - Evaluations of the outcome and process

7. Political and cultural awareness should be a focus for a project manager because she will need to develop and demonstrate the skillful use of politics and power in order to be successful. Additionally, having an awareness of different cultures and the differences each has will enable a project manager to operate more effectively.

8. Advanced negotiation skills are key skills used in several areas in the profession of project management. The goal of any negotiation is an agreement that all parties will benefit from. A win-win outcome is the optimal outcome from a negotiation. Complex negotiations may require specialist skills that the project manager may want to learn, or the project manager may want to bring in experts to complete the negotiations.

EXAM TIP

All negotiations should be entered into in good faith. It is never acceptable to coerce weaker parties in a negotiation into an agreement that may be against their best interests.

9. Underpinning many of the interpersonal skills that a project manager must be able to demonstrate is the ability to build trust. Trust building is necessary to build effective relationships between all stakeholders on the project and without trust, the project manager will experience great difficulty in achieving a lot of their leadership goals. To build trust, a project manager should communicate openly and directly, openly share information, be honest at all times, only make commitments she can keep, and demonstrate a genuine concern for others.

10. Conflict management is an important interpersonal skill for a project manager to have. Dysfunctional conflict may appear within the project team or amongst different stakeholders, and it is the job of the project manager to resolve the conflict to allow the project to continue without distraction. To do this, the project manager will need a wide variety of conflict resolution techniques available and the ability to choose the correct one for the situation. The project manager should first seek to use a collaborative approach to resolve conflict; if this does not work, consider assertiveness, avoidance, compromise, or accommodating conflict resolution techniques.

11. The ability to effectively coach team members to get the best from them is an important interpersonal skill for a project manager. A goal of coaching will be to get the individuals, and subsequently the entire team, to perform at its best. Coaching can be done informally or formally, and the project manager should have the skills to choose the appropriate method of coaching for the individual or team they are leading. When done correctly, coaching can lead to more productive and effective teams.

Training

In order to fully develop individuals on your team, you will have to offer *training* in both technical and nontechnical skills, or soft skills. Training can occur using internal or external trainers and can occur in a classroom environment, on the job, or, increasingly, via remote or online means. Training needs can be agreed upon with team members at regular intervals such as during their performance appraisals, or training can be provided reactively in response to observed needs.

EXAM TIP

You should always assume that you will have to provide training to team members and that you have made a commitment to providing training at all times. This is particularly important if you come across a question in the exam where a team member does not have the right skills to complete an activity. Your first option is always to get them the required training.

Team-building activities

Team-building activities can take many forms, but all have the goal of enhancing the sense of a single team among everyone working on the project. They can be informal or formal, planned or spontaneous, structured or free-flowing. It is important to realize that team-building activities are not a one-time event; they are instead a continual and ongoing process.

Real world

I have always found that having a constant series of both organized and spontaneous team-building activities that appeal to the team members is not only an important way to increase a sense of camaraderie and productivity, but also a great way to develop a unique sense of a team identity and culture.

The *Tuckman five-stage model* is a convenient way to describe the stages a team of people will go through: forming, storming, norming, performing, and adjourning. Although many models show these as linear stages in team development, this isn't always the case; any of the behaviors can be observed at any time. Also, teams can cycle between and within an area, and providing awareness of the model and stages to team members can help propel your team to the performing stage faster. The key point about the model is that your goal is to get your team to the performing stage and keep them there with proactive team management.

Figure 7-9 shows the different stages of the Tuckman five-stage model against performance and time. Although the diagram may indicate an unstoppable linear progression, the reality is that team dynamics can be highly unstable and teams will always be in danger of slipping backward into storming behaviors.

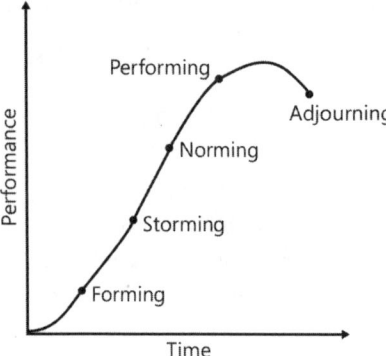

FIGURE 7-9 The Tuckman five-stage model of team development shows the stages of a group process.

When a group meets for the first time, or when new people join a group, there is a period of forming as everybody tries to figure out who the other members are, what common interests they share, where they sit in the hierarchy, and what their role in the team will be.

Fairly soon after a new team forms or a new person joins the team, you will witness storming behaviors. This is the phase in which the team has to work out what direction they will all be going in, which ideas take priority, and which ideas will be cast aside. This phase is often one of conflict and argument; it can also include passive-aggressive behavior as people within the team jostle for position and power. You will also find storming behaviors in the life of an established team when conditions change. Though storming is essential, the core issues must be resolved to allow the team to fully move beyond it.

Norming is the process when the team members explicitly and implicitly define and accept team behaviors and norms. Norming should be the outcome of the storming phase. During the process of norming, if the issues from the storming phase haven't been dealt with, it will be very hard for people to settle down into a normalized culture.

Performing describes the state where the team has moved through the other phases and begins to achieve a high sense of synergy. This is not a static state, however; it's threatened by things such as conflict, team stability, team culture, and external influences. The goal is to keep the team at this stage with constant attention and effort.

Adjourning is the final stage for groups, particularly in project management. It occurs when individuals leave the project as their jobs end, or when the team finally disbands after completing the project. Recognizing and planning for this stage is an important part of the job of the project manager.

Real world

As a project manager I have been lucky enough to have an awareness of teams and their development and have often watched as people go through the stages described in the Tuckman five-stage model of team development. My main focus as project manager has been to make people aware of what was going on and assist them to move to the performing stage. However, I must admit to also being involved in storming behaviors and being totally oblivious to it until the benefit of hindsight revealed it to me. This is one of the main reasons I now often use an independent outsider to assist with regular team-building and assessment activities.

Ground rules

Having a clear set of *ground rules* for expected and accepted group behaviors is an important element of successful team building. Ground rules are more often accepted and enforced by team members if they have had an input into their creation. Common ground rules are around work hours, cooperation, conflict resolution, and participation.

Co-location

Co-location means trying to get as many of the project team members in face-to-face contact with each other as possible by placing them in the same physical location permanently or on a regular basis, such as in team meeting rooms. The purpose of co-location is to enhance team building through better and more effective communication and relationship building. People do these things better when they can see each other. The practice of co-locating people in the same space is often called the creation of a *war room*.

Recognition and rewards

The purpose of *recognition* and *rewards* is to promote acceptable behaviors and discourage unacceptable behaviors from project team members. As covered already, there are several motivation theories that point out that money is not the best way to recognize or reward performance or behavior. There are other ways of recognizing and rewarding people that are much more effective. Team members will appreciate recognition, either publically or privately, for good work, and they will feel valued when the right rewards are given. It is up to the project manager to ensure that he or she is catering to individual needs with appropriate recognition and rewards.

Personnel assessment tools

A key element of any effort to develop individual team members is a defined way to assess individual performances and training needs. *Personnel assessment tools* will assist in formalizing the process of assessing an individual and planning for his or her future professional development. A common means of doing this is via the regular performance appraisal meeting and the use of the 360-degree feedback method. In this method, feedback from an individual's peers, superiors, and those who report to that individual is sought, and then provided in a structured setting in a positive way.

> **Real world**
>
> A poorly carried out 360-degree review can backfire very badly. I recall witnessing a junior manager carrying out his first 360-degree review on a project manager. As part of the team, I was sent a questionnaire that only asked what the project manager's weaknesses were and what that manager had done wrong that had to be improved. The very way the questions were phrased set a poor tone, and I did hear that the project manager walked out of the assessment and refused to take part in another with that manager due to the stream of negative feedback.

Outputs

The major outputs from the Develop Project Team process are the following.

Team performance assessments

The primary output from the Develop Project Team process are the *team performance assessments*, which are prepared by the project manager and document the training activities undertaken and still to be undertaken, any team-building activities undertaken or planned and their outcome, and individual performance assessments. These assessments will be measured against any predefined performance expectations. These predefined performance expectations can include such metrics as staff turnover, length of employment, improvement in individual and team competency, and measures of team cohesiveness.

Team performance assessments go on to be used as an input into the Manage Project Team process.

Enterprise environmental factors updates

The *enterprise environmental factors updates* that will occur as a result of the Develop Project Team process include general organizational personnel employment policies and guidelines.

Quick check

1. Who has responsibility for the ongoing development of the team and individuals within the team?
2. Why is it important that the project manager have a well-developed set of interpersonal skills?
3. If you are witnessing arguments between team members, what phase of the Tuckman five-stage team development model is the team at?
4. What is the most important aspect to recognize when rewarding people for work done or offering rewards as the incentive to do work?
5. What are the two best forms of power a project manager can use?

Quick check answers

1. The project manager has ultimate responsibility for leading the team and taking care of group and individual development needs.
2. The successful development of a team requires a range of interpersonal skills to be utilized by the project manager.
3. The team is at the storming stage.
4. The most important thing to recognize when using rewards is to make them appropriate and meaningful to the individual or team.
5. The two best forms of power the project manager can use are expert, in which the manager is viewed as an expert because of his technical ability, and reward, in which he is able to provide incentives for good work.

Manage Project Team

> **MORE INFO** **MANAGE PROJECT TEAM**
>
> You can read more about the Manage Project Team process in the PMBOK® Guide, 5th edition, in Chapter 9, section 9.4. Table 7-5 identifies the process inputs, tools and techniques, and outputs.
>
> **TABLE 7-5** Manage Project Team process
>
> | Inputs | Tools and techniques | Outputs |
> |---|---|---|
> | ■ Human resource management plan
■ Project staff assignments
■ Team performance assessments
■ Issue log
■ Work performance reports
■ Organizational process assets | ■ Observation and conversation
■ Project performance appraisals
■ Conflict management
■ Interpersonal skills | ■ Change requests
■ Project management plan updates
■ Project documents updates
■ Enterprise environmental factors updates
■ Organizational process assets updates |

The Manage Project Team process is an executing process that uses the human resource management plan, team performance assessments, and work performance reports to monitor team and individual performance, resolve conflicts, and optimize team performance. If as a result of carrying out this process any changes are required, then a change request will be generated.

The Manage Project Team process covers the following domain task:

- 3.6 Maximize team performance through leading, mentoring, training, and motivating team members.

Inputs

The following inputs are used in the Manage Project Team process.

Human resource management plan

The human resource management plan is a critical input into the Manage Project Team process because it provides critical information on how human resources, or people, will be managed, controlled, and assessed. The human resource management plan is an output from the Plan Human Resource Management process.

Project staff assignments

Project staff assignments provide a list of the project team members, their roles, and contact details, all of which are important when managing project team members. Project staff assignments are an output from the Acquire Project Team process.

Team performance assessments

Team performance assessments, which are an output from the Develop Project Team process, contain information about the performance of both individuals and the whole project team. They can include an assessment of how well the team is performing as a whole and also individual assessments, such as key performance indicators (KPIs) from a person's job description, an assessment of interpersonal skills, and an assessment of contribution to the organization's goals. They can identify future training needs and contribute to professional development both while the team members are on the project and also after they leave.

Issue log

The *issue log* is used as an input into this process because it may describe and document relevant issues relating to management of individual team members or the team as a whole. The issue log is an output from the Manage Stakeholder Engagement process.

Work performance reports

Work performance reports, which are an output from the Monitor and Control Project Work process, provide information about how the project team members are actually performing compared to the forecasts made about their performance. Because it is the project team members who are responsible for all aspects of the project that generate other success metrics such as time, cost, quality, and scope, it is important that the work that they are expected to do generates these performance measurements. The work performance reports focus on the performance of the team and individuals.

Organizational process assets

The specific types of organizational process assets that may be useful in managing the project team include any processes or guidelines for acknowledging good work or dealing with poor performance, any financial incentive structures that may be applied to high performance, and any other relevant organizational guidelines on managing team members.

Tools and techniques

The following tools and techniques of this process are able to be used upon the separate inputs to deliver the process outputs.

Observation and conversation

Observation and *conversation* are important tools to use because they allow the project manager, who has ultimate responsibility for managing a project team, to observe team member performance and talk with team members about current performance and planned future performance.

> **Real world**
>
> I have always found that one of the easiest ways to keep team members engaged is regular and ongoing direct communication using face-to-face conversations. You will be surprised what information can be exchanged and how quickly relationships can be built with a simple 10-minute conversation.

Project performance appraisals

Project performance appraisals can occur on a regularly scheduled basis, or on a more spontaneous basis in response to either good or poor performance. They can be conducted formally or informally but should always be viewed as an opportunity to increase good performance and offer assistance, training, and feedback to improve poor performance.

Conflict management

Although conflict can at times be a positive and beneficial tool for soliciting lateral thinking, in most instances conflict is perceived as a negative influence upon team performance and needs to be addressed with successful *conflict management* techniques promptly, openly, and with a view to resolving the core issues in order to ensure that it does not adversely affect team performance. The most common causes of conflict between project team members are time constraints, project priorities, resource availability, differences in technical opinions, administrative processes, project cost and budget, and individual personalities.

It is the role of the project manager to take responsibility first of all for setting in place ground rules for the accepted and expected behaviors in working with the team. If conflict does arise, the project manager must take responsibility for dealing with the conflict. There are six main ways of dealing with conflict, each with a different outcome. They are described in the following list.

- Withdrawal or avoiding simply avoids dealing with conflict. This is definitely not the best way to deal with conflict.
- Forcing involves one party to the conflict pushing his or her viewpoint on another person and trying to have that person adopt it, through the use of various forms of power.

- Smoothing or accommodating tries to resolve conflict by getting parties to agree to disagree and put work ahead of conflict. This approach doesn't deal with the root causes, and therefore the conflict may flare up again at any time.
- Collaboration as a conflict resolution techniques seeks input from all parties to the conflict and seeks to find some form of compromise between the parties involved in the conflict in order to resolve it.
- Compromise is a conflict resolution technique that involves each party giving something up in order to resolve the conflict. Thus, instead of being a win-win solution, the result can often be a lose-lose situation. This approach should be viewed as a second-best option to confronting or problem-solving.
- Confronting or problem-solving is the best option for dealing with any conflict, because it seeks to deal with the conflict in a permanent manner and resolve it openly.

EXAM TIP

You should always assume that conflict is inevitable in any project and that you will have to deal with it. As the project manager, it is your responsibility to always deal with conflict in an open manner that seeks to resolve the core reasons for the conflict. Simply ignoring or sweeping conflict under the carpet is not an acceptable solution because this will eventually manifest in a number of ways, all of which are detrimental to your team's performance and ultimately to the success of the project.

Interpersonal skills

A project manager's interpersonal skills will be very useful in managing the project team, particularly his or her leadership, influencing, and decision-making skills. These were covered in depth in the Develop Project Team process.

Outputs

The major outputs from the Manage Project Team process are the following.

Change requests

As a result of carrying out the Manage Project Team process, you may discover variations between what you had planned in terms of team performance and what is actually occurring. Additionally, you may wish to amend any planned acquisition or development activities in order to optimize team performance. Any of these options will involve the creation of a change request. The change request will be an input into the Perform Integrated Change Control process, where it will be considered as part of the documented change control process.

Project management plan updates

The specific parts of the project management plan that may be updated as a result of the Manage Project Team process are the human resource management plan and the staffing management plan.

Project documents updates

Specific project documents that may be updated as a result of carrying out this process are such things as the issue log and project staff assignments.

Enterprise environmental factors updates

The specific enterprise environmental factors that may be updated include any organizational employee performance appraisal and feedback policies and guidelines.

Organizational process assets updates

The specific organizational process assets that may be updated include any standard templates or processes relating to management of personnel, any templates, and any historical information or lessons-learned documentation.

 Quick check

1. What is the main focus of the Manage Project Team process?
2. Why are observation and conversation important tools in successfully managing a project team?
3. What is the best method to use for successful conflict management?

Quick check answers

1. The main focus of the Manage Project Team process is to analyze team performance against forecast team performance and undertake actions to ensure high team performance by providing feedback and, if necessary, submitting change requests to optimize team performance.
2. Because the management of team performance relies heavily on a project manager's ability to accurately observe what is occurring with individual and team performance, the two tools of observation and conversation are excellent means of gathering information from team members.
3. The best method to ensure successful conflict management is to take a confronting or problem-solving approach that will permanently resolve any conflict being dealt with.

Exercises

The answers for these exercises are located in the "Answers" section at the end of this chapter.

1. Match the management theory on the left with the description on the right.

Quality tool	Definition
1. McGregor's theory X and theory Y	a. A theory that states that certain basic workplace factors must be in place before less tangible factors can be used to motivate staff
2. Tuckman five-stage model of team development	b. A theory that describe the attitude of managers toward staff and separates them into those who believe staff are self-motivated and trustworthy and those who belief staff are lazy and untrustworthy
3. Vroom's Expectancy Theory	c. A theory that states that people will perform at their best when self-actualized but people will want to fulfill the lower-level needs first
4. Herzberg's Motivation-Hygiene Theory	d. A theory that states that the expectation of receiving a reward for a certain accomplishment will motivate people to work harder, but it only works if the accomplishment is perceived to be achievable
5. McClelland's Human Motivation, Achievement, or Three Needs Theory	e. A theory that people will work not for more money, but instead for achievement, power, and affiliation
6. Maslow's hierarchy of needs	f. A process of describing phases that a team can pass through on the way to becoming a high-performing team

2. Arrange the following organizational structures in relation to the power and authority of the project manager, from weakest to strongest.

   1. Strong matrix

   2. Functional

   3. Balanced matrix

   4. Weak matrix

   5. Projectized

3. Take a look at the following list of words. They represent either a type of power a project manager can have, a decision-making style a project manager can use, or a conflict management style that can be used. Sort each of them into one of these three categories: Types of power, decision-making styles, conflict management.

Consensus
Forcing
Referent
Punishment
Coin flip
Command
Compromise
Consultation
Withdrawal
Reward
Collaboration
Problem-solving
Formal
Expert
Smoothing

Chapter summary

- The Human Resource Management knowledge area is focused upon the areas around planning which people you need, obtaining the people that you need when you need them, taking responsibility to continually train and develop your project team members, and monitoring individual and team performance.
- The Plan Human Resource Management process produces the human resource management plan, which guides the three subsequent executing processes.
- The first of the three executing processes in the Human Resource Management knowledge area, the Acquire Project Team process, uses the human resource management plan to obtain the project team members you require, with the appropriate skills, at the time that you need them.

- The Develop Project Team process, which is an executing process, reflects a commitment to understanding the professional development and ongoing training needs of individual team members and the overall team. The goal of this process is to achieve a high-performing project team via a variety of tools and techniques.
- The Manage Project Team process is focused upon using the human resource management plan, which outlines the expected levels of individual and team performance, and checking team performance against it. Providing feedback and making changes and corrective actions is an important part of the Manage Project Team process.

Chapter review

Test your knowledge of the information in Chapter 7 by answering these questions. The answers to these questions, and the explanations of why each answer choice is correct or incorrect, are located in the "Answers" section at the end of this chapter.

1. Which of the following is not an executing process in the Human Resource Management knowledge area?
   A. Manage Project Team
   B. Develop Project Team
   C. Acquire Project Team
   D. Plan Human Resource Management

2. What is the correct order of project role descriptions when ranking from most to least power?
   A. Project manager, project coordinator, project expeditor
   B. Project manager, project expeditor, project coordinator
   C. Project coordinator, project manager, project expeditor
   D. Project coordinator, project expeditor, project manager

3. If you are working in an organization where you continually have to ask another manager if you can spend money allocated to your project, and obtain personnel to work on your project, what sort of organizational structure are you working in?
   A. Projectized organization
   B. Functional organization
   C. Strong matrix organization
   D. Balanced matrix organization

4. What is the best definition of a program of projects?
   A. All projects that the organization is undertaking
   B. An individual project
   C. A group of projects that a portfolio manager oversees
   D. A group of projects that are related in some way

5. What is the primary role of the project sponsor?
   A. To be ultimately accountable for the project
   B. To directly manage the performance of the project manager
   C. To provide financial and political support for the project
   D. To be the primary liaison with the client

6. If you are placing advertisements in local newspapers seeking to recruit project team members, which tool or technique are you using?
   A. Negotiation
   B. Preassignment
   C. Acquisition
   D. Recruitment

7. What information does a resource calendar contain?
   A. The pay rates of project team members
   B. A description of the role of each team member and contact details
   C. The days and times when the project team members are available to work on the project
   D. A description of the work to be done on the project

8. As a project manager, you will have access to different forms of power. When managing your team, what is the worst form of power to use?
   A. Punishment
   B. Expert
   C. Referent
   D. Legitimate

9. What is the generally correct order of stages, or phases, a team will go through according to the Tuckman five-stage model of team development?

    A. Forming, storming, norming, performing, adjourning

    B. Norming, storming, forming, performing, adjourning

    C. Storming, norming, forming, performing, adjourning

    D. Storming, forming, norming, performing, adjourning

10. Which of the following is the lowest of the levels in Maslow's hierarchy of needs?

    A. Physiological

    B. Security

    C. Esteem

    D. Self-actualization

11. You have exhausted all other techniques for making a decision and are making a random decision between two possible options. What style of decision-making technique are you using?

    A. Dice throw

    B. Coin flip

    C. Random assignment

    D. Lucky guess

12. Two project team members are disagreeing strongly about the relevant engineering standards to apply to the design of a particular element in your project. You ask them to carry on working and ignore the problem. What conflict resolution technique are you using?

    A. Problem-solving

    B. Collaboration

    C. Forcing

    D. Avoiding

Answers

This section contains the answers for the "Exercises" and "Chapter review" sections in this chapter.

Exercises

1. Match the management theory on the left with the description on the right.

Quality tool	Definition
1. McGregor's theory X and theory Y	b. A theory that describe the attitude of managers toward staff and separates them into those who believe staff are self-motivated and trustworthy and those who belief staff are lazy and untrustworthy
2. Tuckman five-stage model of team development	f. A process of describing phases that a team can pass through on the way to becoming a high-performing team
3. Vroom's Expectancy Theory	d. A theory that states that the expectation of receiving a reward for a certain accomplishment will motivate people to work harder, but it only works if the accomplishment is perceived to be achievable
4. Herzberg's Motivation-Hygiene Theory	a. A theory that states that certain basic workplace factors must be in place before less tangible factors can be used to motivate staff
5. McClelland's Human Motivation, Achievement, or Three Needs Theory	e. A theory that people will work not for more money, but instead for achievement, power, and affiliation
6. Maslow's hierarchy of needs	c. A theory that states that people will perform at their best when self-actualized but people will want to fulfill the lower-level needs first

2. Arrange the following organizational structures in relation to the power and authority of the project manager, from weakest to strongest.

2. Functional

4. Weak matrix

3. Balanced matrix

1. Strong matrix

5. Projectized

3. Take a look at the following list of words. They represent either a type of power a project manager can have, a decision-making style a project manager can use, or a conflict management style that can be used. Sort each of them into one of these three categories.

Types of power	Decision-making styles	Conflict management
Formal	Command	Withdrawal
Reward	Consultation	Forcing
Punishment	Consensus	Smoothing
Expert	Coin flip	Collaboration
Referent		Compromise
		Problem-solving

Chapter review

1. **Correct answer: D**
   A. **Incorrect:** The Manage Project Team process is an executing process.
   B. **Incorrect:** The Develop Project Team process is an executing process.
   C. **Incorrect:** The Acquire Project Team process is an executing process.
   D. **Correct:** The Plan Human Resource Management process is a planning process.

2. **Correct answer: A**
   A. **Correct:** A project manager has the most power, followed by a project coordinator and then a project expeditor.
   B. **Incorrect:** A project coordinator has more power than a project expeditor.
   C. **Incorrect:** A project manager has more power than a project coordinator.
   D. **Incorrect:** A project manager has more power than both a project coordinator and a project expeditor.

3. **Correct answer: B**
   A. **Incorrect:** In a projectized organization, a project manager has all the power and authority in relation to control of people and budgets.
   B. **Correct:** In a functional organization, it is the functional manager who controls project costs and personnel.
   C. **Incorrect:** In a strong matrix organization, the project manager would have more power than a functional manager.
   D. **Incorrect:** In a balanced matrix organization, the project manager and functional manager would have equal amounts of power over staff and budget.

4. **Correct answer: D**

    A. **Incorrect:** A portfolio best describes all the projects an organization is undertaking.

    B. **Incorrect:** A program is more than just a single project.

    C. **Incorrect:** A portfolio manager oversees a portfolio.

    D. **Correct:** A program of projects are related in some way, and it is the role of the program manager to sort out potential conflicts between projects in a program.

5. **Correct answer: C**

    A. **Incorrect:** The project manager is ultimately accountable for the project, not the project sponsor.

    B. **Incorrect:** It is not generally the project sponsor's role to manage the performance of the project manager, although this can occasionally occur.

    C. **Correct:** The primary role of the project sponsor is to provide financial and political support for the project from initiation through closure.

    D. **Incorrect:** The primary liaison with the client will generally be the project manager, unless there are contractual reasons for it to be somebody else.

6. **Correct answer: C**

    A. **Incorrect:** Negotiation is the process of negotiating with other managers for people to work on your project, or negotiation as part of employment contracts.

    B. **Incorrect:** Preassignment is the process of having people directly allocated to your project.

    C. **Correct:** Acquisition is the tool or technique that actively seeks to recruit project team members.

    D. **Incorrect:** Recruitment may be a particular term used by some in the industry, but it is not the standardized PMBOK® Guide term.

7. **Correct answer: C**

    A. **Incorrect:** The resource calendar will not contain the pay rates of project team members.

    B. **Incorrect:** It is not the resource calendar, but the project staff assignments, that will contain a description of the role of each team member and their contact details.

    C. **Correct:** A resource calendar outlines when project team members are available to work on the project.

    D. **Incorrect:** A description of the work to be done on the project will be found in the scope statement.

8. **Correct answer: A**

   A. **Correct:** The use of punishment will generally result in negative consequences upon team performance; thus it is the worst form of power to use.

   B. **Incorrect:** Expert power is gained from being an acknowledged technical expert in a particular area, and it is a positive form of power to use.

   C. **Incorrect:** Referent power is gained from your personality and charisma, and it is a positive form of power to use.

   D. **Incorrect:** Legitimate power is attributed to the person due to the job description. It is not a long-lasting form of power.

9. **Correct answer: A**

   A. **Correct:** First people come together in the forming phase, then they go through storming behaviors before settling on norming. Then a team can enter the performing stage and finally the adjourning stage.

   B. **Incorrect:** Norming behaviors come after storming behaviors, and forming behaviors come before storming behaviors.

   C. **Incorrect:** Norming behaviors come after storming behaviors.

   D. **Incorrect:** Storming behaviors come after forming and before norming.

10. **Correct answer: A**

    A. **Correct:** Physiological needs like food and water must be satisfied first.

    B. **Incorrect:** Security is the second-lowest level in Maslow's hierarchy of needs.

    C. **Incorrect:** Esteem is the second-highest level in Maslow's hierarchy of needs.

    D. **Incorrect:** Self-actualization is the highest level in Maslow's hierarchy of needs and can only be realized after lower-level needs have been filled.

11. **Correct answer: B**

    A. **Incorrect:** Dice throw is a made-up term and not one of the four basic decision-making techniques.

    B. **Correct:** Coin flip is one of the four basic decision-making techniques.

    C. **Incorrect:** Random assignment does not relate to decision-making techniques.

    D. **Incorrect:** Lucky guess is a made-up term and not one of the four basic decision-making techniques.

12. **Correct answer: D**

   A. **Incorrect:** If you are using problem-solving, you would require the team members to work it out and resolve the dispute, not simply ignore it.

   B. **Incorrect:** If you are using collaboration as a conflict resolution technique, you are asking the team members to work constructively together and, as necessary, to make compromises to achieve an agreeable outcome.

   C. **Incorrect:** Forcing would at least impose a solution and would be an attempt to resolve the conflict.

   D. **Correct:** This is a classic example of avoiding resolving the conflict.

CHAPTER 8

Communications management

This chapter focuses on project communications management. Similar to the other knowledge areas, it begins with a process of planning, which produces a communications management plan. It then has an executing process, Manage Communications, focusing on carrying out the communications management plan, and a monitoring and controlling process, Control Communications, focused on checking whether or not project communications are meeting stakeholder communication requirements.

> ## The PMBOK® Guide processes
>
> ### Project Communications Management knowledge area
>
> The three processes in the Project Communications Management knowledge area are:
>
> - Plan Communications Management (Planning process)
> - Manage Communications (Executing process)
> - Control Communications (Monitoring and Controlling process)

Domain tasks in this chapter:

- Plan Communications Management process:
    - 2.6 Develop a communication plan based on the project organization structure and external stakeholder requirements, in order to manage the flow of project information.
    - 2.12 Conduct a kick-off meeting with all key stakeholders, in order to announce the start of the project, communicate the project milestones, and share other relevant information.
- Manage Communications process:
    - 3.2 Execute the tasks as defined in the project plan, in order to achieve the project deliverables within budget and schedule.

- Control Communications process:
    - 4.6 Communicate project status to stakeholders for their feedback, in order to ensure the project aligns with business needs.

What is project communications management?

Project communications management is focused upon the processes of developing a communications management plan, gathering and distributing project information according to the communications management plan, and checking that you are completing the communications activities in accordance with the plan.

Project communications are absolutely critical for a smooth and successful running of any project, whether you are gathering information or disseminating information. You should assume that a project manager will, in fact, spend 90 percent of his time communicating in different ways, different forms, and to different stakeholders. Of this time spent communicating, 50 percent will be spent communicating with project team members because they are the most important of the stakeholders.

EXAM TIP

You should always assume that communication in its many forms is at the heart of many issues in project management. If you get a question outlining a problem, and one of the potential answers involves better or improved communication, this may be the correct choice.

Real world

I managed a construction project that I soon realized was actually a communications project. At the outset we started off focusing on building the deliverable and reporting on time and cost progress. Very few of the stakeholders were interested in the construction project itself; they were interested in how it would affect their business, and the intended outcome. After about four months of work, on what was a two-and-a-half-year-long project, I was taken aside by the project sponsor and told that despite the project being under budget and ahead of time, many stakeholders considered that the project was a failure because I wasn't communicating effectively with them. I discovered that many of these stakeholders weren't interested in updates about time and cost. They had other communication needs. The project sponsor was correct, and overnight we changed our focus from a construction project to a communications project. We started focusing on what people actually wanted to hear, how they wanted to hear it, when they wanted to hear it, and who they wanted to hear it from. Within a relatively short period of time, the project was judged a success.

EXAM TIP

The project manager should not be in control of every communication, but the project manager should control the communications process.

Plan Communications Management

> **MORE INFO** PLAN COMMUNICATIONS MANAGEMENT
>
> You can read more about the Plan Communications Management process in the PMBOK® Guide, 5th edition, in Chapter 10, section 10.1. Table 8-1 identifies the process inputs, tools and techniques, and outputs.
>
> **TABLE 8-1** Plan Communications Management process
>
> | Inputs | Tools and techniques | Outputs |
> |---|---|---|
> | ■ Project management plan
■ Enterprise environmental factors
■ Organizational process assets | ■ Communications requirements analysis
■ Communications technology
■ Communications models
■ Communications methods
■ Meetings | ■ Communications management plan
■ Project documents updates |

The Plan Communications Management process is a planning process that has the communications management plan as its primary output. In order to develop a successful communications management plan, you will need to gather and analyze information about individual stakeholders and their communication needs in order to be successful.

The Plan Communications Management process covers the following domain tasks:

- 2.6 Develop a communication plan based on the project organization structure and external stakeholder requirements, in order to manage the flow of project information.
- 2.12 Conduct a kick-off meeting with all key stakeholders, in order to announce the start of the project, communicate the project milestones, and share other relevant information.

Inputs

The Plan Communications Management process uses some or all of the following inputs as part of the development of the communications management plan for the project.

Project management plan

The key elements of the project management plan that will be useful as inputs into the Plan Communications Management process are information about project constraints; timeframes; and scope, risk, and stakeholder expectations. The project management plan is an output from the Develop Project Management Plan process.

Enterprise environmental factors

The specific enterprise environmental factor that will be useful as an input into this process is the broader organizational structure, because that will affect how well communications are managed.

Organizational process assets

The specific organizational process assets that may be an important input into the development of your communications management plan include any lessons learned and historical information about successful or unsuccessful communications from past projects, and any blank templates or guidelines for the preparation of the communications management plan.

Tools and techniques

The following tools and techniques are available to be used to develop the inputs into this process in order to produce the communications management plan.

Communications requirements analysis

The purpose of *communications requirements analysis* is to obtain a detailed description of individual stakeholders and their communications needs. In order to identify the communications requirements of individual stakeholders, you can use a variety of techniques to identify the stakeholders. These techniques will allow you to either solicit their requirements from them directly or gather information from other sources about their requirements. The important thing is to gather and document the stakeholder communication requirements so you can then plan how you will meet them.

In order to appreciate the number of potential communications channels that can exist as part of identifying stakeholders on a project, you can use a formula that shows the exponential growth and total number of potential communications channels with every additional stakeholder that is identified. The formula is $n(n-1)/2$, where n equals the number of stakeholders, including yourself.

For example, if you have 4 stakeholders in your project, you would have 6 potential communications channels.

$$\frac{4 \times (4 - 1)}{2} = \frac{4 \times 3}{2} = \frac{12}{2} = 6$$

If you have 5 stakeholders in your project, you would have 10 potential communications channels.

$$\frac{5 \times (5 - 1)}{2} = \frac{5 \times 4}{2} = \frac{20}{2} = 10$$

If you have 20 stakeholders, you will have 190 potential communication channels.

$$\frac{20 \times (20 - 1)}{2} = \frac{20 \times 19}{2} = \frac{380}{2} = 190$$

The number of communications channels will be an important consideration in your communications requirements analysis. Figure 8-1 shows how these communication channels are formed between stakeholders.

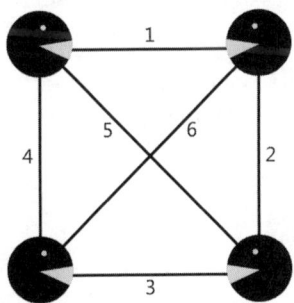
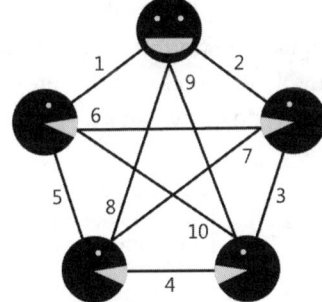

FIGURE 8-1 The number of communications channels in a project increases dramatically when the number of stakeholders increases.

Communications technology

The choice of *communications technology* will depend on several different factors, including urgency, the availability of specific forms of technology and the ease of use of that technology, the project environment and whether the project team members and stakeholders are able to communicate face to face or virtually by using technology, and the sensitivity and confidentiality of information. All of these factors will influence which technologies you choose to use and favor in your communications management plan. It is becoming increasingly common to rely on virtual forms of technology, but nothing is as good as face-to-face communication.

Communications models

Having an awareness of a *communications model*, which outlines how communications can work, is an important skill for a project manager to have. Communications is not just a simple matter of your deciding which information you want to communicate, and assuming that those you want to communicate with will understand what you are actually trying to say. According to the Shannon and Weaver communication model, there is a continual looping process in action, as Figure 8-2 shows. The sender encodes a message according to her own preferences, prejudices, and particular worldview. The sender then transmits this message via whichever communications technology, or medium, she has selected to use. As the message is transmitted, it must pass through a particular medium, and in doing so it will encounter noise. In this instance, noise does not always relate just to acoustic noise, but also includes any other aspects present in the selected medium that may interfere with or change the message being transmitted. It can include the physical environment, participant energy levels, cultural differences, accents, and individual prejudices.

The receiver then receives the message and decodes it according to her own preferences and prejudices. If the receiver then attempts to send the message on to another person, or back to the original sender, it must go through the same obstacles again.

You can begin to recognize how errors in communication can happen very easily even with the best of intent. It is absolutely important that project managers recognize the challenges to effective communication and to try to minimize the potential disruption to the messages they are trying to send.

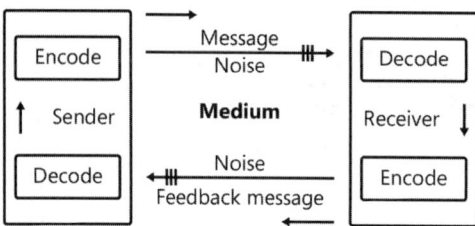

FIGURE 8-2 This communications model shows how a sender encodes and sends a message through a medium to a receiver.

You can mitigate some of the potential negative effects on communication in this model by practicing the following techniques:

- **Active listening** With this technique, the listener takes active steps to ensure that the message was understood correctly. The result of this is that the listener is more engaged and there is a much better transfer of information between sender and receiver.

> **Real world**
>
> Throughout my career as a project manager, the ability to listen and understand what it is that people are actually communicating has played an important role in the success of projects I have managed. I remember when I was younger and perhaps a little more headstrong, and I would simply take shortcuts when receiving information from people, assuming I understood what they were trying to communicate. This, of course, led to many misunderstandings and many inefficiencies and mistakes that affected the chances of project success. I have since learned that being an active listener is more important than being an active talker.

- **Effective listening**   Similar to active listening, this technique also involves the listener or receiver monitoring non-verbal and physical communication.
- **Feedback**   This consists of cues from the receiver to the sender that indicate whether or not the message has been understood.
- **Nonverbal**   This is communication in the form of body language, posture, and similar. You may be surprised to know that most communication is nonverbal and that we are very skilled at picking up nonverbal communication.
- **Paralingual**   This type of communication is vocal but not verbal, and includes tone of voice, inflections, and volume—how the words are said rather than what is said.

Communications methods

There are three broad categories of the types of *communications methods* that you can employ:

- *Interactive communication*   Where all parties in the communications conduct a multidirectional exchange of information concurrently. The most common examples of interactive communication include team meetings, phone calls, and videoconferencing.

- *Push communication*   A form of communication that is sent to recipients. It is an effective means of communication to ensure that information is distributed as planned and includes email messages, reports, memos, press releases, and letters.
- *Pull communication*   Used when recipients can choose to access information at their own discretion. Common examples of pull communication include intranet and Internet sites and e-learning sites.

In addition to these categories of communications, there are also different ways in which the communications can be delivered. These can be formal or informal and verbal or written. Table 8-2 shows the possible combinations of these communications forms and examples of each.

TABLE 8-2 Types of communication

Method	Examples
Informal written	Notes, email messages, memos
Formal written	Contracts, legal notices
Informal verbal	Meetings, discussions, phone calls, conversations
Formal verbal	Speeches, mass communications, presentations

Meetings

Meetings are generally a useful way to bring together members of the project team and other stakeholders so that they can contribute to the development of the communications management plan. Effective meetings feature the use of predistributed agendas, defined start and finish times, agreed ground rules, and a focus on decision-making.

A particular type of meeting that is useful for communicating the end of project planning and the beginning of project execution is the kick-off meeting. The kick-off meeting is held with project team members and relevant stakeholders in attendance, usually on site, and it signifies the start of execution. It is a particularly effective form of communication because it signals to the team and stakeholders that the project is progressing, and contributes to increased team morale.

Outputs

After applying the appropriate tools and techniques to the selected inputs, the Plan Communications Management process has the following outputs.

Communications management plan

The Plan Communications Management process has the *communications management plan* as its primary output. Similar to other management plans, the communications management plan provides a guide for completing the communications management activities in the project.

Your communications management plan will identify individual stakeholders, what information they require, when they require that information, how they will receive information, from whom the information will be received, and any other issues affecting communications.

Your communications management plan may also outline key messages, general communication strategies, how you will review and update the plan, and an overview of the intended outcomes from the communications management plan. The communications management plan is a subsidiary of the project management plan and is used as an input into the other two communications management processes.

> **Real world**
>
> Keep in mind that a lack of communication is in fact a communication in itself. Some stakeholders will take a lack of communication as a sign of arrogance and indifference. I have always found that the absence of communication leads to opinions based on assumptions and gossip. Correcting these opinions takes more energy and time than it would have taken to distribute the correct information in the first place.

Project documents updates

The specific project documents that may be updated as a result of the Plan Communications Management process are the stakeholder register and requirements documentation, scope statement, issue log, and any other relevant documents.

Quick check

1. What is the primary purpose of the communications management plan?
2. If you are working in an organization with nine stakeholders, including yourself, how many potential communications channels would there be?
3. What is the significance of the kick-off meeting?

Quick check answers

1. The main purpose of the communications management plan is to guide your actions in defining what communications the project is going to receive and send, how it is going to identify stakeholders communications requirements, and how information will be tracked and measured.

2. If you have nine stakeholders, including yourself, there are 36 potential communications channels.

$$\frac{9 \times (9 - 1)}{2} = \frac{9 \times 8}{2} = \frac{72}{2} = 36$$

3. The kick-off meeting is used to gather project team members and other relevant stakeholders together and communicate to them that enough planning has occurred for project execution to begin.

Manage Communications

> **MORE INFO MANAGE COMMUNICATIONS**
>
> You can read more about the Manage Communications process in the PMBOK® Guide, 5th edition, in Chapter 10, section 10.2. Table 8-3 identifies the process inputs, tools and techniques, and outputs.
>
> **TABLE 8-3** Manage Communications process
>
> | Inputs | Tools and techniques | Outputs |
> | --- | --- | --- |
> | ■ Communications management plan
■ Work performance reports
■ Enterprise environmental factors
■ Organizational process assets | ■ Communications technology
■ Communications models
■ Communications methods
■ Information management systems
■ Performance reporting | ■ Project communications
■ Project documents update
■ Project management plan updates
■ Organizational process assets updates |

The Manage Communications process is an executing process that gathers the project information so that it can be distributed and stored according to the communications management plan.

The Manage Communications process covers the following domain task:

- 3.2 Execute the tasks as defined in the project plan, in order to achieve the project deliverables within budget and schedule.

Inputs

The Manage Communications process uses some or all of the following inputs.

Communications management plan

The communications management plan is an essential component of the Manage Communications process because it provides direction and guidelines on how to complete this process. The communications management plan is an output from the Plan Communications Management process.

Work performance reports

Work performance reports are a specific presentation of work performance information. The timely dissemination of work performance reports to the right stakeholders is one of the factors influencing project success. All project reports should be tailored to be suitable to their intended audience. Work performance reports are an output from the Monitor and Control Project Work process.

Enterprise environmental factors

The specific types of enterprise environmental factor that will be useful in managing project communications are any broad organizational cultural issues, any relevant government or industry standards, and any licensed software being used to gather and disseminate information.

Organizational process assets

The specific types of organizational process assets that will assist in managing project communications are any blank templates, historical information and lessons learned, and project-specific policies and guidelines relating to communications management.

Tools and techniques

The following tools and techniques are used upon the inputs to deliver the Manage Communications process outputs.

Communications technology

The particular type of communication technology you choose to use to facilitate project communication is an important consideration because each stakeholder will respond differently to the technology chosen. It is up to the project manager to ensure that the correct type of communication technology the selected to ensure that individual project communication requirements can be met. Remember that what works well for one stakeholder may not work for another stakeholder.

> **Real world**
>
> On a project I was managing, we generally disseminated project progress information by way of written and graphical reports. There was one particular senior manager who continued to ask questions about information that was clearly contained in these reports. Answering these questions took up time, so we gave this issue some thought. Ultimately we realized that instead of written reports, this person preferred brief face-to-face updates. So we initiated a regular process of "accidentally" stopping by this manager's office and giving him a brief update.

Communications models

An awareness of how communications work, according to a basic communications model, is important for a project manager to understand so that he or she can avoid the potential obstacles and difficulties in transmitting messages. A more thorough description of communications models was covered earlier in this chapter in the Plan Communications Management process.

Communications methods

Your choice of push communications, pull communications, or interactive communications as a communications method will be dependent on the stakeholder communications requirements. Communications methods were covered in more detail earlier in this chapter in the Plan Communications Management process.

Information management systems

Information management systems are ways of managing and distributing your project information in hard copy and electronic form. Examples of hard copy distribution formats include press releases, memos, and project documents and plans. Increasingly, management and distribution of project information is handled by electronic means such as websites, web publishing, and intranet portals.

Performance reporting

Effective *performance reporting* is a key element in ensuring that a project is successful and that stakeholder communication requirements are met. The way in which you collect and report performance information should be in response to how individual stakeholders want to receive that information. All performance reports should be concise, succinct, and targeted at their intended audience. Performance reports may include simple text reports, or they may be more complex reports featuring a lot of narrative and descriptive text, diagrams, and tables. The content of a performance report can be on any relevant element and metric of the project. You may also choose to report certain elements such as cost and time to one group of stakeholders, while reporting aspects of quality to another group of stakeholders.

Outputs

The Manage Communications process produces some or all of the following outputs.

Project communications

Project communications are the key output from the Manage Communications process. They can take many forms, based on the communications management plan. You may choose to send project communications in different formats, at different times and frequencies, and with different content, according to individual stakeholder communication requirements. Project communications go on to be used as an input into the Control Communications process.

Project documents updates

The specific types of project documents that may be updated as a result of completing the Manage Communications process will be issues logs, stakeholder registers, project schedules, and budget.

Project management plan updates

The specific part of the project management plan that may be updated as a result of the Manage Communications process is the communications management plan, and any document affected by the communications management plan, such as the stakeholder expectation management plan. Additionally, as a result of reporting project performance, parts of the scope management plan, time management plan, and quality management plan may also be updated.

Organizational process assets updates

The specific organizational process assets that may be updated as a result of this process include any generic project performance reports, templates, stored project records, and lessons learned documentation.

> **Quick check**
>
> 1. What is the main purpose of the Manage Communications process?
> 2. What format should be selected, and what content should be included, when reporting project performance?
> 3. In the basic communication model, what can happen to an intended communication between sender and receiver?
>
> **Quick check answers**
>
> 1. The main purpose of the Manage Communications process is to gather project information and distribute and store it in accordance with the communications management plan, which will also reflect individual stakeholder communication requirements.
> 2. When reporting project performance, your choice of format and content will be directly influenced by the intended audience and their communication needs.
> 3. In the basic communication model, a message that is sent can encounter noise in the chosen medium. This noise could be actual audio sound, or it could be any other aspect that impedes, or interferes with, the message being sent.

Control Communications

> **MORE INFO** **CONTROL COMMUNICATIONS**
>
> You can read more about the Control Communications process in the PMBOK® Guide, 5th edition, in Chapter 10, section 10.3. Table 8-4 identifies the process inputs, tools and techniques, and outputs.
>
> **TABLE 8-4** Control Communications process
>
> | Inputs | Tools and techniques | Outputs |
> | --- | --- | --- |
> | ■ Project management plan
■ Project communications
■ Issue log
■ Work performance data
■ Organizational process assets | ■ Reporting systems
■ Expert judgment
■ Meetings | ■ Work performance information
■ Change requests
■ Project documents updates
■ Organizational process assets updates |

The Control Communications process is focused on monitoring and controlling the project communications to ensure that they are in accordance with the communications management plan and individual stakeholder communication requirements.

The Control Communications process covers the following domain task:

- 4.6 Communicate project status to stakeholders for their feedback, in order to ensure the project aligns with business needs.

Inputs

The following inputs are used in the Control Communications process.

Project management plan

The project management plan contains information about how each part of the project will be executed, monitored, and closed, and as such it provides a valuable input into any monitoring and controlling process. The specific part of the project management plan that is most useful for the Control Communications process is the communications management plan. The project management plan is an output from the Develop Project Management Plan process, and the communications management plan is an output from the Plan Communications Management process.

Project communications

Project communications include all forms of communication about project progress, and also any communications that seek to generate political support from stakeholders for the project. As such, project communications can be in many forms and can contain different amounts and types of information. The most common forms of project communications relate to project performance reports about the most popular project metrics: cost, time, and quality. Project communications are an output from the Manage Communications process.

Issue log

The issue log is a useful input into the Control Communications process because it documents and describes issues relating to communication. Additionally, the issue log provides information about who is responsible for resolving and monitoring the issue. Therefore, the issue log is useful both as a repository of project issues and as a communications tool itself that shows stakeholders that issues are being dealt with. The issue log is an output from the Manage Stakeholder Engagement process.

Work performance data

Work performance data is the raw information gathered about how well the project is doing in relation to cost, time, quality, and any other relevant metrics that are being measured. Work performance data will be turned into work performance information in the Control Communications process, and this work performance information in turn will be turned into work performance reports in the Monitor and Control Project Work process. Work performance data is an output from the Direct and Manage Project Work process.

EXAM TIP

Remember the sequence that work performance data becomes work performance information, which becomes work performance reports.

Organizational process assets

The specific organizational process assets that will be of use in the Control Communications process are any templates, policies, and guidelines for project communications that the organization has.

Tools and techniques

The following tools and techniques of this process are able to be used upon the separate inputs to deliver the Control Communications process outputs.

Reporting systems

A *reporting system* is any method that you choose to gather, store, and distribute or disseminate information. Reporting systems can be manual, although they are increasingly electronic and based on software. Reporting systems can be based on text or graphs and pictures. Whatever method you choose, it must be appropriate to the needs of you and your project team, as well as the stakeholders.

EXAM TIP

Microsoft Project is one example of a reporting system that can gather, store, and distribute information in many forms to stakeholders.

Expert judgment

The use of expert judgment in monitoring and controlling communications is a valuable tool, because it makes available to you the experience, wisdom, and skills of groups or individuals within the project team or within the wider group of project stakeholders, or those of external consultants or subject matter experts. It is often important to bring in people external to the project who can bring a sense of objectivity to how well the communications on the project are being monitored and controlled, and how effective and appropriate they are. This is the real strength in using expert judgment as a tool in this process.

Meetings

The Control Communications process is a monitoring and controlling process and, as such, requires careful attention. One of the better ways of giving it the attention that it deserves is through the use of meetings as a tool, where the project team is able to discuss progress with project communications and make decisions on any improvements. Meetings are a form of communication themselves and so should always be run in an effective way to encourage attendance and involvement.

Outputs

The outputs from the Control Communications process are the following.

Work performance information

Work performance information is work performance data that has been organized and summarized in a way that can be used for work performance reports. Work performance information typically organizes raw data and reports on project status in relation to time and cost progress on the project. Work performance information is used as an input into the Monitor and Control Project Work process.

Change requests

As a result of carrying out any monitoring and controlling process, including the Control Communications process, you may come across variations between what you planned to do in the communications management plan and what is actually occurring. You may also come across situations for which corrective or preventive actions are required to ensure that you stay on track. The best way to ensure that any variations or preventive or corrective actions are captured is through a change request. Change requests will then go on to be processed according to your approved change control process in the Perform Integrated Change Control process.

Project documents updates

The specific project documents that may be updated as a result of the Control Communications process include any issues logs, performance reports, and other relevant communications documents.

Organizational process assets updates

The specific organizational process assets that will be updated include any existing templates, guidelines, lessons learned, or historical databases relating to project communications management.

> **Quick check**
>
> 1. What is the main purpose of the Control Communications process?
> 2. Why are reporting systems an important tool or technique in the Control Communications process?
> 3. What is the relationship between work performance data, work performance information, and work performance reports?
>
> **Quick check answers**
>
> 1. The main purpose of the Control Communications process is to assess whether the project communications are being carried out as per the communications management plan and whether or not variations or corrective or preventive actions need to be taken to ensure that you stay on track.
> 2. Reporting systems are the primary tool used in the Control Communications process because they are the manual or electronic means by which you choose to gather and distribute information about project progress to stakeholders.
> 3. Work performance data is the raw data that gets refined and becomes work performance information, which in turn gets further refined to become work performance reports.

Exercises

The answers for these exercises are located in the "Answers" section at the end of this chapter.

1. Match up the communication tool on the left with the description on the right.

Communication tool	Definition
1. Communications technology	a. A tool that recognizes that communications can be interactive, push, or pull
2. Communications requirements analysis	b. A tool that describes how communications moves from sender to receiver through a particular medium
3. Communications models	c. A tool for gathering and documenting the communication requirements of project stakeholders
4. Communications methods	d. A tool that decides the particular form of technology to be used to disseminate information
5. Performance reporting	e. A tool for collecting and disseminating appropriate reporting on project progress to stakeholders
6. Information management systems	f. A tool for the management, storage, and distribution of project information in either hard copy or electronic form

2. You are the project manager on a project that initially identified seven stakeholders, including yourself. You have since identified an additional six stakeholders. How many extra potential communication channels are there?

Chapter summary

- The Communications Management knowledge area is focused upon the successful use of project communications to report project performance, gain political support, and provide stakeholders with their communications requirements.
- The Plan Communications Management process produces the communications management plan, which guides the subsequent communications management processes.
- The Manage Communications process, which is an executing process, uses the communications management plan to gather, store, and distribute project information to stakeholders in the most effective way.
- The Control Communications process, which is a monitoring and controlling process, is like other monitoring and controlling processes in that it assesses actual performance against that forecast in the communications management plan and, if variations or corrective or preventive actions are required, raises a change request.

Chapter review

Test your knowledge of the information in Chapter 8 by answering these questions. The answers to these questions, and the explanations of why each answer choice is correct or incorrect, are located in the "Answers" section at the end of this chapter.

1. Which of the following processes produces the communications management plan?

    A. Develop Project Management Plan

    B. Plan Communications Management

    C. Manage Communications

    D. Develop Communications Management Plan

2. The decision to use a written document to provide project updates is an example of what sort of tool or technique?

    A. Communication technology

    B. Communication models

    C. Expert judgment

    D. Meetings

3. What is the name of the tool that analyzes the individual communication requirements for each of the stakeholders?

    A. Communication models

    B. Information management systems

    C. Communications requirements analysis

    D. Communications technology

4. You are managing a project with 17 stakeholders, including yourself. How many potential communication channels are there?

    A. 17

    B. 136

    C. 272

    D. 34

5. You have decided to send a handwritten update to project stakeholders on the project progress. Some stakeholders complained that they are unable to read your handwriting. This is an example of what?

    A. Bad handwriting
    B. Noise
    C. Interference
    D. Feedback

6. You have set up an intranet site for project team members to be able to download project progress updates. This is an example of which method of communication?

    A. Interactive
    B. Push
    C. Pull
    D. Manual

7. How does the project kick-off meeting act as a means of communication?

    A. The kick-off meeting does not act as a means of communication.
    B. The kick-off meeting signals to the team that enough planning has been completed to begin execution.
    C. The kick-off meeting is completed to start project initiation, and therefore it informs the team that the project is about to start.
    D. The kick-off meeting signals the beginning of project closure and communicates to the team that the job is done.

8. What is the correct sequence of the following terms?

    A. Work performance report, work performance data, work performance information
    B. Work performance information, work performance data, work performance report
    C. Work performance data, work performance report, work performance information
    D. Work performance data, work performance information, work performance report

9. If you are engaged in consciously paying attention to body language and trying to understand the communication from a sender, what are you involved in?

    A. Active listening
    B. Effective listening
    C. Providing feedback
    D. Paralingual communication

Answers

This section contains the answers for the "Exercises" and "Chapter review" sections in this chapter.

Exercises

1. Match up the communication tool on the left with the description on the right.

Communication tool	Definition
1. Communications technology	d. A tool that decides the particular form of technology to be used to disseminate information
2. Communications requirements analysis	c. A tool for gathering and documenting the communication requirements of project stakeholders
3. Communications models	b. A tool that describes how communications moves from sender to receiver through a particular medium
4. Communications methods	a. A tool that recognizes that communications can be interactive, push, or pull
5. Performance reporting	e. A tool for collecting and disseminating appropriate reporting on project progress to stakeholders
6. Information management systems	f. A tool for the management, storage, and distribution of project information in either hard copy or electronic form

2. You are the project manager on a project that initially identified seven stakeholders, including yourself. You have since identified an additional six stakeholders. How many extra potential communication channels are there?

   This question is asking you what the difference is between 7 stakeholders and 13 stakeholders in relation to the number of potential communication channels. You will need to calculate *n(n-1)/2* for each and find what the difference is. The answer is not simply subtracting 7 from 13 and applying the formula to it—that would give you a very wrong answer, but be aware that in the exam that answer may be one of the options.

   $$\frac{7 \times (7-1)}{2} = \frac{7 \times 6}{2} = \frac{42}{2} = 21$$

   $$\frac{13 \times (13-1)}{2} = \frac{13 \times 12}{2} = \frac{156}{2} = 78$$

   78 − 21 = 57 extra potential communication channels

Chapter review

1. **Correct answer: B**

    A. **Incorrect:** The Develop Project Management Plan process produces the project management plan.

    B. **Correct:** The main output from the Plan Communications Management process is the communications management plan.

    C. **Incorrect:** The Manage Communications process uses the communications management plan to gather, store, and distribute project information and communications.

    D. **Incorrect:** Develop Communications Management Plan is a made-up process name.

2. **Correct answer: A**

    A. **Correct:** Any decision you make about the technology used, whether manual or electronic, for the dissemination of project information, is a decision about communication technology.

    B. **Incorrect:** Communication models explain what might happen between sender and receiver.

    C. **Incorrect:** Expert judgment is a tool used to assist with monitoring how well communications are going.

    D. **Incorrect:** Meetings are a tool used to help the project team understand, and contribute to, effective project communications.

3. **Correct answer: C**

    A. **Incorrect:** Communications models explain what may happen to communications between sender and receiver.

    B. **Incorrect:** Information management systems are used to gather and store project information.

    C. **Correct:** Communications requirements analysis is the technique used to determine individual stakeholder communication requirements.

    D. **Incorrect:** Communications technology is a technique used to determine what form the communication will take.

4. **Correct answer: B**

    A. **Incorrect:** This is simply the number of stakeholders, not the number of potential communication channels.

    B. **Correct:** If you use the formula $n(n-1)/2$, you will calculate that there are 136 potential communications channels.

- C. **Incorrect:** This is the answer you get if you only used the first part of the correct formula.
- D. **Incorrect:** This is simply the number of stakeholders multiplied by 2.

5. **Correct answer: B**
   - A. **Incorrect:** In the strictest sense of the word, it is an example of bad handwriting, but according to the basic communications model it is an example of interference with the message, and that is the definition of noise.
   - B. **Correct:** Any element that can interfere with the message is considered to be noise.
   - C. **Incorrect:** This is not the correct answer because noise creates interference.
   - D. **Incorrect:** Feedback is used by the receiver to send confirmation of the message received back to the sender.

6. **Correct answer: C**
   - A. **Incorrect:** Interactive communication is where there is more than one person involved in the communication at the same time.
   - B. **Incorrect:** Push communication involves the sender sending the communication to the receiver.
   - C. **Correct:** This is an example of pull communication because the receivers download the information at their discretion.
   - D. **Incorrect:** Manual communication refers to forms of communication that are not conducted electronically.

7. **Correct answer: B**
   - A. **Incorrect:** The kick-off meeting does act as a means of communication by communicating to the team that enough planning has been done to begin execution.
   - B. **Correct:** The use of the kick-off meeting as both a functional meeting to discuss execution and as a team morale-building exercise means that it is an effective form of communication.
   - C. **Incorrect:** The kick-off meeting is completed after enough planning has been done to begin project execution, and not at the beginning of project initiation.
   - D. **Incorrect:** The kick-off meeting does not begin the process of project closure.

8. **Correct answer: D**
   A. **Incorrect:** Work performance reports come after work performance data and work performance information.
   B. **Incorrect:** Work performance data comes before work performance information.
   C. **Incorrect:** Work performance information comes before work performance reports.
   D. **Correct:** Work performance data, which is the raw data gathered about project performance, in turn gets filtered and refined as understandable work performance information, which in turn is selected to be included in work performance reports.

9. **Correct answer: B**
   A. **Incorrect:** Active listening means that the receiver is actively engaged in trying to understand the message from the sender and does not necessarily involve paying attention to things like body language.
   B. **Correct:** Effective listening takes active listening one step further and has the receiver monitoring nonverbal cues such as body language.
   C. **Incorrect:** Feedback doesn't necessarily involve the interpretation of body language.
   D. **Incorrect:** Paralingual communication involves recognizing and observing vocal but nonverbal communication clues such as expressions, inflections, tone, and volume of voice.

CHAPTER 9

Risk management

This chapter focuses on the topic of Project Risk Management which, like the other knowledge areas, begins with a process of planning, which produces a risk management plan. It then has four further planning process—Identify Risks, Perform Qualitative Risk Analysis, Perform Quantitative Risk Analysis, and Plan Risk Responses—that iteratively develop and refine the risk register. It has a single monitoring and controlling process, Control Risks, which measures the actual risks versus the forecast risks and, if required, generates change requests.

> **The PMBOK® Guide processes**
>
> **Project Risk Management knowledge area**
>
> The six processes in the Project Risk Management knowledge area are:
>
> - Plan Risk Management (Planning process)
> - Identify Risks (Planning process)
> - Perform Qualitative Risk Analysis (Planning process)
> - Perform Quantitative Risk Analysis (Planning process)
> - Plan Risk Responses (Planning process)
> - Control Risks (Monitoring and Controlling process)

Domain tasks in this chapter:

- Plan Risk Management, Identify Risks, Perform Qualitative Risk Analysis, Perform Quantitative Risk Analysis, and Plan Risk Reponses processes:
    - 2.10 Plan risk management by developing a risk management plan, and identifying, analyzing, and prioritizing project risks in the risk register and defining risk response strategies, in order to manage uncertainty throughout the project life cycle.

- Control Risks process:
    - 3.5 Implement approved actions and follow the risk management plan and risk register, in order to minimize the impact of negative risk events on the project.
    - 4.4 Update the risk register and risk response plan by identifying any new risks, assessing old risks, and determining and implementing appropriate response strategies, in order to manage the impact of risks on the project.
    - 4.5 Assess corrective actions on the issue register and determine next steps for unresolved issues by using appropriate tools and techniques in order to minimize the impact on project schedule, cost, and resources.

What is project risk management?

Project risk management is focused upon the processes of developing a risk management plan and a risk register that outlines and identifies how you will deal with project risks or uncertainties. In order to do this effectively, you need to be able to define all potential risks, their causes, and their potential impact, and formulate strategies for dealing with them. After they are identified, you then monitor what you forecasted would occur in relation to risk and what is actually occurring, while looking out for new or changed risks.

Figure 9-1 shows the general linear and highly iterative process of planning for risk and developing the risk register.

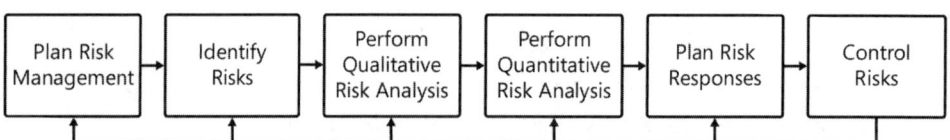

FIGURE 9-1 Developing and controlling a risk register is a sequential and iterative process for risk management.

All projects will experience some degree of risk throughout the project life cycle. How you choose to identity and respond to risk will reflect the level of *risk tolerance* that your project team, or the wider organization, has. If you have a low tolerance for risk, then you either will devote more time and energy to dealing with all risks or choose to not undertake projects with high levels of risk in them. Conversely, if you have a high tolerance for risks, you will either devote less time to proactively planning for risks or choose to take on projects with high degrees of risk, perhaps seeking a high return. It is very important that the project manager spend time assessing the level of risk tolerance key stakeholders such as your organization and the customer have, because this will affect how much time and effort goes into your risk management planning.

EXAM TIP

If you are familiar with ISO 31000 Standard for Risk Management, much of this section will be familiar to you.

Risk is simply a measure of uncertainty that can affect the project either positively or negatively. For example, all of the estimates you have done have some degree of uncertainty—either positive or negative—in them, and this uncertainty represents risk that you need to account for and seek to manage.

EXAM TIP

If you are having trouble understanding exactly what risk management is all about, simply substitute the word "risk" with the word "uncertainty." Risk management focuses on acknowledging that there is uncertainty throughout the entire project, and on planning how to deal with that uncertainty.

If you come across a question in the exam that hints at any amount of uncertainty, you should assume that you will have to perform some level of risk identification and analysis on it.

Risk, or uncertainty, can be positive or negative. If a factor is a potential positive risk, then it is viewed as an opportunity to be maximized through proper selection of risk response strategies. If it is a negative risk, then it is a threat to the project, and your risk response strategies will seek ways to minimize it. Most people tend to think of risks as purely negative events, and though it may be the case that the majority of risks are indeed potentially negative, there are many positive risks. For example, there can be a risk that you will deliver the project under budget by careful procurement of goods and services, in which case you should seek to ensure that you maximize the chances of this risk occurring.

> **Real world**
>
> As a very general rule of thumb, I try to have about two-thirds of my project risk register focused on negative risks, or threats, and about one-third focused upon positive risks, or opportunities. This is a very loose rule, and you may find that your projects are different depending on their industry, size, and complexity. The key point is to make sure that you consider both negative and positive risks on your project.

Plan Risk Management

> **MORE INFO** **PLAN RISK MANAGEMENT**
>
> You can read more about the Plan Risk Management process in the PMBOK® Guide, 5th edition, in Chapter 11, section 11.1. Table 9-1 identifies the process inputs, tools and techniques, and outputs.
>
> **TABLE 9-1** Plan Risk Management process
>
> | Inputs | Tools and techniques | Outputs |
> | --- | --- | --- |
> | - Project management plan
- Project charter
- Stakeholder register
- Enterprise environmental factors
- Organizational process assets | - Analytical techniques
- Expert judgment
- Meetings | - Risk management plan |

The Plan Risk Management process is a planning process with the risk management plan as its sole output. In order to develop a successful risk management plan, you will first need to understand the general level of risks your project faces, as well as the project team or organizational tolerance for risk. Because risk or uncertainty can occur in any part of the project, you will need all the other management plans contained in the project management plan to ensure that you assess and consider all potential sources of risk.

The Plan Risk Management process covers the following domain tasks:

- 2.10 Plan risk management by developing a risk management plan, and identifying, analyzing, and prioritizing project risks in the risk register and defining risk response strategies, in order to manage uncertainty throughout the project life cycle.

Inputs

The Plan Risk Management process uses some or all of the following inputs as part of the development of the risk management plan for the project.

Project management plan

The project management plan will be useful as an input into the Plan Risk Management process because risk can occur at any point from any other aspect of the project. Thus, the already-developed subsidiary plans and baselines contained in the project management plan will highlight areas of uncertainty that can be used to develop the risk management plan. The project management plan is an output from the Develop Project Management Plan process.

Project charter

The project charter, depending on the form it takes, may contain initial descriptions and assessments of known or anticipated risks of the project that provide valuable information for the development of the risk management plan. The project charter is an output from the Develop Project Charter process.

Stakeholder register

The stakeholder register identifies stakeholders in the project, records their roles and contact details, and documents their expectations, all of which are important in including stakeholders in the process of managing risk. The stakeholder register is an output from the Identify Stakeholders process.

Enterprise environmental factors

The specific enterprise environmental factor that will be useful as an input into this process is the broader organizational tolerance for risk. Organizations with a low tolerance for risk will put a lot more effort and energy into managing risk on a project, whereas organizations with a higher tolerance for risk and uncertainty will expend less effort in managing risk and may take on higher-risk projects. International standards such as ISO 31000 may also affect how this process will be carried out and, as such, constitute enterprise environmental factors.

Organizational process assets

The specific organizational process assets that may play an important input in the development of your risk management plan include any templates, processes, or guidelines that the organization has for the development t of a risk management plan and managing risk. Other important organizational process assets are, of course, lessons learned and historical information about successful or unsuccessful risk identification and management from past projects.

Tools and techniques

The following tools and techniques are available to be used to develop the inputs in this process in order to produce the risk management plan.

Analytical techniques

The main purpose of analytical techniques is to determine what the particular approach to risk management on your project will be. This involves checking with stakeholders about their particular appetite and attitude towards risk on the project, and also completing a high-level assessment of risk exposure of the project. Typical analytical techniques are a *stakeholder risk profile analysis*, which can be completed by interviewing individual stakeholders about their attitude and expectations of risk that are suitable for the project. Strategic risk scoring sheets are also used to provide a high-level view of the types and level of risk that the project will encounter.

Expert judgment

Expert judgment is an excellent tool to use when planning your approach to risk management. Utilizing the knowledge and experience of subject matter experts will be invaluable not only in your overall risk management plan, but also in identifying and completing an analysis of risks. Suitable experts who may provide judgment include senior management, stakeholders with relevant experience, and external subject matter experts such as risk professionals, industry groups, and professional associations.

> **Real world**
>
> If your project is likely to be subject to a high number of complex risks, you may want to consider employing the services of a risk management professional. Just as the profession of project management requires a particular skill set, the profession of risk management also employs a particular skill set. I highly recommend the use of risk management professionals for dealing with complex risk issues.

Meetings

Meetings are a great way to bring together project team members, stakeholders, and other experts in order to consider how risk will be managed on the project. There are a number of ways you can run these meetings in order to efficiently get the information that you require. They can be run formally with defined agendas and examination of reports, or they can be run as creative brainstorming sessions. The style of meeting you choose will reflect the participants and your intended outcomes.

> **Real world**
>
> I have often found that meetings are a great way to not only solicit technical input from people with relevant experience but also to generate buy-in and commitment. This is especially important in the area of risk management because giving team members and relevant stakeholders the opportunity to contribute to the management of project risk helps keep them involved and also allows them to understand the importance of being proactive rather than reactive when managing risk.

Outputs

After applying the appropriate tools and techniques to the selected inputs, the Plan Risk Management process has the following output.

Risk management plan

The Plan Risk Management process has the *risk management plan* as its sole output. Similar to other management plans, the risk management plan provides a guide for completing the risk management activities in the project. The risk management plan will probably contain information on the following:

- The particular risk methodology and approach to be taken on the project.
- The individual roles and responsibilities within the team and the wider group of stakeholders.
- Any approved budgets for managing risk, which should then be included in the cost performance baseline.

- An initial analysis of the individual risk categories using a *risk breakdown structure* (RBS). Figure 9-2 shows an example of a risk breakdown structure.

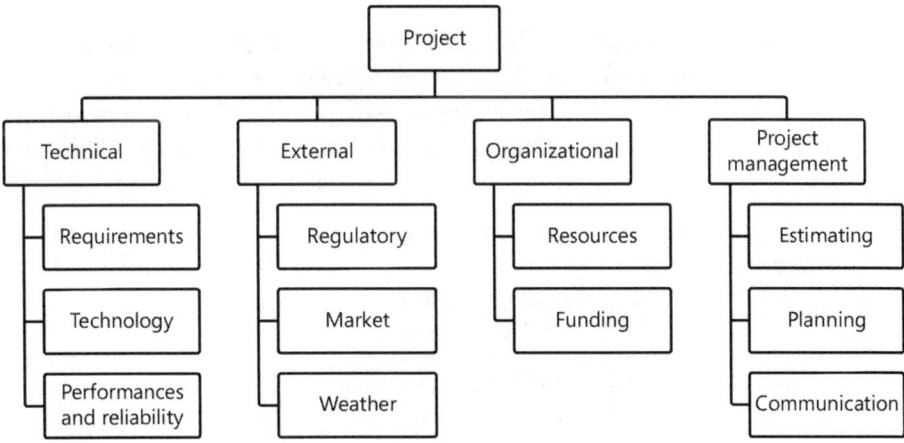

FIGURE 9-2 A risk breakdown structure can be used to develop risk categories.

EXAM TIP

The risk breakdown structure is one of four breakdown structures. The other three are the organizational breakdown structure, work breakdown structure, and resource breakdown structure. Each of the breakdown structures takes a high level concept and breaks it down into its component parts.

- A standardized definition of risk probability and impact is particularly useful for qualitative analysis because the analysis can be quite subjective. Figure 9-3 shows an example of a standardized definition of risk probability and impact.

	Very low or 1	Low or 2	Moderate or 3	High or 4	Very high or 5
Scope	No noticeable change to scope	Minor changes to scope	Significant change to scope	Changes to scope unacceptable to sponsor or client	Changes the complete purpose of the project
Time	No noticeable change to time	Less than 10% increase in time	10–20% increase in time	20–30% increase in time	Greater than 30% increase in time
Cost	No noticeable change to cost	Less than 10% increase in cost	10–20% increase in cost	20–30% increase in cost	Greater than 30% increase in cost

FIGURE 9-3 Standardized definitions of risk probability and impact can be defined in a table.

- A *probability and impact matrix* is useful again for qualitative risk analysis because it allows you to focus on risk activities on those positive or negative risks that present the greatest opportunity or threat. Figure 9-4 shows an example of a probability and impact matrix showing that the highest risks are any with a combined probability and impact greater than 45 percent; these are colored dark grey.

Impact Probability	10%	30%	50%	70%	90%
90%	9%	27%	45%	63%	81%
70%	7%	21%	35%	49%	63%
50%	5%	15%	25%	35%	45%
30%	3%	9%	15%	21%	27%
10%	1%	3%	5%	7%	9%

FIGURE 9-4 A probability and impact matrix shows where the highest risk lies.

- Any predefined formats, processes, guidelines, or templates for risk registers or tracking or reporting of risks.

The risk management plan is a subsidiary of the project management plan and is used as an input into the other five risk management processes.

> **Quick check**
>
> 1. What is the main focus of the Plan Risk Management process?
> 2. Why is it important to also consider positive risk?
> 3. What other areas of the project management plan can risk affect?
>
> **Quick check answers**
>
> 1. The main focus of the Plan Risk Management Process is to formulate your particular approach to how you will manage risks on your project. This is documented in your risk management plan.
> 2. Many people naturally consider risk as a negative event; however, there are many positive risks, which can lead to a project being under budget, ahead of time, delivering greater quality, and delivering higher-than-expected stakeholder expectations.
> 3. Risk management can affect every other aspect of the project because there is generally always uncertainty in all elements of your project.

Identify Risks

> **MORE INFO** **IDENTIFY RISKS**
>
> You can read more about the Identify Risks process in the PMBOK® Guide, 5th edition, in Chapter 11, section 11.2. Table 9-2 identifies the process inputs, tools and techniques, and outputs.

TABLE 9-2 Identify Risks process

Inputs	Tools and techniques	Outputs
- Risk management plan - Cost management plan - Schedule management plan - Quality management plan - Human resource management plan - Scope baseline - Activity cost estimates - Activity duration estimates - Stakeholder register - Project documents - Procurement documents - Enterprise environmental factors - Organizational process assets	- Documentation reviews - Information-gathering techniques - Checklist analysis - Assumptions analysis Diagramming techniques - SWOT analysis - Expert judgment	- Risk register

The Identify Risks process is a planning process that uses a wide variety of inputs and tools and techniques to identify all the risks to the project. It is performed through the life of the project, and the risk register is always updated with newly identified risks or current risks that are reassessed by using the other risk planning processes.

The Identify Risks process covers the following domain task:

- 2.10 Plan risk management by developing a risk management plan, and identifying, analyzing, and prioritizing project risks in the risk register and defining risk response strategies, in order to manage uncertainty throughout the project life cycle.

In addition to being performed throughout the life of the project, risk identification should be completed by all project team members and stakeholders with experience in the area. This enables you to draw on their skills and experience, and it also creates buy-in to the process of risk management. It is important to realize that the process of identifying risks is not a stand-alone process but one that involves many stakeholders in a constant state of communication to get their expertise and experience.

> **Real world**
>
> Despite your best efforts, you will probably miss certain risks. On a project I was working on, we spent a lot of time and money on identifying risks for a particularity complex piece of work that was to occur over a five-day period. We used historical information, consulted experts, reviewed documents and plans, involved the project team members, and conducted tests to prepare what we thought was a completely comprehensive risk register. Within the first two hours of the five-day piece of work, a problem arose that we had not identified. We were able to respond to the situation well in this instance, and we used this information for a new risk register for a similar piece of work to be completed 12 months later. The main lesson we learned is that you need to be ready for the unexpected and not assume that your risk register captures every risk.

You will recognize from the range of inputs into the Identify Risks process that risk can occur in any other part of the project.

Inputs

The Identify Risks process uses some or all of the following inputs.

Risk management plan

The risk management plan is an essential input into the Identify Risks process because it will contain information on your particular approach, or methodology, to identifying risks generally, and more specifically it will contain information derived from the risk breakdown structure on already-identified risk categories. It will also contain a description of the particular risk tolerance for the project, which will assist you in determining the effort that you put into identifying particular risks. The risk management plan is an output from the Plan Risk Management process.

Cost management plan

The cost management plan will contain cost estimates for all elements of the project, and these estimates should reflect the amount of uncertainty in the estimating process. Each of these areas of uncertainties, either negative or positive, represents a risk on the project. The cost management plan is an output from the Plan Cost Management process.

EXAM TIP

All estimates are by their very nature uncertain. They are educated guesses at what the future will be, based on information at hand today. Thus, any baselines, such as cost and time, that are built up using estimates will have a range of uncertainty within them, both negative and positive. In the exam, if you find the word "uncertainty" or "estimate," you should assume that risk will be present.

Schedule management plan

The schedule management plan will refer to areas of uncertainty or risk in the development of the project schedule. This information can be used to identify risks associated with the project time frame. The schedule management plan is an output from the Plan Schedule Management process.

Quality management plan

The quality management plan will identify areas of uncertainty in the delivery of quality on the project. The quality management plan is an output from the Plan Quality Management process.

Human resource management plan

The human resource management plan will identify areas of uncertainty with the definition, recruitment, retention, and development of project team members, all of which represent risks on the project and should be taken into account during the Identify Risks process. The human resource management plan is an output from the Plan Human Resource Management process.

Scope baseline

The scope baseline, made up of the scope statement, the work breakdown structure (WBS), and the WBS dictionary, defines the work to be done on the project and also outlines any areas of uncertainty in the project scope that require further definition. These areas of uncertainty represent risk on the project and should be used to identify individual risks related to the project scope. The scope baseline is an output from the Create WBS process.

Activity cost estimates

Individual activity cost estimates include cost estimates for individual project activities. In addition to the actual dollar amount of the estimate, there will be information about the information used and assumptions made in preparing the estimates, which provides an insight into the range of uncertainty in the estimate. This uncertainty represents risks on the project and should be included in the development of the risk register. Activity cost estimates are an output from the Estimate Costs process.

Activity duration estimates

Activity duration estimates contain information about the individual time estimates prepared for project activities. This estimating information should contain an indication of the range of uncertainty surrounding the estimate, which represents risk to the project. Activity durations estimates are an output from the Estimate Activity Duration process.

Stakeholder register

The stakeholder register is extremely useful in identifying individual risks for two reasons. The first is that the stakeholder register allows you to interview individual stakeholders about their particular attitude towards risk. The second is that each stakeholder will be able to assist from his own unique point of view with the identification of project risks. The stakeholder register is an output from the Identify Stakeholders process.

Project documents

The specific types of project documents that will be useful in the Identify Risks process are things such as work performance reports, network diagrams, and assumptions logs, because they provide information about how the project is performing, the sequence of planned activities, and the assumptions made about different estimates, respectively.

Procurement documents

Procurement documents are a key input into the Identify Risks process because they will outline any contractual obligations that may contribute to uncertainty, and the value of this uncertainty. Procurement documents are an output from the Plan Procurement Management process.

Enterprise environmental factors

The specific types of enterprise environmental factors that will be useful in managing project risk are any broader organizational attitude and tolerance for risk, and any external risk standards that the organization is using.

Organizational process assets

The specific types of organizational process assets that will assist in managing project risk are any blank templates, historical information and lessons learned, and any project-specific policies and guidelines relating to risk management.

Tools and techniques

The following tools and techniques are used upon the inputs to deliver the Identify Risks process outputs.

Documentation reviews

Documentation reviews refer to a structured analysis and review of all relevant project documents and the information they contain to detect any areas of uncertainty or risk on the project. The types of documents reviewed are any part of the project management plan or baselines, documents providing descriptions of any part of the project, and documents outlining the assumptions made in preparing estimates. Documentation reviews are generally carried out by the project manager and project team members.

Information-gathering techniques

There are many different ways to gather information in relation to project risk. Each has its own benefits and will deliver varying degrees of accuracy and thoroughness. Examples of useful *information-gathering techniques* for the Identify Risks process include:

- **Brainstorming**   This is an excellent way to encourage creative thinking about particular risk issues. The intended outcome is a comprehensive list of all the potential risks.
- **Interviewing**   Interviewing experts and people with experience in similar projects and the associated risks is an excellent way to quickly obtain relevant information.
- **Delphi technique**   This is an extremely useful tool to solicit information from experts anonymously, to avoid peer pressure and groupthink. This is particularly useful when you are seeking to encourage a wide range of opinions and assessment of potential project risks.

> **Real world**
>
> One of the few times I've been involved as a participant in a Delphi technique was in the identification of risks on a large and complex IT project. To me as a participant, it was a complex process requiring significant thought, input, and review of other anonymous participants' opinions. After the results were gathered and disseminated to participants, though, I could tell that there had been an extremely comprehensive identification and assessment of all the potential risks that could affect this particular project.

Checklist analysis

Checklist analysis uses historical information gathered from previous projects and presents a list of activities and items that must be checked off to ensure that they have been done as part of a thorough risk identification process.

Assumptions analysis

Any and all assumptions made about any aspect of the project will represent uncertainty and therefore risk for the project. Therefore, *assumptions analysis*, or gathering the assumptions log and testing its accuracy, stability, consistency, and completeness are essential parts of identifying project risks.

Diagramming techniques

The use of *diagramming techniques* is an excellent way to graphically represent the process of identifying individual risks. There are several diagramming techniques that are particularly useful in the identification of risks. They include the cause-and-effect, Ishikawa, or fishbone diagram, which is extremely useful for getting to the root cause of project risks. You saw the use of this particular diagramming technique in Chapter 6, "Quality management," to determine the root cause of quality issues. Figure 9-5 shows a cause-and-effect diagram being used to identify risks associated with cost overruns on a project.

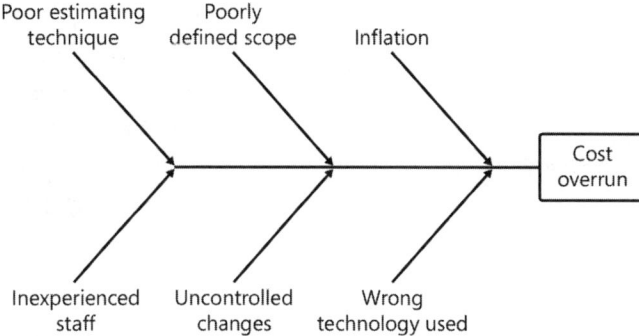

FIGURE 9-5 A cause-and-effect diagram can be used to identify risks.

Another useful diagramming technique is a flowchart, which can show how events are related to each other within a system. By analyzing how different activities or events are interrelated, you can recognize how risk can flow from one part of the project to another.

A third type of diagramming technique that is useful for the identification of risks is an influence diagram, which is a simple graphical representation of cause-and-effect relationships between sequential activities.

SWOT analysis

A key element of any risk identification process is the use of *SWOT analysis*. *SWOT* stands for *strengths, weaknesses, opportunities, and threats*. The idea is to identify and document each of these four areas and then focus on your strengths while making provision for your weaknesses, prepare to take advantage of the opportunities that present themselves, and plan how to respond to identified threats. All of these are key elements in identifying risks.

> **Real world**
>
> I have successfully used SWOT analysis on many occasions to put a framework around a brainstorming session. By getting people to focus on what the current strengths, weaknesses, opportunities, and threats are is an extremely easy way to start people thinking about uncertainty in the project.

Expert judgment

The use of experts and their experience and skills in identifying risks is a key tool during this process because the identification of risks can be quite a complex process. By using the experience of project team members who may have done this sort of project before, or external consultants with expertise in this particular area, you will have a greater chance of identifying all of the risks in the project.

Outputs

The Identify Risks process has the following single output.

Risk register

The risk register is the single output from the Identify Risks process. The development of the risk register is highly iterative, and the risk register itself should be treated as a live document and reviewed regularly. It should be reviewed at all levels from testing the assumptions made right through to the qualitative and quantitative analysis applied to the identified risks. The actual risk register will take many forms depending on your organizational risk tolerance and any existing templates and guidelines. Figure 9-6 shows a generic form of risk register showing risk identification, qualitative analysis, quantitative analysis, and risk responses.

Risk Identification				Qualitative Analysis			Quantitative Analysis		Risk Response Planning
Category	Event	Consequence	+/-	P	I	P x I	P	I$	P x I$	Response

FIGURE 9-6 A risk register is the primary output from the Identify Risks process. The risk register shown here is a generic version.

> **Real world**
>
> As well as providing extremely valuable technical information about your assessment of risk on the project, the preparation and constant revisiting of the risk register keeps risk at the forefront of your project team's minds. I have found time and effort invested in risk management useful not only from a technical point of view in managing risk, but also for obtaining buy-in and helping people to recognize the importance of proactive risk management.

EXAM TIP

The risk register is perhaps the most iterative document in the project because it is constantly undergoing review and being updated. In the exam, you should always assume that the risk register is being referred to often.

> ✓ **Quick check**
> 1. Why is the risk register considered a highly iterative document?
> 2. Who should be involved in the identification of risks?
> 3. What are three types of information-gathering techniques that can be used to identify risks?
>
> **Quick check answers**
> 1. The risk register is a highly iterative document because you will always be updating it as information becomes available, assumptions made are tested and refined, and new risks are identified and old ones closed.
> 2. The project manager will take ultimate responsibility for the Identify Risks process. But the whole project team and relevant external experts should also be involved in the process.
> 3. There are many types of information-gathering techniques useful for many aspects of project management. Techniques specifically mentioned as useful for the Identify Risks process include brainstorming, the Delphi technique, interviewing, and root cause analysis.

Perform Qualitative Risk Analysis

> *MORE INFO* **PERFORM QUALITATIVE RISK ANALYSIS**
>
> You can read more about the Perform Qualitative Risk Analysis process in the PMBOK® Guide, 5th edition, in Chapter 11, section 11.3. Table 9-3 identifies the process inputs, tools and techniques, and outputs.
>
> **TABLE 9-3** Perform Qualitative Risk Analysis process
>
> | Inputs | Tools and techniques | Outputs |
> | --- | --- | --- |
> | ■ Risk management plan
■ Scope baseline
■ Risk register
■ Enterprise environmental factors
■ Organizational process assets | ■ Risk probability and impact assessment
■ Probability and impact matrix
■ Risk data quality assessment
■ Risk categorization
■ Risk urgency assessment
■ Expert judgment | ■ Project documents updates |

The Perform Qualitative Risk Analysis process is a planning process focused on assigning a qualitative, or subjective, analysis of probability and impact to all identified risks.

The Perform Qualitative Risk Analysis process covers the following domain task:

- 2.10 Plan risk management by developing a risk management plan, and identifying, analyzing, and prioritizing project risks in the risk register and defining risk response strategies, in order to manage uncertainty throughout the project life cycle.

EXAM TIP

The key difference between qualitative and quantitative assessment is that qualitative assessment is subjective—that is, it uses opinion and experience—and is done quickly. On the other hand, quantitative assessment involves actual data and figures to support a more objective assessment. For example, you may do a qualitative assessment that the chance of it snowing in winter during your construction project is 7 out of 10 (1 being that it definitely will not snow, and 10 being that it definitely will snow), and that the impact if it does snow is 6 out of 10 (1 being no impact at all, and 10 being a catastrophic impact). This gives a total qualitative assessment of 42 out of a possible 100. You may then decide to spend some time and money doing quantitative risk analysis on this risk and contact the local weather bureau, which tells you that there is a 0.831 chance of it snowing on those dates. Your team members tell you that if it does snow, you will suffer a $10,000 loss. This gives you a total quantitative assessment of $8,310. You can tell that quantitative assessment takes more time and money to get this information, but it is more accurate.

The process of qualitative risk analysis is generally done on all identified risks because it is quick and easy to do. It is simply a matter of assigning a subjective assessment of the probability of the risk occurring and also assigning a subjective assessment of the impact of the risk, using defined scales. The scales used can be numerical, such as 1–10, or text based, such as low, very low, high, and so on.

When these two factors are multiplied together, the result is an individual qualitative risk score for each identified risk, which you can use to prioritize the risks and choose to focus on those that ranked the highest. Additionally, you will go on to perform quantitative risk analysis only on those risks that score the highest.

Inputs

The following inputs are used in the Perform Qualitative Risk Analysis process.

Risk management plan

Obviously one of the key inputs into any of the other risk management planning processes will be the risk management plan because it contains information about how each risk management process, including the Perform Qualitative Risk Analysis process, will be performed. The risk management plan is an output from the Plan Risk Management process.

Scope baseline

The scope baseline is an important input into the Perform Qualitative Risk Analysis process because it describes all the work to be done, and the work not to be done, on the project. With this description of the work, you will get a full picture of the elements of the scope that are clear and defined, and those elements of the scope that are still uncertain and ill defined and that represent risk on the project that needs to be analyzed. The scope baseline is an output from the Create WBS process.

Risk register

The risk register is a key input into the Perform Qualitative Risk Analysis process because, in its first iteration, it is a list of all the risks that have been identified, and the continual development of the risk register includes qualitative risk analysis performed not only once, but on an ongoing basis as new information, new risks, and assumptions are refined. The risk register is an output from the Identify Risks process.

Enterprise environmental factors

The specific types of enterprise environmental factors that will be useful as inputs into the Perform Qualitative Risk Analysis process are any external industry standards, such as ISO 31000, and any external information held by risk professionals, such as risk databases and information about the analysis of individual risks.

Organizational process assets

The specific organizational process assets that will be of use in the Perform Qualitative Risk Analysis process are any historical information that the organization has on similar risks and their probability and impact, and any pre-prepared templates and processes to assist in the qualitative analysis of individually identified risks.

Tools and techniques

The following tools and techniques of this process are able to be used upon the separate inputs to deliver the Perform Qualitative Risk Analysis process outputs.

Risk probability and impact assessment

The primary tool used in the Perform Qualitative Risk Analysis process is *risk probability and impact assessment*. The key here is to assess each identified risk and assign to it a probability of the risk occurring, and an assessment of the impact if the risk does occur, by using a standardized scale that should be included in the risk management plan. Because it is a qualitative analysis, there are several kinds of numerical scales or text descriptions that can be used to standardize the responses assessing probability and impact.

Because the assessments of probability and impact being made are qualitative and therefore somewhat subjective, it is important during this process to document the assumptions that were made based on the information available at the time the assessment was done. Throughout the course of the project you will revisit these assumptions, and you will gain further information, which may change either the assessment of risk probability or impact.

> **Real world**
>
> There are many different ways of assessing qualitative probability and impact on projects. In my career I have used simple numerical scales from 1 to 5, or text-based descriptions such as likely, unlikely, and highly likely.

Probability and impact matrix

A probability and impact matrix standardizes and identifies the risks after they have had a probability and impact assessment performed on them so that individual risks can be ranked very quickly. Figure 9-4, shown earlier in this chapter in the "Plan Risk Management" section, presented an example of a probability and impact matrix as a key component of the risk management plan.

Risk data quality assessment

A key element when performing any sort of risk assessment is the quality of the information being used. Obviously, if the quality of information being used is poor, your subsequent assessment will be poor. Therefore, it is important to use a *risk data quality assessment* technique to evaluate the quality of the data being used to make the assessment.

> **Real world**
>
> In my experience, the quality of information that you use to identify and analyze risks definitely does get better over time, especially if you are doing particular types of work for the first time and you are constantly learning and refining the information you have at hand.

Risk categorization

A useful way of representing and presenting the qualitative risk analysis is with *risk categorization* techniques, which you can use to sort the risks into different categories for easy monitoring and reporting. An excellent example of risk categorization is the risk breakdown structure (RBS) shown earlier in Figure 9-2. You may also choose to categorize your risks by project phase or by relevance to particular stakeholders. However you choose to categorize your risks, you should be able to present them in a document or graphically.

Risk urgency assessment

A *risk urgency assessment* is a tool that takes into account not only an assessment of the probability and impact of the risk, but the urgency of the risk. Urgency has to do with whether the risk is likely to occur in the near future, in which case you will have a high degree of urgency, compared to risks that may or may not manifest until some further point in time. Those risks that may occur in the near future are those that need the greatest attention paid to them. Risks that may occur further off in the project timeframe can have less attention paid to them.

Expert judgment

Again the use of expert judgment is an exceptionally good way to bring a robust level of analysis to your Perform Qualitative Risk Analysis process. Your choice of experts, and the way in which you choose to solicit information from them, will be an important factor in the quality of the advice given.

> **Real world**
>
> It is always important to give a high degree of consideration when selecting those people you will choose to consult with as experts. The types of things you may want to consider are the level of experience, the willingness to share this experience, the availability, the ability to share information concisely, and any costs associated with the use of those experts.

Outputs

The sole output from the Perform Qualitative Risk Analysis process is the following.

Project documents updates

The specific project documents that will be updated are the risk register and the assumptions log. Any time you complete any new qualitative risk assessments, or revise existing qualitative risk assessment based on refined or new information, you will need to update the risk register. Along with updating the risk register with new or revised information is the requirement to update the assumptions log to reflect the new assumptions that have been made.

✓ Quick check

1. What is the main difference between qualitative risk assessment and quantitative risk assessment?
2. What sort of probability and impact assessment is best used for the Perform Qualitative Risk Analysis process?
3. How does risk urgency assessment differ from risk probability and impact assessment?

Quick check answers

1. The main difference between qualitative risk assessment and quantitative risk assessment is that qualitative risk assessment uses subjective assessments of probability and impact, whereas quantitative risk assessment uses objective assessments of probability and impact, usually quantifying it in terms of money or time.
2. There is no one best type of probability and impact assessment to use in the Perform Qualitative Risk Analysis process. The decision whether to use numerical scales or text-based descriptions of qualitative risk analysis is entirely up to you and depends on what is appropriate for your project.
3. Risk urgency assessment takes into account the timeframe in which the risk may manifest, with risks that may manifest in the near future having a higher urgency than risks that may occur in the longer term. Risk probability and impact assessment is applied to all risk and simply assesses the probability of the risk occurring, and the impact if it does occur.

Perform Quantitative Risk Analysis

> **MORE INFO** **PERFORM QUANTITATIVE RISK ANALYSIS**
>
> You can read more about the Perform Quantitative Risk Analysis process in the PMBOK® Guide, 5th edition, in Chapter 11, section 11.4. Table 9-4 identifies the process inputs, tools and techniques, and outputs.

TABLE 9-4 Perform Quantitative Risk Analysis process

Inputs	Tools and techniques	Outputs
- Risk management plan - Cost management plan - Schedule management plan - Risk register - Enterprise environmental factors - Organizational process assets	- Data gathering and representation techniques - Quantitative risk analysis and modeling techniques - Expert judgment	- Project documents updates

The Perform Quantitative Risk Analysis process is a planning process focused on the development of a quantitative, or objective, assessment of individual risk probability and impact, often by using a metric based on money or time.

The Perform Quantitative Risk Analysis process covers the following domain task:

- 2.10 Plan risk management by developing a risk management plan, and identifying, analyzing, and prioritizing project risks in the risk register and defining risk response strategies, in order to manage uncertainty throughout the project life cycle.

Performing quantitative risk analysis generally takes more effort than performing qualitative risk analysis and assessment, and therefore it is generally performed on those risks that are identified as having a higher probability and impact on the project. The intended outcome of the quantitative risk assessment process is to assign a dollar or time amount to specific risks if they occur. You can then aggregate all these individual quantitative estimates to build contingency reserves for time or cost. Because of the complexity of the tools and techniques, and information required for successful quantitative risk analysis, it is often done by risk professionals with experience and access to relevant historical information that can be used in the analysis.

Inputs

The following inputs are used in the Perform Quantitative Risk Analysis process.

Risk management plan

The risk management plan outlines the particular way in which you will approach the process of quantitative risk analysis and, as such, it is an extremely important input to assist in the completion of this process. The risk management plan is an output from the Plan Risk Management process.

Cost management plan

The cost management plan is a useful input into the Perform Quantitative Risk Analysis process because it outlines how financial reserves will be developed and managed. One of the key metrics used in quantitative risk analysis is the use of dollar amounts as a quantity, and cumulatively the individual dollar amounts can be added up to become a cost reserve for the project. The cost management plan is an output from the Plan Cost Management process.

Schedule management plan

Like the cost management plan, the schedule management plan provides guidelines for the development and management of schedule reserve, which is calculated with quantitative risk analysis by using time as a metric. The schedule management plan is an output from the Plan Schedule Management process.

Risk register

The risk register, from the moment it first appears and throughout all its subsequent iterations, is an essential input into the Perform Quantitative Risk Analysis process because the outputs from this process will update the risk register with specific information about individual risk assessment. The risk register is an output from the Identify Risks process.

Enterprise environmental factors

The specific enterprise environmental factors that will be useful in the Perform Quantitative Risk Analysis process are any external industry standards such as ISO 31000 and any risk databases held by risk professionals.

Organizational process assets

The specific organizational process assets that will be of use in the Perform Quantitative Risk Analysis process are any historical information that the organization holds on previous experience with performing quantitative risk analysis and, of course, any blank templates or guidelines the organization has for completing the Perform Quantitative Risk Analysis process.

Tools and techniques

The following tools and techniques of this process are able to be used upon the separate inputs to deliver the Perform Quantitative Risk Analysis process outputs.

Data gathering and representation techniques

A key technique to assist with the execution of the Perform Quantitative Risk Analysis process is the use of *data gathering and representation techniques*. The purpose of using these techniques is to obtain relevant and accurate data that can then be assessed to develop the quantitative metrics of risk probability and impact. These data gathering and representation techniques include the following:

- Interviewing techniques that draw on the experience and skills of experts. The type of information that you will be seeking from experts is their own quantitative assessment of probability and impact of particular risks. You may end up with a range of responses and thus may want to consider the use of three-point estimating, which was covered in the cost and time estimating processes in Chapter 4, "Time management" and Chapter 5, "Cost management."

- Another way to gather quantitative risk data is via the use of established statistical probability distributions. There are many types of probability distributions, but the most commonly used are normal distributions, beta distributions, triangular distributions, and uniform distributions, each with its own statistical distribution of data that can be used to quantify a particular risk probability or impact and the associated range of data. The type of distribution that you use should be based on professional experience and historical information, in order to make sure that it is valid.

Quantitative risk analysis and modeling techniques

In *quantitative risk analysis and modeling techniques,* sophisticated statistical and mathematical approaches are applied to the calculation and range of risk probability and impact. There are a variety of techniques that can be used, but because of their sophistication, they are usually carried out by using software. Of the available types of quantitative risk analysis and modeling techniques, the following are the most popular and useful for quantitative risk analysis:

- ***Sensitivity analysis*** A technique that looks at different aspects of the project and how they have an impact upon project risk, to determine which parts of the project are most sensitive to risk. It may, for example, determine that issues around cost are more sensitive to risk, and more specifically that cost issues related to inflationary pressures on materials over time are most at risk. Sensitivity analysis is a highly complex set of calculations using software and, as such, generally requires specialized knowledge and expertise to carry out.

- ***Tornado diagrams*** Often used to present the results of sensitivity analysis. A tornado diagram is a histogram or bar chart where the data categories are listed vertically instead of horizontally, with the largest category at the top and then the other categories in order of descending size, giving the diagram the appearance of a tornado. Figure 9-7 shows an example of a tornado diagram presenting the results of sensitivity analysis to show which parts of the project are most sensitive to risk, judged by the quantitative impact they will have on the net present value (NPV) of the project.

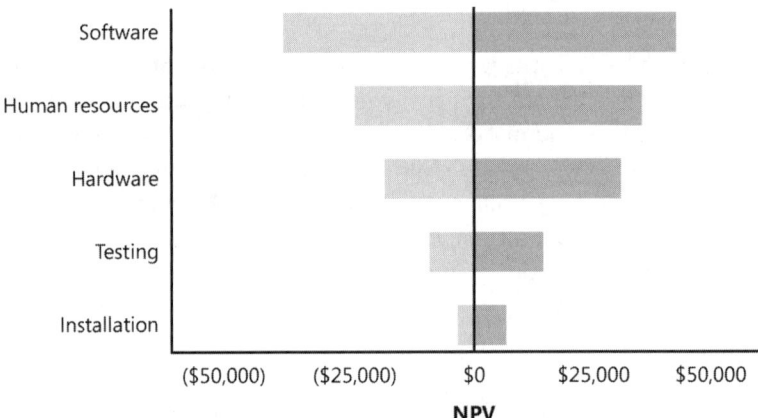

FIGURE 9-7 A tornado diagram shows how different risks might have an impact upon project net present value.

- **Expected monetary value analysis (EMV)**   A way to allocate quantitative numerical probability and impact to particular options and from this to arrive at what the expected monetary value of each option is. Depending on the calculated outcome, you would then be able to quantify your decision. The usual way of graphically representing the expected monetary value analysis is with the use of decision trees. In Figure 9-8, a decision tree shows the calculation of expected monetary value regarding whether to upgrade existing customer ordering software or to develop a completely new piece of software.

Decision Definition	Decision node	Chance node	Net path value
Decision to be made	Input: cost of each option Output: decision made (true, false)	Input: scenario probability, reward if it occurs Output: expected monetary value (EMV)	Computed: (Payoffs minus Costs) along path

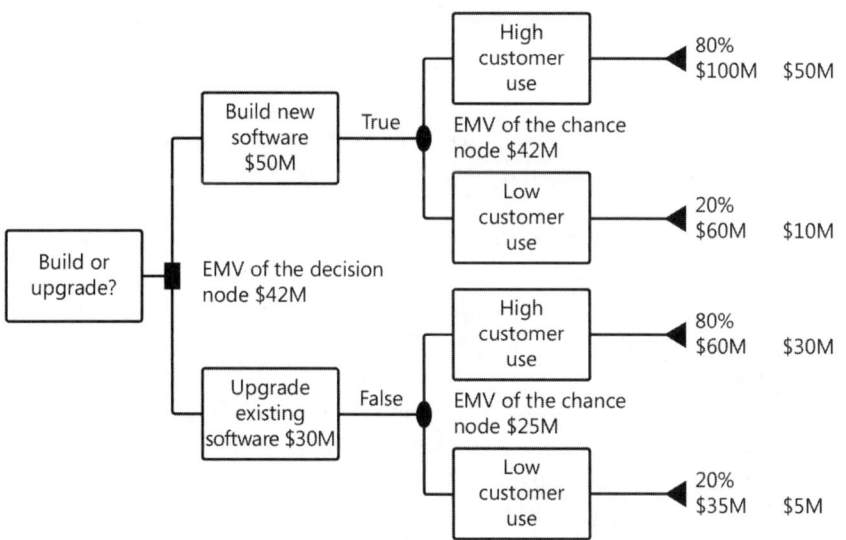

FIGURE 9-8 This decision tree analysis assesses the expected monetary value of building new software versus upgrading existing software.

Figure 9-8 shows that for either decision there is an 80 percent chance of high customer use and a 20 percent chance of low customer use. If you decide to build new software, it will cost $50 million, and if there is high customer use, you will make $100 million, so there is an 80 percent chance of making a net figure of $50 million. By the same token, if you decide to build new software at a cost of $50 million, and there is low customer use, you will only make $60 million, so there is a 20 percent chance of making a net figure of $10 million. You would then add these two calculations together:

(0.8 × $50m) + (0.2 × $10m)

to get an expected monetary value (EMV) of $42 million.

The other option is to upgrade the existing software, which will cost $30 million and has an 80 percent chance of making a net figure of $30 million, and a 20percent chance of making a net figure of $5 million. Therefore, the expected monetary value for this decision is:

(0.8 × $30m) + (0.2 × $5m) = $25m

By using this form of quantitative risk analysis, you can recognize that the best decision is to take the option with the greater expected monetary value, which is to build new software. What is also apparent in this example is that the quality of the calculated outcome is only as good as the quality of the information going into the model. Here is another example of why it is important to document the assumptions that you've made, so that if any of this changes in the future you can quickly recalculate.

EXAM TIP

You may have to calculate a decision tree in the exam, so just remember to calculate the probability of each by the net value—cost minus income.

- **Modeling and simulation** Includes Monte Carlo analysis, which is the most common type. In the Monte Carlo technique, all the potential outcomes are modeled and computed many times, with different input values, to assess the most likely outcomes—that is, those with the highest probability—and to come up with a probability distribution, (normal, uniform, or beta) associated with each of these outcomes. By using Monte Carlo analysis you can find the likely probability of many different risks, and this allows you and your team to determine which risks will have the greatest or least chance of occurring. It is a highly sophisticated form of mathematical modeling and requires the use of software.

EXAM TIP

If you find a question in the exam referring to mathematical modeling of risks, it will be referring to one of these techniques.

Expert judgment

Given the complexity of performing accurate quantitative risk analysis, the use of subject matter experts with relevant experience in this area is very important. Expert judgment is important not only for the quantitative calculations but also for the interpretation of the data produced.

Outputs

The single output from the Perform Quantitative Risk Analysis process is the following.

Project documents updates

The specific project documents that will be updated include the risk register. The types of information that will feature in the risk register updates will include all the calculations generated by the quantitative risk analysis, which includes quantitative probabilities of individual risks, quantitative impacts of individual risks in terms of both cost and time, and subsequently a prioritized list of quantified risks.

Quick check

1. What is the main purpose of quantitative risk analysis?
2. Why is it important to consider the use of experts during the Perform Quantitative Risk Analysis process?
3. What is the main value of using quantitative risk analysis and modeling techniques such as sensitivity analysis and expected monetary value analysis?

Quick check answers

1. The main purpose of quantitative risk analysis is to quantify in either cost or time values the particular probability and impact of individual risks, and the development of reserves for both cost and time.
2. The Perform Quantitative Risk Analysis process can be a highly sophisticated process using complex statistical and mathematical modeling and, as such, in order to extract maximum benefit from quantitative risk analysis it may be necessary to use people with experience in both the preparation and interpretation of quantitative risk data.
3. The main value in using quantitative risk analysis and modeling techniques is that it gives you a standardized and defined means of analyzing and presenting data in a way that can be understood easily.

Plan Risk Responses

> **MORE INFO   PLAN RISK RESPONSES**
>
> You can read more about the Plan Risk Responses process in the PMBOK® Guide, 5th edition, in Chapter 11, section 11.5. Table 9-5 identifies the process inputs, tools and techniques, and outputs.
>
> **TABLE 9-5** Plan Risk Responses process
>
> | Inputs | Tools and techniques | Outputs |
> | --- | --- | --- |
> | - Risk management plan
- Risk register | - Strategies for negative risks or threats
- Strategies for positive risks or opportunities
- Contingent response strategies
- Expert judgment | - Project management plan updates
- Project documents updates |

The Plan Risk Responses process is a planning process that is focused on the development of proactive responses to risks.

The Plan Risk Responses process covers the following domain task:

- 2.10 Plan risk management by developing a risk management plan, and identifying, analyzing, and prioritizing project risks in the risk register and defining risk response strategies, in order to manage uncertainty throughout the project life cycle.

The development of proactive responses is a very effective way of both minimizing the potential effects of negative risk and maximizing the potential benefits of positive risk on a project. Each of the risk responses will seek to influence the risk prior to its possible occurrence, and also to influence the risk if it does occur. In addition to planning responses to identified risk, the Plan Risk Responses process also proactively considers responses to unplanned or unforeseen risks.

Inputs

The following inputs are used in the Plan Risk Responses process.

Risk management plan

The risk management plan contains information about the processes you have decided are most appropriate for the development of risk responses and, as such, it is an essential input into the Plan Risk Responses process. The risk management plan is an output from the Plan Risk Management process.

Risk register

Obviously, in order to develop risk responses you are going to need a list of all the identified risks, their potential consequences, and either the qualitative or quantitative risk analysis for each. All this information is contained within the risk register, which makes it an essential input into the Plan Risk Responses process. The risk register is an output from the Identify Risks process.

Tools and techniques

The following tools and techniques of this process are able to be used upon the separate inputs to deliver the Plan Risk Responses process output.

Strategies for negative risks or threats

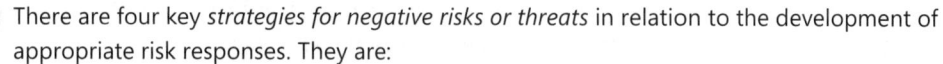

There are four key *strategies for negative risks or threats* in relation to the development of appropriate risk responses. They are:

- **Avoid**   Making plans to avoid the risk occurring. For example, if you have identified that there is a risk of earthquake damage in a building that you plan to construct, an avoid strategy would be to relocate the building to an area that was more geotechnically stable.

- **Transfer**   Making the responsibility and ultimately the consequences of the risk somebody else's responsibility. The most common form of transfer is insurance. For example, after identifying that your building may be subject to damage from an earthquake, you may decide to take out insurance for this event.

- **Mitigate**   Accepting that the risk may occur but attempting to put in place a risk response that minimizes the negative effects of the risk. For example, you may decide to build your multistory building in a known earthquake zone, but choose to mitigate the effects of an earthquake upon the building with the use of base isolators and materials that are impact resistant.

- **Accept**   Simply accepting the consequence of the risk occurring. For example, you may choose not to take out insurance, nor to shift a planned building, nor to use earthquake-resistant building technology, and simply accept that if an earthquake hits you will take responsibility for repairs.

You can have multiple strategies for each risk; often this is the wisest approach because different strategies can be enacted at different times in the timeline of a risk potentially occurring. You will also choose the most appropriate risk strategy, or strategies, for your particular risk and your particular risk tolerance.

Strategies for positive risks or opportunities

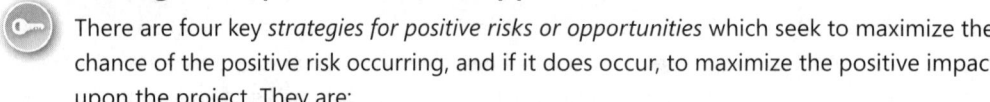
There are four key *strategies for positive risks or opportunities* which seek to maximize the chance of the positive risk occurring, and if it does occur, to maximize the positive impact upon the project. They are:

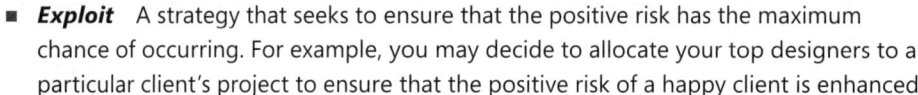
- **Exploit** A strategy that seeks to ensure that the positive risk has the maximum chance of occurring. For example, you may decide to allocate your top designers to a particular client's project to ensure that the positive risk of a happy client is enhanced.

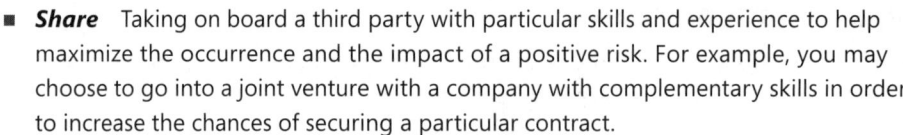
- **Share** Taking on board a third party with particular skills and experience to help maximize the occurrence and the impact of a positive risk. For example, you may choose to go into a joint venture with a company with complementary skills in order to increase the chances of securing a particular contract.

- **Enhance** Being prepared to increase the chances of the positive risk occurring and, if it does occur, the positive impact that it has. For example, you may choose to buy more lottery tickets in order to enhance the chances of your winning.

- **Accept** There will be no changes made to the project management plan and you will simply accept the chances of the positive risk occurring and the impact that it has.

Contingent response strategies

Each of the strategies for negative risk or positive risk discussed previously is developed for clearly identified risks. However, it is highly unlikely that despite your best efforts you will end up identifying all of the risks that may occur on a project, and thus it is prudent to have in place *contingent response strategies*, which are your planned responses to unplanned risk. The contingent response strategies will outline the actions your project team will take if a set of predefined conditions occurs. This set of predefined conditions can refer to particular metrics relating to the project budget or project schedule. Your contingent response strategies will be included in your *contingency plan*.

A further means of dealing with unplanned risks occurring is a *workaround*. The difference between a workaround and contingent response strategies is that a workaround is an unplanned and reactive response to an unplanned risk occurring, whereas a contingent response strategy is a planned and prepared response to an unplanned risk occurring. A workaround is a plan to get around a problem or risk that has arisen and not necessarily fix it. A great way to implement a workaround is to gather experienced people in a single location and get them to brainstorm a solution as fast as possible. The workaround may be a temporary solution to allow you to continue working on the project and, therefore, you should be prepared to revisit the situation with a more permanent solution. Always include your experience of workarounds in your lessons learned so that future projects may anticipate the risk and include it in their risk register.

Expert judgment

Given the complexity of executing a well-defined series of planned risk responses, it is prudent to use expert judgment as a tool in developing your risk responses. The experts that you choose to use will be those people with experience and skills in anticipating and dealing with the identified risks.

Outputs

The outputs from the Plan Risk Responses process are the following.

Project management plan updates

The specific parts of the project management plan that will be updated as a result of your consideration of potential risk responses will include all aspects of the project management plan, such as the schedule, cost, quality, and procurement management plans, as well as the human resource management plan and scope, schedule, and cost baselines. The consideration of different, and appropriate, risk responses will often require you to revisit these foundational documents as a result of the risks identified and the planned responses.

Project documents updates

The specific project documents that will be updated will of course be of the risk register and the assumptions log. It is essential that both of these documents are kept up to date and reflect the latest information about particular risks, the analysis of individual risks, and the planned risk responses.

Quick check

1. What is the main purpose of the Plan Risk Responses process?
2. What are the four risk response strategies for positive risks?
3. What are the four risk response strategies for negative risks?
4. What is the purpose of having contingent response strategies in place?

Quick check answers

1. The main purpose of the Plan Risk Responses process is to give proactive consideration to the actions you will put in place prior to a risk occurring, and actions you will take as a risk occurs, in order to minimize the impact from negative risks and maximize the impact from positive risks.
2. The four risk response strategies for positive risks are enhance, share, exploit, and accept.
3. The four risk response strategies for negative risks are transfer, mitigate, avoid, and accept.
4. The purpose of contingent response strategies is to ensure that you have a proactive response planned to unplanned risk occurring.

Control Risks

> **MORE INFO CONTROL RISKS**
>
> You can read more about the Control Risks process in the PMBOK® Guide, 5th edition, in Chapter 11, section 11.6. Table 9-6 identifies the process inputs, tools and techniques, and outputs.
>
> **TABLE 9-6** Control Risks process
>
> | Inputs | Tools and techniques | Outputs |
> | --- | --- | --- |
> | ■ Project management plan
■ Risk register
■ Work performance data
■ Work performance reports | ■ Risk reassessment
■ Risk audits
■ Variance and trend analysis
■ Technical performance measurement
■ Reserve analysis
■ Status meetings | ■ Work performance information
■ Change requests
■ Project management plan updates
■ Project documents updates
■ Organizational process assets updates |

The Control Risks process is focused on monitoring and controlling the project risk management activities being undertaken to ensure that they are in accordance with the risk management plan and the information contained within the risk register.

The Control Risks process covers the following domain task:

- 3.5 Implement approved actions and follow the risk management plan and risk register, in order to minimize the impact of negative risk events on the project.
- 4.4 Update the risk register and risk response plan by identifying any new risks, assessing old risks, and determining and implementing appropriate response strategies, in order to manage the impact of risks on the project.
- 4.5 Assess corrective actions on the issue register and determine next steps for unresolved issues by using appropriate tools and techniques in order to minimize the impact on project schedule, cost, and resources.

Like all the other monitoring and controlling processes, the Control Risks process checks the implementation of the plan. In this case, you are checking what is occurring against what you planned to occur in relation to risk management. You will be looking out for any variance between what risks you had planned and what risks are occurring, any new risks, and any new information affecting already identified risks, and evaluating the overall risk process.

Inputs

The following inputs are used in the Control Risks process.

Project management plan

The project management plan, and more specifically the risk management plan, contains information about how each part of the project will be executed, monitored, and closed, in relation to risk. The specific part of the project management plan that is most useful for the Control Risk process is the risk management plan. The project management plan is an output from the Develop Project Management Plan process, and the risk management plan is an output from the Plan Risk Management process.

Risk register

The risk register is the key document in this process, because you are checking the information contained in the risk register against what is actually occurring. You are checking that you identified all the risks; that you correctly estimated their consequences, probability, and impact; and that your documented responses were appropriate. You are also using the risk register to check for any risks you may have missed. The risk register is an output from the Identify Risks process.

Work performance data

In order to assess how you are doing against what you had planned to do, you will require work performance data. Work performance data will in turn become work performance reports in the Monitor and Control Project Work process. Work performance data is an output from the Direct and Manage Project Work process.

> **EXAM TIP**
>
> Remember the sequence that work performance data becomes work performance information, which becomes work performance reports.

Work performance reports

Work performance reports are the results of analyzing the work performance information and presenting it in a coherent and easy-to-understand manner in order to give you a comprehensive picture on how well, or how poorly, the project is doing. Work performance reports are an output from the Monitor and Control Project Work process.

Tools and techniques

The following tools and techniques of this process are able to be used upon the separate inputs to deliver the Control Risks process outputs.

Risk reassessment

Risk reassessment is an ongoing process of checking whether there are new risks, whether already-identified risks are still current, whether the analysis of their probability and impact is still accurate, and whether the planned risk responses are still appropriate. The contents of the risk register are highly fluid and subject to a high degree of change as the project progresses and more information is known about existing risks. Thus you should treat the risk register as a live document in constant need of checking and reassessment.

> **EXAM TIP**
>
> Risk reassessment should be viewed as a continual activity led by the project manager and involving the project team.

Risk audits

Generally, audits are a great way to check that processes are working as planned and if there is any room for improvement. In the Control Risks process, *risk audits* are used to check whether the planned risk responses are appropriate and how well the risk management processes are being implemented and if they are appropriate. It is the project manager's responsibility to ensure that risk audits are carried out at appropriate times and with defined objectives. The results of the risk audit will contribute to the ongoing continuous improvement of your project processes.

Variance and trend analysis

Variance and trend analysis is used in other areas as a technique to identify and document what is occurring against what was planned and then extrapolate from that any identifiable trends that may indicate future performance. When it is used in the Control Risks process, you are looking for any divergence from the risk management plan and risk register and examining this to determine if it indicates any trends that you can proactively plan for. For example, you may spot that you have consistently underestimated the magnitude of risks around costs of a certain material and use the variance and trend analysis to reforecast future impact and probability of these risks.

Technical performance measurement

Technical performance measurement means putting in place acceptable parameters around potentially negative risk events, generally those affecting scope, time, and cost, and then checking that the work being performed is within these technical performance measurements. Work being performed outside the defined technical performance measurements represents risk on the project and may require change requests to be prepared and considered, to change parameters if the planed risk response cannot bring the performance back into line. For example, you may have set a range of acceptable costs for development of a new product, but when measuring the actual costs you may find them to be greater than what was planned, and therefore the risk of a cost overrun on the project is greater.

Reserve analysis

During the Perform Quantitative Risk Analysis process you used objective measurements to develop contingency reserves for either cost or time. During the Control Risks process you will check whether these calculations are still accurate and the reserves you have planned for are still appropriate. It may be that new information has come to hand that means that the reserve for either cost or time needs to be changed. It is quite typical that, as a project progresses and estimates become more accurate, the range of contingency calculated by using qualitative risk analysis drops. For example, you may find that extra information gained about an estimate for the range of time taken to perform a certain activity can now be refined and reduced because you have now performed the activity several times. You can then reduce the amount of time reserve allocated to this activity.

Status meetings

You should either make risk management a normal part of regular project meetings or schedule meetings with a special focus on risk management to ensure that you and the team remain focused on risk management activities throughout the life of the project. The purpose of these *status meetings* is to examine all aspects of risk management on the project and ensure they are still appropriate and effective. Additionally, having regular meetings where risk management is a topic of discussion creates greater awareness and buy-in from team members, which in turn results in better risk management.

Outputs

The outputs from the Control Risks process include the following.

Work performance information

As a result of carrying out the Control Risks process you will end up with valuable work performance information about risk management activities. This information will take the form of revised information about risk responses and their effectiveness, the use of planned time and cost contingency reserves, and any defined technical performance measurements. Work performance information is used as an input into the Monitor and Control Project Work process.

Change requests

As a result of completing the Control Risks process and conducting risk audits, variance and trend analysis, technical performance measurements, or reserve analysis, you may discover information that requires a formal change to be made to a part of the project; this will be done via a change request. Change requests will then go on to be processed according to your approved change control process in the Perform Integrated Change Control process.

Project management plan updates

Due to the fact that risk management affects all other areas of the project, you may update many different parts of the project management plan and its baselines. You will most definitely update the risk management plan.

Project documents updates

The specific project documents that will be updated include the risk register and the assumptions log.

Organizational process assets updates

The specific organizational process assets that will be updated include any historical information about risk management and any templates, processes, or guidelines that the organization has in relation to project management.

✓ Quick check

1. What is the main purpose of the Control Risks process?
2. Why is risk reassessment an important tool or technique in the Control Risks process?
3. How does the Control Risks process contribute to the development of contingency reserves for time and cost?

Quick check answers

1. The main purpose of the Control Risks process is to determine if the risk management activities as planned in the risk management plan are being completed as per the plan, if the risks identified in the risk register are manifesting as forecast, and whether the qualitative and quantitative assessments and planned risk responses are still appropriate.
2. In addition to checking whether risk management activities are being completed as per the plan, a key element of the Control Risks process is a complete reassessment of the assumptions made, the risks identified, and whether any new risks have been identified.
3. The Control Risks process allows you to examine the time and cost contingency reserves you have developed and, as part of the reassessment of risks, you may choose to redefine the reserves allowed for time and cost. Usually this process results in a reduction in the reserves for both time and cost. As more information is known, the better the estimate is, and less risk or uncertainty is associated with them.

Exercises

The answers for these exercises are located in the "Answers" section at the end of this chapter.

1. Match up the risk response strategy on the left with the description on the right.

Risk Response strategy	Definition
1. Avoid	a. You are working on an IT project and decide that you will bear the consequences if something goes wrong on the project.
2. Enhance	b. You decide to partner with another organization that has skills and experience that you don't, in order to present a better response to a contract on offer.
3. Transfer	c. You have considered several options for the location of a new manufacturing plant and decide to locate it in a region with plenty of experienced workers, to get around the risk of not having enough people to do the work.
4. Mitigate	d. You are working on a complex IT project and decide to put in place backup data storage so that you can quickly restart should anything occur to the data you are working on during the project.
5. Accept	e. You take out insurance against wet weather delaying your construction project.
6. Exploit	f. You pull your top project manager off other projects and assign her to a new bridge construction project to ensure that it has the greatest chance of success.
7. Share	g. You put all your project staff through a workshop to improve their communications management strategy to minimize the risk of not managing stakeholder expectations effectively.

2. Consider the following five examples of risk analysis and decide whether they are qualitative or quantitative risk analysis methods.

   A. You ask your team members to provide their opinion about whether or not the chance of a storm affecting your construction project next April is very low, low, neither low nor high, high, or very high.

   B. You pay the local meteorological bureau to provide you with the exact probability of there being a storm in April of a magnitude that would affect your construction project.

   C. You gather a team of seven subject matter experts and ask them to provide their opinion of probability and impact of the risk of the selected technology on your IT project. You ask them to select from a standardized scale of probabilities ranging from 0.1, meaning very low probability or impact, up to 0.9, meaning very high probability and impact. You then multiply these two numbers together to obtain a risk score.

D. The quantity surveyor working for your cost estimating team has calculated that over the next two years of your project there is a risk of a 10.3 percent increase in hardware costs, and that this increase could cost you a total of $173,000. He recommends purchasing this hardware now and finding a place to store it to avoid this risk.

E. You have calculated that there is a very high chance that a senior staff member will leave your project within the next three months, and that replacing her will cost $25,000. You decide to offer her a salary increase of $15,000 to get her to stay with the project.

3. Consider the decision tree shown in Figure 9-9 outlining a choice about whether to build a new factory or upgrade an existing factory to take advantage of increased demand for your product. Using expected monetary value analysis, what is the best decision to make?

Decision Definition	Decision node	Chance node	Net path value
Decision to be made	Input: cost of each option Output: decision made (true, false)	Input: scenario probability, reward if it occurs Output: expected monetary value (EMV)	Computed: (Payoffs minus Costs) along path

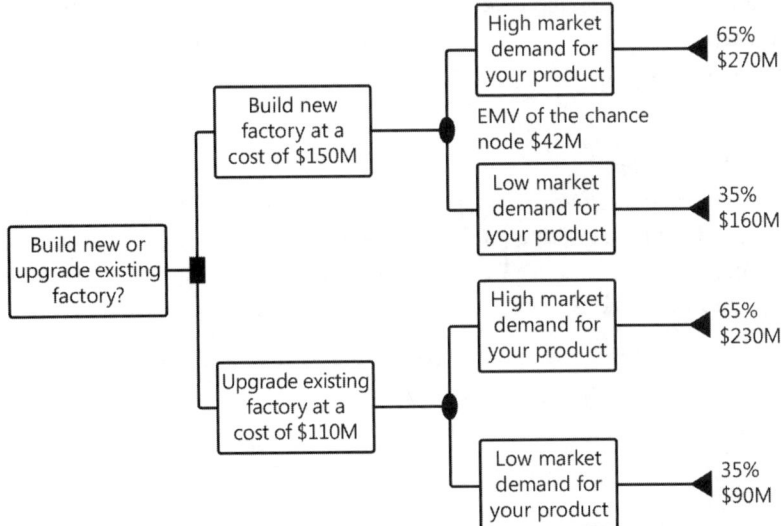

FIGURE 9-9 This decision tree shows the expected monetary value of a new factory versus an upgrade to an existing factory.

Chapter summary

- The Risk Management knowledge area is focused upon the successful use of project risk to report project performance, gain political support, and provide stakeholders with their risk requirements.
- The Plan Risk Management process produces the risk management plan, which guides the subsequent risk management processes.
- The Identify Risks process, which is a planning process, uses the risk management plan to begin the iterative process of developing the risk register by using a variety of tools and techniques to identify all potential negative and positive risks.
- The Perform Qualitative Risk Analysis process is a planning process that seeks to assign a subjective probability and impact assessment to each of the identified risks so that they can be prioritized.
- The Perform Quantitative Risk Analysis process is a planning process that assigns a quantitative and objective analysis, usually based on statistics and factual data, to the individual probability and impact of identified risks, which can lead to the creation of contingency reserves for time and cost.
- The Plan Risk Responses process is a planning process that outlines a proactive response to all identified risks on the project.
- The Control Risks process, which is a monitoring and controlling process, is like other monitoring and controlling processes in that it assesses actual performance against that forecast in the risk management plan, checks whether the risks identified and assessed in the risk register are still accurate, and checks whether there are any new risks.

Chapter review

Test your knowledge of the information in Chapter 9 by answering these questions. The answers to these questions, and the explanations of why each answer choice is correct or incorrect, are located in the "Answers" section at the end of this chapter.

1. Which of the following processes produces the risk management plan?
    - **A.** Develop Project Management Plan
    - **B.** Plan Risk Management
    - **C.** Manage Risk
    - **D.** Develop Risk Management Plan

2. The particular attitude that an organization has toward the amount of risk it is prepared to accept for the project is known as what?

    A. Risk analysis

    B. Risk tolerance

    C. Risk aversion

    D. Risk avoidance

3. Uncertainty that presents opportunities to deliver a project ahead of time is known as what?

    A. Risk threshold

    B. Positive risk

    C. Negative risk

    D. Risk analysis

4. Which of the following documents will contain a description of risk categories?

    A. Risk register

    B. Risk analysis

    C. Risk management plan

    D. Risk progress report

5. You have prepared a grid that shows a standardized representation of probability and impact in order to prioritize individual risks. What is this known as?

    A. Risk breakdown structure

    B. Ishikawa diagram

    C. Probability and impact matrix

    D. Risk register

6. You are in the process of identifying individual risks to your project and are using a technique to discover the underlying causes that lead to a particular risk. What technique are you using?

    A. Brainstorming

    B. Delphi technique

    C. Interviewing

    D. Root cause analysis

7. You have called your team together for a meeting in which you ask them to analyze the strengths, weaknesses, opportunities, and threats your project faces. What tool or technique are you using?

    A. Delphi technique

    B. Brainstorming

    C. SWOT analysis

    D. Root cause analysis

8. After carrying out a particular risk process you end up with a prioritized list of risks, ranking them from highest to lowest priority. Which of the following risk processes produces this list?

    A. Plan Risk Management

    B. Identify Risks

    C. Perform Qualitative Risk Analysis

    D. Perform Quantitative Risk Analysis

9. In carrying out the risk management processes, you will often update particular project documents. What is the most common project document to be updated as a result of completing risk management processes?

    A. Risk register

    B. Risk management plan

    C. Assumptions log

    D. Project management plan

10. You have developed a range of statistical data that demonstrates the characteristics of a beta distribution and are using this information to analyze the probability of a risk occurring. Which risk management process are you carrying out?

    A. Identify Risks

    B. Perform Qualitative Risk Analysis

    C. Perform Quantitative Risk Analysis

    D. Plan Risk Responses

11. If you are using a piece of software to carry out the simulation of the probability of a particular risk occurring over many iterations, what tool are you using?

    A. Expected monetary value analysis

    B. Interviewing

    C. Sensitivity analysis

    D. Monte Carlo analysis

12. The decision to delay the beginning of construction until the end of winter to ensure that team members do not have to contend with the risk of dangerous working conditions is what sort of risk response strategy?

    A. Mitigation
    B. Transference
    C. Avoidance
    D. Acceptance

13. You have identified a potential risk to your project but have decided that you will not conduct an assessment of the probability or impact, or have a proactive response in place. What sort of risk response strategy is this?

    A. Mitigation
    B. Enhancement
    C. Transference
    D. Acceptance

14. You are carrying out a reassessment of the cost reserves built up by using quantitative risk assessment for the procurement of materials for your project, due to new information that reduces the uncertainty in the initial estimates. Which risk management process are you carrying out?

    A. Identify Risks
    B. Perform Quantitative Risk Analysis
    C. Plan Risk Responses
    D. Control Risks

Answers

This section contains the answers for the "Exercises" and "Chapter review" sections in this chapter.

Exercises

1. Match up the risk response strategy on the left with the description on the right.

Risk Response strategy	Definition
1. Avoid	c. You have considered several options for the location of a new manufacturing plant and decide to locate it in a region with plenty of experienced workers, to get around the risk of not having enough people to do the work.
2. Enhance	g. You put all your project staff through a workshop to improve their communications management strategy to minimize the risk of not managing stakeholder expectations effectively.
3. Transfer	e. You take out insurance against wet weather delaying your construction project.
4. Mitigate	d. You are working on a complex IT project and decide to put in place backup data storage so that you can quickly restart should anything occur to the data you are working on during the project.
5. Accept	a. You are working on an IT project and decide that you will bear the consequences if something goes wrong on the project.
6. Exploit	f. You pull your top project manager off other projects and assign her to a new bridge construction project to ensure that it has the greatest chance of success.
7. Share	b. You decide to partner with another organization that has skills and experience that you don't, in order to present a better response to a contract on offer.

2. Consider the following five examples of risk analysis and decide whether they are qualitative or quantitative risk analysis methods.

   A. You ask your team members to provide their opinion about whether or not the chance of a storm affecting your construction project next April is very low, low, neither low nor high, high, or very high.

   Answer: This is an example of quantitative risk analysis because it is using subjective assessment and opinion on a fixed scale.

   B. You pay the local meteorological bureau to provide you with the exact probability of there being a storm in April of a magnitude that would affect your construction project.

   Answer: This is an example of quantitative risk analysis because you are using actual statistical data instead of subjective opinion to calculate probability.

   C. You gather a team of seven subject matter experts and ask them to provide their opinion of probability and impact of the risk of the selected technology on your IT project. You ask them to select from a standardized scale of probabilities ranging from 0.1, meaning very low probability or impact, up to 0.9, meaning very high probability and impact. You then multiply these two numbers together to obtain a risk score.

   Answer: This is an example of qualitative risk analysis because, despite the use of experts using numbers with decimal points in them, it is still an opinion-based assessment on a fixed, predetermined scale.

   D. The quantity surveyor working for your cost estimating team has calculated that over the next two years of your project there is a risk of a 10.3 percent increase in hardware costs, and that this increase could cost you a total of $173,000. He recommends purchasing this hardware now and finding a place to store it to avoid this risk.

   Answer: This is an example of quantitative risk analysis because it uses clear, calculated numbers based on facts to determine probability and impact.

   E. You have calculated that there is a very high chance that a senior staff member will leave your project within the next three months, and that replacing her will cost $25,000. You decide to offer her a salary increase of $15,000 to get her to stay with the project.

   Answer: This is an example of qualitative risk analysis because you have made a subjective assessment of the probability.

3. Consider the decision tree outlining a choice about whether to build a new factory or upgrade an existing factory to take advantage of increased demand for your product. Using expected monetary value analysis, what is the best decision to make? (See the updated decision tree in Figure 9-10.)

Decision	Decision node	Chance node	Net path value
Decision to be made	Input: cost of each option Output: decision made (true, false)	Input: scenario probability, reward if it occurs Output: expected monetary value (EMV)	Computed: (Payoffs minus Costs) along path

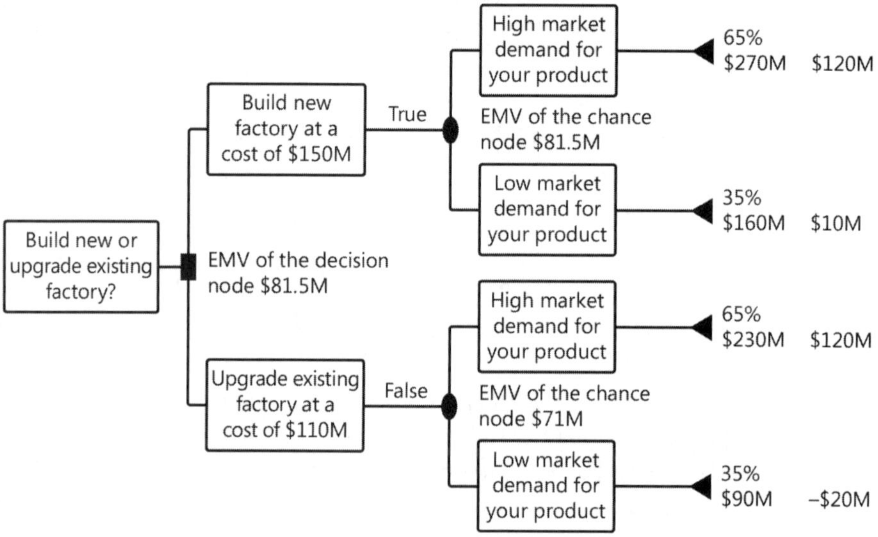

FIGURE 9-10 A decision tree showing the expected monetary value of a new factory versus an upgrade to an existing factory.

Expected monetary value of building a new factory:

(0.65 × $120M) + (0.35 × $10M) = $81.5M

Expected monetary value of upgrading the existing factory:

(0.65 × $120M) + (0.35 × -$20M) = $71M

Therefore, you would choose the build a new factory because it has the higher expected monetary value analysis.

Chapter review

1. **Correct answer: B**
   - **A. Incorrect:** The Develop Project Management Plan produces the project management plan.
   - **B. Correct:** The Plan Risk Management process has the risk management plan as its primary output.
   - **C. Incorrect:** Manage Risk is a made-up process name.
   - **D. Incorrect:** Develop Risk Management plan is a made-up process name.

2. **Correct answer: B**
   - **A. Incorrect:** Risk analysis is the process of analyzing either quantitatively or qualitatively the probability and impact of particular risks.
   - **B. Correct:** Risk tolerance describes the amount of risk an organization is prepared to accept on a project.
   - **C. Incorrect:** Risk aversion is a state of mind whereby an organization would prefer not to undertake high-risk activities.
   - **D. Incorrect:** Risk avoidance is similar to risk aversion and indicates an outcome of assessing risk tolerance.

3. **Correct answer: B**
   - **A. Incorrect:** The risk threshold is the level of risk tolerance that an organization is comfortable with.
   - **B. Correct:** Any uncertainty that presents opportunities constitutes positive risk.
   - **C. Incorrect:** Negative risk is any uncertainty that represents a threat to the project.
   - **D. Incorrect:** Risk analysis is the process of analyzing either quantitatively or qualitatively the probability and impact of particular risks.

4. **Correct answer: C**
   - **A. Incorrect:** The risk register contains a list of the identified risks, probability and impact assessment, and any planned risk responses. It may use risk categories to group individual risks together, but it does not generally contain a description of the risk categories.
   - **B. Incorrect:** Risk analysis is the process of analyzing either quantitatively or qualitatively the probability and impact of particular risks.
   - **C. Correct:** The risk management plan contains a lot of information about the particular approach you will take to managing risk on your project; included in this information is a description of the risk categories.
   - **D. Incorrect:** Any risk progress reports prepared will focus on risk activities completed against risk activities planned, not on a description of risk categories.

5. **Correct answer: C**
   - **A.** **Incorrect:** The risk breakdown structure shows the risk categories in graphical form.
   - **B.** **Incorrect:** An Ishikawa diagram shows the probable causes of particular risk effects.
   - **C.** **Correct:** The probability and impact matrix is a grid that shows a standardized list of both probability on one axis and impact on another axis, and after the two values are multiplied together, presents a graphical analysis of risk priorities.
   - **D.** **Incorrect:** The risk register presents a list of identified risks, probability and impact assessment, and the proactive risk responses.

6. **Correct answer: D**
   - **A.** **Incorrect:** Brainstorming is a technique to gather as much information as possible from project team members or subject matter experts.
   - **B.** **Incorrect:** The Delphi technique is a method of anonymously interviewing and gathering data from experts.
   - **C.** **Incorrect:** Interviewing is a technique used to formally gather data from subject matter experts in a structured format.
   - **D.** **Correct:** Root cause analysis seeks to discover the underlying cause or causes of a particular risk.

7. **Correct answer: C**
   - **A.** **Incorrect:** The Delphi technique is a method of anonymously interviewing and gathering data from experts.
   - **B.** **Incorrect:** Brainstorming is a technique to gather as much information as possible from project team members or subject matter experts.
   - **C.** **Correct:** *SWOT* stands for *strength, weaknesses, opportunities, and threats.*
   - **D.** **Incorrect:** Root cause analysis seeks to discover the underlying cause or causes of a particular risk.

8. **Correct answer: C**
   - **A.** **Incorrect:** The Plan Risk Management process produces the risk management plan.
   - **B.** **Incorrect:** The Identify Risks process produces an iteration of the risk register.
   - **C.** **Correct:** The Perform Qualitative Risk Analysis process uses subjective assessment of probability and impact to give each identified risk a score to enable it to be ranked and prioritized.
   - **D.** **Incorrect:** The Perform Quantitative Risk Analysis uses actual statistical data to calculate probability and impact and produces contingency reserves for either time or cost.

9. **Correct answer: A**

    A. **Correct:** The risk register is a highly iterative document that is constantly updated by most of the risk management planning processes.

    B. **Incorrect:** The risk management plan may be updated as a result of completing risk management activities, particularly the Control Risks process, but the frequency of updates will be less than the updates to the risk register.

    C. **Incorrect:** The assumptions log will be checked and reassessed often, but not as often as the risk register.

    D. **Incorrect:** The project management plan, its subsidiary plans, and its baselines may be updated, but certainly not as often as the risk register.

10. **Correct answer: C**

    A. **Incorrect:** The Identify Risks process does not use any form of either qualitative or quantitative risk analysis.

    B. **Incorrect:** The Perform Qualitative Risk Analysis process uses subjective data rather than statistical data to complete its assessment of probability and impact.

    C. **Correct:** The Perform Quantitative Risk Analysis process uses statistical data and probability distributions such as the beta distribution to calculate quantitative risk.

    D. **Incorrect:** The Plan Risk Responses process is focused upon the development of appropriate responses to identified risks.

11. **Correct answer: D**

    A. **Incorrect:** The expected monetary value analysis analyzes particular options, and the probability and net impact of those options, to determine which has the higher expected monetary value.

    B. **Incorrect:** Interviewing is a technique for gathering information from team members and subject matter experts in a formal setting.

    C. **Incorrect:** Sensitivity analysis is a way of determining which parts of the project are most sensitive to risk.

    D. **Correct:** Monte Carlo analysis is a sophisticated type of mathematical and statistical analysis. It carries out simulations of events occurring, to determine the likely probability and impact.

12. **Correct answer: C**

    A. **Incorrect:** Mitigation is a response that seeks to minimize the impact of risk if it occurs.

    B. **Incorrect:** Transference makes the impact of the risk someone else's responsibility.

    C. **Correct:** The example represents a strategy of avoiding an identified risk.

    D. **Incorrect:** Acceptance would mean doing nothing and accepting the consequences.

13. **Correct answer: D**
    A. **Incorrect:** Mitigation is a response that seeks to minimize the impact of risk if it occurs.
    B. **Incorrect:** Enhancement is a risk response strategy for positive risks that seeks to enhance the probability and impact of the risk.
    C. **Incorrect:** Transference makes the impact of the risk someone else's responsibility.
    D. **Correct:** Acceptance is a strategy whereby you make no provision at all should the risk occur and simply accept the consequences.

14. **Correct answer: D**
    A. **Incorrect:** The Identify Risks process seeks to identify individual risks for inclusion on the risk register.
    B. **Incorrect:** The Perform Quantitative Risk Analysis process conducts a quantitative assessment of probability and impact of individual risks.
    C. **Incorrect:** The Plan Risk Responses process prepares a proactive response to identified risks.
    D. **Correct:** The Control Risks process includes the reassessment of reserves to determine if the uncertainty within them has changed.

CHAPTER 10

Procurement management

This chapter focuses on the topic of project procurement management, which, like the other knowledge areas, begins with a process of planning that, in this case, produces a procurement management plan. It then uses this plan to carry out the procurement work, which involves making decisions about whether or not to procure goods, services, or resources from external sources and if so, how to advertise and award the contract, and what form of contract to use. Procurement management also involves monitoring contractual terms for performance and also includes a process for making sure all contracts are formally closed.

The PMBOK® Guide processes

Project Procurement Management knowledge area

The four processes in the Project Procurement Management knowledge area are:

- Plan Procurement Management (Planning process)
- Conduct Procurements (Executing process)
- Control Procurements (Monitoring and Controlling process)
- Close Procurements (Closing process)

Domain tasks in this chapter:

- Plan Procurement Management process:
    - 2.7 Develop a procurement plan based on the project scope and schedule, in order to ensure that the required project resources will be available.
- Conduct Procurements process:
    - 3.1 Obtain and manage project resources including outsourced deliverables by following the procurement plan, in order to ensure successful project execution.
- Control Procurements process:
    - 4.1 Measure project performance using appropriate tools and techniques, in order to identify and quantify any variances, perform approved corrective actions, and communicate with relevant stakeholders.

- Close Procurements process:
    - 5.3 Obtain financial, legal, and administrative closure using generally accepted practices, in order to communicate formal project closure and ensure no further liability.

What is project procurement management?

EXAM TIP

If you are familiar with the ISO 31000 Standard for Procurement Management, much of this section will be familiar to you. Additionally, much of this topic is based upon formal government procurement processes.

Project procurement management is focused upon planning for and making decisions about whether or not to procure goods and services needed on the project from external sources, which form of contact to choose, how to select sellers to deliver the work, and how to check that the work is being done in accordance with the agreed contracts.

The Plan Procurement Management process results in a procurement management plan, which guides the other procurement management processes. The organization looking to procure goods or services then performs a make-or-buy analysis to determine if it should complete the work internally or source the goods and services from external sources. After the decision has been made to go to external sources, the buying organization then decides what form of *contract* it will use, how it will inform potential sellers of its needs, and how it will select the successful seller.

When the contract has been signed, then both parties take responsibility for checking that the agreed contract terms are being followed and that any changes to the contract are formally documented.

Finally, all contracts must be closed. Contractual closure does not mean project closure because contracts can be closed at any time in a project.

In any contract there are *buyers*, the party looking to acquire the goods or services, and there are *sellers*, the parties with goods or services to sell. There can be multiple sellers, but generally there is a single buyer.

EXAM TIP

In the exam, unless otherwise stated, you should assume that you are the buyer in any contract. But read the question thoroughly to ensure that you understand whether you are the buyer or seller, because your answer to the question may be different depending on which position you are in. You can also be both buyer and seller at different points in the project. So take your time reading the question to understand what perspective you are answering the question from.

Plan Procurement Management

> **MORE INFO** **PLAN PROCUREMENT MANAGEMENT**
>
> You can read more about the Plan Procurement Management process in the PMBOK® Guide, 5th edition, in Chapter 12, section 12.1. Table 10-1 identifies the process inputs, tools and techniques, and outputs.
>
> **TABLE 10-1** Plan Procurement Management process
>
> | Inputs | Tools and techniques | Outputs |
> |---|---|---|
> | ■ Project management plan
■ Requirements documentation
■ Risk register
■ Activity resource requirements
■ Project schedule
■ Activity cost estimates
■ Stakeholder register
■ Enterprise environmental factors
■ Organizational process assets | ■ Make or buy analysis
■ Expert judgment
■ Market research
■ Meetings | ■ Procurement management plan
■ Procurement statement of work
■ Procurement documents
■ Source selection criteria
■ Make or buy decisions
■ Change requests
■ Project documents updates |

The Plan Procurement Management process is a planning process with the procurement management plan and procurement statement of work as its main outputs. The purpose of this process is, as with other planning processes, to enable you and your team to proactively plan your particular approach to procurement requirements on the project.

The Plan Procurement Management process covers the following domain tasks:

- 2.7 Develop a procurement plan based on the project scope and schedule, in order to ensure that the required project resources will be available.

Inputs

The Plan Procurement Management process uses some or all of the following inputs as part of the development of the procurement management plan for the project.

Project management plan

The project management plan is a key input into the Plan Procurement Management process because it contains key information about the scope of work and elements of the scope of work that would need to be considered for external procurement. The description of these potential procurement elements will be described in the scope baseline, which includes the scope statement, work breakdown structure (WBS), and WBS dictionary. The project management plan is an output from the Develop Project Management Plan process.

Requirements documentation

The requirements documentation will include information about specific project requirements that can be taken into consideration when looking at whether or not to make a requirement internally or procure it from external sources and, if the decision is made to procure it from external sources, then what sort of contract is best to use. Requirements documentation is an output from the Collect Requirements process.

Risk register

The risk register is an important input into the Plan Procurement Management process because it identifies specific risks around the decision to make goods or services internally versus the decision to procure them from external sources, and the risks associated with individual contract types. The risk register is an output from the Identify Risks process.

Activity resource requirements

Activity resource requirements contain information about the resources required to complete individually identified activities, and this information can be useful when making decisions about whether or not to procure goods and services externally and the type of contract to use. Activity resource requirements are an output from the Estimate Activity Resources process.

Project schedule

The project schedule is a key input into the Plan Procurement Management process because it outlines the planned deliverable dates of particular activities and tasks, and this information will be used when negotiating contracts. The project schedule is an output from the Develop Schedule process.

Activity cost estimates

Activity cost estimates include the cost estimates of individual activities, which can then be used to anticipate what likely contractual responses will be and assess whether they are reasonable and accurate. Activity cost estimates are an output from the Estimate Costs process.

Stakeholder register

The stakeholder register identifies individual stakeholders and their interest in the project. Thus it is useful in terms of managing stakeholder expectations around which goods and services will be procured externally and the type of contract selected. The stakeholder register is an output from the Identify Stakeholders process.

> **Real world**
>
> The type of contract selected will have an impact on the stakeholders, particularly if stakeholders are to be intimately involved in the administration and execution of the contract. Many types of contracts set up an adversarial relationship with stakeholders, whereas other more modern forms of contract establish a relationship based on trust between stakeholders. Thus, having an in-depth knowledge of how your stakeholders will perceive and react to different contractual decisions is an important consideration in your procurement management process. A style of contract that works for one group of stakeholders may not work for another group of stakeholders. Also, keep in mind that many stakeholders will already have preferred vendors and long-established types of contracts with them.

Enterprise environmental factors

The specific enterprise environmental factors that will be useful as inputs into the Plan Procurement Management process include any marketplace conditions that will determine whether or not there will be a lot of interest in your procurement decisions, the specific types of products and services that will be available in a particular marketplace, the size of the marketplace and whether you can stay local or have to go wider in your search for suppliers, and the expected terms and conditions for contract types with particular industries.

Organizational process assets

The specific organizational process assets that may be an important input into the Plan Procurement Management process include any formal procurement policies that the organization has stating what goods and services will be procured, how the decisions will be made, what sort of contract types will be favored, and who has responsibility in negotiating and administering the contracts.

> **Real world**
>
> I have often found that most organizations have clear procurement policies that specify when external procurement can be or must be used, and the type of contract that the organization prefers. You should always endeavor to familiarize yourself with any procurement policies that your organization has.

EXAM TIP

At all times you must conduct your procurement in accordance with the relevant organizational procurement guidelines. Don't be tempted to act outside of the guidelines; if the guidelines are wrong you can seek to change them, but until they are changed you must adhere to them.

Tools and techniques

The following tools and techniques are available to be used to develop the inputs in this process in order to produce the procurement management plan.

Make or buy analysis

The *make or buy analysis* is a comprehensive description of the decision-making process that an organization goes through when deciding whether it should make the goods or services it requires itself, or seek to acquire goods or services from external sources. There are a number of ways of making the decision, and a number of factors to take into account.

Of the factors that can be taken into account when making a make or buy decision, the following are the most important:

- The risk profile and risk tolerance of the organization
- Ownership of intellectual property
- Availability of suitable sellers
- Availability of internal resources capable of delivering a good or service
- Timeframes for delivery of a good or service
- Length of time that the resource required for the good or service is needed on the project
- Ability to support ongoing changes and technical support

The make or buy process should follow established procedures that take into account the relevant factors, and even assign different weights for different factors to enable you to score factors differently.

In making the make or buy decisions, you may also want to use more quantitative methods such as the *decision tree* analysis used in Chapter 9, "Risk management," in the Quantitative Risk analysis section.

Expert judgment

Expert judgment is an excellent tool to use when planning your approach to procurement management, because utilizing the knowledge and experience of subject matter experts will be invaluable not only in your overall procurement management plan, but also in identifying and completing an analysis of procurements. Suitable experts who may provide judgment include senior management, stakeholders with relevant experience, external subject matter experts such as procurement professionals, industry groups, and professional associations.

One particularly useful type of expert that you should consider using in your procurement management decisions is the legal expert, because your procurement decisions will be supported by legally enforceable contracts and, therefore, it is highly recommended that you involve experts with legal experience in the formation, negotiation, execution, and administration of any procurement contracts.

> **Real world**
>
> I have always found that referring any decisions about contracts to legal experts is a good investment. The wording of contracts can be quite complicated, and it often takes somebody with particular experience in an area to be able to effectively negotiate a contract that is easy to understand and enforce and doesn't place an undue amount of work upon one or the other of the parties involved. Certainly any changes or variations to contracts should involve people with legal expertise.

Market research

Market research is carried out in order to determine the capability and availability of potential sellers in the market and their particular interest in responding to your procurement requests. Additionally, any market research that you carry out may reveal additional ways of delivering goods and services and, as such, it is an important tool in the Plan Procurement Management process.

Meetings

Meetings are a great way to bring together project team members, stakeholders, and other experts in order to consider how procurement will be managed on the project. There are a number of ways you can run these meetings in order to efficiently get the information that you require. They can be run formally with defined agendas and examination of reports, or they can be run as creative brainstorming sessions. The style of meeting you choose to use will reflect the participants and your intended outcomes.

Outputs

After the appropriate tools and techniques have been applied to the selected inputs, the Plan Procurement Management process has the following outputs.

Procurement management plan

The Plan Procurement Management process has the *procurement management plan* as its major output. Similar to other management plans, the procurement management plan provides a guide for completing the procurement management activities in the project. The procurement management plan will probably contain information on the types of contracts to be used, whether or not independent estimates will be used to check responses received, any methods for identifying and selecting sellers, and any other important procurement information that can be used in the other three procurement processes. The procurement management plan goes on to be used as an input into the Conduct Procurements process. Given that it is also a subsidiary plan of the project management plan, is also used as an input into the Control Procurements process and Close Procurements process.

Procurement statement of work

The *procurement statement of work* is an output that describes each good or service that will be procured externally in enough detail to allow potential sellers to determine whether they are interested in, and able to, provide the goods or services sought. You should spend as much time as possible in defining the procurement statement of work because it will form the basis of your procurement contracts, and any omissions or areas that are not sufficiently defined may cause conflict in the administration of the contract.

EXAM TIP

You can think of the procurement statement of work as a type or subset of the project scope of work specifically focused on the work to be done as part of a contract for goods and services.

Procurement documents

There are a variety of key *procurement documents* that will be produced as a result of the Plan Procurement Management process. They are useful in soliciting responses from prospective sellers and will form the basis of the contracts that will eventually be agreed upon. Some of the more common types of procurement documents include the following:

- Request for information (RFI)
- Expression of interest (EOI)
- Invitation for bid (IFB)
- Request for proposal (RFP)
- Request for quotation (RFQ)
- Tender

Real world

If you have ever been involved in any formal seller selection process, you will find this section very straightforward. However, if you have not been involved in the formal contractual negotiation processes, then pay particular attention to this process. It is not uncommon for a project manager to receive negotiated contracts without being involved in the make or buy decisions, seller selection, and contractual negotiations.

Source selection criteria

The point of *source selection criteria* is to enable the buyer to be able to rate individual seller responses. They can include both objective and subjective criteria. The source selection criteria will reflect the criteria that are important to you and your decision-making process for selecting sellers. In addition to the prices submitted, you may also want to take into account a variety of other factors and give them a particular weighting to reflect their importance. Examples of the types of criteria that you may want to take into account include how well the seller understands your needs beyond what you may have described in the procurement statement of work, their technical ability to deliver the requested solution, the financial stability of the organization, their previous experience in doing this type of work, and references from other buyers who may have used this particular seller. You will be able to use the source selection criteria during the Conduct Procurements process.

Real world

There are certain occasions when your only source selection criterion will simply be lowest price; however, there are many other instances when you will want to take into account other criteria in selecting a seller. Typically you will want to look at what experience they have already had, their financial stability, the particular staff members who are allocated to do the work, and other factors such as health and safety and environmental record.

Make or buy decisions

The output from the make or buy analysis will be *make or buy decisions*. These documented decisions outline how you decided to either make the goods or services internally or go to external sources. Make or buy decisions are used as an input into the Conduct Procurements process.

Change requests

As a result of carrying out the Plan Procurement Management process, you may want to change some elements and subsidiary plans or baselines of the project management plan via a change request. All change requests go on to be used as inputs into the Perform Integrated Change Control process.

Project documents updates

The types of project documents that may be updated as a result of completing the Plan Procurement Management process are the project scope, requirements documentation, risk register, and stakeholder register.

> **Quick check**
>
> 1. What is the main focus of the Plan Procurement Management process?
> 2. What are some of the factors that you take into account when conducting a make or buy analysis?
> 3. What are some typical factors included in source selection criteria?
>
> **Quick check answers**
>
> 1. The main focus of the Plan Procurement Management process is to make decisions and provide a documented guideline for the rest of the procurement management processes. This information is contained within the procurement management plan, which is a subsidiary of the project management plan.
> 2. The types of factors that can be taken into account when conducting a make or buy analysis include the risk profile of the organization, the issue of ownership of intellectual property, the timeframe in which the work must be done, the current capability of internal resources, and the cost differential between choosing to make a good or service internally and procuring it externally.
> 3. In addition to the price being included in source selection criteria, you may choose to also include how well the seller understands your actual need, their proposed response and the life-cycle cost, their technical ability to deliver the solution, the staff they have allocated to do the work and their experience, any warranties they offer on the work being completed, the financial capacity and stability of the performing organization, their past performance in doing this type of work, references from others who have used them, and who owns the rights to the work done.

Conduct Procurements

> **MORE INFO** **CONDUCT PROCUREMENTS**
>
> You can read more about the Conduct Procurements process in the PMBOK® Guide, 5th edition, in Chapter 12, section 12.2. Table 10-2 identifies the process inputs, tools and techniques, and outputs.

TABLE 10-2 Conduct Procurements process

Inputs	Tools and techniques	Outputs
- Procurement management plan - Procurement documents - Source selection criteria - Seller proposals - Project documents - Make or buy decisions - Procurement statement of work - Organizational process assets	- Bidder conference - Proposal evaluation techniques - Independent estimates - Expert judgment - Advertising - Analytical techniques - Procurement negotiations	- Selected sellers - Agreements - Resource calendars - Change requests - Project management plan updates - Project documents updates

The Conduct Procurements process is an executing process that seeks to carry out the initial identification of prospective sellers, effectively pass on information about the work required to them, get responses from the sellers, evaluate and select the best seller for the job, and sign an agreement or contract.

The Conduct Procurements process covers the following domain task:

- 3.1 Obtain and manage project resources including outsourced deliverables by following the procurement plan, in order to ensure successful project execution.

Inputs

The Conduct Procurements process uses some or all of the following inputs.

Procurement management plan

The procurement management plan is an important input into the Conduct Procurements process because it outlines exactly how the Conduct Procurements process will be carried out. The procurement management plan is an output from the Plan Procurement Management process.

Procurement documents

The procurement documents are an output from the Plan Procurement Management process and include a range of different documents for soliciting information from prospective sellers. As such, they are an important input into the Conduct Procurements process.

Source selection criteria

Source selection criteria are used during the Conduct Procurements process to enable an evaluation of sellers against predetermined criteria that are important to the organization buying the goods or services. Source selection criteria are an output from the Plan Procurement Management process.

Seller proposals

Seller proposals are documentation received from interested sellers in response to a particular procurement documents package that you have put out to the market. They will be in the form prescribed in the procurement documents and will contain enough information for the buyer to evaluate the response and decide whether the seller is to go on to the next stage in the procurement process.

> **EXAM TIP**
>
> Did you notice that seller proposals are not actually an output from any other process? Instead, they are an independent input into this process.

Project documents

The specific types of project documents that will be useful as inputs into the Conduct Procurements process include risk-related contract decisions captured by the risk register, which is an output from the Plan Risk Responses process.

Make or buy decisions

The documented make or buy decisions are used as an input into the Conduct Procurements process to enable verification of the decisions made about which goods or services to procure externally. Make or buy decisions are an output from the Plan Procurement Management process.

Procurement statement of work

The procurement statement of work is required as an input into the Conduct Procurements process because it forms the basis of any procurement documents to go out to the market for sellers to review and respond to. The procurement statement of work should be as detailed as possible because sellers' responses will only be as detailed as the procurement statement of work. The procurement statement of work is an output from the Plan Procurement Management process.

> **Real world**
>
> A poorly worded procurement statement of work will lead to assumptions about what work is included and what is excluded from the contract, and these assumptions will lead to requests to change the contract, or to contractual disputes. It is a good idea to make the procurement statement of work as detailed as possible to avoid these potential problems.

Organizational process assets

The specific types of organizational process assets that will assist in the Conduct Procurements process include any historical information about market conditions, databases of prospective or prequalified sellers, and any other information about previous experience with sellers.

> **Real world**
>
> Many organizations keep lists or databases of prequalified sellers who have already gone through a selection process and met defined requirements to be able to provide goods or services to the organization. Usually the organization will simply issue procurement requests to these prequalified sellers and only go to the wider market when none of the prequalified sellers is able to provide the required good or service.

Tools and techniques

The following tools and techniques are used upon the inputs to deliver the Conduct Procurements process outputs.

Bidder conference

A *bidder conference* is any type of formal meeting between the buyer and all prospective sellers for the purpose of exchanging further information and answering any questions. Bidder conferences are generally fairly formal with rules to ensure fairness to all sellers participating in the process. They are also increasingly held virtually, with Internet forums being used to solicit questions and provide answers.

It is extremely important that you keep all bidder conferences fair and equitable to all sellers involved in the process. This means that if a seller asks you a question, you must provide the answer to all bidders. As a general rule, you should refuse to go into private talks with any seller during this process unless it is for commercially confidential information. This is not merely a good suggestion but also often a legal, commercial, or organizational requirement in many countries, and failure to follow it could result in your decision being challenged in court.

Proposal evaluation techniques

Proposal evaluation techniques include a range of methods for evaluating and scoring the different responses received from individual sellers. They can make use of the source selection criteria to provide a weighted attribute selection model. They can also take into account any other important elements useful in differentiating and distinguishing between different seller responses.

Independent estimates

Independent estimates are used as a technique to ensure that the seller responses in relation to cost are reasonable. You will want to carry out your own independent estimates to ensure that sellers are not bidding either far too high or too low, both of which indicate potential problems. Sellers bidding high can indicate either collusion between sellers or, more commonly, incorrect information contained within the procurement statement of work, or information that is being misinterpreted.

A range of prices lower than your independent estimates could indicate once again that the procurement statement of work and procurement documents provided are inaccurate, or that an organization is deliberately bidding low in order to win the work. The risk in this case is that the organization may go out of business trying to complete the work or that it is relying on variations to the contract to make the job profitable.

Expert judgment

Expert judgment is an excellent tool to use in evaluating seller proposals. The range of experts that you will use during this process will include people with experience in the procurement response process, contract negotiation and administration process, legal process, finance process, and any other relevant areas of expertise.

Advertising

Advertising is a tool that you may choose to use in order to take your procurement proposals to a wider market. You may choose to advertise in specific industry publications or more broadly in public newspapers. The type of advertising that you choose will reflect the audience you are trying to reach.

Analytical techniques

Analytical techniques involve a detailed analysis of the seller responses to examine them for completeness and accuracy to ensure that the seller is able to carry out the work. You may choose to bring in independent experts to carry out audits of the seller responses and even of the sellers' organizations, particularly in relation to financial capability and stability.

Procurement negotiations

Procurement negotiations can be simple and straightforward, or they can be highly complex affairs requiring teams of experts and a long period of time to work out. The end result is a contract that both parties are happy to commit themselves to.

> **Real world**
>
> Like project management, the world of contract negotiation requires a distinct set of skills and experience. I have found that if you are entering into complex negotiations, you should enlist the help of experts with both technical expertise and also negotiation expertise.

Outputs

The Conduct Procurements process has the following outputs.

Selected sellers

After carrying out the Conduct Procurements process and advertising for sellers, carrying out bidder conferences, evaluating seller responses, and negotiating contracts, you will have the *selected sellers* chosen to provide the goods or services required for the project.

Agreements

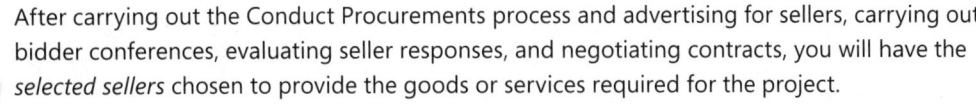

A procurement *agreement* will generally be reflected in a contract between the organizations involved in either buying or selling the goods or services for the project. It is important to keep in mind that a contract is a legally binding document with conditions that must be understood by both parties. Most agreements, or contracts, feature the following content in their terms and conditions:

- Description of the parties to the contract
- The outline of the work to be done as part of the contract
- The timeframe for delivery
- How and where the work is to be performed
- The agreed price
- A description of incentives used
- The terms of payment
- Penalties for nonperformance
- Termination clauses
- Dispute resolution procedures
- Ownership of intellectual property
- Audit, inspection, and acceptance criteria
- How variations will be handled

> **Real world**
>
> I've often found that many project managers do not take the time to read a contract in its entirety. I strongly recommend that if you have any contracts for work on a project, either as a buyer or seller you take the time to read the contract in its entirety and understand the terms and conditions contained within it. If you do not understand certain parts of the contract, you should seek clarification from experts who do.

There are several forms of contract that you can use. The difference between the various forms reflects the risk apportioned to the buyer or the seller. Table 10-3 lists the types of contract, and indicates where risk is apportioned.

TABLE 10-3 Types of contracts

Type of contract	Description	Risk Apportionment
Fixed-price contract (also known as lump sum contract)	A form of contract that includes an agreed, fixed price for the delivery of goods and services. There are several variations, as follows: ■ Firm fixed-price contract (FFP) with no provision at all for cost overruns ■ Fixed-price incentive fee contract (FPIF), which offers an incentive fee for meeting cost or time targets ■ Fixed-price with economic price adjustment contract (FP-EPA), which is often used on longer contracts and allows prices to be amended to reflect changes in inflation rates or exchange rates	Seller has the risk; if the cost to deliver the goods or services is greater than the fixed price, the seller bears the extra costs.
Cost-reimbursable contract	A form of contract that requires the seller to pass on the actual cost of the work to be done. There are several variations, including the following: ■ Cost plus fixed-fee contract (CPFF), which reimburses the seller for actual costs incurred and provides an additional fixed fee ■ Cost plus incentive fee contract (CPIF), which reimburses the seller for actual costs incurred and offers an incentive fee for meeting or exceeding agreed cost or time targets	Risk split between buyer and seller, depending on the actual form and wording of the contract.
Time and material contract (T&M)	A form of contract where the seller charges for all time spent and materials used with no agreed maximum. This form of contract is typically used on projects that are either small and of low complexity or emergency works, or where there is a poorly defined scope of work.	Buyer has the risk because there is no agreed maximum price.

A method for determining where risk lies between buyer and seller cost is to use the calculation for point of total assumption (PTA), particularly when using fixed-price incentive fee (FPIF) forms of contract. The *point of total assumption* is the point in the contract where the seller assumes total responsibility for all cost increases. In order to calculate this, you need a contract that has an agreed maximum ceiling price, target cost to the seller, target price to the buyer, and an agreed ratio between buyer and seller of the percentages of costs over the target cost each party is responsible for.

For example, consider a fixed-price incentive fee contract with a seller that sets a maximum price that the buyer will pay (ceiling price) for the contract of $50,000, a target cost to the seller of $42,000, and a target price to the buyer of $46,000. There is also an agreement that the buyer will pay 60 percent of the cost overrun above the target cost. Using these figures, you can use the following formula to calculate the point of total assumption.

Point of total assumption = Target cost + ((Ceiling price – Target price) / Buyers % share of cost overrun)

For this example:

Point of total assumption = $42,000 + (($50,000 – $46,000)/0.6)
 = $42,000 + ($4 000/0.6)
 = $42,000 + $6,666.67
 = $48,666.67

So the point at which the seller assumes total responsibility for all cost increases is $48,666.67. After this price is reached, the buyer has no further obligations.

Resource calendars

A resource calendar is a useful output from the Conduct Procurements process because it will document the resources committed to delivering the goods and services as part of the contract, and the dates on which those resources are or are not available. The resource calendar goes on to be used as an input into the Estimate Activity Resources, Estimate Activity Duration, Develop Schedule, Determine Budget, and Develop Project Team processes.

Change requests

As a result of carrying out the Conduct Procurements process, you may discover that changes need to be made to the project management plan, subsidiary plans, or baselines to reflect work that has been negotiated and agreed to. Any change requests will be used as inputs into the Perform Integrated Change Control process.

Project management plan updates

The specific parts of the project management plan that may be updated as a result of carrying out the Conduct Procurements process will be the cost baseline, scope baseline, and schedule baseline to reflect any amendments made as a result of contractual negotiations.

Project documents updates

The specific project documents that will be updated include requirements documentation, the risk register, and any historical information.

Quick check

1. What is the main focus of the Conduct Procurements process?
2. Why is it important to keep bidder conferences fair to all prospective sellers?
3. Why is it important to carry out your own independent estimates?
4. Who should be involved in procurement negotiations?
5. What form of contract most favors a buyer in terms of risk?
6. Under what conditions would you generally choose to use a time and materials contract?

Quick check answers

1. The Conduct Procurements process is focused upon carrying out the process documented in the procurement management plan. This involves going to prospective sellers with information about the required goods and services, carrying out a fair and transparent process for selecting the sellers to do the work, and negotiating contracts.

2. In order to solicit professional and fair responses to your procurement process, it is important to treat all potential sellers, or bidders, equitably and provide them all with the same information.

3. There are several benefits to carrying out your own independent estimates. The first is to ensure that the estimates that you are being provided with by potential sellers are neither too high nor too low, perhaps indicating incorrect or insufficient information contained in the procurement statement of work. Another benefit of carrying out your own independent estimates is to independently check the accuracy of responses received from sellers.

4. The project manager should take responsibility for carrying out procurement negotiations, with the assistance of people with both technical, legal, financial, and negotiation skills.

5. The form of contract that most favors a buyer in terms of risk is a fixed-price contract, because in this instance the risk is with the seller, particularly if they have developed estimates upon inaccurate or incomplete information.

6. You would generally choose to use a time and materials form of contract when the work is small and ill defined, or under emergency conditions where the work must be completed quickly and there is not time to negotiate any other form of contract.

Control Procurements

> **MORE INFO   CONTROL PROCUREMENTS**
>
> You can read more about the Control Procurements process in the PMBOK® Guide, 5th edition, in Chapter 12, section 12.3. Table 10-4 identifies the process inputs, tools and techniques, and outputs.
>
> **TABLE 10-4** Control Procurements process
>
> | Inputs | Tools and techniques | Outputs |
> | --- | --- | --- |
> | - Project management plan
- Procurement documents
- Agreements
- Approved change requests
- Work performance reports
- Work performance data | - Contract change control system
- Procurement performance reviews
- Inspections and audits
- Performance reporting
- Payment systems
- Claims administration
- Records management system | - Work performance information
- Change requests
- Project management plan updates
- Project documents updates
- Organizational process assets updates |

The Control Procurements process is a monitoring and controlling process focused on the sometimes complex process of checking that both your procurement process and contracts entered into comply both with your procurement management plan and also with the terms and conditions contained within the negotiated contracts and agreements.

EXAM TIP

It is the responsibility of all parties to a contract to carry out work to ensure that the terms and conditions of the contract are being fulfilled.

The Control Procurements process covers the following domain task:

- 4.1 Measure project performance using appropriate tools and techniques, in order to identify and quantify any variances, perform approved corrective actions, and communicate with relevant stakeholders.

Inputs

The following inputs are used in the Control Procurements process.

Project management plan

The project management plan is a key input into the Control Procurements process, especially the procurement management plan, which is a subsidiary plan. Specific elements of the project management plan that are useful include the scope management plan, the schedule management plan, and the cost management plan. The project management plan is an output from the Develop Project Management Plan process.

Procurement documents

The specific procurement documents that are useful as inputs into the Control Procurements process include any documents from the Conduct Procurements process that result in legal agreements being signed. You will need these documents in addition to the individual agreements to understand the full breadth of agreement that you are monitoring. Procurement documents are an output from the Plan Procurement Management process.

Agreements

You will require any and all binding agreements between parties to all contracts in order to understand what terms and conditions and performance criteria you are monitoring. Agreements are an output from the Conduct Procurements process.

Approved change requests

Approved change requests can affect and modify any agreed terms and conditions of agreements or contracts. They are often referred to as variations, and it is important that as part of the Control Procurements process you check that not only have the changes been approved, or agreed to, but that they are also being carried out as per the agreed change. Approved change requests are an output from the Perform Integrated Change Control process.

Work performance reports

Work performance reports are the result when work performance information interprets work performance data. Work performance reports are useful in determining whether or not the terms and conditions of individual agreements are being met by parties to the agreement. Work performance reports are an output from the Control Project Work process.

Work performance data

Work performance data, specifically that which relates to whether or not quality standards are being met, is important in any assessment of whether or not contractual obligations are being met. Work performance data is an output from the Direct and Manage Project Work process.

Tools and techniques

The following tools and techniques of this process are able to be used upon the separate inputs to deliver the Control Procurements process outputs.

Contract change control system

A *contract change control system*, which includes the processes, guidelines, and tracking systems for reporting all requested changes, all variations, and the decisions made about them, is essential when monitoring the performance, or lack of performance, of any procurement agreements.

EXAM TIP

Any and all changes to a contract need to be recorded formally and in writing to reflect the formal nature of a contract.

Procurement performance reviews

As part of the normal course of administering a negotiated contract, it is common for the buyer to carry out *procurement performance reviews*. This involves comparing the seller's performance against the agreed and documented criteria in the contract. The purpose of the procurement performance reviews is to determine if there is any variance between what was agreed to and what is actually occurring.

EXAM TIP

A procurement performance review is essentially the quality assurance process for any negotiated contracts. It focuses on the agreed processes contained within the negotiated contract and not the actual deliverable.

Inspections and audits

Other key tools and techniques that can be used in the Control Procurements process are inspections and *audits*. Inspections are used to check deliverables, whereas audits are used to check that any agreed processes are being followed. As with other areas that use audits as a tool, it is often a good idea for them to be completed by independent personnel.

Performance reporting

Performance reporting takes information gathered as part of procurement performance reviews, inspections, and audits and presents it to management so that the seller's performance against agreed contractual objectives can be easily communicated. There are a number of methods and formats for reporting performance, including text, graphics, color coding, and pictures.

Payment systems

Payment systems are used to record invoices received and payments made to the seller, and to ensure that they are in accordance with the agreed payment terms in the contract.

> **EXAM TIP**
>
> All payments made as part of a negotiated and agreed contract should be strictly in accordance with the contract. Don't be tempted to make payments outside of the agreed terms.

Claims administration

Claims administration is used when there is a dispute about the amount charged or the work done as part of a contract. It is generally a result of poorly worded contracts or a poorly defined scope of work. Claims can be made by either the buyer or the seller in a contract and are usually made for something to be done outside of the agreed procurement statement of work. If agreement is reached, then the claim ceases and a change is made to the contract. Resolving claims often requires the use of dispute resolution techniques.

> **EXAM TIP**
>
> The word "claim" refers to a disputed cost or change. If you use this word in everyday language to mean something else, you must remember that for the exam, this is the correct definition.

> **Real world**
>
> The process of claims administration is unfortunately a very common and often complex reality of dealing with contracts, generally arising as a result of poorly negotiated or ambiguously worded contracts. Avoiding this potential minefield is a simple process of taking extra time when writing up the original contract and being explicit about as many potential scenarios as possible to avoid extra time spent disagreeing about costs and whether or not work performed constituted an agreed change to the contract.

Records management system

A comprehensive *records management system* is essential for dealing with, and recording, all contract-related agreements and variations. The records management system is a subset of the project management information system.

> **Real world**
>
> Given that contracts are formal, written legal documents you should ensure that your records management system reflects the importance of this and captures information in such a way that it can be retrieved, that it is accurate, and that it will be useful if any disputes escalate to litigation.

Outputs

The Control Procurements process has the following outputs.

Work performance information

As with other monitoring and control processes, the Control Procurements process has work performance information as a major output. The work performance information compiles and presents information gathered as a result of using the Control Procurements tools and techniques and presents it in a way that the intended audience can easily obtain relevant information about the project performance, specifically in relation to contractual administration and compliance. Work performance information can also be used by one contractual party to inform the other party of any areas of noncompliance. Work performance information is used as an input into the Control Project Work process.

Change requests

Change requests are a common output from any monitoring and control process. For the Control Procurements process, change requests relate to both internal project processes and also to change requests for the negotiated contracts.

> **Real world**
>
> It is very important that you document any and all changes, no matter how small, to any contract.

Project management plan updates

As a result of carrying out the Control Procurements process, you may update specific elements of the project management plan, which obviously include the procurement management plan and other plans and baselines such as the scope baseline, cost baseline, and schedule baseline.

Project documents updates

The specific types of project documents that may be updated as a result of carrying out the Control Procurements process are generally focused upon procurement documentation, such as the initial description of work, processes relating to the selection of sellers, and any documents relating to how contracts are monitored.

Organizational process assets updates

The specific organizational process assets that will be updated as a result of the Control Procurements process are any historical information databases, correspondence files, records of payments made, and any internal documentation regarding seller performance.

Quick check

1. What is the main focus of the Control Procurements process?
2. What is the benefit of having a payment system in place?
3. Why is it important to keep well-documented records of any claims made?

Quick check answers

1. The Control Procurements process is focused upon checking that the procurements process is being carried out as per the procurement management plan, and also that the terms and conditions of any contracts being used are being met by both parties.

2. Having a payment system in place ensures that all payments required as part of the agreed contractual terms and conditions are paid on time and records are kept.

3. If a claim has been made, that means that there is a disagreement about performance on a contract. Disagreements can escalate and require dispute resolution. Having well-documented records will assist during any dispute resolution process.

Close Procurements

> **MORE INFO** **CLOSE PROCUREMENTS**
>
> You can read more about the Close Procurements process in the PMBOK® Guide, 5th edition, in Chapter 11, section 12.4. Table 10-5 identifies the process inputs, tools and techniques, and outputs.
>
> **TABLE 10-5** Close Procurements process
>
> | Inputs | Tools and techniques | Outputs |
> |---|---|---|
> | ■ Project management plan
■ Procurement documents | ■ Procurement audits
■ Negotiated settlements
■ Records management system | ■ Closed procurements
■ Organizational process assets updates |

The Close Procurements process is a closing process focused on ensuring that all contracts used in the project are either closed according to the documented terms or conditions, or closed as a result of nonperformance.

The Close Procurements process covers the following domain task:

- 5.3 Obtain financial, legal, and administrative closure using generally accepted practices, in order to communicate formal project closure and ensure no further liability.

Inputs

The following inputs are used in the Close Procurements process.

Project management plan

The project management plan outlines the particular way in which you will carry out the closure of all contracts. Due to the fact that contracts typically reflect many different aspects of the project, there are many subsidiary plans and baselines of the project management plan that will be required in order to successfully close procurements or contracts. The project management plan is an output from the Develop Project Management Plan process.

Procurement documents

Obviously, in order to close any procurements you will require the relevant procurement documents that outline either the agreed terms and conditions for normal contractual closure or the processes for terminating a contract due to nonperformance. You will also want procurement documents that relate to how well the contractual terms have been met, how well the deliverables have been delivered, what payments have already been made and whether there are retention payments, and any other relevant material. Procurement documents are an output from the Plan Procurement Management process.

Tools and techniques

The following tools and techniques of this process are able to be used upon the separate inputs to deliver the Close Procurements process outputs.

Procurement audits

Procurement audits are structured reviews of how both the buyer and seller have carried out the procurement process. From the buyer's point of view, the procurement audit will check that the procurement process has been carried out as planned and documented in the procurement management plan, right through to whether or not the seller met the terms and conditions of a negotiated contract. From the seller's point of view, the procurement audit will determine whether the procurement process as planned and documented has been followed, for everything from responding to initial procurement requests through to product delivery and warranty requirements .

EXAM TIP

Both buyer and seller should carry out procurement audits to ensure that there are no disagreements about which parts of the contract have been met and which haven't, and also for the benefit of developing and documenting any lessons learned for future procurement processes.

Negotiated settlements

Despite your best efforts at documenting and describing contractual processes that include a clear final resolution and closure process, it is not uncommon for all parties to a contract to have to enter into some form of *negotiated settlement* to terminate the contract fully. In this instance, negotiated settlements can reflect obligations and agreements on both buyer and seller as to final payments, warranty obligations, and any other matters to enable the contract to be fully closed. If any disagreements arise as a result of misunderstandings or poorly worded contracts and negotiated settlements cannot be achieved through direct negotiation by all parties to a contract, there may have to be some form of escalation and external dispute resolution used, such as mediation, arbitration, or litigation.

Negotiation is where two or more parties attempt to agree on a solution between themselves. Mediation is when the disagreeing parties bring in an independent person to help them reach an agreement. Arbitration is when the parties agree to allow an independent person to hear both sides of the story and make a binding decision. Litigation is when the parties resolve their disputes through the civil courts system.

EXAM TIP

Contracts should spell out very clearly what the process is for negotiated settlements or dispute resolution. They should include a section on how mediation and arbitration will be carried out and also when and where litigation can occur.

Records management system

The records management system is a way to record and store all records relating to procurement on a project. It is a part of the project management information system, and it should reflect the formal and legal nature of the procurement process.

> **Real world**
>
> You will often find that many countries have statutory requirements for how long contractual documents must be stored. It pays to check what the local requirements are and make sure that you meet them.

Outputs

The outputs from the Close Procurements process are the following.

Closed procurements

The key outputs from the Close Procurements process are *closed procurements*, which include formal documented proof that the contract terms have been met, settlement has been agreed, and thus the contract is now closed. Given that contracts are formal, legal, and written documents, you should have formal, legal, and written proof that the contract has been closed. Contractual closure does not mean project closure. Contracts can be closed at any time in a project. You will want to be sure that before you close a project all contracts are closed.

> **EXAM TIP**
>
> All contracts on a project must be closed. They can be closed as part of normal and agreed processes, or they can be closed as a result of unusual circumstances. This also applies to the situation in which your project is suddenly terminated; you must still ensure that there is some documentation that records that contracts were closed under abnormal circumstances. You may get a question in the exam that presents a scenario that suggests that you have been told to close a project immediately and suggests that perhaps you do not have the authority, money, or time to close contracts formally. This may certainly be the case in relation to formal contract closure, but you should still record that contracts have been closed as a result of abnormal circumstances.

Organizational process assets updates

As a result of carrying out the Close Procurements process, you may want to update particular organizational process assets, including any templates, processes, or guidelines relating to how procurement is carried out and how deliverables are accepted; historical databases; and lessons-learned documentation to use in future procurements.

> ✓ **Quick check**
>
> 1. What is the main focus of the Close Procurements process?
> 2. Why is it sometimes necessary to use negotiated settlements to close contracts?
> 3. What is the purpose of the records management system?
>
> **Quick check answers**
>
> 1. The main purpose of the Close Procurements process is to ensure that all contracts being used on the project are formally closed and recorded as being so.
> 2. Not all contracts end without some form of difference of opinion on what constitutes full and final closure or termination. In these instances, a contract is often terminated or closed as a result of negotiated settlement between both parties.
> 3. The primary purpose of the records management system is to store any documents relating to the procurement process for future use.

Exercises

The answers for these exercises are located in the "Answers" section at the end of this chapter.

1. Unscramble the table below to match up the contract type with its description and the description of risk apportionment.

Type of contract	Description	Risk apportionment
Fixed-price contract	A form of contract that requires the seller to pass on the actual cost of the work to be done	Seller has the risk, and if the cost to deliver the goods or services is greater than the fixed price, the seller bears the extra costs.
Cost-reimbursable contract	A form of contract where the seller charges for all time spent and materials used with no agreed maximum	Buyer has the risk because there is no agreed maximum price.
Time and material contract (T&M)	A form of contract that includes an agreed, fixed price for the delivery of goods and services	Risk split between buyer and seller, depending on the actual form and wording of the contract.

2. You are the project manager working on a construction project using a fixed-price incentive fee (FPIF) form of contract with a selected seller. The agreed contract sets a total ceiling price of $325,000, a target cost to the seller of $280,000, and a target price to you as buyer of $310,000. There is also an agreement that you will pay 70 percent of the cost overruns above the target cost. What is the point of total assumption?

Chapter summary

- The Procurement Management knowledge area is focused upon the development of a plan to guide decisions around external procurement of goods and services, and the execution, monitoring, and control of this plan.
- The Plan Procurement Management process provides a procurement management plan and the procurement statement of work, both of which provide guidance for the subsequent processes for the work to be done as part of agreements.
- The Conduct Procurements process is a planning process that seeks to carry out the procurement management plan in relation to the identification of sellers, the distribution of information about the procurement statement of work to sellers, the selection of sellers to carry out the work, and the type of contract that will be used.
- The Control Procurements process is a monitoring and control process that seeks to both check that the procurement process is being carried out as per the procurement management plan, and also that the contracts are being carried out as per the agreed terms and conditions.
- The Close Procurements process, which is a closing process, seeks to ensure that all contracts entered into as part of a project are formally closed, either as part of normal procedure or as a result of nonperformance or disagreement.

Chapter review

Test your knowledge of the information in Chapter 10 by answering these questions. The answers to these questions, and the explanations of why each answer choice is correct or incorrect, are located in the "Answers" section at the end of this chapter.

1. Which of the following processes produces the procurement management plan?

    A. Close Procurements

    B. Plan Procurement Management

    C. Conduct Procurements

    D. Develop Procurement Management Plan

2. The organization seeking to procure external resources to provide goods or services on a project is known as what?

    A. Procurement specialist

    B. Seller

    C. Lawyer

    D. Buyer

3. You are the seller of a potential good or service, and are responding to an RFP document where there is a poorly defined scope of work. What type of contract would you prefer to enter into?

   A. Fixed-price
   B. Fixed-price incentive fee
   C. Cost-reimbursable
   D. Time and materials

4. The document that describes and defines the portion of the project scope to be included within the related contract is known as what?

   A. Procurement management plan
   B. Organizational process assets
   C. Scope statement
   D. Procurement statement of work

5. A technique that considers a variety of factors in order to determine whether the particular project work is best done by the project team or done by external sources is known as what?

   A. Expert judgment
   B. Market research
   C. Proposal evaluation techniques
   D. Make or buy analysis

6. All of the following could be included as part of your source selection criteria except what?

   A. Intellectual property rights
   B. Technical capability
   C. Financial capacity
   D. Organizational process assets

7. You have decided to engage the services of a quantity surveyor to review the prices received from sellers responding to your procurement requests. What tool or technique are you using?

   A. Delphi technique
   B. Independent estimates
   C. Analytical techniques
   D. Bidder conferences

8. You and your team are in the process of negotiating a contract for a particular service required on your project. Which process are you in?

    A. Plan Procurement Management

    B. Conduct Procurements

    C. Control Procurements

    D. Close Procurements

9. The seller you have engaged to carry out a contract for the provision of services on your project has started submitting multiple change requests, which are escalating into claims. What is the most likely cause of this?

    A. Incomplete risk register

    B. Poorly worded procurement statement of work

    C. Incomplete project management plan

    D. Lack of quality management

10. Who is responsible for carrying out audits on contracts?

    A. Only the buyer

    B. Only the seller

    C. An independent legal professional

    D. Both buyer and seller

11. Which tool or technique would be most useful for storing information about procurement documentation and records?

    A. Records management system

    B. Project management information system

    C. Contract change control system

    D. Procurement performance reviews

12. All of the following conditions can lead to early termination of a contract except what?

    A. Mutual agreement by both parties

    B. Default of one party

    C. Convenience of the buyer if provided for in the contract

    D. An incomplete procurement statement of work

13. Which of the following is not a form of alternative dispute resolution?

    A. Mediation

    B. Arbitration

    C. Litigation

    D. Audit

Answers

This section contains the answers for the "Exercises" and "Chapter review" sections in this chapter.

Exercises

1. Unscramble the table below to match up the contract type with its description and the description of risk apportionment.

Type of contract	Description	Risk apportionment
Fixed-price contract	A form of contract that includes an agreed, fixed price for the delivery of goods and services	Seller has the risk, and if the cost to deliver the goods or services is greater than the fixed price, the seller bears the extra costs.
Cost-reimbursable contract	A form of contract that requires the seller to pass on the actual cost of the work to be done	Risk split between buyer and seller, depending on the actual form and wording of the contract.
Time and material contract (T&M)	A form of contract where the seller charges for all time spent and materials used with no agreed maximum	Buyer has the risk, because there is no agreed maximum price.

2. You are the project manager working on a construction project using a fixed-price incentive fee (FPIF) form of contract with a selected seller. The agreed contract sets a total ceiling price of $325,000, a target cost to the seller of $280,000, and a target price to you as buyer of $310,000. There is also an agreement that you will pay 70 percent of the cost overruns above the target cost. What is the point of total assumption?

   Point of total assumption = Target cost + ((Ceiling price − Target price)/Buyers % share of cost overrun)

   Therefore:

   Point of total assumption = $280,000 + (($325,000 − $310,000)/0.7)
   = $280,000 + ($15,000/0.7)
   = $280,000 + $21,428.57
   = $301,428.57

Chapter review

1. **Correct answer: B**

   A. **Incorrect:** The Close Procurements process is focused upon the administrative and legal closure of all contracts.

   B. **Correct:** The Plan Procurement Management process has the procurement management plan as its primary output.

C. **Incorrect:** Conduct Procurements uses the procurement management plan.

   D. **Incorrect:** Develop Procurement Management Plan is a made-up process name.

2. **Correct answer: D**

   A. **Incorrect:** A procurement specialist may be an expert that you choose to use as part of your decision to procure from external sources.

   B. **Incorrect:** The seller is the organization or individual who is responding to a request from a buyer for the provision of goods and services.

   C. **Incorrect:** A lawyer can act for either buyer or seller.

   D. **Correct:** The buyer is the organization that is requiring goods or services to be performed and is asking for external sources to do the work via a negotiated contract.

3. **Correct answer: D**

   A. **Incorrect:** A fixed-price contract would represent the greatest risk to the seller in the face of a poorly defined scope of work.

   B. **incorrect:** A fixed-price incentive fee contracts does little to remove the risk to the seller with a poorly defined scope of work.

   C. **Incorrect:** A cost-reimbursable form of contract may be preferable to a fixed-price form of contract where there is a poorly defined scope of work, but it still represents more risk to the seller that a time and materials contract.

   D. **Correct:** Given that there is a poorly defined scope of work, you would want to enter into the type of contract that represented the least risk to you, the seller, and this is the time and materials contract.

4. **Correct answer: D**

   A. **Incorrect:** The procurement management plan provides guidelines for carrying out the entire procurement management process.

   B. **Incorrect:** Organizational process assets include templates, historical information, and other guidelines of use in carrying out the procurement management process, but they do not describe or define the work to be done as part of the contract.

   C. **Incorrect:** The project scope statement defines and describes all of the week to be done as part of the project; the procurement statement of work is a subset of the project scope statement specifically related to the work to be done as part of a contract.

   D. **Correct:** The procurement statement of work describes and defines the portion of the project scope to be completed as part of a negotiated contract.

5. **Correct answer: D**
   A. **Incorrect:** Expert judgment is used as a tool and may contribute to the make or buy analysis, but it is not the best answer.
   B. **Incorrect:** Market research is a technique that examines the number of potential sellers and their interest in responding to your procurement documents.
   C. **Incorrect:** Proposal evaluation techniques are used after sellers have responded to your requests, in order to determine which sellers advance in the procurement process.
   D. **Correct:** Make or buy analysis is the technique that takes into account a variety of factors to determine whether you should complete the work in house or outsource it.

6. **Correct answer: D**
   A. **Incorrect:** Intellectual property rights are an important consideration in your source selection criteria, to determine who ultimately owns the work performed as part of a contract.
   B. **Incorrect:** Technical capability will be considered as part of your source selection criteria, in order to ensure that the selected seller has the technical capability to perform the required work.
   C. **Incorrect:** Financial capacity will be considered as part of your source selection criteria, to ensure that the sellers selected are of sufficient financial strength to be able to complete the work.
   D. **Correct:** Organizational process assets may help you with the procurement management processes, but they would not be included as part of your source selection criteria.

7. **Correct answer: B**
   A. **Incorrect:** The Delphi technique is a tool used to solicit information from participants anonymously in order to reach consensus.
   B. **Correct:** Independent estimates are a technique used to determine if prices received from sellers are accurate.
   C. **Incorrect:** Analytical techniques are a particular tool used to evaluate a variety of elements and seller responses, not just prices.
   D. **Incorrect:** Bidder conferences are used to provide information to prospective sellers on a fair and equitable basis.

8. **Correct answer: B**

   A. **Incorrect:** The Plan Procurement Management process is focused on the production of the procurement management plan the procurement statement of work, which will assist with the Conduct Procurements process, which negotiates contracts.

   B. **Correct:** The Conduct Procurements process uses the project management plan and seeks to negotiate contracts with potential sellers.

   C. **Incorrect:** The Control Procurements process monitors the negotiated contracts but does not actually negotiate them.

   D. **Incorrect:** The Close Procurements process closes contracts after they have been negotiated and the terms and conditions have been fulfilled.

9. **Correct answer: B**

   A. **Incorrect:** An incomplete risk register may expose your project to unforeseen risks. But that would not contribute to multiple change requests and an escalating number of claims.

   B. **Correct:** The scenario is most likely to be the result of a poorly worded procurement statement of work, creating ambiguity and disagreement about the work to be performed as part of the contract.

   C. **Incorrect:** An incomplete project management plan may affect several other areas of your project but would not be directly responsible for multiple contractual change requests and claims.

   D. **Incorrect:** A lack of quality management on your project may cause a number of problems but would not be the most likely cause of multiple contractual change requests and claims.

10. **Correct answer: D**

    A. **Incorrect:** The seller is also responsible for carrying out audits on contracts to ensure that both they and the buyer are meeting the agreed terms and conditions.

    B. **Incorrect:** The buyer also has responsibility for carrying out audits of the contracts because they initiated the process and have obligations as well.

    C. **Incorrect:** An independent legal professional may be engaged by either buyer or seller, but the ultimate responsibility lies with both buyer and seller.

    D. **Correct:** Both buyer and seller are responsible for carrying out audits on contracts, because they are both parties to the contract and have responsibilities under the negotiated terms and conditions.

11. **Correct answer: A**

    A. **Correct:** The records management system is a subset of the project management information system devoted to storing information about procurement documentation and records.

    B. **Incorrect:** The project management information system includes the records management system, which is the better answer this question because it specifically focuses upon storing information about procurement documentation and records.

    C. **Incorrect:** The contract change control system records information about requested contractual changes and the status.

    D. **Incorrect:** Procurement performance reviews gather information about whether each party to a contract is carrying out their obligations and responsibilities. Information gathered from procurement performance reviews will be stored in a records management system.

12. **Correct answer: D**

    A. **Incorrect:** Both parties can, by way of mutual agreement, agree to terminate the contract early.

    B. **Incorrect:** The default of one party to a contract is considered sufficient cause for early termination of a contract.

    C. **Incorrect:** There are some forms of contract that have written into them that early termination can occur if it is convenient to the buyer. These contracts normally include some form of compensation to the seller.

    D. **Correct:** An incomplete procurement statement of work may lead to disagreements, change requests, and claims, but not generally to an early termination of the contract except under extreme circumstances.

13. **Correct answer: D**

    A. **Incorrect:** Mediation is a form of alternative dispute resolution that seeks to have both parties reach an agreement.

    B. **Incorrect:** Arbitration is a form of alternative dispute resolution that brings in a third party to make a decision that is binding on both parties.

    C. **Incorrect:** Litigation is a form of alternative dispute resolution that involves some form of court involvement.

    D. **Correct:** An audit is used to determine whether or not parties to a contract are carrying the contract out as per the agreed terms and conditions.

CHAPTER 11

Stakeholder management

This chapter focuses on the topic of project stakeholder management, which begins with an initiating process, Identify Stakeholders, to identify the stakeholders. Next, the process involves developing the stakeholder register that is used in the Plan Stakeholder Management process; this additional process involves developing the stakeholder management plan. The Manage Stakeholder Engagement process carries out the stakeholder management plan, and the Control Stakeholder Engagement process checks planned activities against what is actually occurring in relation to stakeholder management.

> ### The PMBOK® Guide processes
>
> **Project Stakeholder Management knowledge area**
>
> The four processes in the Project Stakeholder Management knowledge area are:
>
> - Identify Stakeholders (Initiating process)
> - Plan Stakeholder Management (Planning process)
> - Manage Stakeholder Engagement (Executing process)
> - Control Stakeholder Engagement (Monitoring and Controlling process)

Domain tasks in this chapter:

- Identify Stakeholders process:
    - 1.3 Perform key stakeholder analysis using brainstorming, interviewing, and other data-gathering techniques, in order to ensure expectation alignment and gain support for the project.
- Plan Stakeholder Management process:
    - 2.6 Develop a communication plan based on the project organization structure and external stakeholder requirements, in order to manage the flow of project information.
    - 2.11 Present the project plan to the key stakeholders (if required), in order to obtain approval to execute the project.
    - 2.12 Conduct a kick-off meeting with all key stakeholders, in order to announce the start of the project, communicate the project milestones, and share other relevant information.

- Manage Stakeholder Engagement process:
    - 3.2 Execute the tasks as defined in the project plan, in order to achieve the project deliverables within budget and schedule.
- Control Stakeholder Engagement process:
    - 4.1 Measure project performance using appropriate tools and techniques, in order to identify and quantify any variances, perform approved corrective actions, and communicate with relevant stakeholders.
    - 4.6 Communicate project status to stakeholders for their feedback, in order to ensure the project aligns with business needs.

What is project stakeholder management?

Project stakeholder management is focused on all the processes involved in identifying as many stakeholders as possible on a project, understanding their expectations and levels of engagement, planning how to proactively engage and influence them, and checking that what you are doing is in accordance with the stakeholder management plan and acting on any deviations or variances.

A *stakeholder* is any person, group, or organization who can affect, or be affected by, your project. Stakeholders can have an impact on your project in both positive and negative ways. All projects have stakeholders interested in the outcomes and impact of the project. It is your job as project manager to identify all of these stakeholders and what their expectations are, keep them engaged, and ensure that stakeholder satisfaction becomes a key project deliverable. The easiest way to do this is to ensure that stakeholder management is a continuous dialogue rather than a one-off event or a series of sporadic events.

A main objective of the stakeholder management process is to get stakeholders to support your project or at least not to oppose it.

In order to effectively understand and manage stakeholders' engagement and expectations, you must be both proactive and influencing. Being proactive means anticipating and planning, and it is the opposite of being reactive. By being proactive you will minimize surprises that stakeholders can bring to the project.

To carry out effective influencing you need to first ensure that you understand where stakeholders currently sit in relation to their expectations and engagement and know where you want them to be. *Influencing* means using a variety of skills and techniques to modify, enhance, or reduce particular aspects of stakeholder engagement and expectations. These skills and techniques include effective communication, highly developed interpersonal skills, and the correct display of technical ability. A skilled project manager chooses which combination to use in order to maximize stakeholder influencing.

EXAM TIP

The success or failure of your efforts to identify and manage stakeholders will have a high degree of impact on whether or not your project is a success or failure. In the exam, you should treat any questions that refer to stakeholders as ones that require you to proactively define, manage, and influence their engagement and expectations.

Real world

I have often found that the actual or perceived success or failure of a project rests on how satisfied stakeholders are rather than the technical measurements around cost or time. This is a sign of just how important it is to keep your stakeholders engaged and to ensure that their expectations are managed.

Identify Stakeholders

MORE INFO   IDENTIFY STAKEHOLDERS

You can read more about the Identify Stakeholders process in the PMBOK® Guide, 5th edition, in Chapter 13, section 13.1. Table 11-1 identifies the process inputs, tools and techniques, and outputs.

TABLE 11-1 Identify Stakeholders process

Inputs	Tools and techniques	Outputs
■ Project charter ■ Procurement documents ■ Enterprise environmental factors ■ Organizational process assets	■ Stakeholder analysis ■ Expert judgment ■ Meetings	■ Stakeholder register

The Identify Stakeholders process is an initiating process with the stakeholder register as its sole output. The stakeholder register contains key information about stakeholders that can be used in the other stakeholder management processes.

The Identify Stakeholders process covers the following domain tasks:

- 1.3 Perform key stakeholder analysis using brainstorming, interviewing, and other data-gathering techniques, in order to ensure expectation alignment and gain support for the project.

Inputs

The Identify Stakeholders process uses some or all of the following inputs as part of the development of the stakeholder register for the project.

Project charter

The project charter will contain information about internal and external stakeholders identified as part of the project initiation, such as the customer, the project sponsor, and any other easily identified stakeholders. The project charter is an output from the Develop Project Charter process.

Procurement documents

The procurement documents will be used as an input into the Identify Stakeholders process if a contract forms the basis of the project, because the parties to the contract are key stakeholders. Procurement documents are an output from the Plan Procurement Management process.

Enterprise environmental factors

The specific enterprise environmental factors that will be useful as inputs into this process are organizational culture and structure, any relevant government or industry standards, and any external cultural aspects of dealing with particular individuals or groups of stakeholders.

Organizational process assets

The specific organizational process assets that may be an important input into the development of your stakeholder register are any blank stakeholder register templates the organization has and lessons learned that your organization has gathered from previous projects.

Tools and techniques

The following tools and techniques are available to be used to develop the inputs in this process in order to produce the stakeholder register.

Stakeholder analysis

There are a number of ways to carry out stakeholder analysis; each of them seeks to identify the stakeholders' interests, expectations, power, influence, and level of engagement in the project. *Stakeholder analysis* begins with the use of information-gathering techniques such as brainstorming, interviewing, and other data-gathering techniques in order to identify stakeholders. The information gathered as part of carrying out stakeholder analysis will enable you to clearly describe the power, interest, influence, impact, and engagement stakeholders have on your project, and then you will be able to develop a robust stakeholder management strategy.

After you have gathered data about stakeholders, there are a number of ways of presenting this data. A very popular way of graphically showing the level of impact, or engagement, a stakeholder has on your project is with a matrix displaying either power and interest, power and influence, or influence and impact on the x-axis and y-axis, respectively. Figure 11-1 shows an example of a power and interest matrix.

		Level of interest	
		Low	High
Power	Low	Monitor	Keep informed
	High	Keep satisfied	Key players, manage closely

FIGURE 11-1 A matrix can be used to categorize stakeholder power and interest.

EXAM TIP

Figure 11-1 is often called a Gardner grid or matrix, named after one of the original authors who developed it.

Another way to represent levels of stakeholder influence on your project is to use the salience model, which maps stakeholders' power, urgency, and legitimacy to place stakeholders into one of seven possible categories, each of which begins with the letter "D." Figure 11-2 shows an example of a salience model and the seven possible categories of stakeholder. It shows that a stakeholder with high levels of power and urgency but with a low level of legitimacy is categorized as dangerous, whereas a stakeholder with legitimacy and power but a low level of urgency is categorized as dominant.

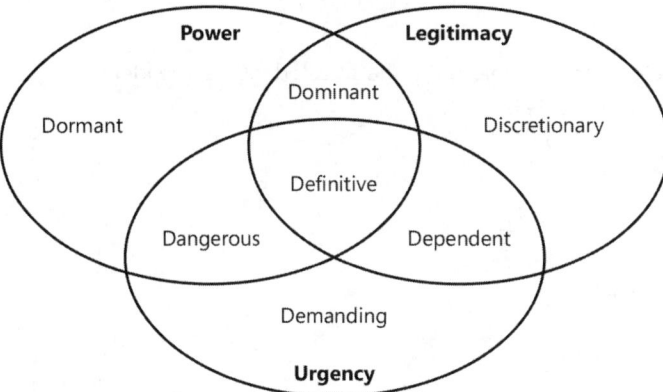

FIGURE 11-2 A salience model can be used to categorize stakeholders.

Identify Stakeholders **CHAPTER 11** **427**

EXAM TIP

The salience model was developed by Ronald Mitchell, Bradley Agle, and Donna Wood. So if you find a question that refers to any form of diagram by these authors, you will know it is referring to the salience model.

Expert judgment

Expert judgment is a key tool to be used in the Identify Stakeholders process because the use of experts with experience in the identification and assessment of stakeholders will ensure that you have a more complete stakeholder register. Particular experts that you may want to consult with include the project sponsor, senior management, the key stakeholders themselves, other people who have worked in similar areas with relevant experience, and any subject matter experts in the area in which you are working.

EXAM TIP

You will recall that when soliciting information from experts there are a wide variety of information-gathering techniques that you are able to use such as interviews, consultation, meetings, surveys, workshops, and focus groups.

Meetings

Meetings are an important tool for gathering, exchanging, and analyzing information gathered about stakeholders and their power, interest, influence, impact, engagement, and expectations.

Outputs

After applying the appropriate tools and techniques to the selected inputs, the Identify Stakeholders process has the following sole output.

Stakeholder register

The Identify Stakeholders process has the stakeholder register as its sole output. The stakeholder register will probably contain information on the following:

- A classification of stakeholder categories so you can distinguish between different stakeholders and their expectations and engagement
- Information about individual stakeholders and their contact details
- A description of the interest that each stakeholder has in the project
- An assessment of the stakeholders' power, impact, influence, engagement, or interest in the project
- A description of the strategy to be employed to gain their support and keep them satisfied
- A description of the frequency and method by which you will revisit the stakeholder register

> **Real world**
>
> Take great care with information that you record in your stakeholder register, and always keep in mind that a stakeholder may one day view the register, so ensure that the information you include about your assessment of the stakeholders' influence, impact, or engagement on the project will not adversely affect your project if the stakeholder reads the register. For example, on a project I worked on, we had one extremely difficult senior manager who was part of the project control group and who constantly failed to read reports, undermined project team members, and had a difficult interpersonal style. He also had the ability to greatly influence the project. As we documented his interest and impact upon the project in the stakeholder register, we had to be careful how we described his interaction with the team, because if we had written what we really thought, it would have caused a lot of problems if he had viewed it.

The stakeholder register is used as an input into a number of processes, including the Collect Requirements process, the Plan Quality Management process, the Plan Risk Management process, the Identify Risks process, the Plan Procurement Management process, and the Plan Stakeholder Management process. This shows how important the stakeholder register is to multiple parts of the project.

Quick check

1. What is the main focus of the Identify Stakeholders process?
2. What is the best definition of a stakeholder?
3. What is your primary objective in identifying and managing stakeholders on your project?
4. How is the Identify Stakeholders process linked to other project management processes?

Quick check answers

1. The main focus of the Identify Stakeholders process is to carry out stakeholder analysis to develop your stakeholder register, which identifies stakeholders, their interest in the project, an assessment of the ways in which they can affect your project, and a consideration of the ways in which you can proactively manage and influence their engagement and expectations.
2. A stakeholder is any individual, group, or organization that can affect, or be affected by, your project.
3. Your primary objective when identifying and managing stakeholders on your project is to ensure that they stay engaged and their expectations are managed in order to ensure that they provide support to your project, or alternatively, that they do not oppose the project.
4. The output from the Identify Stakeholders process is the stakeholder register, which is used as an input into the Collect Requirements process, the Plan Quality Management process, the Plan Risk Management process, the Identify Risks process, and the Plan Procurement Management process, all of which are outside the stakeholder management area. It is also used as an input into the Plan Stakeholder Management process.

Plan Stakeholder Management

> **MORE INFO** **PLAN STAKEHOLDER MANAGEMENT**
>
> You can read more about the Plan Stakeholder Management process in the PMBOK® Guide, 5th edition, in Chapter 13, section 13.2. Table 11-2 identifies the process inputs, tools and techniques, and outputs.
>
> **TABLE 11-2** Plan Stakeholder Management process
>
> | Inputs | Tools and techniques | Outputs |
> |---|---|---|
> | ■ Project management plan
■ Stakeholder register
■ Enterprise environmental factors
■ Organizational process assets | ■ Expert judgment
■ Meetings
■ Analytical techniques | ■ Stakeholder management plan
■ Project documents updates |

The Plan Stakeholder Management process is a planning process that seeks to identify how the project will affect stakeholders, how stakeholders will affect the project, and how the team will proactively manage levels of stakeholder engagement, proactively influence stakeholder expectations, and ensure stakeholder support for the project, its objectives, and deliverables.

The Plan Stakeholder Management process covers the following domain tasks:

- 2.6 Develop a communication plan based on the project organization structure and external stakeholder requirements, in order to manage the flow of project information.
- 2.11 Present the project plan to the key stakeholders (if required), in order to obtain approval to execute the project.
- 2.12 Conduct a kick-off meeting with all key stakeholders, in order to announce the start of the project, communicate the project milestones, and share other relevant information.

> **Real world**
>
> There is a great deal of skill required to be successful in proactively influencing stakeholder engagement and expectations. I strongly recommend that, as part of your own professional development as a project manager, you focus on your ability to proactively influence stakeholders because it is one of the key ways to ensure project success. Conversely, if it is done poorly, it is a surefire way to increase the chances of project failure.

Inputs

The Plan Stakeholder Management process uses some or all of the following inputs.

Project management plan

The project management plan is an input into the Plan Stakeholder Management process because it provides a wealth of information about different aspects of the project that is useful in developing a stakeholder management plan. Specific information that will be useful includes the project life cycle, the methodology selected to execute the project, the specific objectives and deliverables of the project, and the particular forms of communication to be used. All this information can be found in different parts of the project management plan. The project management plan is an output from the Develop Project Management Plan process.

Stakeholder register

The stakeholder register is an extremely important input into the development of the stakeholder management plan because it outlines each of the stakeholders; their interest in the project; their power, interest, impact, and influence; and any particular identified ways of influencing both their engagement and expectations. The stakeholder register is an output from the Identify Stakeholders process.

Enterprise environmental factors

The specific types of enterprise environmental factors that will be useful in the development of the stakeholder management plan will be your particular organizational culture, structures, and internal and external political climate, because all of these will affect the method, frequency, and success or failure of your stakeholder management efforts.

Organizational process assets

The specific types of organizational process assets that will assist in development of the stakeholder management plan include any lessons learned that your organization has gathered about stakeholder management activities from previous projects, any blank templates for the development of a stakeholder management plan, and any other relevant historical information.

Tools and techniques

The following tools and techniques are used upon the inputs to deliver the Plan Stakeholder Management process outputs.

Expert judgment

Expert judgment is an excellent tool to use in the plan stakeholder management process because it allows you to bring together people with experience and skills in the identification of stakeholders and in the development of specific ways in which to manage both their engagement and expectations. You may choose to draw on the expertise of the project sponsor, senior management, other identified key stakeholders, subject matter experts with experience in the area in which your project is operating, and any other relevant experts.

Meetings

Meetings are an excellent tool for bringing together experts and members of the project team to carry out the process of the development and reassessment of your stakeholder management plan throughout the life of your project.

A particularly effective meeting that can be useful in increasing levels of stakeholder engagement and proactively influencing stakeholder expectations is the kick-off meeting. The kick-off meeting is held after enough planning has been completed to enable the first of the project execution work to begin. It is used to bring stakeholders together face to face, to discuss the project and show everyone where the project is going.

Analytical techniques

You may choose to use a variety of analytical techniques in order to assess the level of engagement of individual stakeholders. There are several ways of assessing and documenting different stakeholders and the level of engagement they have with the project. Figure 11-3 shows a stakeholder engagement assessment matrix, which is a popular way of showing whether a stakeholder is unaware of the project, resistant to the project, neutral about the project, supportive of the project, or leading and actively engaged in ensuring that the project will be successful. The letter "C" shows where the stakeholder currently is, and the letter "D" shows where you would like them to be. Getting stakeholders to position "D" is the focus of your stakeholder management activities.

	Unaware	Resistant	Neutral	Supportive	Leading
Stakeholder A		C			D
Stakeholder B				C D	
Stakeholder C			C	D	
Stakeholder D				C	D

FIGURE 11-3 A stakeholder engagement assessment matrix shows stakeholder engagement both now and in the future.

Outputs

The Plan Stakeholder Management process has the following outputs.

Stakeholder management plan

The stakeholder management plan is the key output from the Plan Stakeholder Management process. This plan takes the information gathered from the stakeholder register, and from this provides a plan that identifies stakeholder engagement and expectations and sets out a clear strategy for managing and influencing engagement and expectations to ensure that stakeholders are supportive of the project, or at least do not oppose the project. The stakeholder management plan is used as an input into the Manage Stakeholder Engagement process.

EXAM TIP

Any question that appears in the exam about your interaction with stakeholders will require you to take the position of continuously, and proactively, influencing their engagement and expectations. In order to do this you will require a stakeholder management plan.

Project documents updates

The specific project documents that may be updated as a result of carrying out the Plan Stakeholder Management process include the communications plan, stakeholder register, and any other document that refers to, or relies upon, stakeholder engagement.

Quick check

1. What is the main purpose of the Plan Stakeholder Management process?
2. What sort of information should a stakeholder management plan contain?
3. What does a stakeholder engagement assessment matrix show?
4. How do the activities contained in the Plan Stakeholder Management process interact with other project management knowledge areas?

Quick check answers

1. The Plan Stakeholder Management process seeks to take the information gathered on the stakeholder register and use this to develop a coherent stakeholder management plan that proactively managers and influences stakeholder engagement and expectations to ensure stakeholder support of the project and its objectives.

2. The stakeholder management plan should build upon the information contained in the stakeholder register and contain information about the current and expected engagement levels of key stakeholders, the communications requirements and methods selected for the stakeholders, and the particular strategies to be employed in managing their engagement and expectations.

3. The stakeholder engagement assessment matrix shows the level of engagement of individual stakeholders in the project.

4. The project management plan, which refers to all other areas of the project, is used as an input into the Plan Stakeholder Management process because any information about stakeholders' expectations, requirements, constraints, and engagement that may be included in the project management plan is essential in developing a robust stakeholder management plan.

Manage Stakeholder Engagement

> **MORE INFO** **MANAGE STAKEHOLDER ENGAGEMENT**
>
> You can read more about the Manage Stakeholder Engagement process in the PMBOK® Guide, 5th edition, in Chapter 13, section 13.3. Table 11-3 identifies the process inputs, tools and techniques, and outputs.
>
> **TABLE 11-3** Manage Stakeholder Engagement process
>
> | Inputs | Tools and techniques | Outputs |
> | --- | --- | --- |
> | - Stakeholder management plan
- Communications management plan
- Change log
- Organizational process assets | - Communications methods
- Interpersonal skills
- Management skills | - Issue log
- Change requests
- Project management plan updates
- Project documents updates
- Organizational process assets updates |

The Manage Stakeholder Engagement process is an executing process focused on the execution of the stakeholder management plan in order to ensure that stakeholder engagement and expectations are proactively influenced and managed.

> **EXAM TIP**
>
> By now you will have seen the term "proactive" several times, particularly in the stakeholder management area. In relation to managing stakeholder engagement, being proactive means continuously engaging stakeholders in an appropriate manner to get their support for the project and ensure that you understand their individual expectations of the project and can meet them. Being proactive also means being on constant alert for any concerns that may arise and dealing with them in a manner that stops them from arising or, if they do arise, that minimizes the adverse impact.

The Manage Stakeholder Engagement process covers the following domain task:

- 3.2 Execute the tasks as defined in the project plan, in order to achieve the project deliverables within budget and schedule.

Inputs

The following inputs are used in the Manage Stakeholder Engagement process.

Stakeholder management plan

The key input into the Manage Stakeholder Engagement processes will be the stakeholder management plan because it contains information about stakeholders, their ability to influence the project, their expectations, their level of engagement, and the documented strategies for proactively influencing all of these. The stakeholder management plan is an output from the Plan Stakeholder Management process.

Communications management plan

The communications management plan is an essential input into the Manage Stakeholder Engagement process because it outlines individual stakeholders and the specific methods, frequency, and content of communication with them. It is via the successful use of the information contained in the communications management plan that you will be able to better execute the stakeholder management plan. The communications management plan is an output from the Plan Communications Management process.

Change log

The change log is an important input to have available because you will want to be able to convey to stakeholders any changes that have occurred. The change log is an output from the Perform Integrated Change Control process.

Organizational process assets

The specific organizational process assets that will be of use in the Manage Stakeholder Engagement process are any identified organizational communication methods, change control procedures, lessons learned, and historical information about similar previous projects and how they managed stakeholder engagement.

Tools and techniques

The following tools and techniques of this process are able to be used upon the separate inputs to deliver the Manage Stakeholder Engagement process outputs.

Communications methods

The communications management plan will outline the specific methods and content of communication to be used for each stakeholder. As part of the communications model and methods discussed in Chapter 8, "Communications management," there are several methods of communication that will assist you in managing stakeholder engagement. These methods include interactive communication, which means that all parties to the communication are involved in the exchange of ideas and messages. This is the most common form of communication method for influencing stakeholders, and it relies on all parties involved in the communication having strong interpersonal skills.

Push communication is a one way sender-driven communications method where one party, the sender, sends information to the other party, the receiver, without necessarily checking that it has been received and interpreted correctly. Email messages, letters, and press releases are all examples of push communication. As a communication method it can be a very effective means of distributing information quickly and widely if care is taken to craft the message well.

Pull communication occurs when information is posted so that the recipients can visit and draw the information down at their leisure. Company or project intranet sites are good examples of pull communication.

EXAM TIP

After reading this section on managing stakeholder engagement, you may want to read the communications management chapter (Chapter 8) again because the two subjects are very closely linked.

Interpersonal skills

The process of managing stakeholders is one based on building relationships, and a key tool used in establishing a relationship is the interpersonal skills that a project manager must have. The types of interpersonal skills that you will use include your leadership skills, decision-making skills, conflict resolution skills, change management skills, and active listening.

EXAM TIP

Interpersonal skills were also used as a tool in the Develop Project Team and Manage Project Team processes described in Chapter 7, "Human resource management."

Management skills

In addition to the interpersonal skills already mentioned, there are a range of *management skills* that are more focused on directing and controlling stakeholders; these include your presentation, negotiation, time management, and public speaking skills.

> **Real world**
>
> There is often an artificial distinction made between management and leadership skills, somehow implying that they are separate and used individually. The reality is that as a project manager you will need to develop both your leadership and management skills to high levels and use them concurrently, depending on the situation you are in and the outcomes you are seeking to achieve.

Outputs

The outputs from the Manage Stakeholder Engagement process include the following.

Issue log

As you carry out the process of proactively managing stakeholder engagement, particular issues with individual stakeholders may arise that need to be documented so that they can be recorded and worked on. The best place to record these particular issues is the issue log. The issue log is used as an input into the Control Stakeholder Engagement process, the Manage Project Team process, and the Control Communications process.

Change requests

In addition to issues that may arise, there may also be change requests, including corrective or preventive actions, that need to be documented and assessed via the approved change control process. Change requests are an input into the Perform Integrated Change Control process.

Project management plan updates

The specific parts of the project management plan that may be updated as a result of executing the Manage Stakeholder Engagement process include, obviously, the stakeholder management plan, in addition to the communications management plan, the human resource management plan, and any other parts of the project management plan that are affected by stakeholder expectations and engagement.

Project documents updates

The specific project documents that may be updated are, obviously, the stakeholder register and any other documents specifically affected by stakeholder engagement issues.

Organizational process assets updates

As a result of carrying out the Manage Stakeholder Engagement process, you may want to update your organizational process assets, specifically lessons learned, recording your experience in managing stakeholder engagement, and documents containing stakeholder feedback.

> **Quick check**
>
> 1. What is the main purpose of the Manage Stakeholder Engagement process?
> 2. What is the difference between push and pull forms of communication?
> 3. Why is the issue log a main output from the Manage Stakeholder Engagement process?
> 4. How does the Manage Stakeholder Engagement process interact with other project management knowledge areas?
>
> **Quick check answers**
>
> 1. The main purpose of the Manage Stakeholder Engagement process is the execution of the stakeholder management plan, in order to achieve stakeholder support for the project.
> 2. The difference between push and pull forms of communication is in whether or not the information is sent to specific recipients. In push communication, information is sent from a sender to a recipient, and in pull communication, recipients have to access the information themselves.
> 3. The issue log is a main output from the Manage Stakeholder Engagement process because, while executing the stakeholder management plan, you may identify particular issues with individual stakeholders that need to be recorded and documented in order to ensure that they are monitored and resolved.
> 4. The Manage Stakeholder Engagement process uses the change log from the Perform Integrated Change Control process and the communications management plan from the Plan Communications Management process.

Control Stakeholder Engagement

> **MORE INFO** **CONTROL STAKEHOLDER ENGAGEMENT**
>
> You can read more about the Control Stakeholder Engagement process in the PMBOK® Guide, 5th edition, in Chapter 13, section 13.4. Table 11-4 identifies the process inputs, tools and techniques, and outputs.
>
> **TABLE 11-4** Control Stakeholder Engagement process
>
> | Inputs | Tools and techniques | Outputs |
> | --- | --- | --- |
> | - Project management plan
- Issue log
- Work performance data
- Project documents | - Reporting systems
- Expert judgment
- Meetings | - Work performance information
- Change requests
- Project documents updates
- Organizational process assets updates |

The Control Stakeholder Engagement process is a monitoring and controlling process focused on examining the execution of the stakeholder management plan to ensure that it is being executed correctly and appropriately, and to determine whether or not it needs changing.

The Control Stakeholder Engagement process covers the following domain tasks:

- 4.1 Measure project performance using appropriate tools and techniques, in order to identify and quantify any variances, perform approved corrective actions, and communicate with relevant stakeholders.
- 4.6 Communicate project status to stakeholders for their feedback, in order to ensure the project aligns with business needs.

Inputs

The following inputs are used in the Control Stakeholder Engagement process.

Project management plan

The project management plan contains the stakeholder management plan and other plans and baselines useful for determining whether or not the stakeholder management plan is being executed correctly. The project management plan is an output from the Develop Project Management Plan process.

Issue log

The issue log describes all the issues raised by stakeholders and as such, it can be used to determine whether or not there are issues and subsequently that expectations are being appropriately managed and dealt with. The issue log is an output from the Manage Stakeholder Engagement process.

Work performance data

Work performance data is required to enable you to assess whether the work you have been doing according to the stakeholder management plan is being carried out as planned. Work performance data is an output from the Direct and Manage Project Work process.

Project documents

There are several types of project documents that will be useful in determining whether or not you are controlling stakeholder engagement as per the stakeholder management plan. Examples of relevant project documents include the stakeholder register, change log, communications register, and project schedule.

Tools and techniques

The following tools and techniques of this process are able to be used upon the separate inputs to deliver the Control Stakeholder Engagement process outputs.

Reporting systems

A reporting system is a subset of the project management information system that allows for the documentation, distribution, and storage of information for and about stakeholders. The types of information that the reporting system captures will reflect the particular interests of the stakeholders and may include information about any aspect of the project that can be measured and communicated, including information about project scope, cost, time, quality, risk, or any other relevant factor deemed of interest by stakeholders.

> **Real world**
>
> I have often found that there is a huge disparity between stakeholders when it comes to the types of information that they are actually interested in about the project. Some stakeholders are interested in the traditional cost and time progress of a project, whereas other stakeholders have no interest in these and are more interested in quality measures or issues specific to their interests. It is very important that the project manager determine what particular parts of the project are of importance to individual stakeholders. You also may need to control the amount of information that goes out to certain stakeholders. We had a particular stakeholder on one project who we knew was distributing project information to the media and, because this stakeholder was a senior member of the project control group, he expected to have access to whatever information he required. We had to ensure that he was only given the information he required as a member of the project control group.

Expert judgment

Expert judgment is a valuable tool that can be used in the Control Stakeholder Engagement process. You, as project manager, are one of these experts, as are members of your team. You may choose to draw on the experience of senior management or experts with experience in effectively controlling stakeholder engagement. You may also choose to draw on the expertise of key stakeholders themselves.

Meetings

Meetings between the project manager, project team members, experts, and stakeholders are an excellent way of ensuring that stakeholder engagement levels are kept high. This will only occur if meetings are run appropriately and have the correct people attending for the right reasons. The types of information that may be exchanged at a meeting will be status reports relating to project data that is of interest to the stakeholders.

Outputs

The outputs from the Control Stakeholder Engagement process are the following.

Work performance information

Given that work performance data is an input into this process, you can expect that work performance information is an output because it refines and analyzes the raw work performance data so that it can be presented in an appropriate format and used for decision-making.

Change requests

As a result of carrying out the Control Stakeholder Engagement process, you may discover a variance between what you planned to do and what is actually occurring, and that stakeholder engagement levels are not where you had planned for them to be. Thus, you may raise a change request, which could include changes to the stakeholder management plan or a recommendation for corrective or preventive actions.

Project documents updates

The specific project documents that may be updated as a result of carrying out the Control Stakeholder Engagement process include the stakeholder register and issue logs.

Organizational process assets updates

As a result of carrying out the Control Stakeholder Engagement process, you may discover information that requires you to update organizational process assets to ensure that they better reflect what you have discovered. Specific types of organizational process assets that may be updated include any templates or processes related to stakeholder engagement management, any project records collating feedback from stakeholders, and any lessons-learned documentation.

Quick check

1. What is the main purpose of the Control Stakeholder Engagement process?
2. Why is the issue log an important input into the Control Stakeholder Engagement process?
3. What type of organizational process assets may be updated as a result of carrying out the Control Stakeholder Engagement process?
4. How does the Control Stakeholder Engagement process interact with other project management knowledge areas?

Quick check answers

1. The main purpose of the Control Stakeholder Engagement process is to monitor the overall levels of stakeholder engagement against what is expected and make changes to the stakeholder management plan and the strategies around stakeholder engagement.
2. The issue log describes and documents individual issues raised by stakeholders. Therefore, using it as an input into the Control Stakeholder Engagement process allows you to view the number of issues, the complexity of issues, which stakeholders are raising issues, and whether the issues are being resolved to the satisfaction of stakeholders.
3. The types of organizational process assets that may be updated as a result of the Control Stakeholder Engagement process include any existing processes and templates, project records relating to your stakeholder engagement strategies and results, and of course, your collection of lessons-learned documentation.
4. The Control Stakeholder Engagement process uses inputs from the Develop Project Management Plan process (the project management plan), and also the Direct and Manage Project Work process (work performance data).

Exercises

The answers for these exercises are located in the "Answers" section at the end of this chapter.

1. Match the stakeholder management process on the left to a process key output on the right.

Process	Key output
1. Identify Stakeholders	a. Stakeholder register
2. Plan Stakeholder Management	b. Issue log
3. Manage Stakeholder Engagement	c. Work performance information
4. Control Stakeholder Engagement	d. Stakeholder management plan

2. Categorize each item in the following list as either an interactive, push, or pull method of communication.

   A. Phone calls

   B. Letters

   C. Intranet sites

   D. Video conferencing

   E. Project reports

   F. E-learning site

   G. Meetings

   H. Press releases

Chapter summary

- The Stakeholder Management knowledge area is focused on the identification, management, and proactive influencing of stakeholders' interests, expectations, and engagement to ensure stakeholders' support for the project.
- The Identify Stakeholders process is an initiating process that produces a stakeholder register, which identifies stakeholders in the project.
- The Plan Stakeholder Management process is a planning process that produces a stakeholder management plan, which outlines how stakeholder expectations and engagement will be proactively influenced.
- The Manage Stakeholder Engagement process is an executing process that uses the stakeholder management plan to carry out the activities required to manage and influence stakeholder expectations and engagement.
- The Control Stakeholder Engagement process is a monitoring and control process that reviews the stakeholder management activities against what was planned and updates the stakeholder management plan as required.

Chapter review

Test your knowledge of the information in Chapter 11 by answering these questions. The answers to these questions, and the explanations of why each answer choice is correct or incorrect, are located in the "Answers" section at the end of this chapter.

1. Which of the following processes produces the stakeholder register?
   - **A.** Identify Stakeholders
   - **B.** Plan Stakeholder Management
   - **C.** Manage Stakeholder Engagement
   - **D.** Control Stakeholder Engagement

2. Which of the following is the best definition of a stakeholder?
   - **A.** Your project team members, project sponsor, and client
   - **B.** Any person or group who can affect or be affected by your project
   - **C.** The client, the project sponsor, and external government agencies
   - **D.** Any person or group

3. If you are using a Gardner grid to show the results of stakeholder analysis, what information about stakeholders would you be showing?
   - **A.** How much power, urgency, and legitimacy they have
   - **B.** The amount of risk each stakeholder is willing to share

C. The levels of power and interest of each stakeholder

   D. Their contact details and interest in the project

4. Which of the following documents will contain a description of stakeholder contact details and their requirements for the project?

   A. Stakeholder analysis

   B. Stakeholder register

   C. Gardner grid

   D. Stakeholder management plan

5. At what point in the project should you conduct the kick-off meeting?

   A. As soon as the project is initiated

   B. At the end of the project, to assist with project closure

   C. Only after all the planning work has been completed

   D. After enough planning work has been completed to begin execution

6. If you are assessing the each stakeholder as either unaware, resistant, neutral, supportive, or leading, what technique are you using?

   A. Brainstorming

   B. Delphi technique

   C. Analytical technique

   D. Root cause analysis

7. If you are engaged in carrying out your project work and need to find out the planned timeframe and frequency for distribution of required information to stakeholders, where would be the best place to look?

   A. Project management plan

   B. Stakeholder management plan

   C. Stakeholder register

   D. Issue log

8. Which of the following is not an input into the Manage Stakeholder Engagement process?

   A. Stakeholder management plan

   B. Issue log

   C. Communications management plan

   D. Change log

9. You are sending out regular project updates to stakeholders via email to a list of project stakeholders. This is an example of what sort of communication method?

    A. Verbal
    B. Interactive
    C. Pull
    D. Push

10. Which of the following is not an example of a management skill a project manager may use while managing stakeholder engagement?

    A. Negotiation skills
    B. Public speaking skills
    C. Presentation skills
    D. Conflict resolution skills

11. What is the name of the document that lists any problems that stakeholders may have and records what is being done about them?

    A. Change log
    B. Issue log
    C. Stakeholder register
    D. Stakeholder management plan

12. During which stakeholder management process is work performance data an input, and work performance information an output?

    A. Identify Stakeholders
    B. Plan Stakeholder Management
    C. Manage Stakeholder Engagement
    D. Control Stakeholder Engagement

Answers

This section contains the answers for the "Exercises" and "Chapter review" sections in this chapter.

Exercises

1. Match the stakeholder management process on the left to a process key output on the right.

Process	Key output
1. Identify Stakeholders	a. Stakeholder register
2. Plan Stakeholder Management	d. Stakeholder management plan
3. Manage Stakeholder Engagement	b. Issue log
4. Control Stakeholder Engagement	c. Work performance information

2. Categorize each item in the following list as either an interactive, push, or pull method of communication:

Interactive	Push	Pull
A. Phone calls	B. Letters	C. Intranet sites
D. Video conferencing	E. Project reports	F. E-learning site
G. Meetings	H. Press releases	

Chapter review

1. **Correct answer: A**

    A. **Correct:** The Identify Stakeholders process produces the stakeholder register.

    B. **Incorrect:** The Plan Stakeholder Management process has the stakeholder management plan as its primary output.

    C. **Incorrect:** Manage Stakeholder Engagement does not produce the stakeholder register.

    D. **Incorrect:** Control Stakeholder Engagement does not produce the stakeholder register.

2. **Correct answer: B**

   A. **Incorrect:** Your project team members, project sponsor, and client certainly are stakeholders, but they are a subset of all possible stakeholders and in this case not the best definition of stakeholders offered.

   B. **Correct:** The best definition of a stakeholder is any person or group who can affect or be affected by your project.

   C. **Incorrect:** The client, the project sponsor, and external government agencies may be stakeholders, but this is not the best definition of stakeholders.

   D. **Incorrect:** In order to be considered a project stakeholder, any person or group must be affected by your project or be able to affect the project.

3. **Correct answer: C**

   A. **Incorrect:** A diagram showing power, urgency, and legitimacy of stakeholders would use the salience model.

   B. **Incorrect:** The amount of risk stakeholders are willing to share would be shown in the stakeholder analysis.

   C. **Correct:** A Gardner grid shows the respective levels of power and interest of each stakeholder in order to classify them

   D. **Incorrect:** Stakeholder contracts details and interest in the project would be contained in the stakeholder register

4. **Correct answer: B**

   A. **Incorrect:** Stakeholder analysis is a technique used to gather information about stakeholders, but it is not a document.

   B. **Correct:** The stakeholder register contains information about stakeholders, including their contact details and their requirements for the project.

   C. **Incorrect:** A Gardner grid classifies stakeholders by their levels of power and interest.

   D. **Incorrect:** The stakeholder management plan sets out how stakeholder engagement will be managed.

5. **Correct answer: D**

   A. **Incorrect:** The kick-off meeting does not occur as soon as the project is initiated.

   B. **Incorrect:** The kick-off meeting, as the name suggests, is not used to assist with project closure.

   C. **Incorrect:** You do not need to wait until all planning work has been completed to have a kick-off meeting.

   D. **Correct:** The kick-off meeting is held after enough planning work has been done to begin execution.

6. **Correct answer: C**
   A. **Incorrect:** Brainstorming is an information-gathering technique.
   B. **Incorrect:** The Delphi technique is used to gather information anonymously from experts without peer pressure affecting the outcome.
   C. **Correct:** Categorizing stakeholders in this manner is a sign of using analytical techniques such as a stakeholder engagement assessment matrix.
   D. **Incorrect:** Root cause analysis is used during quality management activities.

7. **Correct answer: B**
   A. **Incorrect:** The project management plan includes the stakeholder management plan but is not the best answer presented.
   B. **Correct:** The stakeholder management plan contains a lot of information about the ways in which stakeholders engagement and expectations will be managed, including the planned timeframe and frequency for distribution of required information to stakeholders.
   C. **Incorrect:** The stakeholder register contains information identifying stakeholders and their requirements and is used as an input into the development of the stakeholder management plan.
   D. **Incorrect:** The issue log documents specific issues raised by stakeholders.

8. **Correct answer: B**
   A. **Incorrect:** The stakeholder management plan is an essential input into the Manage Stakeholder Engagement process because it sets out how stakeholders' engagement and expectations will be managed.
   B. **Correct:** The issue log is an output from, not an input into, the Manage Stakeholder Engagement process.
   C. **Incorrect:** The communications management plan is an input into the Manage Stakeholders Engagement process because it records the communications methods and strategy to be used.
   D. **Incorrect:** The change log is used as an input into the Manage Stakeholders Engagement process because the impact of changes is communicated to stakeholders.

9. **Correct answer: D**
   A. **Incorrect:** Email is not an example of verbal communication.
   B. **Incorrect:** Because there is no two-way communication occurring, this is not an example of an interactive communication method.
   C. **Incorrect:** The method, email, is pushing information to stakeholders, not pulling it from them.
   D. **Correct:** Sending out information without checking whether the receiver understands it is an example of push communication.

10. **Correct answer: D**
    A. **Incorrect:** Negotiation skills are an example of a project manager's management skills.
    B. **Incorrect:** Public speaking skills are an example of a project manager's management skills.
    C. **Incorrect:** Presentation skills are an example of a project manager's management skills.
    D. **Correct:** Conflict resolution skills are an example of leadership, not management skills.

11. **Correct answer: B**
    A. **Incorrect:** The change log records information about change requests and their status.
    B. **Correct:** The issue log records any issues that stakeholders may have and what is being done about them.
    C. **Incorrect:** The stakeholder register records specific information about each stakeholder but does not list any problems or issues they may have.
    D. **Incorrect:** The stakeholder management plan sets out how stakeholders' expectations and engagement will be proactively influenced and managed.

12. **Correct answer: D**
    A. **Incorrect:** The Identify Stakeholders process does not use either work performance data or work performance information.
    B. **Incorrect:** The Plan Stakeholder Management process does not use either work performance data or work performance information.
    C. **Incorrect:** The Management Stakeholder Engagement process does not use either work performance data or work performance information.
    D. **Correct:** The Control Stakeholder Engagement process does use work performance data as an input and has work performance information as an output, as part of the monitoring and controlling activities.

CHAPTER 12

Ethics and professional conduct

This chapter focuses on the topic of ethics and professional conduct, which describes the way that a professional project manager is expected to act in many different situations.

EXAM TIP
The expected and accepted behaviors described this section may differ from your own experience. It is important to remember that, for the exam, the behaviors described here are considered the correct way to act in any situation.

There are no explicit domain tasks that are reflected in this section. Several years ago there were distinct questions about ethics and professional situations in the PMP® exam. However, these questions have now been incorporated into the main body of questions and may lie hidden within a question that appears to be about estimating, or risk, or quality, or customer relations, or any other topic. Thus it is very important that you read the question carefully to determine if it is presenting you with a situation that requires you to specify how you would act ethically and professionally.

Although there are no domain tasks for this topic, there is the Code of Ethics and Professional Conduct from the Project Management Institute (PMI). Both mandatory and aspirational standards are captured in the Code of Ethics and Professional Conduct. The Code of Ethics and Professional Conduct, and the behavior of professional project management practitioners, reflects the vales of responsibility, respect, fairness, and honesty.

The PMI Code of Ethics and Professional Conduct applies to all members of the Project Management Institute. Additionally, it applies to nonmembers who hold a PMI certification, those who apply to commence a PMI certification process, and nonmembers who serve PMI in a volunteer capacity. Beyond these people, whom it directly applies to, it also serves as a guideline for all professional project management practitioners.

A breach of this code can result in an ethics complaint to the Project Management Institute, which has the ability to consider the complaint and take action against anyone found to have breached the code.

453

> **Real world**
>
> I have always found that the Code of Ethics and Professional Conduct serves as a very valuable reference to guide my own decisions and behaviors in real-world situations where perhaps I might be tempted to act differently. It has also served as a guide to the behaviors I expect of other professional project managers. Keep in mind that sometimes the right course of action isn't the easiest course of action. When considering what is best to do in an ethical situation, one approach is to look at what the impact of a bad decision will do to your professional and personal reputation and credibility. Always select an answer that will enhance your credibility and reputation.

Responsibility, respect, fairness, and honesty

The four key foundational values for any project manager are responsibility, respect, fairness, and honesty. Though these may all seem to be fairly straightforward concepts that you think you both understand and apply consistently, you may not fully understand the implications and expected behaviors. Individually they describe specific behaviors, and collectively they present a unified code by which any professional project manager can guide and assess his or her own actions and the actions of others. Therefore, it is worth taking the time to investigate each one and review the specific actions and behaviors that each demands of a professional project manager.

> **EXAM TIP**
>
> Take time when reading a question in the exam to determine if it presenting you with a technical situation or an ethical situation. If it is an ethical situation, then answer according to the Code of Ethics and Professional Conduct.

Responsibility

> **MORE INFO** **RESPONSIBILITY**
>
> You can read more about responsibility in the Project Management Institute Code of Ethics and Professional Conduct.

Responsibility means being personally and professionally accountable for your own actions, being accountable for acting ethically and professionally at all times, and ensuring that others do the same. Responsibility also means that you as the project manager are responsible for the actions of those in your team.

The mandatory standard of responsibility requires you to first make sure that you know and uphold all the relevant policies, rules, regulations, and laws that govern your work, professional, and volunteer activities. If you disagree with any of these rules, you can seek to change them, but until they are changed you must abide by them.

Furthermore, you must always report unethical or illegal conduct to the appropriate people or body. This means that whenever you discover or observe unethical or illegal behavior you must report it to the appropriate authorities. If you discover someone on your project not dealing fairly or honestly with a stakeholder, you must report this to your project team or sponsor. Although your natural inclination maybe to ignore the behavior if you regard it as minor, you must report it no matter how small it is. If the behavior is an ethical breach, you must report it to the Project Management Institute in accordance with the process on their website. Make sure that any complaints you file are substantiated by fact and documented appropriately.

You must also encourage people to do the same and neither retaliate yourself nor let others retaliate against any person who does bring a breach of rules to the attention of the right person or body, or who files an ethical complaint. This is to encourage and support the role of the *whistleblower*.

Real world

There will always be a temptation to avoid responsibility, but I have found that as well as enhancing your professional reputation and credibility, the simple act of taking responsibility also contributes to your ongoing leadership development. Great leadership enhances the chances of project success, and being a great leader requires you to take responsibility and lead by example.

The aspirational standards of responsibility require you to make your decisions and subsequent actions based on the best interests of society, public safety, and the environment and not in your own best interests. The greater good of society, public safety, and the environment must always take precedence over self-interest. This means that if a project you are working on conflicts with or adversely affects society, public safety, or the environment, you should reconsider whether the project is worth doing.

Taking responsibility also means accepting only that project work that is consistent with your background, experience, technical and interpersonal skills, and qualifications. Don't be tempted to exaggerate your own ability; only take on work that you know you are competent to do. After the work is taken on, you must make sure that you fulfill these commitments and see them through to completion.

If you make mistakes, errors, or omissions, you must take responsibility, take ownership, and make corrections as soon as possible. If you discover errors or omissions made by others, you must communicate them to the appropriate body as soon they are discovered. Knowingly acting in error or with information you know is false is considered a breach of this standard.

Finally, taking responsibility means protecting the intellectual property rights, copyright, and confidential information of any person or body. This means that if you are in a situation where you have the opportunity to use intellectual property of a previous client, you should always seek their approval first. Additionally, you should not allow anyone to break any copyright rules, laws, or regulations.

If you do discover anyone breaching these standards, you must report them to the relevant authority. So if you find someone breaking a company standard, you must report them within your organization. If you find someone breaking a PMI standard, you must report them to PMI, and if you find someone breaking the law, you must report them to the appropriate legal authorities.

Quick check

1. What role do you as project manager have in upholding the value of responsibility?
2. What must you do if you disagree with a particular policy that your organization has?
3. What must you do if you discover that a member of your team has made an error?

Quick check answers

1. The project manager must lead by example and take personal and professional responsibility themselves and demand it from others.
2. If you disagree with a policy that your organization has, you must still follow it. You can seek to change it, but until it is changed, you must follow it.
3. Any errors, either by yourself or by another, must be recognized, reported, and acted on immediately.

Respect

> **MORE INFO** **RESPECT**
>
> You can read more about respect in the Project Management Institute Code of Ethics and Professional Conduct.

The value of *respect* means having appropriate regard for yourself and also regard for others personally and professionally. It requires you to negotiate agreements and contracts in good faith and not exercise the power of your expertise or position to influence the decisions or actions of others in order to benefit personally at their expense. This doesn't mean you can't influence people because that is a key skill in stakeholder management and communications activities. It means that you can't seek to benefit personally by taking advantage of others using your position of power.

Respect also means not acting in an abusive manner toward any other person. Keep in mind that abuse can take many forms, from outright verbal and physical abuse to the more insidious forms of gossip, slander, libel, and passive-aggressive behavior. Complying with this standard means observing the golden rule of treating others as you would like to be treated.

Respect also means that you respect the property rights of others, which ties in nicely with the value of responsibility, in which you must protect the intellectual property rights, copyright, and confidential information of any person or body. This means that you must acknowledge the ownership and copyright that others hold on their work.

Demonstrating respect also means being aware of the norms and customs of others and avoiding engaging in behaviors they might consider disrespectful. This is increasingly important in an ever-more globalized economy, where projects are often done internationally. Also, many stakeholders may have different customs from you own, and effective communication and management of stakeholders requires you to understand their customs and treat them with respect. A key element in effective communications with, and expectation management of, stakeholders is the ability to listen to others' points of view and seek to understand them.

When it comes to resolving conflicts or disagreements, respect means dealing directly and in an open manner with those people with whom you have a conflict or disagreement. Seek to deal with the issue and not let personalities get in the way.

Whatever happens around you and whatever the actions of others, respect also means that you always conduct yourself in a professional manner, even when it is not reciprocated.

Real world

I have always found that having respect for myself and for others is a great personal asset. It improves my ability to build genuine relationships with others and understand their point of view. Keep in mind that people will know, either consciously or subconsciously, if you are faking respect, so make sure that it is always genuine.

✓ Quick check

1. If you are given the opportunity to negotiate a contract that would place an undue burden on the other party, what should you do?
2. If you are working in another country and it is a commonly accepted practice to pay bribes to get project work done, what should you do?

Quick check answers

1. In any negotiations, you should seek to get an agreement that both parties can live with. You should not negotiate contracts if you have no intention of honoring them.
2. This is a tricky question. You know that you should always respect the culture and customs of others, but taking precedence over this is the requirement that you should always obey the laws of the country in which you are working. If bribery is illegal, it doesn't matter what the custom is—you simply do not participate in it.

Fairness

> **MORE INFO** FAIRNESS
>
> You can read more about fairness in the Project Management Institute Code of Ethics and Professional Conduct.

 The value of *fairness* deals with conflict of interest, favoritism, and discrimination.

 A *conflict of interest* situation arises when your own personal interest may conflict with the interest of your employer, or you may derive personal benefit from an action undertaken on behalf of another person. *Conflict of interest* can be both real and perceived. Whether it is real or perceived, it should always be fully and openly disclosed as early as possible so that that it can be dealt with in an appropriate manner. You should not participate in any process or project until the disclosure has been made and a decision has been made about the best way to move forward.

Conflict of interest situations can also arise as a result of the business dealings of family members or friends, when they have professional or business connections to your project. In this case, your relationship should always be fully disclosed.

> **Real world**
>
> Many organizations keep a documented conflict of interest register where all employees must disclose and record any real or potential conflict of interest. Often the level of conflict of interest is so small that it can be managed via simple disclosure; at other times it may require those affected to be removed from that particular process or project. Always disclose any real or perceived conflict of interest quickly.

The value of fairness also extends to favoritism and discrimination. To display fairness, you must avoid both favoritism and discrimination, which means that you neither hire nor fire, neither reward nor punish, and neither award nor deny contracts based on your own personal considerations, bias, or benefit. This means that you should treat everyone equally and fairly, regardless of any preconceived notions you may have. It also means that you must not discriminate against anyone based on gender, race, age, religion, disability, nationality, or sexual orientation.

In order to show and prove fairness you must be able to demonstrate transparency and impartiality in your decision-making process and provide equal access to information to those who are authorized to have that information. This is particularly important in legal or contractual matters, because a lack of fairness could be grounds for a legal challenge to your decisions.

> **Quick check**
>
> 1. What should you do if a family member works for a firm submitting a bid for contract work on your project?
> 2. What should you do if you are given the opportunity to provide extra information to a contractor that you really want to award a contract to?
>
> **Quick check answers**
>
> 1. If you, a friend, or family member could benefit, or is perceived to benefit, from a commercial transaction in which you are involved, there is a real or potential conflict of interest. It must first be fully disclosed, and you should not take part in any process until it is resolved.
> 2. You should treat everyone involved in procurement negotiations fairly and equally. Everyone should receive exactly the same information at the same time.

Honesty

> **MORE INFO** **HONESTY**
>
> You can read more about honesty in the Project Management Institute Code of Ethics and Professional Conduct.

Honesty seems like one of those self-evident terms. We all know when we are being honest, and if we aren't being honest, then surely we are being dishonest. Or is there some grey area between honesty and dishonesty?

If you want to act in accordance with the value of honesty, there is no grey area; you are either being honest or dishonest. Telling half-truths or omitting key information is dishonest. In order to meet the standards required by this value, you must be 100 percent honest at all times. This means that you, as a professional project manager, will not engage in or condone behavior in others that is designed to deceive anyone. This includes making misleading or false statements, telling half-truths, providing information out of context, or omitting information that, if known, would make your statements misleading or incomplete.

The value of honesty also ties in with other values of responsibility, respect, and fairness, and demands of us that we do not engage, condone, or participate in dishonest behavior with the intention of personal gain or at the expense of another.

> **EXAM TIP**
>
> If you are ever presented with a question that asks you what is best to do in a situation where you suspect dishonesty, the answer is always to disclose this, then investigate and rectify the situation with honesty.

Displaying honesty means being prepared to ensure that the information you are basing your decisions upon or providing to others is accurate, reliable, and timely. Being honest also means being prepared to share bad news even when it may be poorly received.

> **Real world**
>
> Being honest will sometimes have repercussions that will test your skill as a relationship builder and influencer. You may even lose some credibility in the short term. But over the long term, you will develop a reputation based on honesty, and this will serve you better than a reputation of someone who isn't always honest.

Displaying the value of honesty also means you only make promises you can keep, and you keep the promises you make. By leading the way and acting honestly at all times, you will create a culture of honesty that encourages and expects it all times. Ultimately it will be your reputation and credibility that is enhanced by sticking to this value at all times.

> **Quick check**
>
> 1. If giving the truth about the status of your project to your project sponsor and client would result in the project being terminated when you are sure that the problem is short-lived and can be fixed, what should you do?
> 2. If you are halfway through a complex set of contractual negotiations with a potential vendor and your sponsor tells you that the project is likely to be cancelled, what should you do in relation to the contractual negotiations?
>
> **Quick check answers**
>
> 1. In order to be honest, you must openly share all information that you have. Communicating half-truths and omissions about the status of your project to buy time to fix the problems is dishonest.
> 2. This question relates not only to the value of honesty, but also to responsibility, fairness, and respect. You have a duty to not continue the negotiations until the future of the project is decided, and to inform the vendor of the reasons.

Exercise

The answers for this exercise are located in the "Answers" section at the end of this chapter.

1. Categorize each statement from the PMI Code of Ethics and Professional Conduct in the following list as a value associated with either responsibility, respect, fairness, or honesty.

    A. We report unethical or illegal conduct to appropriate management and, if necessary, to those affected by the conduct.

    B. We negotiate in good faith.

    C. We provide accurate information in a timely manner.

    D. We do not act in an abusive manner toward others.

    E. We proactively and fully disclose any real or potential conflicts of interest to the appropriate stakeholders.

    F. We protect proprietary or confidential information that has been entrusted to us.

    G. We provide equal access to information to those who are authorized to have that information.

    H. We make opportunities equally available to qualified candidates.

    I. We do not exercise the power of our expertise or position to influence the decisions or actions of others in order to benefit personally at their expense.

    J. We do not engage in or condone behavior that is designed to deceive others.

- **K.** We inform ourselves and uphold the policies, rules, regulations, and laws that govern our work, professional, and volunteer activities.
- **L.** We do not engage in dishonest behavior with the intention of personal gain or at the expense of another.

Chapter summary

- This chapter outlines the expected and accepted behaviors of a professional project manager. It outlines the four key values of responsibility, respect, fairness, and honesty, which define the behavior of a project manager and that person's behavior toward others.
- The key value of responsibility requires a project manager to take personal and professional responsibility for his or her own actions, acting ethically and professionally at all times, and ensuring that others do the same.
- The key value of respect requires professional project managers to display respect for themselves and others. It requires that they refrain from abusive behaviors and understand different customs and cultures.
- The key value of fairness seeks to avoid either real or potential conflict of interest situations and avoid favoritism and discrimination by treating everyone equally and openly.
- The key value of honesty requires a project manager to be completely truthful at all times and not engage in half-truths or omission of information.

Chapter review

Test your knowledge of the information in Chapter 12 by answering these questions. The answers to these questions, and the explanations of why each answer choice is correct or incorrect, are located in the "Answers" section at the end of this chapter.

1. What are the four foundational values upon which the PMI Code of Ethics and Professional Conduct is built?

    A. Trust, honesty, respect, fairness

    B. Honesty, respect, responsibility, fairness

    C. Integrity, trust, respect, honesty

    D. Respect, truthfulness, responsibility, transparency

2. You are the project manager on a project that is behind schedule and over budget. You have gathered your team together to think of ways that you can make up time and save money. A team member who has recently joined your organization says that he has access to design drawings from his previous employer that are very similar to your current project, and using them would save both time and cost. What should you do?

   A. Use the drawings and acknowledge where they came from in your project reports.

   B. Refuse to use the drawings.

   C. Use the drawings without acknowledging where they came from.

   D. Refuse to use the drawings during the team meeting, then during a one-on-one conversation with your team member, encourage him to use them.

3. Your husband is working for a company that is submitting a bid for a contract you are managing on your project. Your husband's role within the company has nothing to do with the bid process. What should you do?

   A. You don't need to do anything because your husband can have no impact nor can he derive any benefit from the process.

   B. Refuse to allow your husband's organization to participate in the bid process.

   C. Resign from the project.

   D. Disclose the potential conflict of interest to your project sponsor.

4. You are working on a project in a country where bribery is the norm, and the only way to get a permit you need processed is to pay a bribe to a local official. Your project cannot continue without this permit, and the amount of the bribe is relatively small. What should you do?

   A. Pay the bribe but lodge a complaint with local officials.

   B. Pay the bribe.

   C. Do not pay the bribe.

   D. Do not pay the bribe and continue your project without obtaining the permit.

5. You are about to walk into a meeting with your project sponsor and client to report progress on your project, and you notice that the financial figures you are about to present to them do not look correct and present an overly optimistic view of your project. What should you do?

   A. Go ahead with the meeting and point out the mistakes.

   B. Tell you project sponsor and client that you can't proceed with the meeting until you are sure you have the correct information.

   C. Go ahead with the meeting and hope they don't notice the error.

   D. Cancel the meeting without explanation.

6. You and several of your colleagues are studying to take the Project Management Professional (PMP®) examination when one of your colleagues admits that she has downloaded a copy of a copyrighted study book by using a peer-to-peer file sharing network, without paying for it. She offers a copy to you and recommends the text as a great way to help you pass the exam. What should you do?

   A. Gratefully accept the study aid.
   B. Offer to pay her for it.
   C. Refuse the offer and report her to the author of the work.
   D. Use the book for your study and delete it once finished.

7. Your project sponsor has asked you to lead a project and has given you a deadline of six months to deliver the product. After completing the time estimating processes with your team, you discover that the fastest you can deliver the project is nine months. Your project sponsor asks you to start the project anyway and still try to deliver the project within six months. What should you do?

   A. Start working on the project, looking for ways to save three months.
   B. Start working on the project, knowing that it will take nine months regardless of what you do.
   C. Refuse to work on the project.
   D. Explain to your project sponsor that you cannot make a promise you can't keep, and that the project should not start without accurate and agreed timeframes.

8. You discover that a colleague of yours whom you have worked alongside for 12 years lied on his CV to get the job and does not have the engineering degree he claims to have. However, he has proven himself as more than competent to design and manage engineering projects over the 12 years you have worked with him. What should you do?

   A. Talk with your colleague and encourage him to disclose this information to management.
   B. Report this information immediately to your employer.
   C. Do nothing because he has proven himself as competent.
   D. Refuse to work on projects with this person.

9. You are managing a project to build a new motorway next to land that your parents have owned for 50 years. As a result of the new motorway, the value of your parents' land will increase significantly. What should you do?

   A. Go ahead with the project because the land was there before the planned motorway.

   B. Keep your parents informed on project progress so they know the best time to sell.

   C. Disclose this to your project sponsor and ask him or her what the best course of action is.

   D. Do nothing because you will not personally benefit from this.

10. You are acting as a volunteer for the Project Management Institute and, during a meeting in your capacity as a volunteer, the people that you are meeting with discover that you are a skilled project management trainer and ask you to provide training services to them. What should you do?

    A. After you have spoken to them about PMI business, start discussing ways you can help them as a trainer.

    B. Explain to them that you are there on PMI business and it is not appropriate to discuss commercial possibilities at this time.

    C. Explain to them that you are there on PMI business, then explain the situation to PMI and seek guidance on the best way forward.

    D. Try to get a contract for your training services signed before you leave.

11. You are the project manager on a project and, during the business feasibility phase, you discover that your project will have large and irreversible effects upon a natural wetlands area. Your project sponsor asks you to keep quiet about this because it will mean that the project will not proceed. What should you do?

    A. Report the effects of the project to the local government agency responsible for the environment.

    B. Resign from the project.

    C. Keep managing the project because that is what you promised you would do.

    D. Manage the project and try to minimize the impact upon the environment.

12. You are preparing to give a talk to your team about how to improve your risk management planning and identification processes, and you plan to use an article you have downloaded for free from the Project Management Institute website. The article is freely available to members for download and for their professional development. During the presentation, what should you do?

A. Deliver a great presentation without making reference to the article.

B. Acknowledge the article and attribute the authors' ideas during your presentation.

C. Hand out a copy of the original article to all team members.

D. Decide not to use the article because it would be a breach of copyright.

13. You have successfully managed a large, complex project for a client and they are very happy with the results and your leadership. As a thank-you gift, they send you a brand new car with a note expressing their gratitude. What should you do?

A. Make sure the ownership papers have been transferred into your name correctly.

B. Refuse the gift because it does not align with your company's policy on receiving gifts.

C. Sell the car and split the proceeds among all project team members.

D. Have the car delivered to your home without telling anyone.

14. You are managing a large team whose members come from many different countries. Among your team members there are several who observe a particular religious holiday at a time when your team is scheduled to be delivering part of the final deliverable. The team members have asked for time off to observe the holiday. What should you do?

A. Allow the team members the time off and use factors such as this as constraints in the resource calendar.

B. Give all team members the time off so that everyone is treated equally.

C. Do not approve the time off because it will adversely affect your project.

D. Do not approve the time off because you are working in a country that does not recognize that particular holiday as a public holiday.

Answers

This section contains the answers for the "Exercise" and "Chapter review" sections in this chapter.

Exercise

1. Categorize each statement from the PMI Code of Ethics and Professional Conduct in the following list as a value associated with either responsibility, respect, fairness, or honesty.

    A. We report unethical or illegal conduct to appropriate management and, if necessary, to those affected by the conduct.

    RESPONSIBILITY

    B. We negotiate in good faith.

    RESPECT

    C. We provide accurate information in a timely manner.

    HONESTY

    D. We do not act in an abusive manner toward others.

    RESPECT

    E. We proactively and fully disclose any real or potential conflicts of interest to the appropriate stakeholders.

    FAIRNESS

    F. We protect proprietary or confidential information that has been entrusted to us.

    RESPONSIBILITY

    G. We provide equal access to information to those who are authorized to have that information.

    FAIRNESS

    H. We make opportunities equally available to qualified candidates.

    FAIRNESS

I. We do not exercise the power of our expertise or position to influence the decisions or actions of others in order to benefit personally at their expense.
RESPECT

J. We do not engage in or condone behavior that is designed to deceive others.
HONESTY

K. We inform ourselves and uphold the policies, rules, regulations, and laws that govern our work, professional, and volunteer activities.
RESPONSIBILITY

L. We do not engage in dishonest behavior with the intention of personal gain or at the expense of another.
HONESTY

Chapter review

1. **Correct answer: B**

   A. Incorrect: Trust is not one of the four foundational values of the Code of Ethics and Professional Conduct.

   B. Correct: Honesty, respect, responsibility, and fairness are the four foundational values of the Code of Ethics and Professional Conduct.

   C. Incorrect: Integrity is not one of the four foundational values of the Code of Ethics and Professional Conduct. Having integrity is an important value, though, because it means having a set of values and sticking to them.

   D. Incorrect: Transparency and truthfulness are not part of the four foundational values of the Code of Ethics and Professional Conduct.

2. **Correct answer: B**

   A. Incorrect: It would be unethical to use drawings that belong to someone else, even if you acknowledge where they came from. You should always seek permission and negotiate terms of use of someone else's intellectual property.

   B. Correct: The best option in this instance is to refuse to use the drawings. You may also want to educate your new employee about expected ethical standards.

   C. Incorrect: It would be unethical to use drawings that belong to someone else.

   D. Incorrect: This answer displays a level of dishonesty and is not correct.

3. **Correct answer: D**
   A. **Incorrect:** It doesn't matter whether there is an impact or not. What matters is whether there is a perceived or potential impact. So in this case, you do need to disclose your relationship.
   B. **Incorrect:** This answer does not address the issue of potential conflict and puts your husband's organization at a disadvantage.
   C. **Incorrect:** Resigning from the project will not address the issue.
   D. **Correct:** The first step is to disclose the potential conflict of interest and seek advice on how best to manage it.

4. **Correct answer: C**
   A. **Incorrect:** You cannot pay the bribe because it is illegal, and lodging a complaint with officials will not make it okay to pay the bribe.
   B. **Incorrect:** Paying the bribe is illegal and thus you cannot do it.
   C. **Correct:** Your only choice here is to not pay the bribe, because it is an illegal payment.
   D. **Incorrect:** Not paying the bribe is correct, but proceeding without a legally required permit would be illegal and, as such, is not an option.

5. **Correct answer: B**
   A. **Incorrect:** You have an obligation to be honest at all times, and if you know or suspect that information is incorrect, you must address this, so you cannot go ahead with the meeting.
   B. **Correct:** This answer presents the most honest approach to dealing with the situation.
   C. **Incorrect:** This would be dishonest.
   D. **Incorrect:** Canceling the meeting without explanation is not the best option because you should be honest about the reason for the cancellation.

6. **Correct answer: C**
   A. **Incorrect:** She has downloaded a copy of a book without paying for it, and this is both illegal and dishonest, so this is not the correct answer.
   B. **Incorrect:** Paying her for it does not change the fact that it is an illegal copy.
   C. **Correct:** Your only option here is to refuse her offer and then report her illegal activity.
   D. **Incorrect:** You cannot use the book because it is an illegal copy.

7. **Correct answer: D**

   A. **Incorrect:** Starting to work on a project that you know can't be delivered is unethical.

   B. **Incorrect:** This option begins the project with dishonesty.

   C. **Incorrect:** Refusing to work on the project may be a last option, but it is not the best answer in resolving this dilemma.

   D. **Correct:** Being very honest about the situation is the best option.

8. **Correct answer: B**

   A. **Incorrect:** When you are aware of an unethical or illegal act, you must report it. You should not wait for him to disclose this.

   B. **Correct:** When you are aware of an unethical or illegal act, you must report it.

   C. **Incorrect:** When you are aware of an unethical or illegal act, you must report it. Doing nothing is no longer an option.

   D. **Incorrect:** Refusing to work with this person does not address the issue of fake credentials.

9. **Correct answer: C**

   A. **Incorrect:** This situation is an example of a real or potential conflict of interest and, as such, it must first be disclosed before the project can proceed.

   B. **Incorrect:** When the conflict of interest has been disclosed, you would not be able to give your parents any special information.

   C. **Correct:** Because this is either a real or potential conflict of interest, you must disclose it first.

   D. **Incorrect:** It doesn't matter whether you benefit from it directly; your actions could benefit a member of your family, and thus there is a conflict of interest.

10. **Correct answer: C**

    A. **Incorrect:** This situation requires you to be clear about the role you have. You would have to clearly separate your PMI activities from you commercial interests and explain that you are there on PMI business, not your own business.

    B. **Incorrect:** This may be a good answer in the absence of answer C.

    C. **Correct:** This is the best answer because it directs you to seek guidance on how to deal with this situation.

    D. **Incorrect:** Mixing PMI interests and your commercial interest is not permissible because it is a clear conflict of interest.

11. **Correct answer: A**
    - **A. Correct:** You have a responsibility to protect the natural environment, and thus this is the best answer.
    - **B. Incorrect:** Resigning from the project does not address the damage to the environment that the project will do. It may be a last-resort option, though.
    - **C. Incorrect:** You cannot be silent about this after you know about it.
    - **D. Incorrect:** This option requires you to be dishonest and, as such, is not a good choice.

12. **Correct answer: B**
    - **A. Incorrect:** You must acknowledge the authorship and ownership of the article during your presentation.
    - **B. Correct:** You must acknowledge the authorship and ownership of the article, and you should also check with PMI as to whether it is OK to use it in this way.
    - **C. Incorrect:** Handing out a copy to your team members does not address the issues of ownership and authorship.
    - **D. Incorrect:** You can use the article as long as you follow the standard use of copyright articles such as acknowledging authorship and ownership.

13. **Correct answer: B**
    - **A. Incorrect:** You should first check your company's policy on receiving gifts. Many organizations have clear guidelines forbidding the acceptance of gifts, to ensure a lack of conflict of interest and promote fairness.
    - **B. Correct:** If the gift does not align with your organization's policy, then you must refuse it.
    - **C. Incorrect:** This does not address issues of honesty and fairness.
    - **D. Incorrect:** This does not address issues of honesty and fairness.

14. **Correct answer: A**
    - **A. Correct:** This is a common situation, and you should be prepared to allow for different customs in your team members.
    - **B. Incorrect:** This is not about treating everyone equally but about respecting the customs of everyone. Other team members may observe different holidays.
    - **C. Incorrect:** Not approving the time off shows disrespect for other people's customs.
    - **D. Incorrect:** Not approving the time off shows disrespect for other people's customs.

Glossary

A

accept A risk response strategy for either positive or negative risks that involves simply accepting the consequences of risk occurring.

accepted deliverable A project deliverable that has been through both validation and quality control to ensure that it meets the requirements and specifications.

accuracy How close the measured value is to the actual value; compare with *precision*, which refers to how uniform measurements are.

acquisition The tool of advertising externally for project team members.

active listening A communications technique in which the listener takes active steps to ensure that the message was understood correctly.

activity attributes Detail provided about activities on the activity list.

activity cost estimates The cost estimates developed for each identified activity.

activity durations estimate The estimate of the duration of a defined activity.

activity list The list of identified activities developed as part of the schedule management processes.

activity network diagram A tool used in quality planning to show relationships between interdependent activities and calculate the paths of activities and their durations. The generic term for all network diagrams, including those used in scheduling management.

activity-on-arrow An arrow diagramming method that represents activities on arrows and uses dummy activities to represent multiple predecessor and successor relationships between activities.

activity-on-node A precedence diagramming method that represents activity information on nodes and uses arrows to indicate the relationship between activities.

activity resource requirements The resources requires to complete the work of identified activities.

actual cost The actual incurred cost of completing project work.

additional quality planning tool In quality management, a generic referral to those quality tools not captured in the seven basic quality tools; includes the seven new quality tools.

advertising A tool for promoting a project's procurement requirements to a particular audience.

affinity diagram A graphical representation of ideas and similar concepts grouped by their relationship to each other. One of the seven new quality tools.

agreements Any and all formal contracts that initiate a project.

alternative analysis A consideration of all the possible different ways that a potential outcome may be achieved and making a decision about which method is best.

alternatives generation A process tool that considers many potential alternatives in order to determine whether you have selected the most efficient and appropriate one.

analogous estimating An estimating process that takes a similar activity and compares it to a planned activity to generate the estimate.

analytical techniques A group of mainly mathematical techniques used to forecast potential outcomes based upon known data.

approved change request A change request that has been through the documented change control process and received approval.

approved change requests review A tool to determine whether approved change requests have been implemented as planned.

assumptions analysis An analysis of the assumptions made when calculating estimates.

audit A tool for carrying out an assessment of whether or not a defined process has been followed.

avoid A risk response strategy for negative risk that involves putting in place measures to avoid the risk occurring.

B

backward pass The process of calculating the late finishes and late starts in a network diagram. After calculating the backward pass, the amount of total float for each activity and the critical path can be identified.

balanced matrix A type of matrix organizational structure in which power is equally shared between the functional manager and the project manager.

basis of estimates Supporting documentation for activity cost estimates that provides additional information about assumptions, constraints, uncertainty, and estimating techniques used.

benchmarking Comparing a project, or parts of a project, against other projects to judge how they compare.

bidder conference A forum or meeting where all potential bidders on a procurement request can ask questions of the buyer for clarification.

bottom-up estimating The process of aggregating individual activity estimates upward to arrive at a total cost.

brainstorming A technique for gathering information that encourages creative and thorough thinking.

budget at completion The original approved project budget to complete all the work.

business case A document that examines the objectives, cost, benefits, strategic goals, constraints, and assumptions and provides s justification for an organization to approve a project.

business value The sum of all tangible and intangible value in an organization.

buyer The person or organization procuring external goods or services.

C

cause-and-effect diagram Also called a fishbone or Ishikawa diagram; a graphical representation of a known and identified effect and the potential causes of the effect. One of the seven basic quality tools.

change control board A panel of people with experience to consider and make decisions upon any requested changes as part of the change control process.

change control meeting A meeting that is defined and scheduled by the documented change control process. Change control meetings typically occur at regular intervals, and attendees at the meetings have the necessary skills and authority to make decisions about change requests.

change control tool Any tool defined by the change control process that can help define and manage the change requests received.

change log A log used to document change requests received and manage their status.

change request A request made in response to new or amended requirements, or as a result of variances discovered.

checklist analysis A technique of having a predefined checklist of steps, or activities, that must be completed and ensuring that they are.

checksheet A standardized list of activities, process, and steps that need to be completed during quality management activities. One of the seven basic quality tools.

claims administration A tool for recording and assessing any claims made by either party to a contract.

closed procurement A documented output that provides a formal record that a contract has been completed and closed.

co-location Putting project team members within the same physical location so that they can see each other and work together more effectively.

communications management plan The management plan that guides project communications.

communications method A tool that recognizes that communications can be interactive, push, or pull.

communications model A tool that describes how communications move from sender to receiver through a particular medium.

communications requirements analysis A tool for gathering and documenting the communication requirements of project stakeholders.

communications technology A tool that decides the particular form of technology to be used to disseminate information.

conflict management The process of resolving conflict.

conflict of interest A situation in which an individual may benefit personally from decisions or actions they undertake while acting in the best interests of another party.

context diagram A method of graphically representing how users interact with a process.

contingency plan A documented plan of contingent responses to a unplanned risk occurring.

contingency reserves The reserve developed, usually as a result of quantitative risk analysis, for known unknowns for time or cost.

contingent response strategy A risk response strategy for unplanned risk.

continuous improvement An iterative process of always seeking to improve your overall approach to quality management and the specific results obtained from quality management processes.

contract A formal agreement, usually in writing, between two or more parties with obligations, roles, and responsibilities clearly defined.

contract change control system A technique for defining how the procurement process can be changed.

control chart A graphical representation of data points mapped over time against an expected mean or average; upper and lower control limits are set three standard deviations either side of the mean, and beyond the control limits there are upper and lower specification limits. One of the seven basic quality tools.

control limit A limit used on a control chart, set three standard deviations either side of the expected mean to get the upper and lower control limit.

conversation A tool used to communicate with team members about their performance.

corrective action An action that seeks to realign the project performance with the project management plan.

cost aggregation The technique of adding up lower-level cost estimates to arrive at a total cost estimate for higher-level deliverables.

cost baseline The approved project cost over time.

cost-benefit analysis A tool for analyzing the expected costs to be incurred against the expected benefits to be gained. Benefits should outweigh costs.

cost forecast A forecast that contains the project costs for a project or part of a project based on the available information.

cost management plan The management plan outlining how you will plan, monitor, and control changes to your project costs.

cost of quality A consideration of the impacts of manufacturing high quality or low quality over the life of the product.

cost performance index A relative measure of cost performance calculated by dividing earned value by actual cost.

cost variance A measure of variance between what was planned and what is occurring in relation to project cost performance, calculated by subtracting actual cost from earned value.

crashing A schedule compression technique that involves allocating more resources to an activity to speed its completion. It usually involves additional cost.

D

data gathering and representation techniques Techniques and methods of collecting and presenting data in graphical form for further analysis.

decision tree A tool for making decisions about which option to select based on known probabilities and outcomes, to calculate the expected monetary value of each.

decomposition The technique of breaking down high-level descriptions into their component parts. When used in the creation of a WBS, decomposition is used down to the work package level.

defect repair A required activity to repair a discovered defect.

deliverable A unique and verifiable product, service, or result produced by the project.

Delphi technique An estimating technique that involves soliciting information from experts anonymously to avoid peer pressure.

dependency determination The consideration given to whether activities represent mandatory, discretionary, external, or internal dependencies.

design of experiments A tool for determining quality by using a known set of variables, designing an experiment, and being able to control different variables to determine the variable responsible, or most responsible, for quality issues.

diagramming techniques A variety of techniques of using diagrams to show relationships between related activities, events, causes, and effects.

document analysis A technique of analyzing existing documents to gather information.

documentation reviews A technique of thoroughly examining documents that serve as inputs into processes to fully understand and review them.

dummy activity A relationship, represented by a dotted line, between multiple activities in an activity-on-arrow (AOA) diagram.

E

early finish The earliest an identified activity can finish. Calculated by adding the duration of the activity to the early start.

early start The earliest an activity can start.

earned value The value of the work completed.

earned value management A technique for analyzing past performance and utilizing formulas to forecast future performance based on planned value, earned value, and actual cost.

effective listening Similar to active listening, a communications technique that also includes the listener or receiver monitoring nonverbal and physical communication.

enhance A risk response strategy for positive risks that seeks to enhance the probability or impact of a risk occurring.

enterprise environmental factor A factor that is external to a project that can influence the success of a project.

enterprise environmental factors update An update to the enterprise environmental factors as a result of completing processes.

estimate at completion The formula for calculating what the forecast cost estimate at the completion of the project will be.

estimate to complete The calculation to estimate how much more money there is to be spent on the project to reach the estimate at completion.

expected monetary value analysis A mathematical technique, often using decision trees, of calculating the probability and impact of a particular decision in order to calculate expected monetary value.

expert judgment The advice and decisions from people with specialist knowledge in a particular area.

exploit A risk response strategy for positive risks that seeks to put in place strategies to ensure that if a positive risk occurs you are ready to exploit it.

exploratory study An initial assessment and review of an issue to gain a preliminary understanding of potential ways to address it.

F

facilitated workshop A workshop with a focus on a particular issue, directed by an independent facilitator.

facilitation techniques A broad range of techniques designed to solicit information from groups of people with the objective of accomplishing project activities.

fairness One of four key values underpinning the ethical and professional conduct expected of a project manager. It seeks to avoid conflict of interest, favoritism, and discrimination. See also *responsibility*, *respect*, and *honesty*.

fast tracking A schedule compression technique that involves performing activities in parallel that were originally scheduled in sequence.

feedback Cues from the receiver to the sender that indicate whether or not the message has been understood.

Fielder's Contingency Theory A theory that states that leadership effectiveness is contingent on whether the situation is stressful or calm and whether the leader is task-oriented or relationship-oriented.

final product, service, or result The deliverable, product, or service produced by the project and handed over to operations.

fishbone diagram Also called a cause-and-effect diagram or Ishikawa diagram; a graphical representation of a known and identified effect and the potential causes of the effect. One of the seven basic quality tools.

flowchart A tool for showing in graphical form the steps in a process. One of the seven basic quality tools.

focus group A gathering of a group of stakeholders or participants to address a particular issue or provide specific feedback.

forecasting The technique of extrapolating from past performance what likely future performance will be.

forward pass The calculation of early starts and early finishes in a network diagram that results in the project duration.

free slack or free float The amount of time an activity can be delayed before it affects the next activity on the path.

functional manager A general manager or team leader in charge of a functional area in an organization.

functional organization An organization that is structured into its separate functional areas, each having its own technical specialty and manager or leader.

funding limit reconciliation A technique for reconciling forecast funding requirements against actual funding limits.

G

grade A measure of the amount of features a product has. Low grade means the product has few features, whereas high grade means it has lots of features.

ground rules Rules established by the project manager and project team members for accepted and expected behaviors for being part of the team.

group creativity techniques A range of techniques used to get a group of people to generate and consider a wide range of possible options.

group decision-making techniques A range of techniques to enable a group of people to reach a decision.

grouping method A particular method of deciding how results will be categorized for easy assessment and prioritization.

H

Herzberg's Motivation-Hygiene Theory A theory that states that hygiene factors will not motivate, but their absence will make staff unsatisfied, and that motivation will motivate, but only if hygiene factors are in place.

histogram Also called a bar chart; a tool for showing amount or frequency of a variable. One of the seven basic quality tools.

historical relationships Any past information about interactions between variables used in an estimating process.

honesty One of four key values underpinning the ethical and professional conduct expected of a project manager. See also *responsibility*, *respect*, and *fairness*.

human resource management plan The management plan for planning, acquiring, developing, and controlling human resources on the project.

I

independent estimate A technique that uses an independent professional to provide advice on what seller responses in relation to cost should reasonably be.

influencing The technique of understanding, modifying, and changing the expectations and engagement of stakeholders to ensure that they support your project or do not oppose it.

information gathering techniques A variety of techniques for gathering information from project team members, subject matter experts, and other stakeholders, and other sources of information.

information management system A tool for the management, storage, and distribution of project information in either hard copy or electronic form.

inspection The tool of physically checking work that has been done.

interactive communication A form of communication where multiple parties communicate concurrently.

interpersonal skills A range of technical, personal, and conceptual skills that a project manager should have and be able to display at appropriate times in order to increase his or her effectiveness.

interrelationship digraph A tool for graphically showing the many relationships that exist between different variables or steps in a process. One of the seven new quality tools.

interview A formal and structured meeting between small groups of people to solicit specialist information.

Ishikawa diagram Also called a cause-and-effect diagram or a fishbone diagram; a graphical representation of a known and identified effect and the potential causes of the effect. One of the seven basic quality tools.

issue log A document that lists and describes issues that have been identified and the status of those issues.

J

just in time A tool for controlling inventory in which inventory is delivered just as it is needed. Can be used as a quality management tool, because lack of inventory in stock exposes mistakes very fast and provides a reason to improve quality.

K

kaizen The loose Japanese translation of *continuous improvement*, which means always seeking to improve your quality processes and products.

kick-off meeting A meeting held before project execution activities start.

L

lag The amount of time an activity must wait after its predecessor finishes before it can start.

late finish The latest an activity can finish.

late start The latest an activity can start.

lead The amount of time before the finish of its predecessor that an activity can start.

M

make or buy analysis A tool for assessing whether work should be done by the project team or procured from an external source.

make or buy decision The output from the make or buy analysis that decides whether an organization will make the required goods or services or buy them from an external provider.

management reserves A reserve of cost or time for unknown unknowns; under the control of management.

management skills A set of skills a project manager should have that include presentation, negotiation, time management, and public speaking skills.

market research As tool for examining and assessing current marketplace conditions in order to assess the impact upon procurement decisions.

Maslow's hierarchy of needs A theory that states that a person will always be motived by lower needs before being motivated by higher-order needs.

matrix diagram A tool for graphically showing how one set of variables on a vertical axis interacts with other variables on a horizontal axis. One of the seven new quality tools.

matrix organization A type of organizational structure in which projects are completed across functional lines and a project manager draws on different technical specialties from different functional areas.

McClelland's Human Motivation, Achievement, or Three Needs Theory A theory that states that people will work not for more money, but instead for achievement, power, and affiliation.

McGregor's theory X and theory Y A set of theories that states that managers either view employees as trustworthy and self motivated (theory Y) or untrustworthy and needing constant motivation (theory X).

meeting A gathering of a group of people for a defined purpose and agenda.

methodology A defined set of processes, tools, techniques, and templates for managing projects in a particular way.

milestone list A high-level graphical representation of the milestones to be achieved on the project.

mitigate A risk response strategy for negative risks that seeks to minimize the probability and impact of a particular risk.

modeling techniques A variety of mathematical and computer-based techniques to forecast possible outcomes based on several different inputs.

Monte Carlo Analysis A statistical and complex mathematical method of extrapolating from observed data what a likely future scenario or scenarios will be.

multicriteria decision analysis A tool used to assess the different attributes of prospective team members, and give each attribute a particular weight so that the overall ranking of the preferred team member can be assessed.

N

negotiated settlement A technique for arriving at an agreed means of terminating and closing a contract between parties to the contract.

negotiation A tool for interacting with another party and attempting to come to a mutually beneficial agreement.

networking A tool used to build relationships between individuals and groups based on mutual benefit.

nominal group technique A method of using group members to vote on which ideas generated from a brainstorming session are most worthy of investigating or using further.

nonverbal Communication in the form of body language, posture, and similar.

O

observation A tool used to observe team members' performance so that performance appraisals can be completed; also the technique of physically observing how people act in the environment and how they might use a particular product, service, or result.

organizational chart A hierarchical and graphical representation of the way that an organization is structured, identifying specific roles and their reporting lines.

organizational process asset Any formal or informal process that the performing organization has in place to assist in delivery of the project.

organizational process assets update Any update that will be made to existing organizational process assets as a result of information gathered or observations made during the execution of the project.

organizational project management maturity A method of assessing the level of organizational maturity in relation to the use of portfolio, program, and project management processes, tools, templates, and methodologies.

organizational theory A range of theories describing the way people and organizations interact.

Ouchi's Theory Z A theory that states that employee loyalty and productivity can be increased by offering a job for life and providing full care.

P

padding The unjustifiable increase in estimates of time or cost.

paralingual Communication that is vocal but not verbal, and includes tone of voice, inflection, and volume.

parametric estimating An estimating technique that multiplies a known quantity by a known metric.

Pareto diagram A tool for showing the frequency of events individually, and also cumulatively, so that the 20 percent of events responsible for 80 percent of the effects can be identified. One of the seven basic quality tools.

payment system A tool for ensuring that payments due under the terms of a contract are properly paid and recorded.

performance reporting A tool for collecting and disseminating appropriate reporting on project progress to stakeholders.

performance reviews The process of measuring, comparing, and analyzing actual project performance.

personnel assessment tools A range of tools and techniques that enable project managers and team members to assess individual and team performance, strengths, and weaknesses.

phase A defined part of a project marked by a milestone, stage gate, phase gate, or major decision point.

plan-do-check-act (PDCA) cycle An iterative cycle developed by Shewhart and Deming to describe continuous planning and checking processes.

planned value The value of work that should have been completed at a certain point in time.; calculated by multiplying the budget at completion by percentage of time elapsed.

PMBOK® Guide A collection of what is considered good practice in the profession of project management, providing a framework from which to draw appropriate processes, tools, and techniques for managing projects.

point of total assumption The price point in a contract where the seller assumes total responsibility for all cost increases.

portfolio The range of projects being undertaken by an organization.

portfolio manager The person responsible for managing a portfolio of projects; the portfolio manager typically operates at strategic level.

position description A document that sets out the required responsibilities, skills, and experience for a particular role on the project team.

preassignment A tool that allocates project team members to a project based on their specific experience or contractual agreements.

precedence diagramming method A graphical representation of activities in the project with arrows indicating the relationship between them. The most common type of precedence diagram is the activity-on-arrow (AOA) diagram.

precision The degree to which measurements are clustered together rather than scattered. Compare to *accuracy*.

predecessor An activity that comes immediately before another activity.

preventive action An action to stop work that will cause the project to deviate from the project management plan.

prioritization matrix A tool for prioritizing and weighting issues and events and displaying the results graphically. One of the seven new quality tools.

probability and impact matrix A graphical means of displaying the combined probability and impact of risks in a standardized manner.

process analysis A tool that follows steps in a process to determine whether they are appropriate and can be improved upon.

process decision program chart A tool that links ideas together and graphically represents them as a means to achieve a particular goal. One of the seven new quality tools.

process improvement plan A plan that identifies the way in which project processes will be defined, analyzed, and improved. A subset of the project management plan.

procurement audit A tool for auditing whether or not procurement processes and contracts are being carried out as per the approved documentation.

procurement documents A range of documents produced by the procurement processes that provide additional advice or record decisions made about the procurement process.

procurement management plan A management plan that provides guidance on how the procurement management processes will be carried out.

procurement negotiation A technique of entering into negotiations with prospective sellers that results in an agreed contract.

procurement performance review A technique for carrying out a structured review of a seller's performance and progress against an agreed contract.

procurement statement of work A defined and documented description of the scope of work to be completed as part of the procurement process.

product analysis The technique of breaking a defined product down into its component parts to fully understand it.

program A number of projects that are interrelated in some way.

Program Evaluation and Review Technique (PERT) A graphical technique developed to evaluate the time and cost elements of a project and the relationship and interdependencies between them.

program manager The person responsible for managing a program of projects.

progressive elaboration A process of iteratively defining and planning work to be done on a project.

project A temporary activity to deliver a unique product, service, or result.

project calendars The times that activities on the project can and cannot be carried out in completing project deliverables.

project charter The foundational document for the project; it provides political and financial support for the project.

project communications The output from the Manage Communications process that includes all information created, stored, and disseminated by the project.

project coordinator A person given a leadership role in managing a project with less power and authority than a project manager.

project documents update An update to any project documents as a result of information gathered, or observations made during the execution of the project.

project expeditor A person given a leadership role in managing a project with very little power and authority.

project funding requirements The documented timing of when project funding will be required.

project life cycle The defined stages of initiating, planning, executing, monitoring and controlling, and closing a project.

project management The proactive application of professional project management practices to deliver a project.

project management information system Any system the project utilizes to gather, store, record, and disseminate information about the project.

project management office The center of excellence for project management within an organization.

project management plan The collection of all planning documents used to guide project execution.

project management plan update Any update to any part of the project management plan or its subsidiary plans.

project management software Any software that provides monitoring and reporting capability for managing a project.

project manager The person ultimately responsible for all aspects of the project.

project performance appraisal A tool used to assess individual and team performance against expected performance, provide feedback to team members, identify individual training needs, and use this information to plan future team and individual performance.

project schedule The expected timeframe the project will take.

project schedule network diagram A graphical representation of all the activities to be completed on a project and the relationships between them.

project scope statement The description of all the work to be done, and the work not to be done, as part of the project.

project staff assignments A document outlining which project staff members are allocated to the project, their roles, and contact details.

project steering committee An oversight group made up of senior managers providing high-level advice, support, and governance to the project.

projectized organization An organizational structure that reflects an organization that is divided and structured along project lines.

proposal evaluation technique A technique for assessing and scoring all proposals received as part of a procurement process.

prototype A technique of producing an example of the finished product, service, or result to seek feedback from stakeholders.

published estimating data A database of known quantities or costs relating to completion of activities in the project. Such databases are usually available commercially.

pull communication A form of communication where information is downloaded and accessed by the receivers when they want it.

push communication A form of communication where information is sent to the receiver.

Q

quality The degree to which a set of inherent characteristics fulfills requirements.

quality audit A tool for checking conformity to defined process to ensure that they are being followed.

quality checklist An input/output that provides a standardized list of steps to be taken. Compare with *checksheets*, which are used as a quality tool.

quality control measurement An input/output that describes the result of Control Quality activities.

quality management plan A subset of the project management plan that describes how quality management will be defined, document, measured, and improved in a project.

quality metric An input/output that describes a particular product or project attribute in detail and how the Quality Control process will measure it.

quantitative risk analysis and modeling techniques A variety of tools and techniques for performing quantitative risk analysis.

questionnaires and surveys Formal documented methods of asking for information and feedback from stakeholders.

R

RACI chart A type of responsibility assignment matrix (RAM) that identifies particular team members and activities to be completed, and defines whether the team members are responsible, accountable, consulted, or informed.

recognition A tool for acknowledging the performance of team members.

records management system A tool used to record, store, and distribute information relating to procurement processes and decisions.

reporting system A tool for gathering, storing, and distributing project information.

requirements The attributes, condition, or capability that a stakeholder requires from a product, service, or result, produced as part of the project.

requirements documentation A document that describes individual requirements and their priority; developed in consultation with stakeholders.

requirements management plan The document that sets out how you will define, document, and manage your project requirements.

requirements traceability matrix A document that maps individual project requirements to specific business objectives and stakeholders.

reserve analysis An analysis, usually using quantitative risk analysis, that results in the provision of either a contingency or management reserve for time and cost.

resource breakdown structure A breakdown, using the process of decomposition, of the categories and types of resources required to complete the project.

resource calendars The specific time periods that a particular resource is available to be used on the project.

resource leveling The process of optimizing and making most efficient use of resources over a given period of time.

resource optimization techniques Any of the techniques that enable a more efficient use of resources on the project.

resource smoothing A resource optimization technique that seeks to optimize the use of resources without extending the total float of any activity.

respect One of four key values underpinning the ethical and professional conduct expected of a project manager. It seeks to ensure that respect is provided for. See also *responsibility*, *fairness*, and *honesty*.

responsibility One of four key values underpinning the ethical and professional conduct expected of a project manager. It seeks to ensure that a project manager takes full personal and professional responsibility for all actions and decisions. See also *respect*, *fairness*, and *honesty*.

responsibility assignment matrix A tool for displaying particular roles in a project and the responsibilities each role has.

rewards A tool for compensating high performance.

risk audit A technique for determining if the processes outlined in the risk management plan for conducting risk management activities are being followed.

risk breakdown structure (RBS) A graphical representation of different risk categories and subcategories.

risk categorization A technique for assigning similar and interrelated risks into identified categories.

risk data quality assessment A technique for examining the quality and certainty of data being used in risk analysis.

risk management plan The particular management plan that outlines how you will approach the planning, monitoring, and controlling of risk management activities on your project. It is a subsidiary of the project management plan.

risk probability and impact assessment A tool for assigning likely probability and impact to individual identified risks on the project.

risk reassessment A technique for continually reassessing the information used to identify individual risks, their probability and impact, the prepared risk responses, and any new risks that may have arisen.

risk register The documented list, analysis, and planned responses to identified risks on the project.

risk tolerance The maximum level of risk that an organization is prepared to tolerate on a project.

risk urgency assessment A technique for assessing those risks that are likely to occur in the short term, and prioritizing those over risks that will occur at a further point in time.

rolling wave planning A form of progressive elaboration that focuses on planning the immediate future in more detail than timeframes further off.

rule of seven A guide for determining when a process may be out of control in a control chart. If seven consecutive data points appear above or below the mean and within the control limits, this may indicate that the process is out of control or is about to go out of control.

S

scatter diagram A tool for graphically representing the results of two variables. One of the seven basic quality tools.

schedule baseline The developed and approved project timeframe.

schedule compression Any technique that reduces individual activity or the total project duration.

schedule data The collection of information describing and controlling the schedule, including the schedule milestones, schedule activities, activity attributes, and any schedule contingency reserves.

schedule forecast The estimated time the project, or parts of the project, will take based on available information.

schedule management plan The plan developed to guide the development, monitoring, and control of the project schedule. It forms part of the overall project management plan.

schedule network templates Any templates that an organization has for assisting with developing a schedule network.

schedule performance index A calculation measuring the time performance on the project. Calculated by dividing earned value by planned value.

schedule variance The difference between what was planned and what is actually occurring in relation to the project schedule.

scheduling tool Any manual or automated tool that focuses on the project schedule.

scope baseline The scope statement, work breakdown structure (WBS), and WBS dictionary.

scope management plan The document that sets out how you will define, document, and manage changes to your project scope statement.

selected sellers The group of sellers chosen to participate in the procurement process either by being prequalified or by completing a stage in the procurement process.

seller The individual or organization responsible for delivery of externally contracted goods or services.

seller proposal A formal response to a procurement request from a prospective seller.

sensitivity analysis A mathematical technique for determining which parts of the project are most sensitive to risk.

seven basic quality tools Initially developed by Ishikawa, graphical ways of showing complex text based or numerical information. They are the cause-and-effect diagrams, flowcharts, checksheets, Pareto diagrams, histograms, control charts, and scatter diagrams.

seven new quality tools A further seven ways to show information in graphical form. They are affinity diagrams, process decision program charts, interrelationship digraphs, tree diagrams, prioritization matrices, activity network diagrams, and matrix diagrams.

share A risk response strategy for positive risks that seeks to increase the probability or impact of a risk occurring by sharing experience and capabilities with another organization.

simple average A mathematical average obtained by adding a set of numbers and dividing the total by the amount of numbers.

Six Sigma A proprietary approach to quality management which seeks to reduce defects and errors to as close to zero as possible. Named after six standard deviations, which includes 99.999 percent of a population.

source selection criteria A tool for developing a range of approved criteria for assessing seller responses to procurement requests.

specification limit A limit used on a control chart outside the control limits set by the customer. Any product manufactured outside either the upper or lower specification limit will not be accepted by the customer.

sponsor The person who provides financial and political support for the project, appoints the project manager, and authorizes the project charter.

staffing management plan An important component of the human resource management plan that specifically addresses the skills required, the time people are able to work on the project, and how and when project team members will be obtained to work on the project.

stakeholder Any person or group that can affect or be affected by your project.

stakeholder analysis A technique for identifying and documenting stakeholders' interests, expectations, power, influence, and level of engagement in the project.

stakeholder management plan The document that sets out how you will define, document, and manage stakeholders and their expectations.

stakeholder register A register of all project stakeholders and information about their interest in the project, the power they have to influence the project, their expectations, and how their expectations will be managed.

stakeholder risk profile analysis An assessment of individually identified stakeholders' attitudes toward risk on the project.

standard deviation A measurement about how widespread a particular set of data is from the mean.

statement of work A high-level narrative description of the work to be done on the project.

statistical sampling A tool for sampling a small subset of a large population and extrapolating the result to the entire population. Used when testing the entire population is not possible or when destructive testing is involved.

status meetings Regularly scheduled meetings that focus upon a particular project status metric.

strategies for negative risks or threats A range of suitable options for dealing with negative risks, including transfer, mitigate, avoid, and accept.

strategies for positive risks or opportunities A range of suitable options for dealing with positive risks, including enhance, exploit, share, and accept.

strong matrix A type of matrix organization in which the project manager has most of the power and authority, and the functional manager has little power and authority.

successor An activity that comes immediately after another activity.

SWOT analysis A technique that analyzes strengths, weaknesses, opportunities, and threats.

T

tailoring The process of taking and using only those processes, tools, and techniques that provide benefit to managing your project.

team-building activities A wide range of activities designed to enhance team performance via the creation of team morale, culture, and ground rules.

team performance assessment A tool used to develop a formal or informal assessment of a project team's effectiveness.

technical performance measurement A technique for checking whether predetermined parameters for initiating particular risk strategies have been met.

template Any blank preformed document that can be used to complete processes, documents, or forms on a project.

three-point estimating A formula taken from the Program Evaluation and Review Technique (PERT) that calculates a weighted average of the optimistic, most likely, and pessimistic estimates. The formula is (O+(4 x M) + P)/6.

to-complete performance index The rate at which you must perform to achieve either the budget at completion or the estimate at completion.

tornado diagram A tool for graphically representing the results of sensitivity analysis in hierarchal form to identify those parts of the project to be affected by risk, from most likely down to least likely.

total quality management (TQM) A management-led philosophy and approach to quality that involves everyone in the organization and seeks to continuously improve all aspects of quality within an organization and a project.

total slack or total float The amount of time an activity can be delayed before it affects the total project duration.

training A tool used to increase the level of skills a team member has through formal learning.

transfer A risk response strategy for negative risks, which involves making the probability and impact of the risk someone else's responsibility.

tree diagram A tool for showing the systemic breakdown of concepts or issues. Used as a quality management tool and also is the generic term for breakdown structures such as the work breakdown structure and organizational breakdown structure.

trend analysis A technique for identifying any trends and observed data and extrapolating from this a likely future outcome.

Tuckman's five-stage model of team development A theory that describes the five stages of forming, storming, norming, performing, and adjourning that a team goes through.

V

validated change An approved change that has been acted upon and checked for accuracy.

validated deliverable A deliverable that has previously been verified and has been checked with stakeholders to ensure it meets stakeholder requirements and expectations.

variance The difference between what was planned and what is actually occurring.

variance analysis The technique of checking what you planned to do against what you are actually doing and spotting any difference between the two.

variance and trend analysis The technique of checking what you planned to do against what you are actually doing and using this information to forecast likely future trends.

variance at completion The difference between the budget at completion and the estimate at completion.

variance formula The formula used to determine the mathematical variance; calculated by multiplying the standard deviation by itself.

vendor bid analysis The technique of getting an independent assessment of prices submitted by vendors to check for accuracy.

verified deliverable A deliverable that has previously been verified and has been checked with stakeholders to ensure it meets stakeholder requirements and expectations.

virtual team A tool that recognizes that project team members may come from different geographic locations but can still work together by using technology.

Vroom's Expectancy Theory A theory that states that the expectation of receiving a reward for a certain accomplishment will motivate people to work harder, but that this only works if the accomplishment is perceived to be achievable.

W

war room A specific form of co-location activity that places team members in the same room.

weak matrix A type of matrix organization in which the functional manager has much more power and authority than a project manager.

weighted average A mathematical average calculated by adding a set of numbers and prescribing different weights to each of the numbers, then dividing by the sum of the weights given; used to calculate three-point estimates.

what-if scenario analysis A complex mathematical model which examines the probability of different scenarios.

whistleblower Someone who reports illegal or unethical behavior within an organization.

work breakdown structure (WBS) A hierarchical graphical representation of the work to be done on the project, broken down to work package level.

work breakdown structure (WBS) dictionary A document providing additional information about each node in a WBS.

work package An amount of work that can have time and cost accurately estimated; the lowest level of the WBS.

work performance data The raw data gathered as part of observations and inspections.

work performance information The refined work performance data presented in a relevant form.

work performance reports The presentation of work performance information to stakeholders.

workaround An acceptable response to unplanned risk, which involves creating a makeshift solution to allow work to continue.

Index

Symbols

80:20 rule, 237
360-degree feedback method, 294

A

AC (actual cost), 210
accepted deliverables
    Close Project or Phase process, 73
    Validate Scope process, 111
accuracy, 150, 230–231
Acquire Project Team process, 143, 203
    inputs, 279–280
    outputs, 282–283
    overview, 279
    tools and techniques, 280–281
acquisition, 281
active listening technique, 316
activity attributes
    Define Activities process, 134
    Develop Schedule process, 158
    Estimate Activity Durations process, 148
    Estimate Activity Resources process, 143
    Sequence Activities process, 136
activity cost estimates
    Determine Budget process, 202
    Estimate Activity Resources process, 144
    Estimate Costs process, 200
    Identify Risks process, 345
    Plan Procurement Management process, 390
activity duration estimates
    Develop Schedule process, 159
    Estimate Activity Durations process, 155
    Identify Risks process, 346

activity list
    Define Activities process, 133
    Develop Schedule process, 158
    Estimate Activity Durations process, 148
    Estimate Activity Resources process, 143
    Sequence Activities process, 136
activity network diagrams, 247
activity-on-arrow (AOA) diagrams, 140, 141
activity-on-node (AON) diagrams, 137, 140, 161, 247
activity resource requirements
    Develop Schedule process, 158
    Estimate Activity Durations process, 148
    Estimate Activity Resources process, 145
    Plan Human Resource Management process, 268
    Plan Procurement Management process, 390
actual cost (AC), 210
ACWP (actual cost of work performed), 214
adjusting leads, 172
administrative closure, 74
advertising, 400
affinity diagrams, 245
agreements
    Conduct Procurements process, 401–403
    Control Procurements process, 406
    Determine Budget process, 203
    Develop Project Charter process, 40–41
alternative analysis, 144
alternatives generation, 101
analogous estimating
    Estimate Activity Durations process, 150
    Estimate Costs process, 197
analytical techniques
    Close Project or Phase process, 73
    Conduct Procurements process, 400
    Monitor and Control Project Work process, 61–63
    Plan Cost Management process, 191
    Plan Risk Management process, 339

AOA (activity-on-arrow) diagrams

    Plan Schedule Management process, 129
    Plan Stakeholder Management process, 433–434
AOA (activity-on-arrow) diagrams, 140, 141
AON (activity-on-node) diagrams, 137, 140, 161, 247
applying leads, 172
approved change requests
    Control Procurements process, 406
    Control Quality process, 253
    Direct and Manage Project Work process, 54
    Perform Integrated Change Control process updates, 69
arbitration, 412
audits, 407, 412

B

BAC (budget at completion), 209
backward pass, 161
balanced matrix organization, 275
bar charts, 238
basis of estimates
    Determine Budget process, 202
    Estimate Costs process, 200
BCR (Benefit-Cost Ratio), 37
BCWP (budgeted cost of work performed), 214
BCWS (budgeted cost of work scheduled), 214
benchmarking
    Collect requirements process, 97
    Plan Quality Management process, 235–239
Benefit-Cost Ratio (BCR), 37
beta distributions, 359
bidder conference, 399–400
bottom-up estimating
    Estimate Activity Resources process, 145
    Estimate Costs process, 197
brainstorming, 42, 49, 153, 347
Budget at completion (BAC), 209
budgeted cost of work performed (BCWP), 214
budgeted cost of work scheduled (BCWS), 214
budget vs. cost, 190
buffer time, 164
business case
    Develop Project Charter process, 39–40
    vs. project charter, 43
business value, 11
buyers, 388

C

cause-and-effect diagram, 235
CEO (chief executive officer), 272, 274
change control board, 68
change control meetings, 68
change control tools, 69
change log
    Manage Stakeholder Engagement process, 437
    Perform Integrated Change Control process updates, 69
change requests
    Conduct Procurements process, 403
    Control Communications process, 327
    Control Costs process, 216
    Control Procurements process, 409
    Control Quality process, 251, 254
    Control Risks process, 372
    Control Schedule process, 174
    Control Scope process, 114
    Control Stakeholder Engagement process, 443
    Direct and Manage Project Work process updates, 57
    Manage Project Team process, 299
    Manage Stakeholder Engagement process, 439
    Monitor and Control Project Work process, 63
    Perform Integrated Change Control process, 67–68
    Perform Quality Assurance process, 249
    Plan Procurement Management process, 396
    Validate Scope process, 111
checksheets, 236
claim, 408
claims administration, 408
closed procurements, 413
Close Procurements process, 72
    inputs, 411
    outputs, 413–414
    overview, 411
    tools and techniques, 412–413
Close Project or Phase process
    accepted deliverables, 73
    analytical techniques, 73
    expert judgment, 73
    final product, service, or result transition, 74
    meetings in, 73
    organizational process assets, 73
    organizational process assets updates, 74–75
    overview, 70–72
    project management plan, 72

Collect Requirements process, 233
    inputs, 94–95
    outputs
        overview, 97
        requirements documentation, 97–98
        requirements traceability matrix, 98–99
    overview, 93–94
    tools and techniques
        benchmarking, 97
        context diagrams, 97
        document analysis, 97
        facilitated workshops, 95
        focus groups, 95
        group creativity techniques, 95
        group decision-making techniques, 96
        interviews, 95
        observations, 96
        overview, 95
        prototypes, 96
        questionnaires and surveys, 96
co-location, 293
communications
    Manage Project Team process, 298
    Manage Stakeholder Engagement process, 438
communications management
    Control Communications process, 324–327
    defined, 312–313
    Manage Communications process, 320–323
    overview, 311–312
    Plan Communications Management process, 313–318
        inputs, 313–314
        outputs, 318–319
        overview, 313
        tools and techniques, 314–317
communications management plan
    Manage Communications process, 320
    Manage Stakeholder Engagement process, 437
    Plan Communications Management process, 318–319
communications methods
    Manage Communications process, 322
    Plan Communications Management process, 317–318
communications models
    Manage Communications process, 321
    Plan Communications Management process, 316–317

communications requirements analysis, 314–315
communications technology
    Manage Communications process, 321
    Plan Communications Management process, 315
Conduct Procurements process, 203, 394–395
    inputs
        make or buy decisions, 398
        organizational process assets, 399
        overview, 397
        procurement management plan, 397
        procurement statement of work, 398–399
        project documents, 398
        seller proposals, 398
        source selection criteria, 398
    outputs
        agreements, 401–403
        change requests, 403
        overview, 400–401
        project documents updates, 403–404
        project management plan updates, 403
        resource calendars, 403
        selected sellers, 400–401
    overview, 397
    tools and techniques
        advertising, 400
        analytical techniques, 400
        bidder conference, 399–400
        expert judgment, 400
        independent estimates, 400
        overview, 399
        procurement negotiations, 400–401
conflict management, 298–299
conflict of interest, 458, 459
conflict resolution
    defined, 43
    importance of, 49
context diagrams, 97
contingency plan, 366
contingency reserve, 154
contingent response strategies, 366
continuous improvement, 230
contract change control system, 407
contracts, 388
contractual closure, 74, 388
control charts, 238–239
Control Communications process, 322
    inputs, 324–325
    outputs, 326–327

Control Costs process

    overview, 324
    tools and techniques, 325–326
Control Costs process
    change requests, 216
    costs forecasts, 60, 216
    earned value management, 209–211
    forecasting, 212–214
    organizational process assets, 208
    organizational process assets updates, 216–217
    overview, 207
    performance reviews, 215
    project document updates, 216
    project funding requirements, 208
    project management plan, 208
    project management plan updates, 216
    project management software, 215
    reserve analysis, 215
    TCPI, 214
    work performance data, 208
    work performance information, 215
control limits, 238
Control Procurements process
    inputs, 406
    outputs, 409–410
        change requests, 409
        organizational process assets updates, 410
        overview, 409
        project documents updates, 410
        project management plan updates, 409
        work performance information, 409
    overview, 405
    tools and techniques
        claims administration, 408
        contract change control system, 407
        inspections and audits, 407
        overview, 407
        payment systems, 408
        performance reporting, 407
        procurement performance reviews, 407
        records management system, 408–409
Control Quality process, 56, 60
    inputs, 251–252
    outputs, 253–256
    overview, 250–251
    tools and techniques, 252–253
Control Risks process
    inputs
        overview, 369
        project management plan, 369
        risk register, 369
        work performance data, 369
    outputs
        change requests, 372
        organizational process assets updates, 372–373
        overview, 371
        project documents updates, 372
        project management plan updates, 372
        work performance information, 371
    overview, 368
    tools and techniques
        overview, 370
        reserve analysis, 371
        risk audits, 370
        risk reassessment, 370
        status meetings, 371
        technical performance measurement, 371
        variance and trend analysis, 370
Control Schedule process, 60
    inputs, 169–170
    outputs, 173–175
    overview, 169
    tools and techniques, 170–172
Control Scope process, 98, 112–115
Control Stakeholder Engagement process
    inputs
        issue log, 441
        overview, 441
        project documents, 442
        project management plan, 441
        work performance data, 442
    outputs
        change requests, 443
        organizational process assets updates, 443–444
        overview, 443
        project documents updates, 443
        work performance information, 443
    overview, 441
    tools and techniques
        expert judgment, 443
        meetings, 443
        overview, 442
        reporting systems, 442
control tools, 245–248
conversation, 298
corrective action, 57, 63
cost aggregation, 204
cost baseline, 205–206

cost-benefit analysis, 234
cost forecasts
    Control Costs process, 216
    Monitor and Control Project Work process, 60
cost management plan
    Determine Budget process, 202
    Estimate Costs process, 195
    Identify Risks process, 344–345
    Perform Quantitative Risk Analysis process, 358
    Plan Cost Management process, 192
cost of quality
    Estimate Costs process, 199
    Plan Quality Management process, 234–235
cost performance index (CPI), 211
cost plus fixed-fee contract (CPFF), 402
cost plus incentive fee contract (CPIF), 402
cost-reimbursable contract, 402
cost variance (CV), 211
cost vs. budget, 190
CPFF (cost plus fixed-fee contract), 402
CPI (cost performance index), 211
CPIF (cost plus incentive fee contract), 402
crashing technique, 166
Create WBS process, 91, 98, 132, 195, 346
    inputs
        enterprise environmental factors, 104
        organizational process assets, 105
        overview, 104
        project scope statement, 104
        requirements documentation, 104
        scope management plan, 104
    outputs
        overview, 106
        project document updates, 108
        scope baseline, 106–107
    overview, 103–104
    tools and techniques
        decomposition, 105
        expert judgment, 106
        overview, 105
critical chain method, 164
critical path method, 160–163
CV (cost variance), 211

D

data gathering and representation techniques, 359
decision tree analysis, 361
decomposition
    Create WBS process, 105
    Define Activities process, 133
defect repair, 57, 63
Define Activities process
    inputs, 132
    outputs
        activity attributes, 134
        activity list, 133
        milestone list, 134–135
        overview, 133
    overview, 131
    tools and techniques
        decomposition, 133
        expert judgment, 133
        overview, 132
        rolling wave planning, 133
defined, 62
Define Scope process, 91, 99–103
deliverables, 110
    Control Quality process, 252
    Direct and Manage Project Work process, 56
Delphi technique, 153–154, 347
Deming, William Edwards, 232
dependency determination, 139
design of experiments tool, 240
Determine Budget process
    activity cost estimates, 202
    agreements, 203
    basis of estimates, 202
    cost aggregation, 204
    cost baseline, 205–206
    cost management plan, 192, 202
    expert judgment, 204
    funding limit reconciliation, 205
    historical relationships, 204
    overview, 201–202
    project document updates, 206–207
    project funding requirements, 206
    project schedule, 203
    reserve analysis, 204
    resource calendars, 203
    risk register, 203
    scope baseline, 202

Develop Project Charter process, 89
    agreements, 40–41
    business case, 39–40
    enterprise environmental factors, 41
    expert judgment, 42
    facilitation techniques, 42–43
    organizational process assets, 41–42
    overview, 35–38
    project charter output, 43–44
    SOW, 39
Develop Project Management Plan process, 89, 233, 441
    expert judgment, 48–49
    facilitation techniques, 49
    organizational process assets, 48
    outputs from other processes as inputs, 46–47
    overview, 45–46
    project charter input, 46
    project management plan output, 50–52
Develop Project Team process, 284–294
    inputs, 284–285
    outputs, 294
    overview, 284
    tools and techniques, 285–294
        co-location, 293
        ground rules, 293
        interpersonal skills, 285–290
        overview, 285
        personnel assessment tools, 293
        recognition and rewards, 293
        team-building activities, 291–293
Develop Schedule process, 157–168
    inputs, 158–160
    outputs, 166–168
    overview, 157
    tools and techniques, 160–166
        critical chain method, 164
        critical path method, 160–163
        leads and lags, 165
        modeling techniques, 165
        overview, 160
        resource optimization techniques, 164
        schedule compression, 165–166
        schedule network analysis, 160
        scheduling tool, 166
Direct and Manage Project Work process, 442
    approved change requests, 54
    change requests, 57
    deliverables, 56
    Direct and Manage Project Work process deliverables, 56
    enterprise environmental factors, 54
    expert judgment, 55
    meetings in, 55
    organizational process assets, 54
    overview, 52–53
    project document updates, 57–58
    project management information system, 55
    project management plan, 53–54
    project management plan updates, 57
    work performance data, 56
direct costs, 194
discretionary dependencies, 139
document analysis, 97
documentation reviews, 347

E

EAC = AC + ((BAC-EV)/(CPI × SPI)) formula, 213
EAC = AC + (BAC-EV) formula, 212
EAC = AC+ ETC formula, 212
EAC = BAC/CPI formula, 212
EAC (estimate at completion), 173, 212
early finish (EF), 161
early start (ES), 161
earned value management, 209–211
Economic Value Add (EVA), 37
EF (early finish), 161
effective listening technique, 317
EMV (expected monetary value) analysis, 361
enterprise environmental factors, 14
    Acquire Project Team process, 280
    Create WBS process, 104
    Define Activities process, 132
    Develop Project Charter process, 41
    Develop Project Management Plan process, 47
    Develop Project Team process, 294–295
    Develop Schedule process, 159
    Direct and Manage Project Work process, 54
    Estimate Activity Durations process, 149
    Estimate Activity Resources process, 144
    Estimate Costs process, 196
    Identify Risks process, 346
    Identify Stakeholders process, 426
    Manage Communications process, 321

expert judgment

Manage Project Team process, 300
Monitor and Control Project Work process, 61
Perform Integrated Change Control process, 68
Perform Qualitative Risk Analysis process, 353
Perform Quantitative Risk Analysis process, 358
Plan Communications Management process, 314
Plan Cost Management process, 190
Plan Human Resource Management process, 268
Plan Procurement Management process, 391
Plan Quality Management process, 233–234
Plan Risk Management process, 338–339
Plan Schedule Management process, 128
Plan Scope Management process, 89
Plan Stakeholder Management process, 432
Sequence Activities process, 136
EOI (expression of interest), 394
equation models, 62
ES (early start), 161
Estimate Activity Duration process, 346
    inputs, 148–149
    outputs, 155–156
    overview, 147
    tools and techniques
        analogous estimating, 150
        expert judgment, 149
        group decision-making techniques, 153–154
        overview, 149
        parametric estimating, 150
        reserve analysis, 154–155
        three-point estimating, 150–153
Estimate Activity Resources process, 142–146, 268
estimate at completion (EAC), 173, 212
Estimate Costs process, 278, 346
    activity cost estimates, 200
    analogous estimating, 197
    basis of estimates, 200
    bottom-up estimating, 197
    cost management plan, 192, 195
    cost of quality, 199
    enterprise environmental factors, 196
    expert judgment, 196
    group decision-making techniques, 200
    human resource management plan, 195
    organizational process assets, 196
    overview, 193–195
    parametric estimating, 197
    project document updates, 200–201
    project management software, 199
    project schedule, 195
    reserve analysis, 198–199
    risk register, 196
    scope baseline, 195
    three-point estimating, 197–198
    vendor bid analysis, 199
estimates
    accuracy of, 150
    Estimate Activity Durations process, 150–153
    Estimate Activity Resources process, 144–145
    padding, 154
estimate to complete (ETC), 173, 213
ETC (estimate to complete), 173, 213
ethics and professional conduct
    fairness, 458–459
    honesty, 460–461
    overview, 453–454
    respect, 457–458
    responsibility, 454–456
EVA (Economic Value Add), 37
EV (earned value), 210. *See also* earned value management
expected monetary value (EMV) analysis, 361
expert judgment
    Close Project or Phase process, 73
    Conduct Procurements process, 400
    Control Communications process, 326
    Control Stakeholder Engagement process, 443
    Create WBS process, 106
    Define Activities process, 133
    Define scope process, 101
    Determine Budget process, 204
    Develop Project Charter process, 42
    Develop Project Management Plan process, 48–49
    Direct and Manage Project Work process, 55
    Estimate Activity Durations process, 149
    Estimate Activity Resources process, 144
    Estimate Costs process, 196
    Identify Risks process, 349
    Identify Stakeholders process, 428
    Monitor and Control Project Work process, 61
    Perform Integrated Change Control process, 68
    Perform Qualitative Risk Analysis process, 355
    Perform Quantitative Risk Analysis process, 363
    Plan Cost Management process, 191
    Plan Human Resource Management process, 277
    Plan Procurement Management process, 393
    Plan Risk Management process, 339

exploratory study

    Plan Risk Responses process, 366
    Plan Schedule Management process, 129
    Plan Scope Management process, 90
    Plan Stakeholder Management process, 433
exploratory study, 62
expression of interest (EOI), 394
external dependencies, 139

F

facilitated workshops
    Collect requirements process, 95
    Define scope process, 101
facilitation techniques
    Develop Project Charter process, 42–43
    Develop Project Management Plan process, 49
failure mode and effect analysis (FMEA), 62, 240
fairness, 458–459
fast tracking, 166
feedback, 317
FF (finish-to-finish) relationship, 138
FFP (fixed-price contract), 402
Fielder's Contingency theory, 286
final product, service, or result transition, 74
finish-to-finish (FF) relationship, 138
finish-to-start (FS) relationship, 137
fishbone diagram, 235
five nines reliability, 231
five-stage model, Tuckman, 291
fixed costs, 193
fixed-price contract (FFP), 402
fixed-price incentive fee contract (FPIF), 402
fixed-price with economic price adjustment contract
    (FP-EPA), 402
float, 161
flowcharts, 235–236
FMEA (failure mode and effect analysis), 62, 240
focus groups, 95
forecasting, 212–214
formal communication, 318
FP-EPA (fixed-price with economic price adjustment
    contract), 402
FPIF (fixed-price incentive fee contract), 402
FS (finish-to-start) relationship, 137
functional manager, 268–269
functional organizational structure, 274
funding limit reconciliation, 205
FV (future value), 37–38

G

Gantt (graphical analysis and numerical tracking
    tool), 50, 127, 166–167
Gardner grid, 427
gold plating, 66, 102
grade, 231
graphical analysis and numerical tracking tool
    (Gantt), 50, 127, 166–167
ground rules, 293
group creativity techniques, 95
group decision-making techniques
    Collect requirements process, 96
    Estimate Activity Durations process, 153–154
    Estimate Costs process, 200
    Validate Scope process, 110
grouping methods, 62

H

Herzberg's Motivation-Hygiene Theory, 287
histograms, 238
historical information, 128
historical relationships, 204
honesty, 460–461
human resource management
    Acquire Project Team process, 279–283
    defined, 267–278
    Develop Project Team process
        inputs, 284–285
        outputs, 294
        overview, 284
        tools and techniques, 285–293
    Manage Project Team process
        inputs, 296–297
        outputs, 299–300
        overview, 296
        tools and techniques, 297–299
    Plan Human Resource Management process
        inputs, 267–268
        outputs, 278
        overview, 267
        tools and techniques, 268–277
Human Resource Management knowledge area, 143
human resource management plan, 278
    Acquire Project Team process, 279–280
    Develop Project Team process, 284

in Estimate Costs process, 195
Identify Risks process, 345
Manage Project Team process, 296

I

Identify Risks process, 203, 233
    inputs
        activity cost estimates, 345
        activity duration estimates, 346
        cost management plan, 344–345
        enterprise environmental factors, 346
        human resource management plan, 345
        organizational process assets, 346
        overview, 344
        procurement documents, 346
        project documents, 346
        quality management plan, 345
        risk management plan, 344
        schedule management plan, 345
        scope baseline, 345
        stakeholder register, 346
    outputs
        overview, 349
        risk register, 350
    overview, 343–344
    tools and techniques
        checklist analysis, 348
        documentation reviews, 347
        expert judgment, 349
        information-gathering techniques, 347
        overview, 347
        SWOT analysis, 349
Identify Stakeholders process, 36, 233, 432
    inputs
        enterprise environmental factors, 426
        organizational process assets, 426
        overview, 425
        procurement documents, 426
        project charter, 425
    outputs
        overview, 428
        stakeholder register, 429–430
    overview, 425
    tools and techniques
        expert judgment, 428
        meetings, 428
        overview, 426
        stakeholder analysis, 426–428
IFB (invitation for bid), 394
impact matrix, 342
independent estimates, 400
indirect costs, 194
influence diagram, 349
influencing, 424
informal communication, 318
information-gathering techniques, 347
information management systems, 322
inputs
    Acquire Project Team process, 279–280
    Close Procurements process, 411
    Collect requirements process, 94–95
    Conduct Procurements process
        make or buy decisions, 398
        organizational process assets, 399
        overview, 397
        procurement documents, 398
        procurement management plan, 397
        procurement statement of work, 398–399
        project documents, 398
        seller proposals, 398
        source selection criteria, 398
    Control Communications process, 324–325
    Control Procurements process, 406
    Control Quality process, 251–252
    Control Risks process, 369–370
    Control Schedule process, 169–170
    Control Scope process, 113–114
    Control Stakeholder Engagement process
        issue log, 441
        overview, 441
        project documents, 442
        project management plan, 441
        work performance data, 442
    Create WBS process
        enterprise environmental factors, 104
        organizational process assets, 105
        overview, 104
        project scope statement, 104
        requirements documentation, 104
        scope management plan, 104
    Define Activities process, 132
    Define scope process
        organizational process assets, 101
        overview, 100

inputs

        project charter, 100
        requirements documentation, 100
        scope management plan, 100
    Develop Project Team process
        human resource management plan, 284
        overview, 284
        project staff assignments, 285
        resource calendars, 285
    Develop Schedule process, 158–160
    Estimate Activity Durations process
        activity attributes document, 148
        activity list, 148
        activity resource requirements, 148
        enterprise environmental factors, 149
        organizational process assets, 149
        overview, 148
        project scope statement, 148–149
        resource breakdown structure, 149
        resource calendars, 148
        risk register, 149
        schedule management plan, 148
    Estimate Activity Resources process
        activity attributes, 143
        activity cost estimates, 144
        activity list, 143
        enterprise environmental factors, 144
        organizational process assets, 144
        overview, 143
        resource calendars, 143
        risk register, 144
        schedule management plan, 143
    Identify Risks process
        activity cost estimates, 345
        activity duration estimates, 346
        cost management plan, 344–345
        enterprise environmental factors, 346
        human resource management plan, 345
        organizational process assets, 346
        overview, 344
        procurement documents, 346
        project documents, 346
        quality management plan, 345
        risk management plan, 344
        schedule management plan, 345
        scope baseline, 345
        stakeholder register, 346
    Identify Stakeholders process
        enterprise environmental factors, 426
        organizational process assets, 426
        overview, 425
        procurement documents, 426
        project charter, 425
    Manage Communications process, 320–321
    Manage Project Team process, 296–297
    Manage Stakeholder Engagement process, 437
    Perform Qualitative Risk Analysis process
        enterprise environmental factors, 353
        organizational process assets, 353
        overview, 352
        risk management plan, 352
        risk register, 352
        scope baseline, 352
    Perform Quality Assurance process, 244
    Perform Quantitative Risk Analysis process
        cost management plan, 358
        enterprise environmental factors, 358
        organizational process assets, 359
        overview, 358
        risk management plan, 358
        risk register, 358
        schedule management plan, 358
    Plan Communications Management process, 313–314
    Plan Human Resource Management process, 267–268
    Plan Procurement Management process
        activity cost estimates, 390
        activity resource requirements, 390
        enterprise environmental factors, 391
        organizational process assets, 391–392
        project management plan, 389
        project schedule, 390
        requirements documentation, 390
        risk register, 390
        Stakeholder register, 390–391
    Plan Quality Management process, 233–234
    Plan Risk Management process
        enterprise environmental factors, 338–339
        organizational process assets, 339
        overview, 338
        project charter, 338
        project management plan, 338
        stakeholder register, 338
    Plan Risk Responses process
        overview, 364
        risk management plan, 364
        risk register, 365

Plan Schedule Management process
  enterprise environmental factors, 128
  organizational process assets, 128
  overview, 127
  project charter, 128
  project management plan, 128
Plan Scope Management process
  enterprise environmental factors, 89
  organizational process assets, 90
  overview, 89
  project charter, 89
  project management plan, 89
Plan Stakeholder Management process
  enterprise environmental factors, 432
  organizational process assets, 433
  project management plan, 432
  stakeholder register, 432
Sequence Activities process
  enterprise environmental factors, 136
  milestone list, 136
  organizational process assets, 136
  project scope statement, 136
Validate Scope process
  overview, 109
  project management plan, 109
  requirements documentation, 109
  requirements traceability matrix, 110
  verified deliverables, 110
  work performance data, 110
inspections
  Control Procurements process, 407
  Control Quality process, 252
  technique, 110
interactive communication, 317
internal dependencies, 139
Internal Rate of Return (IRR), 37
International Organization for Standardization (ISO), 2, 230
interpersonal skills
  Develop Project Team process, 285–290
  Manage Project Team process, 299
  Manage Stakeholder Engagement process, 438
interrelationship digraphs, 246
interviews, 95, 347
invitation for bid (IFB), 394
IRR (Internal Rate of Return), 37
Ishikawa diagram, 235
Ishikawa, Kaoru, 239

ISO 9000 standard, 244
ISO/IEC 15288 standard, 104
ISO (International Organization for Standardization), 2, 230
issue log
  Control Communications process, 325
  Control Stakeholder Engagement process, 441
  Manage Project Team process, 297
  Manage Stakeholder Engagement process, 439

J

JAD (joint application design/development sessions), 95
JIT (just in time), 231
joint application design/development sessions (JAD), 95
Juran, Joseph, 232, 237
just in time (JIT), 231

K

kaizen, 230
key performance indicators (KPIs), 297
kick-off meeting, 63, 433
KJ Methods diagrams, 245
KPIs (key performance indicators), 297

L

lags
  Control Schedule process, 172
  Develop Schedule process, 165
  Sequence Activities process, 139–140
late finish (LF), 161
late start (LS), 161
leads
  Control Schedule process, 172
  Develop Schedule process, 165
  Sequence Activities process, 139–140
LF (late finish), 161
linear programming, 38
litigation, 412
LS (late start), 161
lump sum contract, 402

M

make or buy analysis
    Conduct Procurements process, 398
    Plan Procurement Management process, 392, 395
Manage Communications process
    inputs, 320–321
    outputs, 322–323
    overview, 320
    tools and techniques, 321–322
management reserve, 154
management skills, 439
Manage Project Team process
    inputs, 296–297
    outputs, 299–300
    overview, 296
    tools and techniques, 297–299
Manage Stakeholder Engagement process, 434
    inputs, 437
    outputs
        change requests, 439
        issue log, 439
        organizational process assets updates, 440
        overview, 439
        project documents updates, 440
        project management plan updates, 439
    overview, 436
    tools and techniques
        communications methods, 438
        interpersonal skills, 438
        management skills, 439
        overview, 437
mandatory dependencies, 139
market research, 393
Maslow's hierarchy of needs, 287
mathematical modeling, 362
matrix, 427
matrix diagrams, 248
matrix organization, 275
McClelland's Human Motivation, Achievement, or Three Needs Theory, 288
McGregor's Theory X and Theory Y, 288
mediation, 412
meetings
    Close Project or Phase process, 73
    Control Communications process, 326
    Control Stakeholder Engagement process, 443
    Direct and Manage Project Work process, 55
    Identify Stakeholders process, 428
    making productive, 49
    management of, 43
    Monitor and Control Project Work process, 63
    Perform Integrated Change Control process, 68–69
    Plan Communications Management process, 318
    Plan Cost Management process, 191
    Plan Human Resource Management process, 277
    Plan Procurement Management process, 393
    Plan Quality Management process, 240
    Plan Risk Management process, 340
    Plan Schedule Management process, 129
    Plan Scope Management process, 90
    Plan Stakeholder Management process, 433
memorandum of understanding (MOU), 40
methodologies, of project management, 16
milestone list
    Define Activities process, 134–135
    Sequence Activities process, 136
minus sign (-), 140
modeling techniques
    Control Schedule process, 171–172
    Develop Schedule process, 165
Monitor and Control Project Work process, 253
    analytical techniques, 61–63, 73
    change requests, 63
    cost forecasts, 60
    enterprise environmental factors, 61
    expert judgment, 61
    meetings in, 63
    organizational process assets, 61
    overview, 58–59
    project document updates, 64–65
    project management information system, 63
    project management plan, 59
    project management plan updates, 64
    schedule forecasts, 60
    validated changes, 60
    work performance information, 60–61, 215
Monte Carlo analysis, 165, 172, 362
MOU (memorandum of understanding), 40
multicriteria decision analysis, 281

N

negotiated settlements, 412
negotiation, 281, 412

Net Present Value (NPV), 38, 360
networking, 273
n(n-1)/2 formula, 314–315
non-linear programming, 38
nonverbal communication, 317
normal distributions, 359
NPV (Net Present Value), 38, 360

O

observations
    Collect requirements process, 96
    Manage Project Team process, 298
OBS (organizational breakdown structure), 105
operations management, 11–12
Opportunity Cost, 38
organizational breakdown structure (OBS), 105
organizational charts, 268–273
organizational influences, 13–15
organizational process assets, 14
    Acquire Project Team process, 280
    Close Project or Phase process, 73
    Conduct Procurements process, 399
    Control Communications process, 325
    Control Costs process, 208
    Control Quality process, 252
    Control Schedule process, 170
    Control Scope process, 114
    Create WBS process, 105
    Define Activities process, 132
    Define scope process, 101
    Determine Budget process, 203
    Develop Project Charter process, 41–42
    Develop Project Management Plan process, 48
    Develop Schedule process, 160
    Direct and Manage Project Work process, 54
    Estimate Activity Durations process, 149
    Estimate Activity Resources process, 144
    Estimate Costs process, 196
    Identify Risks process, 346
    Identify Stakeholders process, 426
    Manage Communications process, 321
    Manage Project Team process, 297
    Manage Stakeholder Engagement process, 437
    Monitor and Control Project Work process, 61
    Perform Integrated Change Control process, 68
    Perform Quantitative Risk Analysis process, 359
    Plan Communications Management process, 314
    Plan Cost Management process, 190
    Plan Human Resource Management process, 268
    Plan Procurement Management process, 391–392
    Plan Quality Management process, 234
    Plan Risk Management process, 339
    Plan Schedule Management process, 128
    Plan Scope Management process, 90
    Plan Stakeholder Management process, 433
    Sequence Activities process, 136
    updates to
        Close Procurements process, 413–414
        Close Project or Phase process, 74–75
        Control Communications process, 327
        Control Costs process, 216–217
        Control Procurements process, 410
        Control Quality process, 255
        Control Risks process, 372–373
        Control Schedule process, 175
        Control Scope process, 115
        Control Stakeholder Engagement process, 443–444
        Manage Communications process, 323
        Manage Project Team process, 300
        Manage Stakeholder Engagement process, 440
        Perform Quality Assurance process, 249–250
organizational project management maturity, 7
organizational strategy, 11–12
organizational theory, 274–277
Ouchi's theory Z, 288
outputs
    Acquire Project Team process, 282–283
    Close Procurements process
        closed procurements, 413
        organizational process assets updates, 413–414
        overview, 413
    Collect requirements process
        overview, 97
        requirements documentation, 97–98
        requirements traceability matrix, 98–99
    Conduct Procurements process
        agreements, 401–403
        change requests, 403
        overview, 400–401
        project documents updates, 403–404
        project management plan updates, 403
        resource calendars, 403
        selected sellers, 400–401

outputs

Control Communications process, 326–327
Control Procurements process
    change requests, 409
    organizational process assets updates, 410
    overview, 409
    project documents updates, 410
    project management plan updates, 409
    work performance information, 409
Control Quality process, 253–256
Control Risks process
    organizational process assets updates, 372–373
    overview, 371
    project documents updates, 372
    project management plan updates, 372
    work performance information, 371
Control Schedule process, 173–175
Control Scope process, 114
Control Stakeholder Engagement process
    change requests, 443
    organizational process assets updates, 443–444
    overview, 443
    project documents updates, 443
    work performance information, 443
Create WBS process
    overview, 106
    project document updates, 108
    scope baseline, 106–107
Define Activities process
    activity attributes, 134
    activity list, 133
    milestone list, 134–135
    overview, 133
Define scope process
    overview, 102
    project document updates, 102–103
    project scope statement, 102
Develop Project Team process, 294
Develop Schedule process, 166–168
Estimate Activity Durations process
    activity duration estimates, 155
    overview, 155
Estimate Activity Resources process
    activity resource requirements, 145
    overview, 145
    project documents updates, 146
    resource breakdown structure, 145–146
Identify Risks process
    overview, 349
    risk register, 350

Identify Stakeholders process
    overview, 428
    stakeholder register, 429–430
Manage Communications process, 322–323
Manage Project Team process, 299–300
Manage Stakeholder Engagement process
    change requests, 439
    issue log, 439
    organizational process assets updates, 440
    overview, 439
    project documents updates, 440
    project management plan updates, 439
Perform Qualitative Risk Analysis process
    overview, 355
    project documents updates, 355–356
Perform Quality Assurance process, 249–250
Perform Quantitative Risk Analysis process, 363
Plan Communications Management process, 318–319
Plan Human Resource Management process, 278
Plan Procurement Management process
    change requests, 396
    make or buy decisions, 395
    overview, 394
    procurement documents, 394–395
    procurement management plan, 394
    procurement statement of work, 394
    project documents updates, 396
    source selection criteria, 395
Plan Quality Management process, 240–242
Plan Risk Management process
    overview, 340
    risk management plan, 341–343
Plan Risk Responses process, 367
Plan Schedule Management process
    overview, 129
    schedule management plan, 129–130
Plan Scope Management process
    overview, 90
    requirements management plan, 91–92
    scope management plan, 91
Plan Stakeholder Management process
    overview, 434
    project documents updates, 434–435
    stakeholder management plan, 434
Sequence Activities process
    overview, 140
    project documents updates, 141–142
    project schedule network diagrams, 140–141

Validate Scope process
    accepted deliverables, 111
    change requests, 111
    overview, 111
    project documents updates, 111–112
    work performance information, 111

P

padding estimates, 154
paralingual communication, 317
parametric estimating
    Estimate Activity Durations process, 150
    Estimate Costs process, 197
Pareto principle, 237
Payback Period, 38
payment systems, 408
PDCA (Plan-Do-Check-Act) cycle, 16
PDM (precedence diagramming method), 135
PDPC (process decision program chart), 246
performance reporting
    Control Procurements process, 407
    Manage Communications process, 322
performance reviews
    Control Costs process, 215
    Control Schedule process, 170–171
Perform Integrated Change Control process, 114, 254, 372, 437
    approved change requests, 54, 69
    change control tools, 69
    change log, 69
    change requests, 67–68
    enterprise environmental factors, 68
    expert judgment, 68
    meetings in, 68–69
    organizational process assets, 68
    overview, 65–67
    project document updates, 70
    project management plan, 67
    project management plan updates, 69
    work performance reports, 67
Perform Qualitative Risk Analysis process
    inputs
        enterprise environmental factors, 353
        organizational process assets, 353
        overview, 352
        risk management plan, 352
        risk register, 352
        scope baseline, 352
    outputs
        overview, 355
        project documents updates, 355–356
    overview, 351–352
    tools and techniques
        expert judgment, 355
        overview, 353
        probability and impact matrix, 354
        risk categorization, 354
        risk data quality assessment, 354
        risk probability and impact assessment, 353
        risk urgency assessment, 355
Perform Quality Assurance process, 240
    inputs, 244
    outputs, 249–250
    overview, 243–244
    tools and techniques
        overview, 245
        process analysis, 249
        quality audits, 248–249
        quality management and control tools, 245–248
Perform Quantitative Risk Analysis process
    inputs
        cost management plan, 358
        enterprise environmental factors, 358
        organizational process assets, 359
        overview, 358
        risk management plan, 358
        risk register, 358
        schedule management plan, 358
    outputs, 363
    overview, 357
    tools and techniques
        data gathering and representation techniques, 359
        expert judgment, 363
        overview, 359
        quantitative risk analysis and modeling techniques, 360–362
personnel assessment tools, 293
PERT (Program Evaluation and Review Technique), 150, 153, 197
phases, within projects, 15
Plan Communications Management process, 437
    inputs, 313–314
    outputs, 318–319

Plan Cost Management process

    overview, 313
    tools and techniques
        communications methods, 317–318
        communications models, 316–317
        communications requirements analysis, 314–315
        communications technology, 315
        meetings, 318
        overview, 314
Plan Cost Management process
    analytical techniques, 191
    cost management plan, 192
    enterprise environmental factors, 190
    expert judgment, 191
    meetings in, 191
    organizational process assets, 190
    project management plan, 189
Plan-Do-Check-Act (PDCA) cycle, 16, 232
Plan Human Resource Management process, 278
    inputs, 267–268
    outputs, 278
    overview, 267
    tools and techniques
        expert judgment, 277
        meetings, 277
        networking, 273
        organizational charts and position descriptions, 268–273
        organizational theory, 274–277
planned value (PV), 209
Plan Procurement Management process, 98
    inputs
        activity cost estimates, 390
        enterprise environmental factors, 391
        organizational process assets, 391–392
        overview, 389
        project management plan, 389
        project schedule, 390
        requirements documentation, 390
        risk register, 390
        Stakeholder register, 390–391
    outputs
        change requests, 396
        make or buy decisions, 395
        overview, 394
        procurement documents, 394–395
        procurement management plan, 394
        procurement statement of work, 394
        project documents updates, 396
        source selection criteria, 395

    overview, 389
    tools and techniques
        expert judgment, 393
        make or buy analysis, 392
        market research, 393
        meetings, 393
        overview, 392
Plan Quality Management process, 98
    inputs, 233–234
    outputs, 240–242
    overview, 232–233
    tools and techniques
        additional quality planning tools, 240
        benchmarking, 235–239
        cost-benefit analysis, 234
        cost of quality, 234–235
        design of experiments, 240
        design of experiments tool, 240
        meetings, 240
        overview, 234
        seven basic quality tools, 235–239
        statistical sampling, 240
Plan Risk Management process
    inputs
        enterprise environmental factors, 338–339
        organizational process assets, 339
        overview, 338
        project charter, 338
        project management plan, 338
        stakeholder register, 338
    outputs
        overview, 340
        risk management plan, 341–343
    overview, 338
    tools and techniques
        analytical techniques, 339
        expert judgment, 339
        meetings, 340
        overview, 339
Plan Risk Responses process
    inputs
        overview, 364
        risk management plan, 364
        risk register, 365
    outputs, 367
    overview, 364
    tools and techniques
        contingent response strategies, 366
        expert judgment, 366

procurement management

    overview, 365
    strategies for negative risks or threats, 365
    strategies for positive risks or opportunities, 366

Plan Schedule Management process
    inputs
        enterprise environmental factors, 128
        organizational process assets, 128
        overview, 127
        project charter, 128
        project management plan, 128
    outputs
        overview, 129
        schedule management plan, 129–130
    overview, 127
    tools and techniques
        analytical techniques, 129
        expert judgment, 129
        meetings, 129
        overview, 128

Plan Scope Management process
    inputs
        enterprise environmental factors, 89
        organizational process assets, 90
        overview, 89
        project charter, 89
        project management plan, 89
    outputs
        overview, 90
        requirements management plan, 91–92
        scope management plan, 91
    overview, 88
    tools and techniques, 90

Plan Stakeholder Management process, stakeholder management
    inputs
        enterprise environmental factors, 432
        organizational process assets, 433
        overview, 432
        project management plan, 432
        stakeholder register, 432
    outputs
        overview, 434
        project documents updates, 434–435
        stakeholder management plan, 434
    overview, 431
    tools and techniques
        analytical techniques, 433–434
        expert judgment, 433
        meetings, 433
        overview, 433

plus sign (+), 140
PMBOK® Guide, 2–4
PMI Code of Ethics and Professional Conduct, 453–454
PMI (Project Management Institute), 7, 48, 453
PMO (Project Management Office), 7, 42
PMP (Project Management Professional) certification, 4
point of total assumption (PTA), 402–403
portfolio manager, 270
portfolios, 5–8
preassignment, 280
precedence diagramming method (PDM), 135, 137–138
precision, 230
predecessor relationship, 137
Present Value, 37
preventive action, 57, 63
prioritization matrices, 247
proactive, 436
probability and impact matrix, 342, 354
probability distributions, 359
process analysis, 249
process decision program chart (PDPC), 246
process improvement plan
    Perform Quality Assurance process, 244
    Plan Quality Management process, 241
procurement agreement, 401
procurement audits, 412
procurement documents
    Close Procurements process, 411
    Conduct Procurements process, 398
    Control Procurements process, 406
    Identify Risks process, 346
    Identify Stakeholders process, 426
    Plan Procurement Management process, 394–395
procurement management
    Close Procurements process
        inputs, 411
        outputs, 413–414
        overview, 411
        tools and techniques, 412–413
    Conduct Procurements process
        inputs, 397–399
        outputs, 401–403
        overview, 397
        tools and techniques, 399–401
    Control Procurements process
        inputs, 406
        outputs, 409–410

procurement management plan

    overview, 405
    tools and techniques, 407–409
  defined, 388
  overview, 387
  Plan Procurement Management process
    inputs, 389–392
    outputs, 394–396
    overview, 389
    tools and techniques, 392–393
procurement management plan
  Conduct Procurements process, 397
  Plan Procurement Management process, 394
procurement negotiations, 400–401
procurement performance reviews, 407
procurement statement of work
  Conduct Procurements process, 398–399
  Plan Procurement Management process, 394
product analysis, 101
Program Evaluation and Review Technique (PERT), 150, 153, 197
program manager, 270
program of projects, 5–8
progressive elaboration, 9
project calendars
  Control Schedule process, 170
  Develop Schedule process, 167
project charter
  Collect requirements process, 94
  Define scope process, 100
  Develop Project Charter process, 43–44
  Develop Project Management Plan process, 46
  Identify Stakeholders process, 425
  Plan Cost Management process, 190
  Plan Risk Management process, 338
  Plan Schedule Management process, 128
  Plan Scope Management process, 89
project communications
  Control Communications process, 325
  Manage Communications process, 322
Project Communications management group, 18
project coordinator, 269
project cost management
  Control Costs process
    change requests, 216
    costs forecasts, 216
    earned value management, 209–211
    forecasting, 212–214
    organizational process assets, 208
    organizational process assets updates, 216–217
    overview, 207
    performance reviews, 215
    project document updates updates, 216
    project funding requirements, 208
    project management plan, 208
    project management software, 215
    reserve analysis, 215
    TCPI, 214
    work performance data, 208
    work performance information, 215
  Determine Budget process
    activity cost estimates, 202
    agreements, 203
    basis of estimates, 202
    cost aggregation, 204
    cost baseline, 205–206
    cost management plan, 202
    expert judgment, 204
    funding limit reconciliation, 205
    historical relationships, 204
    organizational process assets, 203
    overview, 201–202
    project document updates, 206–207
    project funding requirements, 206
    project schedule, 203
    reserve analysis, 204
    resource calendars, 203
    risk register, 203
    scope baseline, 202
  Estimate Costs process, 200–201
    activity cost estimates, 200
    analogous estimating, 197
    basis of estimates, 200
    bottom-up estimating, 197
    cost management plan, 195
    cost of quality, 199
    expert judgment, 196
    group decision-making techniques, 200
    human resource management plan, 195
    organizational process assets, 196
    overview, 193–195
    parametric estimating, 197
    project management software, 199
    project schedule, 195
    reserve analysis, 198–199
    risk register, 196
    scope baseline, 195

project integration management

    three-point estimating, 197–198
    vendor bid analysis, 199
  overview, 187–188, 189
  Plan Cost Management process
    analytical techniques, 191
    cost management plan, 192
    enterprise environmental factors, 190
    expert judgment, 191
    meetings in, 191
    organizational process assets, 190
    overview, 189
    project charter, 190
    project management plan, 189
Project Cost management group, 18
project documents
  Conduct Procurements process, 398
  Control Quality process, 252
  Control Stakeholder Engagement process, 442
  Identify Risks process, 346
  Perform Quality Assurance process, 244
project document updates
  Control Costs process, 216
  Determine Budget process, 206–207
  Direct and Manage Project Work process, 57–58
  Estimate Costs process, 200–201
  Monitor and Control Project Work process, 64–65
  Perform Integrated Change Control process, 70
project expeditor, 269
project funding requirements
  Control Costs process, 208
  Determine Budget process, 206
Project Human Resource management group, 18
project integration management
  Close Project or Phase process
    accepted deliverables, 73
    analytical techniques, 73
    expert judgment, 73
    final product, service, or result transition, 74
    meetings in, 73
    organizational process assets, 73
    organizational process assets updates, 74–75
    overview, 70–72
    project management plan, 72
  Develop Project Charter process
    agreements, 40–41
    business case, 39–40
    enterprise environmental factors, 41
    expert judgment, 42
    facilitation techniques, 42–43
    organizational process assets, 41–42
    overview, 35–38
    project charter output, 43–44
    SOW, 39
  Develop Project Management Plan process
    enterprise environmental factors, 47
    expert judgment, 48–49
    facilitation techniques, 49
    organizational process assets, 48
    outputs from other processes as inputs, 46–47
    overview, 45
    project charter input, 46
    project management plan output, 50–52
  Direct and Manage Project Work process
    approved change requests, 54
    change requests, 57
    deliverables, 56
    enterprise environmental factors, 54
    expert judgment, 55
    meetings in, 55
    organizational process assets, 54
    overview, 52–53
    project document updates, 57–58
    project management information system, 55
    project management plan, 53–54
    project management plan updates, 57
    work performance data, 56–57
  Monitor and Control Project Work process
    analytical techniques, 61–63
    change requests, 63
    cost forecasts, 60
    enterprise environmental factors, 61
    expert judgment, 61
    meetings in, 63
    organizational process assets, 61
    overview, 58–59
    project document updates, 64–65
    project management information system, 63
    project management plan, 59
    project management plan updates, 64
    schedule forecasts, 60
    validated changes, 60
    work performance information, 60–61
  overview, 31–33
  Perform Integrated Change Control process
    approved change requests, 69
    change control tools, 69

Project Integration management group

    change log, 69
    change requests, 67–68
    enterprise environmental factors, 68
    expert judgment, 68
    meetings in, 68–69
    organizational process assets, 68
    overview, 65–67
    project document updates, 70
    project management plan, 67
    project management plan updates, 69
    work performance reports, 67
Project Integration management group, 17
projectized organizations, 275
project life cycle, 15–19
project management
    organizational influences on, 13–15
    overview, 8–10
    versus operations management, 11
project management information system
    Direct and Manage Project Work process, 55
    Monitor and Control Project Work process, 63
Project Management Institute (PMI), 7, 48, 97, 453
project management methodologies, 16
Project Management Office (PMO), 7, 42
project management plan
    Close Procurements process, 411
    Close Project or Phase process, 72
    Control Communications process, 324
    Control Costs process, 208
    Control Procurements process, 406
    Control Risks process, 369
    Control Schedule process, 169
    Control Scope process, 113
    Control Stakeholder Engagement process, 441
    Develop Project Management Plan process, 50–52
    Direct and Manage Project Work process, 53–54
    Monitor and Control Project Work process, 59
    Perform Integrated Change Control process, 67
    Plan Communications Management process, 314
    Plan Human Resource Management process, 267
    Plan Procurement Management process, 389
    Plan Quality Management process, 233
    Plan Risk Management process, 338
    Plan Schedule Management process, 128
    Plan Scope Management process, 89
    Plan Stakeholder Management process, 432
    updates to
        Acquire Project Team process, 282–283
        Conduct Procurements process, 403
        Control Costs process, 216
        Control Procurements process, 409
        Control Quality process, 254
        Control Risks process, 372
        Control Schedule process, 174
        Control Scope process, 115
        Develop Schedule process, 168
        Direct and Manage Project Work process, 57
        Manage Communications process, 323
        Manage Project Team process, 300
        Manage Stakeholder Engagement process, 439
        Monitor and Control Project Work process, 64
        Perform Quality Assurance process, 249
        Plan Risk Responses process, 367
        Validate Scope process, 109
Project Management Professional (PMP) certification, 4
project management software
    Control Costs process, 215
    Control Schedule process, 171
    Estimate Activity Resources process, 145
    Estimate Costs process, 199
project manager, 268
project mandate, 43
project performance appraisals, 298
project phases, 15
project procurement management. *See* procurement management
Project Procurement management group, 19
Project Quality management group, 18
Project Risk management group, 18
projects, 5–8
project schedule
    Control Schedule process, 170
    Determine Budget process, 203
    Develop Schedule process, 166–167
    Estimate Costs process, 195
    Plan Procurement Management process, 390
project schedule network diagrams
    Develop Schedule process, 158
    Sequence Activities process, 140–141
Project Scope management. *See* Scope management
Project Scope management group, 17
project scope statement
    Create WBS process, 104
    Define scope process, 102
    Develop Schedule process, 159
    Estimate Activity Durations process, 148–149
    Sequence Activities process, 136
project selection process, 36

project sponsor, 271
project staff assignments
  Acquire Project Team process, 282
  Develop Project Team process, 285
  Develop Schedule process, 159
  Manage Project Team process, 297
Project Stakeholder Identification Management, 36
project stakeholder management. *See* stakeholder management
Project Stakeholder management group, 19
project steering committee, 271
Project Time management group, 18
proposal evaluation techniques, 400
prototypes, 96
PTA (point of total assumption), 402–403
published estimating data, 144–145
pull communication, 317, 438
push communication, 317, 438
PV (planned value), 209

Q

QFD (quality function deployment), 95
qualitative risk analysis, 352
quality, 231
quality audits, 248–249
quality checklists
  Control Quality process, 251
  Plan Quality Management process, 242
quality control measurements
  Control Quality process, 253
  Perform Quality Assurance process, 244
quality function deployment (QFD), 95
quality management, 232
  Control Quality process, 250–255
  defined, 230–232
  overview, 229
  Perform Quality Assurance process
    inputs, 244
    outputs, 249–250
    overview, 243–244
    tools and techniques, 245–249
  Plan Quality Management process
    inputs, 233–234
    outputs, 240–242
    overview, 232–233
    tools and techniques, 234–240

quality management plan, 232
  Control Quality process, 251
  Identify Risks process, 345
  Perform Quality Assurance process, 244
  Plan Quality Management process, 241
quality metrics
  Control Quality process, 251
  Perform Quality Assurance process, 244
  Plan Quality Management process, 242
quality planning tools, 240
quantitative risk analysis and modeling techniques, 360–362
questionnaires and surveys, 96

R

RACI chart, 273
RAM (responsibility assignment matrix), 273
RBS (resource breakdown structure), 105
RBS (risk breakdown structure), 105, 341, 354
recognition, 293
records management system
  Close Procurements process, 413
  Control Procurements process, 408–409
regression analysis, 62
reporting systems
  Control Communications process, 326
  Control Stakeholder Engagement process, 442
request for information (RFI), 394
request for proposal (RFP), 394
request for quotation (RFQ), 394
requirements, defined, 93
requirements documentation
  Collect requirements process, 97–98
  Control Scope process, 113
  Create WBS process, 104
  Define scope process, 100
  Plan Procurement Management process, 390
  Plan Quality Management process, 233
  Validate Scope process, 109
requirements management plan
  Collect requirements process, 94
  Plan Scope Management process, 91–92
requirements traceability matrix
  Collect requirements process, 98–99
  Control Scope process, 113
  Validate Scope process, 110

reserve analysis
- Control Costs process, 215
- Control Risks process, 371
- defined, 62
- Determine Budget process, 204
- Estimate Activity Durations process, 154–155
- Estimate Costs process, 198–199

resource breakdown structure (RBS), 105
- Develop Schedule process, 159
- Estimate Activity Durations process, 149
- Estimate Activity Resources process, 145–146

resource calendars
- Acquire Project Team process, 282
- Conduct Procurements process, 403
- Determine Budget process, 203
- Develop Project Team process, 285
- Develop Schedule process, 158
- Estimate Activity Durations process, 148
- Estimate Activity Resources process, 143

resource leveling, 164

resource optimization techniques
- Control Schedule process, 171
- Develop Schedule process, 164

resource smoothing, 164
respect, 457–458
responsibility, 454–456
responsibility assignment matrix (RAM), 273
Return on Invested Capital (ROIC), 38
Return on Investment (ROI), 38
rewards, 293
RFI (request for information), 394
RFP (request for proposal), 394
RFQ (request for quotation), 394
risk audits, 370
risk breakdown structure (RBS), 105, 341, 354
risk categorization, 354
risk data quality assessment, 354
risk management
- Control Risks process
  - inputs, 369–370
  - outputs, 372–373
  - overview, 368
  - tools and techniques, 370–371
- defined, 336–337
- Identify Risks process
  - inputs, 344–346
  - outputs, 350
  - overview, 343–344
  - tools and techniques, 347–349

- overview, 335
- Perform Qualitative Risk Analysis process
  - inputs, 352–353
  - outputs, 355–356
  - overview, 351–352
  - tools and techniques, 353–355
- Perform Quantitative Risk Analysis process
  - inputs, 358–359
  - outputs, 363
  - overview, 357
  - tools and techniques, 359–363
- Plan Risk Management process
  - inputs, 338–339
  - outputs, 341–343
  - overview, 338
  - tools and techniques, 339–341
- Plan Risk Responses process
  - inputs, 364–365
  - outputs, 367
  - overview, 364
  - tools and techniques, 366

Risk Management knowledge area, 233
risk management plan
- Identify Risks process, 344
- Perform Qualitative Risk Analysis process, 352
- Perform Quantitative Risk Analysis process, 358
- Plan Risk Management process, 341–343
- Plan Risk Responses process, 364

risk probability and impact assessment, 353
risk reassessment, 370
risk register
- Control Risks process, 369
- Determine Budget process, 203
- Develop Schedule process, 159
- Estimate Activity Durations process, 149
- Estimate Activity Resources process, 144
- Estimate Costs process, 196
- Identify Risks process, 350
- Perform Qualitative Risk Analysis process, 352
- Perform Quantitative Risk Analysis process, 358
- Plan Procurement Management process, 390
- Plan Quality Management process, 233
- Plan Risk Responses process, 365

risk tolerance, 336
risk urgency assessment, 355
ROIC (Return on Invested Capital), 38
ROI (Return on Investment), 38
rolling wave planning, 9, 133
rule of seven, 238

S

salience model, 427–428
scatter diagrams, 239
schedule baseline, 166
schedule compression, 165–166, 172
schedule data
    Control Schedule process, 170
    Develop Schedule process, 167
schedule forecasts
    Control Schedule process, 173–174
    Monitor and Control Project Work process, 60
schedule management plan
    Define Activities process, 132
    Develop Schedule process, 158
    Estimate Activity Durations process, 148
    Estimate Activity Resources process, 143
    Identify Risks process, 345
    Perform Quantitative Risk Analysis process, 358
    Plan Schedule Management process, 129–130
    Sequence Activities process, 136
schedule network analysis, 160
schedule performance index (SPI), 173, 211
schedule variance (SV), 173, 211
scheduling tool
    Control Schedule process, 172
    Develop Schedule process, 166
scope baseline
    Create WBS process, 106–107
    Define Activities process, 132
    Determine Budget process, 202
    Estimate Costs process, 195
    Identify Risks process, 345
    Perform Qualitative Risk Analysis process, 352
scope creep, 66, 102
scope management
    Collect requirements process
        inputs, 94–95
        outputs, 97–99
        overview, 93–94
        tools and techniques, 95–97
    Control Scope process
        inputs, 113–114
        outputs, 114
        overview, 112–113
        tools and techniques, 114
    Create WBS process
        inputs, 104–105
        outputs, 106–108
        overview, 103–104
        tools and techniques, 105–106
    defined, 86–88
    Define scope process
        inputs, 100–101
        outputs, 102–103
        overview, 99–100
        tools and techniques, 101
    overview, 85
    Plan Scope Management process
        inputs, 89–90
        outputs, 90–92
        overview, 88
        tools and techniques, 90
    Validate Scope process
        inputs, 109–110
        outputs, 111–112
        overview, 108–109
        tools and techniques, 110
Scope Management knowledge area, 233
scope management plan
    Collect requirements process, 94
    Create WBS process, 104
    Define scope process, 100
    Plan Scope Management process, 91
S-curve, 205
SD (standard deviations), 151–152
selected sellers, 400–401
seller proposals, 398
sellers, 388
sensitivity analysis, 360
Sequence Activities process
    inputs, 136–137
    outputs
        overview, 140
        project documents updates, 141–142
        project schedule network diagrams, 140–141
    overview, 135–136
    tools and techniques
        applying leads and lags, 139–140
        dependency determination, 139
        overview, 137
        precedence diagramming method, 137–138
SF (start-to-finish) relationship, 138
simple average, 197
SIPOC (Suppliers, Inputs, Process, Outputs, and Customers), 236
Six Sigma, 152, 231
slack, 160–161

source selection criteria
    Conduct Procurements process, 398
    Plan Procurement Management process, 395
SOW (statement of work), 39
specification limit, 238
SPI (schedule performance index), 173, 211
SS (start-to-start) relationship, 138
staffing management plan, 278
stakeholder analysis, 426–428
stakeholder engagement assessment matrix, 433–434
stakeholder management
    Control Stakeholder Engagement process
        inputs, 441–442
        outputs, 443–444
        overview, 441
        tools and techniques, 442–443
    defined, 424–425
    Identify Stakeholders process
        inputs, 426
        outputs, 428–430
        overview, 425
        tools and techniques, 426–428
    Manage Stakeholder Engagement process
        outputs, 439–440
        overview, 436
        tools and techniques, 437–439
    overview, 423
    Plan Stakeholder Management process
        inputs, 432–433
        outputs, 434–435
        tools and techniques, 433–434
Stakeholder Management knowledge area, 233
stakeholder management plan
    Collect requirements process, 94
    Manage Stakeholder Engagement process, 437
    Plan Stakeholder Management process, 434
stakeholder register
    Collect requirements process, 95
    Identify Risks process, 346
    Identify Stakeholders process, 429–430
    Plan Procurement Management process, 390–391
    Plan Quality Management process, 233
    Plan Risk Management process, 338
    Plan Stakeholder Management process, 432
stakeholder risk profile analysis, 339
stakeholders, 424
standard deviations (SD), 151–152
start-to-finish (SF) relationship, 138
start-to-start (SS) relationship, 138

statement of work (SOW), 39
statistical sampling, 240
status meetings, 371
strategies for negative risks or threats, 365
strategies for positive risks or opportunities, 366
strong matrix organization, 275
successor relationship, 137
sunk costs, 194
Suppliers, Inputs, Process, Outputs, and Customers (SIPOC), 236
SV (schedule variance), 173, 211
SWOT analysis, 349

T

tailoring, 3
TCPI (to-complete performance index), 214
team-building activities, 291–293
team performance assessments
    Develop Project Team process, 294
    Manage Project Team process, 297
technical performance measurement, 371
techniques. *See* tools and techniques
three-point estimating
    Estimate Activity Durations process, 150–153
    Estimate Costs process, 197–198
time and material contract (T&M), 402
time management
    Control Schedule process
        inputs, 169–170
        outputs, 173–175
        overview, 169
    Define Activities process
        inputs, 132
        outputs, 133–135
        overview, 131
        tools and techniques, 132–133
    defined, 126–127
    Develop Schedule process
        inputs, 158–160
        outputs, 166–168
        overview, 157
        tools and techniques, 160–166
    Estimate Activity Durations process
        inputs, 148–149
        outputs, 155–156
        overview, 147

Estimate Activity Resources process
    inputs, 143–144
    outputs, 145–146
    overview, 142–143
    tools and techniques, 144–145
overview, 125
Plan Schedule Management process
    inputs, 127–128
    outputs, 129–131
    overview, 127
    tools and techniques, 128–129
Sequence Activities process
    outputs, 140–142
    overview, 135–136
    tools and techniques, 137–140
T&M (time and material) contract, 402
tools and techniques
    Acquire Project Team process, 280–281
    Close Procurements process
        negotiated settlements, 412
        overview, 412
        procurement audits, 412
        records management system, 413
    Collect requirements process
        benchmarking, 97
        context diagrams, 97
        document analysis, 97
        facilitated workshops, 95
        focus groups, 95
        group creativity techniques, 95
        group decision-making techniques, 96
        interviews, 95
        observations, 96
        overview, 95
        prototypes, 96
        questionnaires and surveys, 96
    Conduct Procurements process
        advertising, 400
        analytical techniques, 400
        bidder conference, 399–400
        expert judgment, 400
        independent estimates, 400
        overview, 399
        procurement negotiations, 400–401
        proposal evaluation techniques, 400
    Control Communications process, 325–326
    Control Procurements process
        claims administration, 408
        contract change control system, 407
        inspections and audits, 407
        overview, 407
        payment systems, 408
        performance reporting, 407
        procurement performance reviews, 407
        records management system, 408–409
    Control Quality process, 252–253
    Control Risks process
        overview, 370
        reserve analysis, 371
        risk audits, 370
        risk reassessment, 370
        status meetings, 371
        technical performance measurement, 371
        variance and trend analysis, 370
    Control Schedule process, 170–172
    Control Scope process, 114
    Control Stakeholder Engagement process
        expert judgment, 443
        meetings, 443
        overview, 442
        reporting systems, 442
    Create WBS process
        decomposition, 105
        expert judgment, 106
        overview, 105
    Define Activities process
        decomposition, 133
        expert judgment, 133
        overview, 132
        rolling wave planning, 133
    Define scope process, 101
    Develop Project Team process
        interpersonal skills, 285–290
        overview, 285
        personnel assessment tools, 293
        recognition and rewards, 293
        team-building activities, 291–293
    Develop Schedule process
        critical path method, 160–163
        leads and lags, 165
        modeling techniques, 165
        resource optimization techniques, 164
        schedule compression, 165–166
        schedule network analysis, 160
        scheduling tool, 166
    Estimate Activity Durations process
        analogous estimating, 150
        expert judgment, 149

tools and techniques

    group decision-making techniques, 153–154
    overview, 149
    parametric estimating, 150
    reserve analysis, 154–155
    three-point estimating, 150–153
    tools and techniques, 149–155
Estimate Activity Resources process
    alternative analysis, 144
    bottom-up estimating, 145
    expert judgment, 144
    overview, 144
    project management software, 145
    published estimating data, 144–145
Identify Risks process
    documentation reviews, 347
    expert judgment, 349
    information-gathering techniques, 347
    overview, 347
    SWOT analysis, 349
Identify Stakeholders process
    expert judgment, 428
    meetings, 428
    overview, 426
    stakeholder analysis, 426–428
Manage Communications process, 321–322
Manage Project Team process, 297–299
Manage Stakeholder Engagement process
    communications methods, 438
    interpersonal skills, 438
    management skills updates, 439
    overview, 437
Perform Qualitative Risk Analysis process
    expert judgment, 355
    overview, 353
    probability and impact matrix, 354
    risk categorization, 354
    risk data quality assessment, 354
    risk probability and impact assessment, 353
    risk urgency assessment, 355
Perform Quality Assurance process
    control tools, 245–248
    overview, 245
    process analysis, 249
    quality audits, 248–249
Perform Quantitative Risk Analysis process
    data gathering and representation techniques, 359
    expert judgment, 363

    overview, 359
    quantitative risk analysis and modeling techniques, 360–362
Plan Communications Management process
    communications methods, 317–318
    communications models, 316–317
    communications requirements analysis, 314–315
    communications technology, 315
    meetings, 318
    overview, 314
Plan Human Resource Management process
    meetings, 277
    networking, 273
    organizational charts and position descriptions, 268–273
    organizational theory, 274–277
    overview, 268
Plan Procurement Management process
    expert judgment, 393
    make or buy analysis, 392
    market research, 393
    meetings, 393
    overview, 392
Plan Quality Management process
    basic tools, 235–239
    benchmarking, 235–239
    cost-benefit analysis, 234
    cost of quality, 234–235
    meetings, 240
    overview, 234
    quality planning tools, 240
    statistical sampling, 240
Plan Risk Management process
    analytical techniques, 339
    expert judgment, 339
    meetings, 340
    overview, 339
Plan Risk Responses process
    contingent response strategies, 366
    expert judgment, 366
    overview, 365
    strategies for negative risks or threats, 365
    strategies for positive risks or opportunities, 366
Plan Schedule Management process
    analytical techniques, 129
    expert judgment, 129
    meetings, 129
    overview, 128

Plan Scope Management process, 90
Plan Stakeholder Management process
    analytical techniques, 433–434
    expert judgment, 433
    meetings, 433
    overview, 433
Sequence Activities process
    applying leads and lags, 139–140
    dependency determination, 139
    overview, 137
    precedence diagramming method (PDM), 137–138
Validate Scope process, 110
tornado diagrams, 360
total float, 160
TQM (total quality management), 231
tree diagram, 247
trend analysis, 62, 171
triangular distributions, 359
Tuckman five-stage model, 291

U

uniform distributions, 359
updates
    change request type, 57
    enterprise environmental factors
        Develop Project Team process, 294–295
        Manage Project Team process, 300
    organizational process assets, 74–75
        Close Procurements process, 413–414
        Control Communications process, 327
        Control Costs process, 216–217
        Control Procurements process, 410
        Control Quality process, 255
        Control Risks process, 372–373
        Control Schedule process, 175
        Control Scope process, 115
        Control Stakeholder Engagement process, 443–444
        Manage Communications process, 323
        Manage Project Team process, 300
        Manage Stakeholder Engagement process, 440
        Perform Quality Assurance process, 249–250
    project document
        Control Scope process, 115
        Create WBS process, 108
        Define scope process, 102–103
        Validate Scope process, 111–112
    project documents
        Conduct Procurements process, 403–404
        Control Communications process, 327
        Control Procurements process, 410
        Control Quality process, 255
        Control Schedule process, 174
        Control Stakeholder Engagement process, 443
        Develop Schedule process, 168
        Estimate Activity Durations process, 155–156
        Estimate Activity Resources process, 146
        Manage Communications process, 323
        Manage Project Team process, 300
        Manage Stakeholder Engagement process, 440
        Perform Qualitative Risk Analysis process, 355–356
        Perform Quality Assurance process, 249
        Perform Quantitative Risk Analysis process, 363
        Plan Communications Management process, 319
        Plan Procurement Management process, 396
        Plan Quality Management process, 242
        Plan Risk Responses process, 367
        Plan Stakeholder Management process, 434–435
        Sequence Activities process, 141–142
        updates, Control Risks process, 372
    project management plan
        Acquire Project Team process, 282–283
        Conduct Procurements process, 403
        Control Costs process, 216
        Control Procurements process, 409
        Control Quality process, 254
        Control Risks process, 372
        Control Schedule process, 174
        Control Scope process, 115
        Develop Schedule process, 168
        Manage Communications process, 323
        Manage Project Team process, 300
        Manage Stakeholder Engagement process, 439
        Monitor and Control Project Work process, 64
        Perform Quality Assurance process, 249
        Plan Risk Responses process, 367

V

VAC (variance at completion), 213
validated changes
  Control Quality process, 253–254
  Monitor and Control Project Work process, 60
validated deliverables, 254
Validate Scope process, 91, 98, 254
  inputs
    overview, 109
    project management plan, 109
    requirements documentation, 109
    requirements traceability matrix, 110
    verified deliverables, 110
    work performance data, 110
  outputs
    accepted deliverables, 111
    change requests, 111
    overview, 111
    project documents updates, 111–112
    work performance information, 111
  overview, 108–109
  tools and techniques, 110
validation vs. verification, 60
values
  fairness, 458–459
  honesty, 460–461
  respect, 457–458
  responsibility, 454–456
variable costs, 193
variance
  analysis, 114, 370
  calculating, 153
variance at completion (VAC), 213
vendor bid analysis, 199
verification vs. validation, 60
verified deliverables, 110
virtual teams, 281
Vroom's Expectancy Theory, 287

W

war room, 293
WBS (work breakdown structure), 104–107, 193, 195, 202, 272, 346
weak matrix organization, 275
weighted average, 197
what-if scenario analysis, 165, 172
whistleblower, 455
workaround, 366
work breakdown structure (WBS), 104–107, 193, 195, 202, 272, 346
work order, 43
work packages, 105
work performance data
  Control Communications process, 325
  Control Costs process, 208
  Control Procurements process, 406
  Control Quality process, 251
  Control Risks process, 369
  Control Schedule process, 170
  Control Scope process, 113
  Control Stakeholder Engagement process, 442
  Direct and Manage Project Work process, 56
  Validate Scope process, 110
work performance information
  Control Communications process, 326
  Control Costs process, 215
  Control Procurements process, 409
  Control Quality process, 254
  Control Risks process, 371
  Control Schedule process, 173
  Control Scope process, 114
  Control Stakeholder Engagement process, 443
  Monitor and Control Project Work process, 60–61
  Validate Scope process, 111
work performance reports
  Control Procurements process, 406
  Manage Communications process, 320
  Manage Project Team process, 297
  Perform Integrated Change Control process, 67

About the author

SEAN WHITAKER is an experienced project manager, author, and trainer who has successfully delivered projects in the construction, telecommunications, and IT industries, making him a truly professional project manager. He began his project management career as a residential land developer, then moved on to the construction of wireless telecommunications networks, and then mission-critical hardware and software projects for large infrastructure organizations before returning to the construction industry. What began as a part-time teaching opportunity has now become his full time occupation as teacher, trainer, speaker, and author about project management. He holds the Project Management Professional (PMP®) credential in addition to Bachelor of Arts (BA), Master of Science (MSc), and Master of Business Administration (MBA) academic degrees. He regularly attends and presents at national and international project management conferences, and he currently provides project management training and teaching across a wide range of industries and at all levels. He gives back to the profession via his regular blogs and mentoring and is the author of several project management books, including *PMP® Rapid Review* (Microsoft Press, 2013). He has been a volunteer leader with the Project Management Institute for many years.

How To Download Your eBook

Thank you for purchasing this Microsoft Press® title. Your companion PDF eBook is ready to download from O'Reilly Media, official distributor of Microsoft Press titles.

To download your eBook, go to
http://go.microsoft.com/FWLink/?Linkid=224345
and follow the instructions.

Please note: You will be asked to create a free online account and enter the access code below.

Your access code:

VDXVDHL

PMP® Training Kit

Your PDF eBook allows you to:
- Search the full text
- Print
- Copy and paste

Best yet, you will be notified about free updates to your eBook.

If you ever lose your eBook file, you can download it again just by logging in to your account.

Need help? Please contact:
mspbooksupport@oreilly.com
or call 800-889-8969.

Please note: This access code is non-transferable and is void if altered or revised in any way. It may not be sold or redeemed for cash, credit, or refund.

Microsoft • Cisco • CISSP • CIW • CompTIA • HRCI • Linux • Oracle • PMI • SCP • VMware

Practice. Practice. Practice. Pass.

Get more practice with MeasureUp® & ace the exam!

You've practiced — but have you practiced enough? The disk included with this book has dozens of quality questions from the publisher to get you started. MeasureUp offers additional practice tests with more than 100 new and different questions at MeasureUp.com. And when you use our practice test you'll pass — guaranteed.

- Performance-based simulation questions – similar to the ones found on Microsoft exams – are available online and via download.

- Study Mode helps you review the material with detailed answers and references to help identify areas where you need more study.

- Certification Mode simulates the timed test environment.

Get certified today! Purchase your complete practice test at **www.measureup.com**.

For tips on installing the CD software located in this Training Kit, visit the FAQ section at MeasureUp.com. For questions about the content, or the physical condition of the CD, visit **microsoft.com/learning/en/us/training/format-books-support.aspx**.

Save 20% on MeasureUp Practice Tests!

Prepare for your **IT Pro**, **Developer** or **Office** certification exams with MeasureUp Practice Tests and you'll be ready to pass, we guarantee it. Save 20% on MeasureUp Practice Tests when you use this coupon code at checkout:

Coupon Code: **MSP020112**

www.measureup.com
*excludes VMware

Now that you've read the book...

Tell us what you think!

Was it useful?
Did it teach you what you wanted to learn?
Was there room for improvement?

Let us know at http://aka.ms/tellpress

Your feedback goes directly to the staff at Microsoft Press, and we read every one of your responses. Thanks in advance!